# INTELLECTUAL LIFE IN THE MIDDLE AGES

# INTELLECTUAL LIFE IN
# THE MIDDLE AGES

ESSAYS PRESENTED TO MARGARET GIBSON

EDITED BY LESLEY SMITH

AND BENEDICTA WARD

THE HAMBLEDON PRESS

LONDON   AND   RIO GRANDE

Published by The Hambledon Press 1992

102 Gloucester Avenue, London NW1 8HX (U.K.)

P.O. Box 162, Rio Grande, Ohio 45672 (U.S.A.)

ISBN 1 85285 069 8

A description of this book is available from
the British Library and from the Library of Congress.

Typeset by York House Typographic Ltd., London.
Printed on acid-free paper and bound in
Great Britain by Cambridge University Press.

# Contents

# Acknowledgements

The energy and enthusiasm of Margaret Gibson's many friends have made the production of this book run smoothly; our one dismay was that space prevented us from approaching so many others who might have been included.

We would like to thank Sir Richard and Lady Southern, Giles Constable, Barbara Harvey, Nigel Ramsay, Richard Sharpe and Pat Starkey for their advice and encouragement. We are grateful for the practical help of Henry Mayr-Harting and St. Peter's College, Kristian Jensen, and Patricia Stirnemann. Carlotta Dionisotti and Michael Crawford achieved the thought-to-be-impossible task of photographing Gibson. Martin Kauffmann has radiated good sense and cheerful patience. The Sisters of the Love of God and the British Academy gave us the means to make the editing of this book possible. The editors and the publisher are most grateful to Susan Hall for compiling the indexes with such exemplary efficiency and despatch.

Finally, the personal interest of Martin Sheppard of the Hambledon Press, both in vigorous copy-editing and in relations with contributors, has been invaluable.

Lesley Smith
Benedicta Ward

Oxford, 1992

Margaret Gibson

# *Preface*

This volume is offered to Margaret Gibson by her friends as an expression of gratitude and admiration for the contribution she has made to the study of medieval thought and learning. Year by year since 1969 she has produced a stream of sparkingly clear and concise additions to our knowledge of central personalities and problems in the intellectual disciplines of the middle ages. In particular, and in precise detail, she has illuminated the period of transition from the Carolingian to the Scholastic periods by her observations about the changes in the study of the liberal arts which heralded and made possible the wider aims and outlook of later centuries. While doing this, she has also inspired and directed large enterprises covering the whole period from late antiquity to the fifteenth century, designed to provide exact knowledge about the manuscripts which were the vehicles linking the ancient with the modern world.

Her own articles and the enterprises which she has planned would have sufficed to make her widely known and valued as a creative scholar. But she has a further claim on the gratitude of her contemporaries. Much of her work has been inspired by the generous intention of completing work that others had left incomplete – in particular, Helen Clover's edition of Lanfranc's *Letters*, and Richard Hunt's long awaited doctoral thesis on Alexander Nequam – and of bringing the varied knowledge of different scholars to bear on great themes. The volumes which she has edited on Boethius and Charles the Bald are monuments to this aspect of her scholarly vision.

Everything that she has done has been inspired by her large view of many minds working together to provide a fuller understanding of the central themes of medieval intellectual development. Her selfless dedication to this task has given her a position of unique influence among medievalists, and the production of this volume has been inspired by a common desire, shared both by contributors and by many others who have supported the editors in their project, to express the affection and gratitude of medievalists in many parts of the world.

R.W. Southern

# Bibliography of M.T. Gibson

## Books

*Medieval Learning and Literature: Essays Presented to R.W. Hunt*, ed., with J.J.G. Alexander (Clarendon Press, Oxford 1976), xiv + 455 pp.

*Lanfranc of Bec* (Clarendon Press, Oxford 1978), xii + 266 pp.

*The Letters of Lanfranc, Archbishop of Canterbury*, Latin text by the late V.H. Clover; introduction, revision of the Latin text, translation and notes by M.T. Gibson (Oxford: Oxford Medieval Texts, 1979), xiv + 204 pp.

*Charles the Bald: Court and Kingdom*, ed. with J.L. Nelson and contrib. (British Archaeological Reports, Oxford, 1981), xii + 406 pp. (2nd edition Variorum, 1990).

*Boethius: His Life, Thought and Influence*, ed. and contrib. (Oxford, Blackwell 1981), xxv + 451 pp.

*Liverpool Ivories*; slide booklet with text (Merseyside Country Museums, Liverpool, 1982).

*English Romanesque Art, 1066-1200* (Arts Council, London 1984), 24 pp. with plates

*The Schools and the Cloister: The Life and Work of Alexander Nequam*, by R.W. Hunt; revised and ed. M.T. Gibson (Clarendon Press, Oxford, 1984) xiii + 165 pp.

*Joseph Mayer of Liverpool, 1803-1886*, ed. with S.M. Wright and contrib. (London, Society of Antiquaries Occasional Papers, n.s., xi, 1988) xiii + 244 pp.

*The Eadwine Psalter*, ed. with T.A. Heslop and R.W. Pfaff (London, Modern Humanities Research Association and Pennsylvannia State University Press, 1992).

*Biblia Latina cum Glossa Ordinaria*, facsimile edition with K. Froehlich (Brepols, Louvain, 1992).

## Contributions to Books

'The *Artes* in the Eleventh Century', *Arts libéraux et philosophie au moyen âge: actes du quatrième congrès international de philosophie médiévale* (Montreal/Paris, 1969), pp. 120-26.

Historical introduction to J.E. Tolson, *The 'Summa' of Petrus Helias on Priscianus Minor* (Copenhagen: Cahiers de l'Institut du Moyen Age grec et latin, 27-28, 1978), pp. 159-66.

'Pre-Scholastic Learning', *Manuscripts at Oxford: Exhibition in Memory of R.W. Hunt*, ed. A.C. de la Mare and B.C. Barker-Benfield (Bodleian Library, Oxford, 1980), pp. 45-46; fig. 28-29.

'RAG Reads Priscian', *Books*, 4 (1981), pp. 311-16.

'The *Opuscula Sacra* in the Middle Ages', *Books*, 5(1981), pp. 214-34.

'History at Bec in the Twelfth Century', *Medieval Historiography: Essays Presented to R.W. Southern*, ed. J.M. Wallace-Hadrill et al. (Cambridge University Press, Cambridge, 1982), pp. 167-86.

'Who Designed the Eadwine Psalter?', *Art and Patronage in the English Romanesque*, ed. S. Macready and F.H. Thompson (London, Society of Antiquaries Occasional Papers, n.s., viii, 1986), pp. 71-76.

'Adelard of Bath': *Adelard of Bath: An English Scientist and Arabist of the Early Twelfth Century*, ed. C.S.F. Burnett (London, Warburg Institute Surveys and Texts, xiv, 1987), pp. 7-16.

'Joseph Mayer of Liverpool', 'Late Antique And Medieval Ivories', 'Limoges Enamel', *Books*, 9 (1988), pp. 1-27, 106-13, 114-17.

'Letters and Charters Relating to Berengar of Tours', *Auctoritas und Ratio: Studien zu Berengar von Tours*, ed. P. Ganz, R.B.C. Huygens and F. Niewöhner, Wolfenbütteler Mittelalterstudien, 2 (1990), pp. 5-23.

'Before the *Glossa Ordinaria*', *Papers of the Conference 'Ad litteram'*, ed. K. Emery and M. Jordan (Notre Dame, IN, 1992).

'1066-1220': *The History of Canterbury Cathedral*, ed. N.F. Ramsay (Oxford, 1992).

'The Image of Lanfranc', *Papers of the Colloquium 'Lanfranco di Pavia'*, ed. G. d'Onofrio (Milan, 1993).

## Articles

'The Study of the *Timaeus* in the Eleventh and Twelfth Centuries', *Pensamiento*, xxv (1969), pp. 183-94.

'Theodore of Mopsuestia: Fragment in Bodleian Library', *Journal of Theological Studies*, n.s., xxi (1970), pp. 104-5.

'Lanfranc's Commentary on the Pauline Epistles', *Journal of Theological Studies*, n.s., xxii (1971), pp. 86-112.

'Lanfranc's Notes on Patristic Texts', *Journal of Theological Studies*, n.s., xxii (1971), pp. 435-50.

'The Case of Berengar of Tours', *Studies in Church History*, vi (1971), pp. 61-68.

'Priscian, *Institutiones Grammaticae*: A Handlist of Manuscripts', *Scriptorium*, xxvi (1972), pp. 105-24.

'A Picture of "Sapientia" from S Sulpice, Bourges', *Transactions of the Cambridge Bibliographical Society*, vi (1973), pp. 260-61, with plate.

'The Continuity of Learning, *c.* 850-1050', *Viator*, vi (1975), pp. 1-13.

'The Collected Works of Priscian: The Printed Editions, 1470-1859', *Studi Medievali*, 3 ser., xviii (1977), pp. 1-15.

'The Early Scholastic Glosule to Priscian, *Institutiones Grammaticae*: The Text and its Influence', *Studi Medievali*, 3 ser., xx (1979), pp. 235-54.

'Boethius in the Carolingian Schools', *Transactions of the Royal Historical Society*, 5 ser., xxxii (1982), pp. 43-56.

[with S.P. Hall], 'R.W. Hunt, *The History of Grammar in the Middle Ages*: Additions and Corrections', *Bodleian Library Record*, xi, i (1982), pp. 9-19.

'Latin Commentaries on Logic before 1200', *Bulletin de Philosophie Médiévale*, xxiv (1982), pp. 54-64.

[with M. Lapidge and C. Page], 'Neumed Boethian Metra from Canterbury: A Newly-Recovered Leaf of Cambridge, University Library, Gg.5.35 (the 'Cambridge Songs' Manuscript)', *Anglo-Saxon England*, xii (1983), pp. 141-52.

' "Tradizioni Perdute" of the *De Consolatione Philosophiae*: Comments on a Recent Book', *Revue des Etudes Augustiniennes*, xxx (1984), pp. 274-78.

'*Codices Boethiani*', *Revue d'Histoire des Textes*, xiv (1984), pp. 71-5.

' "Through the Looking Glass": A Gothic Ivory Mirror-Case in the Liverpool Museum', *Chaucer Review*, xxi (1986), pp. 213-16.

[with N.F. Palmer and D.R. Shanzer], 'The Manuscripts of Alan of Lille, *Anticlaudianus* in British Libraries', *Studi Medievali*, xxviii (1987), pp. 905-1001.

'The Twelfth-Century Glossed Bible', *Studia Patristica*, xxiii (1989), ed. E.A. Livingstone, pp. 232-44.

[with E.C. Southworth], 'Radiocarbon Dating of Ivory and Bone Carvings', *Journal of the British Archaeological Association*, cxliii (1990), pp. 131-33, plates xxiii-xxiv.

'Milestones in the Study of Priscian', *Viator* (1992).

'A Fragment of "Liberal Arts" Embroidery', *Journal of the Warburg and Courtauld Institutes* (1992).

'The Psalter-Commentary Attributed to Bruno, Bishop of Würzburg', *Studi Medievali* (1992).

'Boethius in the Tenth Century', *Mittellateinisches Jahrbuch* (1992).

# List of Contributors

| | |
|---|---|
| Martin BRETT | Robinson College, Cambridge |
| Christopher BROOKE | Gonville and Caius College, Cambridge |
| Alan COBBAN | Liverpool University |
| David d'AVRAY | University College, London |
| Christopher de HAMEL | Sotheby's, London |
| Valerie FLINT | University of Auckland |
| David GANZ | University of North Carolina, Chapel Hill |
| Margaret HARVEY | Durham University |
| Colette JEUDY | I.R.H.T., Paris |
| Donald MATTHEW | Reading University |
| Henry MAYR-HARTING | St. Peter's College, Oxford |
| Rosamond McKITTERICK | Newnham College, Cambridge |
| Alexander MURRAY | University College, Oxford |
| Janet NELSON | King's College, London |
| Richard PFAFF | University of North Carolina, Chapel Hill |
| Marjorie REEVES | St. Anne's College, Oxford |
| Richard and Mary ROUSE | UCLA |
| Lesley SMITH | Linacre College, Oxford |
| Richard SOUTHERN | St. John's College, Oxford |
| John VAN ENGEN | University of Notre Dame |
| Benedicta WARD | Oxford |

# Abbreviations

BRUO          A.B. Emden, *A Biographical Register of the University of Oxford to A.D. 1500*, 3 vols. (Oxford, 1957-59)
CCCM          *Corpus Christianorum, Continuatio Medievalis*
CCSL          *Corpus Christianorum, Series Latina*
CSEL          *Corpus Scriptorum Ecclesiasticorum Latinorum*
MGH           *Monumenta Germaniae Historica*
PL            J.-P. Migne, *Patrologia Latina*

# The Intellectual in Politics: Context, Content and Authorship in the Capitulary of Coulaines, November 843

## Janet L. Nelson

At Verdun, in August 843, Louis the Pious's three sons, Lothar, Louis and Charles, finally ended three years of conflict when, along with their nobility, they agreed a division of the Carolingian Empire. This was effectively a new beginning for the reign of Charles the Bald,[1] now acknowledged ruler of a western kingdom comprising roughly the area of modern France. Yet many problems remained. It was not just that Lothar, the firstborn, had not really reconciled himself to Charles' acquiring a substantial share of Frankish heartlands between the rivers Scheldt and Seine: Lothar also had supporters further west, in Neustria (the region between Seine and Loire), and especially in the lower Loire valley and in Brittany, longstanding trouble-spots for Carolingian rulers.[2] After Verdun, the Breton leader Nominoë remained in contact with Lothar. In May 843 Lambert, a Neustrian noble whose kinsmen had been among Lothar's henchmen in earlier conflicts (in the 830s), allied with Nominoë, slew Charles's faithful man Rainald and seized Nantes.[3]

---

[1] Recent reassessments of Charles the Bald, and of the scholars who were his contemporaries, owe an incalculable debt to Margaret Gibson's work. This essay is offered to her in affectionate gratitude for inspiration over many years. In the footnotes the following abbreviations are used:

T.     G. Tessier, *Receuil des Actes de Charles II le Chauve*, 3 vols. (Paris, 1944-1955)
AB     *The Annals of St-Bertin*, translated and annotated by J.L. Nelson (Manchester, 1991)
Nithard     Nithard, *Historiarum Libri IV*, ed. as *Histoire des fils de Louis le Pieux*, by P. Lauer (Paris, 1926), with French translation.
Lupus     Lupus of Ferrières, *Epistolae*, ed. L. Levillain, *Loup de Ferrières, Correspondance*, 2 vols. (Paris, 1927-35), with French translation.

[2] See now the admirable study of J.M.H. Smith, *Province and Empire: Brittany and the Carolingians* (Cambridge, 1992). Lothar also continued to support Charles' Carolingian rival in Aquitaine, his nephew Pippin II: see further J.L. Nelson, *Charles the Bald* (London, 1992), chap. 5.

[3] *AB* 843, p. 55.

Rennes too was apparently now in Breton hands.[4] No wonder Charles's first major action after Verdun was to lead an army towards the Breton border. En route at Laurière, just north of Angers, in October, the Neustrian bishops met in council and promulgated four decrees threatening with anathema 'anyone found to be a public subverter of divine law, a despiser of ecclesiastical just and reasonable judgements, or a puffed-up and proud contradicter of ecclesiastical warnings and the decrees of the holy fathers'; 'anyone proved to have tried to act cunningly, craftily and wickedly against the royal dignity'; 'anyone who attempts with contumacious and puffed-up spirit contrary to authority and reason wickedly to go against the royal power, which, as the Apostle says, "is from God alone", and refuses to obey unquestioningly its just and reasonable commands'; and, finally, 'whoever, inflamed by the brands of pride or stuffed with insolence, may try to violate or by any argument to breach those things which have been laid down by us unanimously for the tranquillity of Holy Mother Church, by priestly rigour and royal dignity, and confirmed by our own hands'.[5]

The *capitula* of Laurière, for all their ecclesiastical tone, emanated not from the chapter-house or library but from the camp. The bishops were part of Charles's host, and were accompanied by military contingents. In the host also travelled clerks, with styli and wax-tablets, pens and parchment. The Carolingian elite was a small one, and its members – churchmen, scholars, warlords, scholar-warlords – operated much of the time in the same milieu, as the king's companions (*commilitones*): hence, in the *capitula* of Laurière, the deployment of ecclesiastical authority in the king's service, and the combination of ideological punch, in the blunt assertion of the king's executive power, with political topicality, in the implicit reference to the problem of faction. For while Lambert and Nominoë were no doubt the prime targets of the bishops' wrath, as of the campaign itself, the *capitula* hint at dissension among Charles's lay supporters – dissension that had gone beyond the normal jostling for influence at court.

Of those most influential in Charles's kingdom at this time, Warin had been an opponent of Lothar back in 834, and consistently supported Charles after 840.[6] He had been able to ensure that his counties, Chalon and Mâcon, ended

---

[4]   T. 28: issued 'in the tents by the *civitas* of Rennes'. But H. Guillotel, 'L'action de Charles le Chauve vis-à-vis de la Bretagne de 843 a 851', *Mémoires de la Société d'Histoire et d'Archéologie de Bretagne*. 53 (1975-6), pp. 5-32, at p. 10 n. 12, points out that this does not necessarily indicate a siege.

[5]   843, *MGH Conc*, iii, *Die Konzilien der karolingischen Teilreiche, 843-859*, ed. W. Hartmann (Hanover, 1984), 2, pp. 8-9, with text (incorporated into the decrees of the council of Meaux-Paris) at p. 72. Hartmann retains the identification of the place-name as 'Loiré', without considering the convincing arguments of Guillotel, 'L'action de Charles', p. 12 for Laurière (dep. Maine-et-Loire, arrond. Angers).

[6]   Nithard i, 5, p. 22 (describing Warin's unsuccessful defence of Chalon against Lothar during the last throes of the revolt of Louis the Pious's sons aginst him in 833-4); ii, 5, p. 50.

up on Charles's side of the line in the division of Verdun,[7] and would use his position as a *potens* (powerful man) to build up his regional power.[8] He was to be the first magnate to put his hand to the Capitulary of Coulaines.[9] A more contentious figure was Adalard, count of Tours and lay-abbot of St-Martin. In the spring of 843 he had been bitterly denounced by the soldier-historian Nithard, best-known of the intellectuals at Charles's court in the period before Verdun. According to Nithard, the reason that Charles the Bald had married Adalard's niece in December 842 was 'to win over the greatest part of the lesser aristocracy', whose support Adalard had won by lavish distribution 'to each of whatever he wanted of public resources'.[10] Nithard, who had fulfilled his commission from Charles in 841 to write propagandistic contemporary history, now felt himself excluded not only from royal favour but (and this is what rankled) from the magic circle of Adalard's patronage.[11]

In the summer of 843, the monk-scholar Lupus, favoured in the 830s at the court of Charles' parents and recipient of the abbacy of Ferrières from Charles in 840, warned the young king against 'subjecting yourself to one man, so that you do everything according to his will'. The reference may well be, again, to Adalard.[12] And yet this same Lupus, scarcely before the year was out, wrote in warmly appreciative tones of 'the most influential Adalard', whose intervention had persuaded Charles to promise restoration of property to Ferrières.[13]

Adalard's position in Charles's kingdom was problematic for Adalard himself. Originally from Middle Francia, his reception of offices and lands in Neustria had not extinguished his interests east of the Meuse,[14] hence in the area that in 843 was assigned to Lothar. A letter addressed to Lothar's wife, the Empress Ermengard, probably by Adalard not long before Verdun seems to show him hedging his bets, keeping open the option of return to Middle

---

[7]  See P. Classen, 'Die Verträge von Verdun und Coulaines, 843, als politische Grundlagen des westfränkischen Reiches', *Historische Zeitschrift*, 196 (1963), pp. 1-35, at p. 10.

[8]  T. 98 (847), 117 (849) are grants to Burgundian vassals at Warin's request. Cf. T. 10, 11 both of August 842, and issued from Agen and Castillon-sur-Dordogne respectively, for two laymen apparently from Burgundy, perhaps also Warin's men. Nithard iv, 4, p. 132, suggests that Warin *quidam dux* had been campaigning with Charles in Aquitaine in August, and that he was left in charge of that *patria* when Charles withdrew.

[9]  See below, n. 69.

[10]  Nithard iv, 6, p. 142.

[11]  See J.L. Nelson, 'Public *Histories* and Private History in the Work of Nithard', *Speculum*, 60 (1985), pp. 251-93, reprinted in Nelson, *Politics and Ritual in Early Medieval Europe* (London, 1986), pp. 195-238.

[12]  *Ep.* 31, p. 142. Cf. ibid., pp. 142-44: Lupus urged Charles to make his regime one that would 'frighten *potentes*', and 'not to fear the *potentes* whom you yourself have made and whom, if you want, you can diminish'.

[13]  *Ep.* 32, p. 148, with reference to an extant charter: T. 30 (27 December 843).

[14]  T. 20 (23 February 843) is a grant made at the request of 'Adalard abbot of St-Martin'. See K.F. Werner, 'Untersuchungen zur Frühzeit des französischen Fürstentums', *Die Welt als Geschichte*, 18 (1958), pp. 256-89, at p. 274.

Francia.[15] Adalard was with Charles in September, attesting a monastic privilege as 'abbot of Tours'.[16] But could Charles count on him to hold the lower Loire valley, a region peculiarly vulnerable to attack from Lothar's supporters?

While Adalard was an outsider in western Neustria, another of the leading men of 843, Vivian, by contrast hailed from that region. His kinsman (?father) and namesake had been killed fighting for Charles's father against Lothar's men on the Breton March in 834,[17] and another probable kinsman (?uncle) was Rainald who had recently died in battle against Lambert in the same area.[18] Vivian is first documented in February 843, when he requested a charter as Charles's chamberlain. During the remainder of that year, no fewer than four of Charles's charters, three of them grants of Neustrian fisclands to laymen,[19] were issued at Vivian's request, while the beneficiary of a fifth was Vivian's brother Rainald, abbot of Marmoutier, near Tours.[20] Charles's promotion of Vivian in 843 can have been no coincidence: the king was trying to reduce his dependence on Adalard – even, to cut Adalard down to size. Vivian with his Neustrian background was likely to be able to establish a strong position in that region. Yet Charles did not want to provoke Adalard into abandoning his kingdom for Lothar's.[21]

Perhaps because Charles's opponents were well aware of these problems (and in touch with Lothar), there was little to show for the autumn campaign: neither Nominoë nor Lambert sued for peace. From Rennes the host fell back to Coulaines near Le Mans, the thence Charles went to St-Martin, Tours.

---

[15] *MGH Epp. Karolini Aevi*, v, *Epp.* Variorum no. 27, pp. 343-45.

[16] *MGH Conc.* iii, no. 1, p. 6.

[17] Nithard i, 5 p. 20.

[18] *AB* 843, p. 55, n. 1.

[19] T. 19, for Gailo; T. 24, for Count Harduin, apparently a Neustrian; and T. 28, for Atto. The beneficiary of T. 30, also requested by Vivian, was Lupus of Ferrières.

[20] T. 31. See F. Lot and L. Halphen, *Le règne de Charles le Chauve* (Paris, 1909), pp. 89 and 157 n. 2.

[21] This happened in 844, however: Lupus, *Ep.* 36, written August/Sept 844, refers to Adalard as 'just about to leave'. The dating of T. 60-63 is crucial for dating Adalards's replacement at St-Martin by Vivian. Lot and Halphen, *Le règne*, p. 88 n. 1, dated these charters, and so Adalard's departure for Lothar's kingdom, to December 843/January 844. Tessier, *Recueil*, 1, pp. 170-71, questioned this for three reasons: (a) these four charters are dated to Charles's fifth year, which would give dates of December 844/January 845; (b) the indictional dating, which might suggest the period 1 September 843 to 31 August 844, and was accepted by Lot and Halphen, should not be preferred to the reign-year dating because errors in indictional calculation are frequent, and in any case Charles's chancery may not have used an indictional style dating from 1 September. (Tessier could have added that the argument of Lot and Halphen would require that the same error was made in charters by two different notaries, Jonas (T. 60), and Bartholomew (T. 61-3)); (c) Jonas subscribed T. 30 as *notarius*, and T. 60 as *diaconus*, and 'il n'y a aucune raison liturgique de placer la collation d'un ordre sacré entre le 27 et le 30 décembre'. (Jonas did, however, subscribe his next charter after T. 30, namely T. 33 (5 April 844) as *diaconus*.) Tessier's arguments were reaffirmed by K.F. Werner, 'Untersuchungen', pp. 274-75, n. 89, but without reference to other crucial evidence; Lupus, *Ep.* 32, and T. 30: see next note.

Despite the military stalemate, Charles achieved a measure of political success: he spent Christmas at Tours attended by both Vivian and Adalard.[22]

Also in attendance on Charles that Christmas was Lupus of Ferrières.[23] Six months later, Lupus would be taken captive campaigning in Aquitaine on Charles's behalf; Nithard was to die in the same battle.[24] The intellectual making his way in a court society, whether like Nithard a layman lacking the church's institutional support, or like Lupus an ecclesiastical appointee of the king, was more or less dependent on royal favour, and often dependent too on those very *potentes* against whom he warned the king. The splitting of the Carolingian Empire, multiplying royal consumers, should have tilted the market in favour of the 'sellers of wisdom'.[25] It is striking, therefore, that Charles the Bald, still more of a 'Carolingian Renaissance Prince' than his father and grandfather, was more successful than either of his brothers in his recruitment and retention of scholars to serve him.[26] To patronise learning was no affectation, no mere Theodosian pose: Charles had grasped, early on, the political uses of wisdom, and the role of the written word in forming an elite. Scholars who sang for their supper were guilty of no *trahison des clercs*. Rather, their production and preservation of written records of political decision-making and action was a unique and durable contribution to the forming of a new, self-conscious political community. Nithard in 842 recorded, and may have drafted, the Strasbourg Oaths in which Charles the Bald and Louis the German mobilised their aristocracy in the quest for peace.[27] In 844, Lupus wrote up the decrees of an assembly summoned by Charles to his palace at Ver.[28] In both these cases, the text was at once a public and a private

[22] T. 30, 31, dated 27 and 29 December, were both issued from St-Martin. Vivian appears as formal requester (*impetrator*) of T. 30 (cf. n. 19 above), a grant made as a result of Adalard's intervention: see above, p. 4, and n. 13.

[23] See above nn. 19 and 22.

[24] *AB* 844, p. 59; Nelson, *Politics and Ritual*, pp. 235-7.

[25] I borrow the expression from Notker, *Gesta Karoli Magni* i, c. i, ed. H.F. Haefele, *MGH SS rerum germanicarum in usum scholarum*, n.s. 13, revd. edn (1980), pp. 1-2 (describing Irish scholars in Charlemagne's realm): its scriptural origin is appreciated in a fine paper by D. Ganz, 'Humour as History in Notker's *Gesta Karoli Magni*', in E.B. King, J.T. Schaefer and W.B. Wadley ed., *Monks, Nuns and Friars in Mediaeval Society* (Sewanee, 1989), pp. 171-83.

[26] J.M. Wallace-Hadrill, 'Charles the Bald: a Carolingian Renaissance Prince', in *Proceedings of the British Academy* 64 (1978), pp. 155-84. Cf. P. Godman, *Poetry of the Carolingian Renaissance* (1985), and idem, *Poets and Emperors* (1987); J.L. Nelson, 'Charles le Chauve et les utilisations du savoir', in D. Iogna-Prat, C. Jeudy and G. Lobrichon ed., *L'école carolingienne d'Auxerre* (Paris, 1991), pp. 37-54.

[27] Nithard iii, 5, pp. 102-8. See further J.L. Nelson, 'Literacy in Carolingian Government', in R. McKitterick ed., *The Uses of Literacy in Early Mediaeval Europe* (Cambridge, 1990), pp. 258-96. Cf. for the aims and output of a ninth-century intellectual working not for but against Charles, D. Ganz, '*The Epitaphium Arsenii* and Opposition to Louis the Pious', in P. Godman and R. Collins ed., *Charlemagne's Heir: New Perspectives on the Reign of Louis the Pious* (Oxford, 1990), pp. 537-50.

[28] Lupus, *Ep.* 43, p. 182.

document: the king and his faithful men set an agenda, and took decisions, but what was preserved as the official record embodied a good deal of the recorder's own concerns. This dual character was shared, especially in the ninth century, by many Carolingian capitularies, blending as they did the legislative and the administrative. Each has the timeless generality and anonymity of law yet, at the same time, reflect a particular historical conjuncture and authorial presence. Fortunately, and fortuitously, that presence can be identified in the texts emanating from Strasbourg and Ver. Between those events came the assembly of Coulaines. Now that its context has been sketched that capitulary's particular content invites exploration.

The capitulary issued at Coulaines in November 843 provides a snapshot of a political crisis resolved.[29] Charles showed his preparedness to act against an overmighty magnate. But Coulaines was about more than damage-limitation. At stake had been the political future of Charles himself: his new-made kingdom, scarcely four months old, created by one Carolingian's artifice, vulnerable to a rival Carolingian's subversion, now received a belated birth-certificate. Charles defused faction within the realm by mobilising (rather than yielding to) the force of aristocratic opinion and ecclesiastical authority. The draftsman of the capitulary generalised from the particular: he acknowledged the *fideles* (faithful men), ecclesiastical and lay, as the king's 'constituency'.

The document shows some formal inconsistencies: the king uses now the royal 'we', now the first person singular;[30] he speaks sometimes for himself alone, sometimes for the aristocracy as well; he makes a concession that is in effect a promise; he issues a unilateral decree that is, at the same time, a bilateral and a trilateral pact. But capitularies typically show such formal irregularities: they can hardly be forced into the strait-jacket of any chancery norm. The style and content of the Coulaines *capitula* in some ways recall those of Laurière (likewise drawn up by a participant-observer), with their scriptural quotation, and reference to a written document 'confirmed by our own hands'. Still more strongly does the Coulaines text recall the 823/25 *ordinatio* of Louis the Pious: there too were references to the church's *honor*, the *honor* of emperor and *regnum*, and the *honor* of Louis' *missi*, and by implication of his counts too – holders of *honores* who must make themselves honoured.[31] The *ordinatio* foreshadows Coulaines with its stress on the notion of participation in the governing of the state by persons designated 'associates'

---

[29] Ed. Hartmann, *MGH Conc.*, iii, 3, pp. 10-17.

[30] Cf. a similar shift in Louis the Pious's capitulary of 823/825, c. 3, cited from the text of Ansegis, in *MGH Capit.*, i, p. 415. See O. Guillot, 'Une *ordinatio* méconnue: le capitulaire de 823-825', in Godman and Collins ed., *Charlemagne's Heir*, pp. 455-86.

[31] Capitulary of 823/25, cc. 6, 11, 13, *MGH Capit.*, i, pp. 416-7, discussed by Guillot, 'Une *ordinatio*', at pp. 477, 485. There is (*pace* Guillot's implication) no explicit reference to the *honor* of counts, though that may well be implicit in the idea of the count's *ministerium*. Cf. *cc.* 13, 16, p. 417, for the inverse notion of *inhonoratio regni et regis*.

(*socii*), and more generally, 'every one of you' (*unusquisque vestrum*), and to operating through assemblies (*placita*).[32] Louis's *tria capitula* of 823/25 in turn echo Charlemagne's prescriptions for him a decade before, when a kind of 'coronation oath' was extracted before Louis was crowned co-emperor.[33]

For all that there are continuities with the past, the Coulaines text does more than elaborate earlier political ideas. In 843, alongside the *honor* of church and the *honor* of the king (both notions already present in the 823/25 capitulary), appears something new: the collective *honor* of the lay *fideles*. While churches have been placed by God under the jurisdiction of the king's government, churchmen need royal power *and lay vigour* in order to carry out their ministry.[34] The operations of royal power depend in turn on the 'counsel and aid' supplied by 'episcopal authority and the unanimity of the *fideles*'.[35] Lay *fideles* depend for their security on the king: to guarantee that security the king undertakes to preserve for each his *lex competens* (due law), and not to deprive anyone of office and lands and status (the term *honor* includes all three) without just cause.[36] The assertion that a relationship of mutual obligation existed between king and each of his (lay) *fideles* was not new – Charlemagne had given assurances of 'his will that every man should have his law fully kept'[37] – but had never before been so explicit or so specific.[38] Still more important here though is the 'horizontal' covenant that establishes a political community. A mutual agreement (*convenientia*) has been entered into by all with all, the *fideles*, lay and ecclesiastical, 'coming together into a single thing' (*venientes in unum*). *Convenientia* means both, literally, the meeting of men and, metaphorically, the arrangements made through a 'meeting' of minds and wills. For this the church is the model, the inspiration coming explicitly from

[32] Capitulary of 823/25, c. 2, c. 3, p. 415: 'Sed quamquam summa huius ministerii in nostra persona consistere videatur, tamen et divina auctoritate et humana ordinatione ita per partes divisum esse cognoscitur, ut unusquisque vestrum in suo loco et ordine partem nostri ministerii habere cognoscatur'. See Guillot, 'Une *ordinatio*', pp. 464-66. For echoes in the Coulaines text of the decrees of the 829 council of Paris, see H.H. Anton, 'Zum politischen Konzept karolingischer Synoden', *Historisches Jahrbuch*, 99 (1979), pp. 55-132, at p. 80.

[33] Thegan, *Vita Hludowici imperatoris* c. 6, *MGH SS*, ii, pp. 591-2. Guillot, 'Une *ordinatio*', p. 485, notes the line leading from this capitulary to later coronation oaths.

[34] Coulaines c. 1, *MGH Conc.*, iii, no. 3, p. 15, 'illustrorum virorum strenuitas seu reipublicae administratores'.

[35] *MGH Conc.*, iii, 3, c, 2, p. 16. This is the earliest appearance of the expression *consilium et auxilium*: see J. Devisse, 'Essai sur l'histoire d'une expression qui a fait fortune', *Le Moyen Age*, 74 (1968), pp. 179-205.

[36] This recalls Charlemagne's warning to Louis in 813 (see n. 33): 'nullum ab honore suo sine causa discretionis eiecisset'. *Honor* has a crucial sociological dimension: cf. Devisse, *Hincmar Archevêque de Reims*, 3 vols. (Geneva, 1975-6), ii, p. 1109, with n. 219, citing Montesquieu: 'l'honneur est la pierre angulaire des régimes monarchiques'. See already T. Hobbes, *Leviathan*, chapter 10, ed. M. Oakeshott (Oxford, 1960), pp. 56-63.

[37] *MGH Capit.*, i, no. 25, p. 67.

[38] Guillot, 'Une *ordinatio*', p. 476, notes the reference in 823/25 c. 6, p. 416, to each count's having promised *fides* to the ruler.

St. Paul.[39] There is also a striking allusion to the Vulgate Book of Maccabees 12: 50, which tells how the people of Israel, deprived of their commander, 'encouraged one another': the prelude, in the scriptural story, to Israel's revival under a new leader. The *convenientia*, which sustains royal authority, and to which the king then agrees to apply his power ('nos nostramque potestatem eorum bonae convenientiae . . . sociam et comitem fore . . . spopondimus': 'We promised that we and our power would be a collaborator and companion to their *convenientia*')[40] curiously foreshadows Hobbes' hypothetical history of a social covenant and its sequel, the authorising of a sovereign.[41] The similarity is real, for beyond both Caroline and Carolingian texts lie biblical authority and patristic (especially Augustinian) thought;[42] motivating the authors of both texts was the same horror of recently-experienced internecine conflict, the same quest for what the Coulaines draftsman, following Augustine, calls tranquillity.[43] But whereas Hobbes asserted the futility of covenants without the sword, and so backhandedly justified the absolute power of the Leviathan,[44] the Coulaines author wanted both to affirm the indispensability of royal power and to ensure that it could operate in an even-handed and acceptable manner. Everyone who had joined in the *convenientia* owed *sinceritas*, 'straightforwardness', to his fellows and to the king: consequently, so the king was made to declare, 'whoever knows that someone is clearly (*manifeste*) plotting against us and against this agreed straightforwardness (*contra nos et contra hanc pactam sinceritatem*) is to

---

[39] See especially Ephesians 4: 3-6, 15-16; I Corinthians 12: 12-27; Colossians 1: 18. Note also the allusion (unremarked by previous editors or commentators) to John 12: 26 ('Si quis mihi ministraverit, honorificabit eum Pater meus') in c.3 ('a quibus honorem suscipimus, eos iuxta dictum dominicum honoremus'.) This identification of the *dictum dominicum* seems more persuasive than those of Hartmann, *MGH Conc.*, iii, p. 16, n. 26 (citing Romans 13: 7 and 15: 7). Note also above n. 30, the association between the count's *ministerium* and his *honor*, in the 823/25 capitulary.

[40] *MGH Conc.*, iii, p.15.

[41] Hobbes, *Leviathan*, chapter 17, pp. 109-13.

[42] *De civitate Dei* xv, 8, *CSEL* 40(ii), p. 74: 'Civitas . . . nihil est aliud quam hominum multitudo aliquo societatis vinculo conligata'; *Enarratio in Ps.*, 24, 21 *CCSL* 38, p. 140: 'Recti corde non praesentia corporali miscentur tantum, sicut mali, sed consensione cordis . . . adhaerent mihi'. The parallel between Augustine and Hobbes was acutely observed by M.J. Wilks, 'St. Augustine and the General Will', in F.L. Cross ed., *Studia Patristica*, 9 (Berline, 1966), pp. 487-522. For Augustine's use of the term *pactum* in *Confessions*, iii, 8 ('generale quippe pactum est societatis humanae obedire regibus suis'; 'pactum inter se civitatis aut gentis, consuetudine vel lege firmatum'), see J.W. Gough, *The Social Contract*, 2nd edn (Oxford, 1957), p. 24.

[43] Coulaines, preface, pp. 14, 15. Cf. Augustine, *De civitate Dei* xix, 13, *CSEL* 40(ii), p. 395: 'pax omnium rerum tranquillitas ordinis'. See R.A. Markus, *Saeculum: History and Society in the Theology of St. Augustine* (Cambridge, 1970), pp. 83, 95-96.

[44] *Leviathan*, chapters 17, p. 109, 18, pp. 115, 119-20. The concept of authorisation here is of course distinctively Hobbesian.

denounce that person openly (*aperte*)'.[45] The problems of the West Frankish *regnum* in 843 resembled those which eight centuries later would shatter the United Kingdom: the Coulaines document, frank about the workings of private and sectional interests (as indeed had been the capitulary of 823/25),[46] showed how these could be inhibited and overridden, how *sinceritas* could vanquish deviousness (*calliditas*). It was the *fideles*, not the young king, who were held to blame for such selfish and underhand conduct, whether on their own part, or through their bad influence and inordinate requests. Royal authority was to be respected by the *fideles* because of its assurance for their individual and collective rights (*lex competens, honor*). This was a blueprint for a monarchy not enfeebled but strengthened by its commitment to the politics of consensus.[47] If, the king said, the *fideles* 'keep to what you promised in your *convenientia*', then 'our authority can be more readily and strictly observed'. Coulaines recorded a double transaction: the preceding covenant of the *fideles* with one another and, in the document itself, the compact (*foedus*) between king and *fideles*.

Charles the Bald himself, learned in secular and canon law, no doubt already *au fait* with his father's capitularies, may well have had a hand in the Coulaines text.[48] But so rich are the scriptural, and still more the Augustinian, resonances here (the latter rather neglected by modern commentators) that they seem to reflect the mind of an ecclesiastical draftsman. The text's opening passage, with the arresting metaphor of the church as a ship on a stormy sea,

---

[45] Coulaines c. 2, *MGH Conc.*, iii, p. 16. For similar notions of concord and singleheartedness in Augustine, see P. Brown, 'St. Augustine', in B. Smalley ed., *Trends in Medieval Political Thought* (Oxford, 1965), pp. 1-21; idem, *The Body and Society* (New York, 1988), chap. 19.

[46] Cf. Coulaines c. 4, *MGH Conc.*, iii, p. 16, denouncing advice given 'pro quacumque privata commoditate aut reicienda cupiditate sive alicuius consanguinitate vel familiaritatis seu amicitiae coniunctione', with 823/25 capitulary, c. 6, *MGH Capit.*, i, familiaritatis seu amicitiae coniunctione', with 823/25 capituarly, c. 6, *MGH Capit.*, i, p. 416, admonishing counts 'nulla quaelibet causa aut munerum acceptio aut amicitia cuiuslibet vel odium aut timor vel gratia ab statu rectitudinis vos deviare compellat'.

[47] See Classen, 'Die Vorträge', pp. 26-27; E. Magnou-Nortier, *Foi et fidelité* (Toulouse, 1976), pp. 98-108; and cf. the sometimes perverse but always thought-provoking comments of Devisse, *Hincmar*, i, pp. 287-90, 309. For a ninth-century treatise on consensus politics, see below, p. 12.

[48] The earliest use in one of Charles's capitularies of Ansegis' capitulary collection does not occur until 853, however: see Nelson, *Politics and Ritual*, p. 95. For Charles's legal knowledge, see Nelson, ' "Not Bishops' Bailiffs but Lords of the Earth": Charles the Bald and the Problem of Sovereignty', in D. Wood ed., *The Church and Sovereignty: Essays in Honour of Michael Wilks* (Oxford, 1991), pp. 23-24. Anton, 'Zum politischen Konzept', p. 83, n. 104, points to similarities between the Coulaines text and Walahfrid Strabo's *Libellus de exordiis et incrementis*: for the suggestion that Walahfrid's treatise had been used in the education of the young Charles the Bald, see Nelson, *Charles the Bald*, chap. 4.

was very probably inspired by a passage in Augustine's *Commentaries on the Psalms*.[49] Could this offer a clue as to the likely author of the capitulary of Coulaines? Though the question of authorship has been thought unresolvable,[50] it may be worth posing once more.[51]

The style (wordy and unclassical) of the Coulaines text is certainly not that of Lupus of Ferrières.[52] Another candidate for authorship was all but proposed by Jean Devisse: Hincmar, future archbishop of Rheims. Devisse had been struck by the fact that the capitulary of Coulaines was the earliest text to use the expression *consilium et auxilium*, which was to become something of a Hincmar hallmark.[53] But Devisse rejected the possibility of Hincmar's authorship, on the grounds that Hincmar himself, describing his own early career in a letter to Pope Nicholas I in 867, implied that he had remained in the monastery of St-Denis after 840 right up until his ordination as archbishop of Rheims in 845, and so could not have been with Charles at Coulaines.[54] Elisabeth Magnou-Nortier pursued Devisse's idea, though she concluded that Charles could well have written the capitulary himself, using Hincmar's advice.[55] The most recent commentator, Wilfried Hartmann, comes out firmly against Hincmar's authorship.[56] I think the argument for Hincmar's authorship is worth reviving.

In 833 Abbot Hilduin of St-Denis joined the rebellion of Louis the Pious's sons, and ordered Hincmar as a monk of that community to follow suit.

[49] Augustine, *Enarrationes in Ps.*, 103, iv, 5, on verse 26, *CCSL* 40, pp. 1524-25. See also H. Rahner, *Symbole der Kirche: Die Ekklesiologie der Väter* (Salzburg, 1964), p. 354, and pp. 359-60. I am very grateful to Lynne Grundy for help in identifying the likely source of this passage. There is a further instance of the ship metaphor in the preface to the *capitula* of Yütz (Thionville), *MGH Conc.*, iii, no. 6, p. 29 and n. 6 (Hartmann notes verbal parallels here to the Coulaines preface).

[50] Devisse, *Hincmar*, ii, p. 1095: 'la preuve materielle manquera sans doute toujours'.

[51] Guillot, 'Une *ordinatio*', surprisingly does not pose the question of authorship in the case of the 823/25 capitulary, which he apparently regards as the direct reflection of the views of Louis the Pious.

[52] Lupus's authorship was alleged by Lot and Halphen, *Le règne de Charles*, p. 96, n. 2, but rightly rejected as stylistically impossible by Classen, 'Die Vorträge', p. 21, n. 1 and Hartmann, *MGH Conc.*, iii, p. 10. Lupus, who subscribed the synodal diploma issued in September or October by an assembly at Germigny (dep. Loiret), *MGH Conc.*, iii, no. 1, p. 7, and was with Charles at Tours in December (see above, n. 19), may well have been with him at Coulaines, however.

[53] Devisse, 'Essai sur l'histoire d'une expression', pp. 179-81; idem, *Hincmar*, i, pp. 287-90, ii, pp. 1095, 1109-10.

[54] Devisse, 'Essai', p. 192, makes the inference, with evident reluctance, from Hincmar, *Ep.* 198, in *MGH Epp.*, viii(i), p. 210, adding: 'Eut-il été présent à Coulaines, aurait-il eut le crédit nécessaire, l'influence suffisante pour y imposer une nouvelle expression?' Devisse immediately goes on to raise the possibility of collective work (without suggesting who the other worker(s) might have been), yet in n. 56, hankers still for Hincmar's authorship: 'Le style due préambule . . . se rapproche beaucoup de celui d'Hincmar', noting that the citation from Matthew 10: 20 is given in 'la version qu 'Hincmar cite souvent de 856 à 860'.

[55] *Foi et fidelité*, pp. 102, 106-7.

[56] *MGII Conc.*, iii, p. 10, citing Hincmar's 868 letter, above n. 53.

Hincmar refused, and instead remained loyal to the emperor.[57] Many years later (in the letter of 867) Hincmar recalled that he had 'joined the emperor's personal service and attended episcopal assemblies', perhaps before as well as after Louis' restoration in 834.[58] Hilduin, now pardoned, may well have had Hincmar's collaboration in the mid 830s in producing his Life of St. Denis.[59] But Hincmar had apparently 'again sought the quiet of the monastery for some years',[60] before emerging from St-Denis to join Charles the Bald – the question is, when?[61]

Hincmar was certainly present (along with Abbot Louis of St-Denis) at the council summoned by the king at his palace of Ver in December 844.[62] Hincmar was not responsible for writing up these *capitula* – where the elegant Latin and aggressive tone on the subject of lay abbacies in c. 12 show Lupus' hand.[63] The style and content of the capitulary of Toulouse in June 844 are arguably Hincmarian, however.[64] Hincmar can be identified as the recipient of a grant of fisc-lands in the Poissy area (dep. Seine-et-Oise), issued in the Auvergne on 12 August.[65] Thus Charles had had Hincmar in his entourage in Aquitaine, perhaps taking him south at the outset of the ill-fated Toulouse campaign in February 844. Hincmar's Aquitanian connexions are probably relevant here. Bernard, count of Toulouse in the 860s, was his *propinquus*,[66] and Bernard was the nephew of Fredelo, *custos* of Toulouse in 849 and perhaps

---

[57] Flodoard *Historia Remensis ecclesiae* iii, c. 1, in *MGH SS*, xiii, p. 475. In 831, though, Hincmar had followed his *nutritor into exile*.

[58] *MGH Epp.*, viii(i) p. 210.

[59] J.M. Wallace-Hadrill, 'History in the Mind of Archbishop Hincmar', p. 47.

[60] *MGH Epp.*, viii(i), p. 210.

[61] Hincmar's reference to Verdun in his Letter to Charles's son and heir Louis, in 877, *PL* 125, col. 985, need not imply he was there.

[62] *MGH Conc.*, iii, no. 7, p. 38.

[63] *MGH Conc.*, iii, p. 36. Hartmann points out that cc. 1 and 12 were probably written by Lupus, but he may have done no more than tidy up cc. 4-11. Cf. Lupus, *Ep.* 43, p. 182: 'canones eosdem sive, ut vos vocatis, capitula meo stilo tunc comprehensa vobis direxi'.

[64] Nelson, 'Making Ends Meet: Wealth and Poverty in the Carolingian Church', *Studies in Church History*, 24 (1987), pp. 25-35, at p. 30, argues this on the grounds of similarities of style and substance between the 844 capitulary and Hincmar's *Collectio de ecclesiis et capellis*, written in c.859, now available in the fine edition by M. Stratmann, *MGH Fontes iuris Germanici antiqui in usum scholarum*, 14 (Hanover, 1990). Stratmann, *Hinkmar von Reims als Verwalter von Bistum und Kirchenprovinz* (Sigmaringen, 1991), pp. 34, 35, seems close to making the same link.

[65] T. 57, to the 'venerabilis vir, Hincmarus presbyter'. Tessier, *Recueil*, ii, p. 58 n. 1, identifies this estate with the *Mansus Adalingi* in the Poissy area, mentioned in a charter for St-Denis, T. 247 (19 September 862), as that which 'Hincmarus, venerabilis archiepiscopus Remensis ecclesiae, a nostra largitate in jus proprium per regale praeceptum consecutus fuerat, idemque per nostram licentiam fratribus in eodem loco infirmis benigne contulerat'. Both T. 57 and T. 247 survive as originals, from the St-Denis archive.

[66] Flodoard, *Hist.*, iii, c. 26, *MGH SS*, xiii, p. 543.

already in 844.[67] Very soon after becoming archbishop of Rheims in 845, Hincmar wrote to Fredelo, committing to his protection Rheims' property in Aquitaine.[68] It seems clear, therefore, that Hincmar in 844 was already well-acquainted with the political scene in Aquitaine. Professor Magnou-Nortier has detected a specifically Aquitanian usage in the term *convenientia*.[69] There is nothing distinctively Aquitanian about it though:[70] in fact it appears as a synonym for 'sworn association' (*adunatio*) in the capitulary of Herstal of 779, and in the general sense of 'political arrangement' in Charlemagne's *Divisio regni* of 806.[71] But Magnou-Nortier is surely right to stress the Coulaines author's familiarity with legal language. As noted above, he seems to have been familiar with earlier capitularies, notably that of 823/25, and probably also the decrees of the council of Paris of 829.[72] It is relevant to recall, therefore, that Hincmar 'certainly by 830 was playing a part in public affairs under the eye of Abbot Hilduin',[73] who held the post of archchaplain at the palace of Louis the Pious through the years from 819 to 830. Those 'public affairs' included attendance at assemblies. At least by June 844 Hincmar (if the attribution of the Toulouse *capitula* is correct) was capable of drafting a capitulary, and certainly by December of that year, he had well-known ideas about what *capitula* should look like.[74] He was, by 844, nearing forty, and he had not refused Charles's summons to serve him in Aquitaine. Altogether, it seems quite likely that even before the 844 campaign, and hence perhaps from 843, Hincmar (alongside Lupus) was in the king's entourage, ready for the moment when Charles moved against his nephew Pippin II. In any event, Hincmar's presence in Aquitaine in 844 is sufficient to dispose of the argument that he went straight from St-Denis to the archiepiscopal throne in April 845.

Hincmar almost certainly played a part in the transmission of the capitulary of Coulaines. MS Hague 10 D 2, written at Rheims in the third quarter of the

[67] T. 339 shows that Bernard's father was Raymund. He had succeeded his brother Fredelo as count of Toulouse in the early 850s: see L. Levillain, 'Les Nibelungen historiques et leurs alliances de famille', *Annales du Midi*, 50 (1938), pp. 5-52, at 20-21.

[68] Flodoard, *Hist.*, iii, c. 20, p. 513: 'quas res Frigidoloni viro illustri tutandas commisit'. If Fredelo was in charge of Toulouse, it was as Pippin II's man: hence Hincmar does not address him as count.

[69] *Foi et fidelité*, pp. 86, 95, invoking the 'connaissance du droit romain' characteristic of the Midi.

[70] The one example cited by Magnou-Nortier, *Foi et fidelité*, pp. 28-29, is from the formulary of Angers.

[71] *MGH Capit.*, i, no. 20, c. 16, p. 51; no. 45, c. 16, p. 129: 'statuta vel convenientiae'. Cf. *MGH Capit.*, ii, no. 194, p. 23 (division project of 831); and no. c. 7, p. 178 (the 847 Council of Mainz, referring to agreements between bishops and laity over the protection of church property).

[72] See Hartmann, *MGH Conc.*, iii, p. 10.

[73] Wallace-Hadrill, 'History of the Mind of Hincmar', p. 43.

[74] Cf. above, n. 62.

ninth century, contains a series of capitularies starting with that of Coulaines which can plausibly be seen as copied from a collection made by Hincmar, or on his orders.[75] This of course does not prove that Hincmar drafted all these capitularies, but his interest in the Coulaines text is proved by the use made of it in a number of subsequent capitularies, including some which he almost certainly wrote himself – notably the oaths exchanged by Charles and his *fideles* at Quierzy in March 858.[76] Further, in a work addressed to Charles in 868, Hincmar referred to 'what had been agreed at Coulaines', implying (he had evidently seen the document) that Warin's had been the first of the magnates' confirmations, and adding that a copy had been sent to Louis the German, taken by Richwin.[77]

Several traits in the capitulary of Coulaines may be seen as characteristically Hincmarian. There is the emphasis on the production, and subscription, of a written document.[78] Then there is c. 1's insistence on the safeguarding of church property: widespread though this concern was among ninth-century churchmen, it was Hincmar who was later, in an important treatise on this subject, to base his demand for royal observance of ecclesiastical rights on Coulaines c. 1.[79] As for the role of lay consensus in the politics of the realm, Hincmar's personal interest came through loud and clear not only in a string of *capitula* and royal speeches which he composed wholly or in part, but in *The Government of the Palace* where aristocratic assemblies were discussed at length as means whereby 'the good condition (*status*) of the whole realm was

[75] Classen, 'Die Verträge', pp. 28-31; Nelson, *Politics and Ritual*, p. 94. Hartmann, *MGH Conc.*, iii, p. 12, argues that the collection of the Hague MS could not have originated in the royal chancery, as it includes the capitulary of Ver which was otherwise 'nicht rezipiert'. But a hard-and-fast distinction between 'public' and 'private' archives is anachronistic for the ninth century: cf. Nelson, *Politics and Ritual*, pp. 94, 97, and idem, 'Literacy', pp. 288-89. Hincmar's role straddles those categories. For Rheims connexions of one of the other two MSS containing the Coulaines text, Paris, B.N. Lat. 4638, see Nelson, *Politics and Ritual*, p. 96, n. 25.

[76] *MGH Capit.*, ii, no. 269, pp. 295-7. See also the *Consilium* of 856, *MGH Capit.*, ii, no. 295, pp. 424-5. See further Nelson, *Politics and Ritual*, pp. 147, 148 and nn. 1 and 2.

[77] *Pro ecclesiae libertatum defensione*, PL 125, col. 1066, quoting Coulaines, c. 1 *in extenso*. Hincmar's reference here to the *consensus Warini et aliorum optimatum* echoes that of the text's rubric in the Hague MS. Classen, 'Die Verträge', pp. 24-25, suggests alternative interpretations for Warin's singular position: either that he was the dominant figure at Coulaines, or that he was clinging on grimly to a threatened position at court which he in fact lost soon after. I suggest that Warin's role in November 843 was as a power-broker between rival magnates: see above, p. 2. It is not clear, *pace* Classen, that he was thereafter 'in the background of West Frankish politics'. For Richwin, see *AB* 844, p. 59, n. 19.

[78] Notably in the preface ('hoc scriptum fieri proposuimus') and in c. 6 ('hoc foedus concordiae salubris, quod propter pacis caritatisque custodiam inivimus et cirographi virtute subscripsimus . . . ') M. Stratmann, *Hincmar von Reims als Verwalter*, pp. 5-19, 65-69, shows the difficulty of assessing how typical or otherwise of ninth-century West Frankish bishops Hincmar was in his concern with *Schriftlichkeit*, yet gives the impression that she thinks he was in some ways exceptional. See also Devisse, *Hincmar et la loi* (Dakar, 1962), pp. 87-90: Nelson, *Politics and Ritual*, p. 145 and n. 2, 151, 154-55.

[79] Above, n. 76.

maintained'.[80] Ruling with the 'counsel and aid' (*consilium et auxilium*) of bishops and lay *fideles*, a phrase first recorded at Coulaines, was indeed, in Devisse's phrase, an expression with a future: it was to appear repeatedly in Hincmar's later works, including capitularies.[81] Finally, there is in both the form and the content of the Coulaines text an Augustinian flavour that brings Hincmar particularly to mind. Many Carolingian scholars were acquainted with some of Augustine's writings, but few had internalised them as thoroughly as Hincmar, and fewer still over such a range: during his pontifical career between 845 and 882, Hincmar was to quote from thirty-eight distinct works, in some cases more than thirty times.[82] Of all these the one he most often cited, and the one from which the flow of citations is fairly constant through Hincmar's writings (though his extant output is unevenly distributed, with relatively little datable to the first decade or so of his pontificate), is the *Commentaries on the Psalms*. From time to time, Hincmar would put himself through a crash course in one or another of Augustine's treatises to tackle (usually at the king's request) a particular theological or canonical issue; but his thought had been permanently and profoundly shaped, long before he became archbishop of Rheims, but Augustine's unhurried reflections on the primary text of early medieval education and personal piety. To apply fundamentals of Christian learning to the problems of secular political life, to respond positively (like Augustine's wise judge in *The City of God*, xix, 6) to the claims of earthly society, to achieve peace of a kind: such was the essence of Hincmar's life-work – and of the capitulary of Coulaines.

[80] *De ordine palatii* c. 29, ed. T. Gross and R. Schieffer, *MGH Fontes iuris Germanici antiqui in usum scholarum*, 3 (Hanover, 1980), p. 82. Hincmar's interest is proven, whether he wrote this passage himself or revised an earlier work: cf. Nelson, *Politics and Ritual*, p. 106. It's worth stressing that Hincmar's political ideas were not entirely coherent, or consistent, throughout his long life: the Coulaines text could be seen as an early, 'experimental' work, only some of whose themes were developed later.

[81] Devisse, 'Essai sur l'histoire d'une expression', pp. 182-95.

[82] Devisse, *Hincmar*, iii, pp. 1358-63. Cf. J.N. Hillgarth, 'L'influence de la *Cité de Dieu* de saint Augustin au haut moyen âge', *Sacris Erudiri*, 28 (1985), pp. 5-34.

# 2

## Continuity and Innovation in Tenth-Century Ottonian Culture[*]

### Rosamond McKitterick

Comparisons drawn between Carolingian and Ottonian culture, the artistic achievement excepted, at one stage were almost invariably to the disparagement of the latter.[1] Now, however, not only the art, architecture, metal work and ivory sculpture is fully appreciated,[2] but far more is known and understood of the intellectual activities of the Ottonian monasteries and bishoprics and of their religious aspirations.[3] Any past underestimation of the culture of

---

[*] It is with affection and gratitude for Margaret's friendship over the last two decades, in particular for the generous help she gave me in the early years when I was a very green research student, and in tribute to her fine contribution to the study of mediaeval learning, that I offer this essay.

[1] Bishop Burnet called the tenth century a 'very age of lead' and many have since followed his lead.

[2] Adolf Goldschmidt, *German Illumination*, ii, *Ottonian Period* (Florence, 1928); Albert Boekler, *Abendländische Miniaturen bis zum Ausgang der romanischen Zeit* (Berlin, 1930) and 'Ottonische Kunst in Deutschland', *I problemi comuni dell'Europa postcarolingia*. Settimane di studio del centro Italiano di studi sull'alto medioevo, 2 (Spoleto, 1955), pp. 329-53; Victor Elbern, *Das erste Jahrtausend: Kultur und Kunst im werdenden Abendland an Rhein und Ruhr* (Düsseldorf, 1962) Louis Grodecki, *L'architecture ottonienne: au seuil de l'art roman* (Paris, 1958); Louis Grodecki, Florentine Mütherich, Jean Taralon and Francis Wormald, *Le siècle de l'an mil* (Paris, 1973) and the new exhibitions on Theophanu, *Vor dem Jahr 1000: Abendländische Buchkunst zur Zeit der Kaiserin Theophanu*. ed. Anton von Euw and Gudrun Sporbeck, Austellungskataloge, Schnütgen Museum, Cologne 12 April-16 June 1991 (Cologne, 1991) and now Henry Mayr-Harting, *Ottonian Manuscript Illumination*, 2 vols. (London, 1991). Nevertheless, more effort has been concentrated on elucidating the Salian period; and even there, less emphasis is placed on book production and intellectual activity: see for example, *Die Salier und das Reich*, ed. Stefan Weinfurter, 3 vols. (Sigmaringen, 1991).

[3] See, for example, the useful assessments by Heinz Hofmann, 'Profil der lateinischen Historiographie im zehnten Jahrhundert' and Peter Christian Jacobsen, 'Formen und Strukturen der lateinischen Literatur der Ottonischen Zeit', in: *Il secolo di ferro: mito e realta del secolo X*, Settimane di studio del centro Italiano di studi sull'alto medioevo, 38 (Spoleto, 1991). See also *Kaiserin Theophanu: Begegnung des Ostens und Westens um die Wende der ersten Jahrtausends*. 2 vols. (Cologne, 1991). Only a small section of these volumes is concerned with intellectual life in the East Frankish kingdom itself. Most of the recent output concerned with intellectual life in the tenth century has largely concerned itself with the west Frankish or French and Lotharingian

tenth-century Germany may have been in part a consequence of the evident lack of interest on the part of the Ottonian kings, at least as far as the patronage of book production and intellectual culture are concerned. There is no sign, for instance, of any of the Ottonian rulers having emulated the Carolingians in actually sustaining groups of artists, scribes and craftsmen associated with the royal court over a long period of time in order to create books and artefacts for their particular objectives.[4] Only for Otto III and Henry II can evidence of a royal library be assembled, and even then it is quite striking how few of the books in that library were produced in contemporary Germany.[5] Patronage by the Carolingian rulers, moreover, was primarily for the promotion of their royal power as Christian kings and for the consolidation of the Christian faith by disseminating the key texts on which that faith was based.[6] Such motives have not as yet been discerned in relation to the Ottonian rulers.

It may be that fuller examination of the manuscripts of the tenth century may yet reveal evidence of kingly promotion of book production. As I have argued elsewhere, however, while it was not the kings but the queens and princesses of the Ottonian house who were the active royal participants in, and occasional promoters of, Ottonian intellectual life, it appears to have been episcopal patronage which was the deciding factor in the degree of educational and artistic achievement in the East Frankish kingdom in the tenth century.[7] The intellectual achievements of the Ottonian schools are certainly better appreciated than they were, and full credit in particular has been accorded the remarkable contribution to historiographical writing made by East Frankish writers in the tenth century such as Thietmar, Widukind and Hrotsvit.[8] The

regions: see for example, *Haut moyen-âge. Culture, education et société: études offerts à Pierre Riché*, ed. M.Sot (Paris, 1990).

[4] The Carolingians' activity is clear from the work of Bernhard Bischoff, collected together above all in his *Mittelalterliche Studien*. 3 vols. (Stuttgart, 1966, 1967 and 1981) and Wilhelm Koehler and Florentine Mütherich, *Die Karolingische Miniaturen* (Berlin 1935– ). For an assessment of Carolingian royal patronage see Rosamond McKitterick, 'Royal Patronage of Culture in the Frankish Kingdoms under the Carolingians: Motives and Consequences', *Committenti e produzione artistico-letteraria nell'alto medioevo occidentale*. Settimane di studio del centro italiano di studi nell'alto medioevo, 39 (Spoleto), pp. 1-40.

[5] Florentine Mütherich, 'The Library of Otto III', in *The Role of the Book in Medieval Culture*, ii, ed. Peter Ganz, Bibliologia. Elementa ad librorum studia pertinentia, 4 (Turnhout, 1986), pp. 11-26 and Rosamond McKitterick, 'Ottonian Intellectual Culture in the Tenth Century and the Role of Theophanu', in *Keizerin Theophano, Byzantium en het Westen 950-1050*. ed. Bert Groen, Victoria van Aalst and Andrew Palmer, forthcoming.

[6] McKitterick, 'Carolingian Royal Patronage'.

[7] Eadem, 'Ottonian Intellectual Culture'.

[8] See the recent survey by Franz-Josef Schmale, *Funktion und Formen mittelalterliche Geschichtsschreibung: Eine Einführung* (Darmstadt, 1985) and his references, as well as Wilhelm Wattenbach and Robert Holtzmann, *Deutschlandsgeschichtsquellen im Mittelalter: Die Zeit der Sachsen und Salier*, i, *Das Zeitalter des Ottonischen Staates (900-1050)*. ed. F.J. Schmale (Darmstadt, 1978), which also gives due space to the impressive number of saints' lives and episcopal biographies from this period.

implications for the extent of continuity or innovation in tenth-century intellectual culture in Ottonian Germany of episcopal and monastic book production, however, have still to be explored. In this essay, therefore, I make some preliminary observations and raise some specific questions about the apparent emphases in and concentrations of tenth- and early eleventh-century manuscripts from the Ottonian realm. I hope thereby to contribute a little to the understanding of the continuity of learning and the availability of essential texts in the early middle ages which Margaret Gibson has herself done so much to elucidate.[9]

The essential foundation for the study of Ottonian book production has been provided by Hartmut Hoffmann in a masterly survey of the principal groups of 'schools of script' or *Schreibschulen* into which surviving manuscripts can be divided on palaeographical grounds.[10] Twelve main *Schreibschulen* have been identified, at Corvey, Fulda, Hersfeld, Lorsch, Mainz, Regensburg, Reichenau, Würzburg, St. Gall, Seeon, Tegernsee and Trier, with subsidiary groups associated with an 'unknown Saxon scriptorium', the 'Sankt Gallische Zweigschule' in Mainz, Freising, Niederaltaich, St. Eucharius and St. Martin in Trier and Echternach. Yet this catalogue at once raises questions. Nearly all these houses are the well-established ones, founded in the late Merovingian or early Carolingian period, and some of them with not only a long history of book production behind them, but also well-established 'house-styles' of script and layout and concentrations of expertise.[11] Given the enormous number of new monastic foundations in Ottonian Germany, partly in association with the reform movement emanating from Lotharingia,[12] partly in association with lay piety and the aristocratic foundation of many new religious houses,

---

[9] See, for example, Margaret Gibson, 'The Continuity of Learning, circa 850 – circa 1051', *Viator* 6 (1975), pp. 1-13 and eadem, 'Priscian, "Institutiones Grammaticae": A Handlist of Manuscripts', *Scriptorium*, 26 (1972), pp. 105-24.

[10] Hartmut Hoffman, *Buchkunst und Königtum im ottonischen und frühsälischen Reich. MGH Schriften*, 30 (Stuttgart, 1986).

[11] On Fulda, for example, see the articles in *Von der Klosterbibliothek zur Landesbibliothek*, ed. A. Brall (Fulda, 1978); on Freising, Tegernsee, Regensburg and Niederaltaich see Bernhard Bischoff, *Die südostdeutschen Schreibschulen und Bibliotheken in der Karolingerzeit*, i, *Die Bayerischen Diözesen*. 3rd. ed. (Wiesbaden 1974); on Lorsch, see B. Bischoff, *Lorsch im Spiegel seiner Handschriften* (Munich, 1974); on Würzburg see B. Bischoff and J. Hofmann, *Libri Sancti Kyliani: Die Würzburger Schreibschule und die Dombibliothek im VIII. und IX. Jahrhundert* (Würzburg, 1952); on St. Gall see Albert Bruckner, *Scriptoria Medii Aevi Helvetica: Denkmäler schweizerischer Schreibkunst des Mittelalters*, ii, *Schreibschulen der Diözese Konstanz. St. Gallen*, i, (Geneva, 1936) *St. Gallen*, ii, (Geneva, 1938). On the general character and problems of the later Carolingian scriptoria and the notion of a 'house style' see R. McKitterick, 'Carolingian Book Production: Some Problems', *The Library*, Sixth Series, 12 (1990), pp. 1-33.

[12] The literature on this subject is enormous. The recent collection of papers, *Monastische Reformen im 9 und 10 Jahrhundert*, ed. Raymund Kottje and Helmut Maurer, Vorträge und Forschungen, 38 (Sigmaringen, 1989) will direct readers to the necessary literature.

especially convents for women,[13] why are there so few new houses discernable among the identified scriptoria? Certainly we witness in the establishment of new bishoprics and religious houses a prodigious effort, in which the royal house joined, to create a network of monasteries and churches to the farthest reaches of the realm. Are the absence of all but a handful of new centres among the ateliers of Ottonian Germany and the relatively small number of identifiable houses illusions? Were some houses with scribes trained by older foundations in fact responsible for the establishment of new scriptoria who then produced books which appear to us to originate from the older houses? Or is it that Ottonian book production was concentrated in a few centres which then had as their function the supply of books to the new houses? That is, was it the case that the older houses simply supplied the new ones with books when they contributed monks? Can we discern the process of a provision of guidance in organising a library of a school? Was it never the case that a new house might set out to become a centre for book production to supply its own needs, let alone those of a patron, commissioner or neighbouring monastery or church? In other words, can we observe in the extant evidence any sign at all of the fundamental provision for learning and education of any kind, namely the copying of texts, being associated with these new foundations, and book production in the Ottonian world being organised with these considerations in mind?

Such a relentless series of questions constitutes an agenda for future research and only a beginning can be made in response to them here. It embraces, furthermore, other considerations. Not only do we have to reckon with the possible provision of scribes, training of new scribes, and the provision of exemplars, we also have to acknowledge that a selection process of available texts may have occurred, in order to transmit to the new Ottonian houses some proportion of the canon of learning the Carolingians had done so much to define as well as some appreciation of the Carolingian organisation of knowledge.[14] Further, there is the problem of new scribes learning techniques of writing and layout for the copying of books developed in the ninth century and passed on.[15] To what extent were these techniques simply received and preserved in the tenth century rather than being further developed?

Some interesting indications emerge from Hoffmann's magisterial survey, particularly the palaeographical evidence for the mobility of scribes in the tenth century. As far as collaboration between well-established houses for the

[13] Some useful comments on this are to be found in Michel Parisse, 'Les chanoinesses dans l'empire germanique (IXe-XIe siècle)', *Francia* 6 (1978), pp. 107-27 and Karl Leyser, *Rule and Conflict in an Early Medieval Society* (London, 1979), pp. 63-74.

[14] R. McKitterick, *The Carolingians and the Written Word* (Cambridge, 1989), especially pp. 165-210.

[15] For developments in layout in response to the requirements of the contents of the text as it is perceived in different contexts see the examples provided in *Mise en page et mise en texte du livre manuscrit*, ed. Henri-Jean Martin and Jean Vezin (Paris, 1990).

exchange of books, information and expertise is concerned, Hoffmann himself is the first to stress how such classification does not leave space for the number of instances of scribes clearly trained to write in one place collaborating with scribes from another on the copying of books.[16] Hoffmann cites examples of Reichenau and St. Gall collaboration as well as Mainz and Fulda, evidenced for example in the Gospels now in The Hague (Koninklijke Bibliotheek, MS 135 F. 10).[17] He raises too the possibilities of scribes learning to write together in one centre and then returning to their home monasteries and copying books in the essentially 'foreign' style they had learnt or of scribes going from one centre to teach others to write.[18]

Proximity did not necessarily ensure related script styles, as is clear from a comparison of Reichenau and St. Gall scripts, each of which is entirely distinctive. The occasional intense rivalry between the two monasteries, moreover, did not prevent them from collaborating, as in the Book of Maccabees now in Leiden Universiteitsbibliothek (MS Periz. F 17).[19]

Hoffmann posits also the deliberate exchange of particular expert scribes in order to fulfil certain commissions, or even, as in the case of Paris, B.N., MS lat 13313, a Mainz pontifical, how a scribe might be sent from Metz to Mainz in order to copy a book required by his own bishop.[20] Pursuit of particular texts, or editions of certain texts, was clearly a major imperative in such exchange. The recension of the Vulgate in use at Fulda, for example, was used for the copying of Berlin, MS theol. lat. fol. 336 at Werden.[21] One centre, particularly a cathedral might draw heavily on the general scribal expertise of another, likely to be a nearby monastery, in order to build up its own resources; as Mainz drew on Fulda and as Regensburg and Freising may have drawn on St. Emmeram and Tegernsee.[22] It is this aspect that needs to be explored more fully. We have to consider how the many new foundations of female and some male monasteries would have equipped themselves with the books they needed and whether or not they could themselves have acquired the skills of writing from living teachers from other centres or used older books as silent teachers.

Let us look, therefore, at the example of Essen, which gets no discussion as a scriptorium by Hoffmann at all, nor does he entertain the possibility anywhere

---

[16] Hoffman, *Buchkunst*, p. 96.

[17] Ibid., pp. 97 and 239.

[18] Ibid., pp. 98-99 and see Christine Eder concerning the role of Froumund of Tegernsee in this respect: 'Die Schule des Klosters Tegernsee im frühen Mittelalter im Spiegel der Tegernseer Handschriften, *Studien und Mitteilungen zur Geschichte des Benediktiner-Ordens*, 83 (1972), pp. 6-155 at pp. 37 and 44.

[19] Hoffmann, *Buchkunst*. p. 97 gives other examples.

[20] Ibid., pp. 98 and 254-55.

[21] Ibid., pp. 143-44 and W. Stüwer, *Das Erzbistum Köln*, 3, *Die Reichsabtei Werden an der Ruhr*. Germania Sacra, Neue Folge, 12 (Berlin, 1980) p. 70.

[22] Hoffman, *Buchkunst*, pp. 226-30, 276-303, 416-41.

in his book that some of the remarkable convents where there was so much literary activity may also have produced their own books as well as books for others.[23] Study of the books of Essen provenance in the late ninth and the tenth centuries reveals literate nuns annotating their books. From a list of the non-liturgical books at Essen compiled *c.* 900 (Düsseldorf Universitätsbibliothek, MS B4), moreover, we can see that the literary interests of the nuns were very similar to those of comparable male foundations, namely, patristic and Carolingian theology and biblical exegesis. Whether the nuns at Essen were later able to develop their own atelier for book production has not yet been established, but no less than eight tenth- and eleventh-century manuscripts can be associated with Essen, none of which has been attributed to any centre other than Essen itself. The palaeography of these books, pointing to a north-west German origin, makes location to Essen a distinct possibility. The texts copied include the sermons of Gregory the Great and Augustine, the letters of Gregory the Great and a sacramentary, Isidore of Seville's *Etymologiae* and two Gospel books. As far as the contents of the books are concerned, Essen, like all other German ecclesiastical centres, continued the emphases of the Carolingian collections, with biblical and liturgical books, works of exegesis and theology predominating.

The pattern of survival indicated in surviving books from Essen with books from elsewhere forming the ninth-century portion of the library, and books, possibly from Essen itself for the tenth century and later, is entirely consistent with the development of a scriptorium at Essen in the later part of the ninth and early tenth centuries. The influence of Werden script is so clear it is possible that it is thence that the Essen nuns acquired their teachers of script. Similarly, in relation to many of the other new foundations, the extant manuscripts need to be scrutinised without the assumption that they are to be linked with a few main centres. Literate nuns and monks in these new foundations may not at first have organised a scriptorium in order to build up a library or serve the needs of a school, but have acquired their books instead from elsewhere. Only later in their history may the first steps towards personal production of books have been made, with guidance offered from master scribes in longer-established communities. In the codices associated with Hitda, abbess of Meschede and Uta, abbess of Niedermünster, for example, we have books decorated in distinctive Cologne and Regensburg styles (Darmstadt, Hessische Landesbibliothek MS 1640 and Munich, Bayerische Staats-

---

[23] Work is in progress on Essen by Gerhard Karpp; a preliminary study is his 'Bemerkungen zum Bücherbesitz des Essener Damenstifts um 900', in *Octogenario: Dankesgabe für Heinrich Karpp überreicht von Schülern Verwandten und Bekannten.* ed. Jurgen Honscheid and Gerhard Karpp (Düsseldorf, 1988), pp. 51-115. For what follows I draw also on my discussion of Essen in the context of female literacy in the middle ages: 'Frauen und Schriftlichkeit im Frühmittelalter', in *Weibliche Lebensgestaltung im früheren Mittelalter.* ed. Hans-Werner Goetz (Cologne, 1991), pp. 65-118 at pp. 87-90.

bibliothek, Clm. 13601).[24] These may point to the sources of instruction for the scribes rather than the origins of the manuscripts themselves.

A further example of a new scriptorium is to be seen in the books of Seeon. Founded in 999, Seeon was a remarkably small community numbering, as far as we know, only seventeen monks, four laymen and a *puer*.[25] Yet, at the beginning of the eleventh century, a small group of scribes there produced an astonishing number of beautiful liturgical books, mostly Gospel books and sacramentaries, in addition to a copy of the Rule of Benedict, a *computus* and two copies of Boethius's *Consolatio philosophiae*. These books show clear signs of an independent and distinctive development of a script type based on the Regensburg script. They suggest the deliberate setting up of a scriptorium, with help initially from Regensburg.

In methods of book production, the script type, the development of higher ranking scripts for display, the idea of a house style of script being associated with a particular scriptorium, the methods of scribal organisation and the types of text copied, we can indeed observe clear continuity with the Carolingian west Frankish writing centres as well as with east Frankish scriptoria such as Würzburg and Fulda, Cologne and Corvey, Reichenau and St. Gall, which appear to have provided guidance to some new establishments setting up their own scriptoria and building their libraries. This is particularly evident in the case of Corvey. Originally founded from Corbie in Picardy, it might be expected that the ninth-century manuscripts first produced there would show close familiarity with the methods of, and with the texts produced at, Corbie.[26] In the tenth century it is clear that there was scholarly work being done at Corvey, evident, for example, in the glossed Bible now in Bamberg (Staatsbibliothek, MS 96): that the book was designed for study is suggested by the copious marginal notes and the careful layout of the manuscript pages to accommodate it.[27] That the monks of Corvey produced books for other centres as well as for their own consumption, however, is suggested by the extraordinary number of Gospel books and sacramentaries that can be attributed to it in the tenth and eleventh centuries such as the Gospels in Baltimore (Walters Art Gallery, MS W 751), the Gregorian sacramentary now in Munich, Bayerische Staatsbibliothek Clm. 10077 and the meagre fragment of a large-format Bible in Stuttgart, Württemburgische Landesbibliothek, Cod. fragm. 77.

We have no idea whether Corvey's activity was a self-appointed mission to supply the essential texts for priests in their ministry. At the risk of making a subjective judgement, these Gospel books and liturgical texts are not in the

[24] Hoffman, *Buchkunst*, p. 295.

[25] Ibid., pp. 402-16.

[26] Ibid., pp. 127-29. On Corbie, David Ganz, *Corbie in the Carolingian Renaissance*. Beihefte der Francia, 20 (Sigmaringen, 1990).

[27] Hoffman, *Buchkunst*, pp. 128 and plates 1-3.

first rank of sumptuous codices; most look like texts for everyday use. Corvey's book production may have been the result of commissions from clergy unable to provide the books themselves and be one crucial indication of the service a monastic scriptorium could provide for the Ottonian church and ecclesiastical hierarchy.

Reichenau's book production, on the other hand, is notable for the enormous number of sumptuous Gospel books it produced. Of the one hundred or so extant manuscripts, well over fifty are Gospel books, Gospel lectionaries, sacramentaries and other liturgical books. Some were presented to kings. Others represent gifts or commissions, such as the tonary now in Cleveland (Museum of Art, J.H. Wade Collection, MS 52.88); the Gero codex in Darmstadt (Landesbibliothek, MS 1948) produced for Cologne, the Leipzig Gospels (Leipzig Universitätsbibliothek, MS Rep. I 4° 57) presented to Corvey; the Paris Gospels (Bibliothèque d'Arsenal, MS 610) probably produced for Worms; a sacramentary in Paris (B.N., MS lat. 18005) for a see in the archdiocese of Trier; the Hornbach Sacramentary now in Solothurn (St. Ursus Cod. U 1) produced for Abbot Adalbert of Hornbach; a Gospel book for Utrecht (Rijksmuseum, Het Catharijnconvent Bernulphuscodex); and the Gospel book, now Paris, B.N., MS lat. 10514, produced for the monastery of Poussay. Even among the non-liturgical books there is evidence of commissioned or donated books, such as Berno of Reichenau's tracts on prayer for Henry II, now Montpellier, Bibliothèque Municipale, MS 303 and a copy of the *Vita Udalrici* possibly written for presentation to Augsburg, now Vienna, Österreichische Nationalbibliothek, MS 573. Very little of Reichenau's total book production in the tenth and eleventh centuries appears to have been for home consumption; the greater proportion of its scribal expertise was expended on books for export.[28]

By contrast, such centres as Fulda, while also producing a quantity of liturgical books, also copied an impressive number of patristic and Carolingian texts, presumably for use in the school, though one aspect of tenth- and eleventh-century Fulda manuscript production that merits further investigation is the number of Bibles it produced such as Kassel, Landesbibliothek, MS 2° theol. 284. Although mostly only fragments of these massive books survive, including Kassel Landesbibliothek, MS 4° Mus. 111/1-4 and Mscr. Hass. Fol. 57e.I. Abth.Heft 5) work is needed to ascertain the degree to which Fulda was working on an edition of the Bible in this period and whether it can be set

---

[28] For details see Hoffmann, *Buchkunst*, pp. 303-55 and the discussion in many contexts by Mayr-Harting, *Ottonian Manuscript Illumination*.

beside the remarkable activity in this respect in the Carolingian period in west Francia, not least at Metz, the royal court and Tours.[29]

At Regensburg, on the other hand, efforts appear to have been concentrated on the production of sacramentaries and Mass texts. Fifteen out of thirty-four liturgical books attributed to Regensburg in the tenth and eleventh century are Mass books. Unfortunately in very few cases is there an indication in the subsequent history of the recipients of these books. A small group of manuscripts may indicate other than exclusively liturgical activities, such as the Rule of Caesarius of Arles for nuns, probably written for the convent of Niedermünster (Berlin, MS theol. lat. qu.199), and the *Traditionscodex* written under Abbot Ramvold (975-1000) (Munich, Hauptstaats Archiv, Regensburg St. Emmeram, MS Lit. 5 1/2).[30]

Hersfeld and Lorsch, too, continued to produce books for the use of the monks in their library, such as Cicero's *De officiis* and *De inventione*, Macrobius, Prudentius, Boethius's *De arithmetica* and Philo's *Antiquitates biblicae*, as well as standard theological books such as Gregory's Dialogues and Homilies on the Gospels from Hersfeld, and Quintus Curtius Rufus's *Historia Alexandri*, Isidore of Seville's *Sententiae*, and a striking number of historical works (Jordanes, Orosius, Gregory of Tours, Einhard and the royal Frankish annals) from Lorsch. Only a small proportion of their output was devoted to liturgical books.[31]

At Mainz, episcopal needs were well represented. Besides a fair number of Gospel books, possibly produced to supply churches in the diocese, there is an impressive array of classical and patristic texts and a notable concentration on canon and royal law, as well as such texts as Regino of Prüm's *De synodalibus causis* (Wolfenbüttel, Herzog August Bibliothek, MS Guelf. 83.21 Aug.2°) and pseudo-Alcuin's *De divinis officiis* (Vienna, Nationalbibliothek Cod. 983).[32] Würzburg on the other hand, produced hardly any liturgical books at all. Most of its tenth- and eleventh-century books are of classical and late antique authors: Cicero, Persius, Horace, Juvenal, Martianus Capella and Plato.

At St. Gall we are able to trace the clearest lines of continuity. Many of its liturgical books include music. It is also likely that some were produced for export elsewhere. A notable clutch of texts is the number of saints' lives (such as London, B.L., MS Add. 21170) as well as the school books produced. Similarly, at Tegernsee there was extensive copying of standard patristic

---

[29] See David Ganz, 'Copying the Tours Bibles' and Rosamond McKitterick, 'Carolingian Bible Production: The Tours Anomaly', in *Mediaeval Bible Production*, ed. Richard Gameson (Cambridge, forthcoming). Above all, however, see Bonifatius Fischer, 'Bibeltext und Bibelreform unter Karl dem Grosse', in *Karl der Grosse: Lebenswerk und Nachleben*, ii, *Das geistliche Leben*. ed. B. Bischoff (Düsseldorf, 1965) pp. 156-216.

[30] Hoffmann, *Buchkunst*, pp. 276-7.

[31] For full details ibid., pp. 180-226.

[32] Ibid., p. 265-66.

authors, and classical texts such Cicero, Lucan, Ovid, Statius, Macrobius and Boethius.[33] At St. Maximin of Trier, on the other hand, the extant books reveal a far greater concentration on patristic authors – Jerome, Augustine, Gregory and Cassiodorus – as well as Carolingian biblical exegesis. Of the eighty or so manuscripts of the late tenth and early eleventh centuries, thirty-five are of patristic authors.

If it is feasible to generalise about the light the extant manuscripts of the Ottonian scriptoria shed on intellectual culture in the tenth and early eleventh centuries, it is notable how essentially conservative that culture was. Very little in the way of new texts was being copied. The texts are of the standard classical authors familiar from the Carolingian schools and of the mainline patristic authors we find listed in our Carolingian library catalogues. Very occasionally a work stands out from the general run of familiar texts. Examples of such new work are the treatises of Berno of Reichenau and Regino of Prüm, new saints' lives and histories, new collections of canon law, and some of the late ninth- and early tenth-century Carolingian authors, such as Remigius and Haimo of Auxerre, John the Deacon and his Life of Gregory, the great works of Notker Balbulus and Notker Labeo of St. Gall, or Tietland of Einsiedeln's commentary on the Epistles of St. Paul (Bamberg, Staatsbibliothek, MS Bibl. 89). Some interest in Greek is evident in the so-called Greek grammar included in a general collection of grammars made by Froumund of Tegernsee at the end of the tenth century.[34] Apart from the Gospel book of the second half of the tenth century now in Vienna, but possibly written in Constantinople itself, there is hardly any sign of an interest in, or knowledge of, Greek culture to any greater an extent than was evident in the Carolingian world.[35] What we do have, are very interesting concentrations of interest, and an impression of many houses equipping churches with the essential texts they needed. The examples of Essen and Seeon indicate the way in which members of new houses could be taught scribal skills. Among many of the other groups of manuscripts, products of new churches, convents and monasteries of the Ottonian realm may be represented. At present there appears to be a remarkable continuity in centres, and in methods, of book production. Whether this impression is correct remains to be explored.

[33] Further on Tegernsee in Eder, 'Tergernsee.'

[34] But see W.J. Aerts, 'The Knowledge of Greek in Western Europe at the Time of Theophano and the Greek Grammar Fragment in MS Vindob. 114', *Byzantium and the Low Countries in the Tenth Century*, ed. V. van Aaist (Hernen, 1985), pp. 78-103.

[35] Walter Berschin, *Griechisch-lateinisches Mittelalter* (Bern and Munich, 1980).

# 3

# 'Pando quod Ignoro': In Search of Carolingian Artistic Experience[1]

## David Ganz

Carolingian theological authors discussed the function of religious images, and Carolingian artists produced images of biblical and hagiographical, and sometimes of secular scenes. Yet between the image and the theology there seems to be a gulf. It is easy to find exegesis of the psalter which will clarify the meanings of images in illustrated psalters, but much harder to suggest ways in which these images were prized. In this essay I shall explore evidence of how Carolingian authors describe such images, in search of a vocabulary which conveys contemporary responses to works of art.[2] This treatment does not seek to be either comprehensive or definitive: we have little evidence, and what we do have does not supply a coherent set of categories. But at a time when historians of Carolingian art are exploring those features which make that art distinctive it seems worth investigating what contemporaries saw. Carolingian art was seldom autonomous; we must evaluate it in a context in which the response of the spectator was seldom concerned with beauty.

The famous letters of Gregory the Great to Bishop Serenus of Marseilles provide the classic expression of an attitude to images widely quoted by Carolingian authors.[3] Gregory saw images as a source of knowledge of biblical stories for persons ignorant of letters. 'A picture is displayed in churches on this account, in order that those who do not know letters may at

---

[1] *MGH Poeta*, ii, p. 396. This one-line poem by Walahfrid Strabo, for his wax tablet (*tabula*), 'Pando quod ignoro nec contradico petenti', one of a series of *tituli* preserved in three Carolingian manuscripts, seems to convey the problems of this piece.

[2] The classic anthology of sources, on which I have drawn frequently remains J. von Schlosser, *Schriftquellen zur Geschichte der karolingischen Kunst* (Vienna, 1892; reprinted Hildesheim, New York, 1974). The classic model for this type of enquiry, though for a much richer period, is M. Baxandall, *Painting and Experience in Fifteenth-Century Italy* (Oxford, 1972).

[3] The letters are most recently edited by D. Norberg, *CCSL* 140-40A (Turnhout, 1982), pp. 873-76, and translated with a most important commentary by C. Chazelle, 'Pictures, books and the illiterate: Pope Gregory I's letters to Serenus of Marseilles', *Word and Image*, 6 (1990), pp. 138-53.

least read by seeing on the walls what they are unable to read in books.' They were for instruction, not adoration:

> For it is one thing to adore a picture, another through a picture's story to learn what must be adored. For what writing offers to those who read it, a picture offers to the ignorant who look at it, since in it the ignorant see what they ought to follow, in it they who do not know letters read; whence especially for gentiles a picture stands in place of reading.

Elsewhere Gregory compares colours and the things depicted with the words and meanings of Scripture. To concentrate on colours or words is foolish, this is the letter which kills.[4] Images of sacred subjects offer 'something whereby the ignorant may gather knowledge of the story', and may guide the viewer to virtue and the worship of God. Gregory's letter was quoted in the *Libri Carolini* and in the arguments of Agobard of Lyons and Dungal in response to the iconoclastic stance of Claudius of Turin.[5] Walahfrid Strabo saw pictures as a kind of writing for the unlettered, 'useful for commemorating past deeds, as pictures do for stories, or for impressing love of those whose likenesses are presented more firmly on the minds of the viewers, as with the images of the lord and his saints'. Images can lead the simple and rude to love of invisible things.[6] But the doctrine of images as a teaching tool and an incitement to virtue and to adoration of God only offers a partial explanation of how these images might appear to an observer.

A Gospel book copied at Tours in 849 for the Emperor Lothar has a full page illumination of the enthroned emperor facing a set of verses, copied in golden capitals on purple vellum, in which Sigilaus asks God to exalt, protect and adorn the ruler. He tells how Lothar commissioned the volume, ordering the monks of St. Martin to write it beautifully and ornament it with gold and pictures. 'So that they might pray for the ruler he was painted on this page, so that whoever saw the face of the Augustus might humbly say "Praise to eternal God: may Lothar deserve to have eternal rest through our Lord Christ who reigns everywhere."'[7] On the following page are images of Pope Damasus and Jerome, with verses telling how the shaped image of blessed Damasus shines (*rutilat*) and the form of blessed Jerome shines (*splendet*).[8] Though they are in a volume copied at a major centre for an imperial patron, all of these verses are more concerned with the function than with the form of the image. In the great Bibles copied for Charles the Bald verse inscriptions detail the content and message of Scripture, and the virtues of the sovereign, but are as general in

---

[4] *Expositiones in Canticum Canticorum*, *CCSL* 144, ed., P. Verbraken (Turnhout, 1963), p. 5.

[5] *MGH Concilia*, ii, pp. 81-82, and note the use of this passage in the 825 council of Paris, *MGH Concilia*, II, ii, pp. 487-88, 527-29. For Agobard and Dungal, *Agobardi opera*, *CCCM*, lii, pp. 171-72 and Dungal in *PL* 105:468-69.

[6] *MGH Capitularia*, ii, pp. 482-84.

[7] *MGH Poetae*, ii, pp. 676-77; Paris, B.N., MS Lat 266, fo. 2.

[8] W. Kohler, *Die karolingischen Miniaturen, i, Die Schule von Tours* (Berlin, 1933), pl. 98-100.

their accounts of the images which they describe. David the psalmist shines (*resplendet*).[9] At the end of the first Bible of Charles the Bald, Charles also shines, and is addressed thus: 'You are portrayed here by the high study of art, but because this image is so shining (*rutilans*) that does not make it a true image of you to whom every image of man yields'. The facing picture shows Abbot Vivian and his flock presenting the Bible to Charles, with a verse describing how the picture reveals how Vivian the hero offers this work.[10] The image is a sign of new attitudes to the monarch's links with the abbey, but the verses address the king, they do not treat of the illustration. In the *Codex Aureus* of St. Emmeram the texts describing the opening illumination of Charles the Bald, enthroned with Francia and Gothia bringing tribute, seem to use no vocabulary for the craftsmanship of their work. Charles is adorned by piety and love of goodness. This codex shines with the gold and the rule of this man who constructed many good things with God's favour.[11] The illustration of prophets and evangelists is described as a 'page which shows with beautiful splendour how the eight creatures make echo with a pious mouth.'[12]

This silence about works of art may be paralleled in many Carolingian *tituli*. Poems from St. Riquier describing scenes of the Annunciation, Nativity, Passion and Ascension,[13] from Saint Gall designed to accompany a set of paintings of the life of Christ[14]; *tituli* from St. Riquier with scenes of the Fall;[15] *tituli* from Weissenburg for scenes from the life of Christ and St. Peter;[16] poems composed by Sedulius Scottus as *tituli* for Archbishop Gunther of Cologne with scenes of cherubim, the evangelist symbols, angels and the disciples,[17] or for a painted room with scenes of the Annunciation, Nativity, Flight into Egypt and John the Baptist,[18] all describe the scenes, but are silent about features of the depiction which show the treatment that the artist adopted.

Yet there can be no doubt about the importance of these *tituli*. Hrabanus Maurus, describing the altar of St. Boniface, urges the reader who wants to know the name of the saint to look at the picture and to read the *titulus*.[19] Without a *titulus* the image was incomplete.

In two poems Sedulius Scottus describes the rooms in the episcopal palace of

[9] *MGH Poetae*, iii, p. 248; Paris, B.N., MS Lat. 1, fo. 215 v.

[10] Kohler, *Miniaturen*, pp. 220-31 and pl. 74-77; *MGH Poetae*, iii, pp. 250-51.

[11] *MGH Poetae*, iii, p. 252; Munich, MS Clm. 14000, fo. 5 v.

[12] *MGH Poetae*, iii, p. 253; Munich, MS Clm. 14000, fo. 6 v. On the verses of the manuscript cf. P.E. Dutton, E. Jeauneau, 'The Verses of the Codex Aureus of Saint Emmeram', *Studi Medievali*, 3rd series, xxiv (1983), pp. 75-120.

[13] *MGH Poetae*, i, pp. 413-15.

[14] Ibid., ii, pp. 480-82.

[15] Ibid., iii, pp. 347-48.

[16] Ibid., iv, pp. 1047-50.

[17] Ibid., iii, pp. 231-32.

[18] Ibid., iii, p. 210.

[19] Ibid., ii, p. 215; Hrabani *Carmina*, 49, v.

Hartgar of Liège. The roofs shine freshly painted with skill, and many new pictures shine, their colours are listed, in contrast to the dark rooms of the poet.[20] In the second poem the colours of the rainbow are linked to the splendour of the room filled with sunlight.[21] The gold, the green of spring, purple and blue of the heavens, found in the order of the rainbow, are fitting for God who rules the heavens. The red and green are linked to the Crucifixion (the red blood and the green wood of the cross), the gold and blue to the sceptres of God.

Clearly the *tituli* placed beside images of rulers and of biblical scenes must be supplemented by other testimony. In his *De universo*, the revision of Isidore's *Etymologiae*, Hrabanus Maurus included definitions of beauty (*venustas*) and pictures (*pictura*) in Book XXI. Beauty is defined as whatever is added to buildings for ornament or fineness (*ornamentis et decoris causa*) like the gold painted laquearia or precious slabs of marble or pictures of colours.[22] A picture, in the same chapter, is defined as an image expressing the likeness of anything, which when it is seen leads the mind back to recollection.[23] The chapter continues with a section on colours and their symbolism. These definitions come straight from Isidore and transmit classical teaching. In the *Liber glossarum*, the encyclopedic glossary transmitted in some ten Carolingian manuscripts from Corbie, Fleury, Lorsch, Tours, Regensburg, Monza and Milan, the definitions of *pictura* supplement Isidore's account with excerpts from Book XXXV Pliny's *Natural History* detailing the history of painting in antiquity from Egypt to Rome.[24]

Sometimes passages of Carolingian exegesis supply hints as to how works of art were perceived. Both Angelomus of Luxeuil and Hrabanus Maurus explain the colours of the rainbow as symbols of security and fear, the colours of water and fire are shown together, blue on one side and red on the other as witnesses of both judgements, the one which has been and the one to come, that is when the world will be burned in fire.[25] In explaining the second commandment Hrabanus, in his commentary on Exodus, quotes Origen on idols, which are distinguished from likenesses:

> If someone gives gold, silver, wood or stone the shape of a quadruped, a snake or a bird and sets it up to be adored, he makes a likeness and not an idol, nevertheless if he sets up a picture for this purpose it is a likeness. Someone makes an idol when he,

[20] Ibid., iii, p. 169.
[21] Ibid., iii, pp. 198-99.
[22] *PL* 111:562:68. The text is Isidore *Etymologiae*, 19, xv, xi.
[23] *PL* 111:563. The text is Isidore *Etymologiae*, 16, i.
[24] *Glossaria latina, i, Glossarium Ansileubi*, ed. W.M. Lindsay et al. (Paris, 1926), p. 442. I have used the *Liber glossarum* text in London, BL, MS Harley 2735.
[25] Angelomus *In Genesim*, *PL* 115:162. This is quoted by Hrabanus *De universo*, 9, xx, *PL* 111:277-78. It derives from Isidore *De rerum natura*, xxxi, 2 and is also quoted by Bede. In the same passage Isidore describes a rainbow coloured red for the heavens, purple for the waters, white for air and black for earth.

(according to the Apostle's teaching 'An idol is nothing'[I Corinthians 8:4]) makes what does not exist. What is it that does not exist? An image which no eye has seen, but which the spirit has imagined. For example, if you imagine a dog's or a ram's head on human limbs, or if you put two faces on one man or join a man's torso to the lower parts of a horse or a fish.[26]

Earlier in the same work Hrabanus quoted Origen defining the likeness of the elect to the Lord in John's first Epistle.[27] 'If we say a picture is like the person whose image is depicted in the picture, if you look at the beauty (*gratia*) it is like, if you look at the reality it is very unlike. One is the image of flesh and a living body, the other is a mass of colours and wax placed on pictures lacking in feeling.[28]

This silence may be set in a context of Carolingian legislation. A capitulary of Charlemagne, issued in 811, says that 'although it is good if churches are beautifully built, the adornment and summit of good life is to be preferred to buildings; for as it seems to us the structure of churches conveys something of the old law, but correction of life truly pertains to the discipline of the New Testament.'[29]

A celebrated poem in which Hrabanus addresses his successor Haito serves as a classic statement of the relative status of painting and writing. The recent discussion of this poem by Hans Haefele has clarified Hrabanus's stance and his attitude to painting. Haefele reminds us that the poem has not survived complete. Haito is urged not to despise writing, singing or reading though he prefers painting:

The sign of writing is worth more than the form of an image and offers more beauty to the soul than the false picture with colours, which does not show the figures of things correctly. For script is the perfect and blessed norm of salvation and it is more important in all things and is more use to everyone. It is tasted more quickly, is more perfect in its meaning, and is more easily grasped by human senses. It serves ears, lips and eyes, while painting only offers some consolation to the eyes. It shows the truth by its form, its utterance, its meaning, and it is pleasant for a long time. Painting delights the gaze when it is new, but when it is old it is a burden, it vanishes fast and it is not a faithful transmitter of truth.[30]

Hrabanus was not uninterested in imagemaking, his *De laudibus sanctae crucis* is an elaborate set of acrostic images which depict the crucified Christ, Louis the Pious, the evangelical symbols around the lamb, images of the cross, and

---

[26] Hrabanus, *PL* 108:95, Origen *Homelia*, viii, 1 (*Origène, Homélies sur l'Exode*, ed. M. Borret (Paris, 1985), pp. 250-52). This homily is also quoted by Jonas of Orleans, *PL* 106:321, 159.

[27] *PL* 108:71, Origen *Homelia*, vi, 5, *Origène, Homélies*, pp. 182-84.

[28] Migne reads *caetera*, but Origen has *cera*.

[29] *MGH Capitularia*, i, c. 11, p. 164.

[30] *MGH Poetae*, ii, p. 196, Hrabani *Carmina*, 38 as revised by H. Haefele in *Tradition und Wertung: Festschrift Franz Brunhölzl*, ed. G. Bernt, F. Raedle, G. Silagi (Sigmaringen, 1989), pp. 59-74 at pp. 68-71.

Hrabanus in prayer before the cross.[31] But the texts which accompany these images explain their meaning, not their beauty.

One of the most remarkable and moving accounts of a response to Carolingian religious images is found in the life of St. Maura, written by Bishop Prudentius of Troyes, who had known her himself:

> From her earliest years the young Maura would spend all day from matins to sext in the church of the Apostles where, as you know, the image of the Lord and Saviour is depicted in three ways, for he is shown as a boy sitting in the lap of his mother, and like a great lord sitting on a throne of majesty and like a youth hanging on the standard of the cross. Blessed Maura observed this custom from her earliest years, that she did not cease daily to ponder: first prostrating her whole body before the infant, then before the youth, thirdly before the king; nor could she be dragged from there for any reason, for each day she tirelessly observed the Lord with her bodily eye. Prudentius asked her, and often repeated the question, why she prostrated herself before the images of the Saviour in this way. At last, asked frequently, she replied, not without great difficulty, 'Happy church of the Apostles in which I frequently heard the boy crying on his mother's lap and the youth groaning on the cross and the king terribly thundering on his throne, but giving me his golden rod in a friendly way.'[32]

For Maura the images miraculously took on life; Prudentius sees this as the measure of her faith.

Religious images are discussed in terms of their subject matter, and sometimes in terms of correct responses to that subject matter. The craftsmanship of goldsmiths or of weavers is appraised: it can be wondrous, of remarkable workmanship, it may shine or sparkle. This corresponds to Rhabanus's definition of beauty as an ornament, and of a picture as a spur to contemplation.

Some works of Carolingian art are described in terms which convey an appreciation of their artistry. At Aniane, Benedict equipped his church with seven candelabra *fabrili arte mirabiliter producta*, with spears, globes, lilies, reeds and scyphi and seven lamps hung before the altar of wondrous and most beautiful inestimable work, which experts who saw them said were *Salomoniaco conflatae*.[33] Heiric's account of the wax model prepared before the construction of the crypts at the shrine of St. Germanus of Auxerre in 841 speaks of that beauty and that subtlety which was worthy of the king of men

---

[31] The interpretation of this work has been transformed by the recent studies of Elizabeth Sears and Celia Chazelle. E. Sears, 'Louis the Pious as *Miles Christi*: The Dedicatory Image in Hrabanus Maurus's *De laudibus sanctae crucis*', in P. Godman and R. Collins, eds., *Charlemagne's Heir: New perspectives on the Reign of Louis the Pious* (Oxford, 1990), pp. 605-28. I am very grateful to Dr. Chazelle for letting me read her 1985 Yale dissertation 'The Cross, the Image and the Passion in Carolingian Thought and Art', which is being revised for publication.

[32] Prudentius, *De vita et morte beatae gloriosae virginis Maurae, PL* 115:1372. The text is printed from the same source in *Acta Sanctorum September VI*, col. 576.

[33] *Vita Benedicti, MGH Scriptores*, xv, p. 206.

and angels, the assembly of the saints, the majesty of that place.[34] But Einhard, known as an artist, uses only *pulchritudo* in the *Vita Karoli*, both to describe the palace chapel and to describe the table with a map of the world which Charlemagne had owned.[35] Such terminology seems not to be used of images, only of craftsmanship.

Hrabanus's view was authoritative to Carolingian writers, so that they discuss images as if they were windows onto the subject. But to convey knowledge of their subject matter these images needed and received *tituli*, indeed more *tituli* than images have survived. The Last Judgement, or the complex iconographic programme of Einhard's cross reliquary, are explained by prominent inscriptions. For Bede, such religious images were living reading of the Lord's story, as it were, for the Greek for *pictura* is indeed 'living writing'.[36] Writing is always the cognitive model for the interpretation of images. In a remarkable letter preserved in a Carolingian manuscript from Fleury the author, who identifies himself only with the initial A., writes to his master E. and sends him *tituli* to be placed beside the paintings in the refectory.[37] A. says that the paintings of deer are as if dumb, for their superscription in no way edifies the hearers. He has sent verses to be written there, after E. has corrected them and if the brothers and the dean Fulcoaldus approve. He wanted Cerberus added to the pictures of the deer. Cerberus and the deer signify the human fall and return. (For Ambrose, Cerberus was a symbol of the devil and the deer a symbol of Christ.[38]) The snare of death represented by Cerberus turns the body to dust, but the other returning seeks the stars and heaven. It can reject the snakes and their law. In the second verse, which was for the facing wall, there is a reference to how the painter wanted to match the figures of Apelles. The deer and the three mouths of Cerberus should remind the reader to avoid death and, like the swift deer, expel the poison of the serpent and seek the bank and the fountain of salvation. The poem reveals a complexity of allegorical explanation worthy of the friend of Manno of Lyons, John the Scot and Isaac, bishop of Langres, reader of Aulus Gellius, Jerome, Terence and Martianus Capella. But though he

---

[34] 'Ea pulchritudine, ea subtilitate quae digna angelorum hominumque Rege, quae sanctorum collegio, quae ipsius etiam loci maiestate erat.' *Miracula S. Germani*, c. 5, *MGH Scriptores*, xiii, p. 402. Cf. *St. Germain d'Auxerre. Intellectuels et Artistes dans l'Europe Carolingienne IXe-XIe siècles* (Auxerre, 1990), pp. 121-60.

[35] *Vita Karoli*, c. 26: 'plurimae pulchritudinis basilicam extruxit . . . atque . . . adornavit.'; c. 33: 'tertiam, quae ceteris et operis pulchritudine multum excellit . . . totius mundi descriptionem subtili ac minuta figuratione conplecitur.'

[36] Bede, *De templo*, CCSL 19a, p. 213. This passage is quoted by Agobard and Walahfrid.

[37] Leiden, MS Voss, Lat. 0 88, *MGH Epistolae*, vi, pp. 182-86. The verses are also edited in *MGH Poetae*, iv, p. 1051. See also John Contreni, 'Three Carolingian Texts Attributed to Laon: Reconsiderations', *Studi Medievali*, 3e serie, xvii (1976), pp. 798-802 which links the text to Fleury.

[38] Ambrosius, *De interpellatione Job et David*, ii, 4, *CSEL*, 32, pp. 269-70.

explains the new images, and refers to the rivalry with Apelles, he has little to say about the image: it is the *titulus* which will edify the reader.

Images may shine in splendour, they may be admired for their beauty or elegance. They can be like their subject in beauty, but are not like in their substance, just as men can be said to be like God. If they depend on imagination alone, and do not represent what exists, they are not images but idols. So representation is a crucial category. Pictures may console the eye, especially if they are new, but they cannot transmit truth. They may however affect the viewer, especially if he cannot read. To understand them, words must provide a medium of explanation: to convey not only an account of biblical scenes but also to elaborate allegory which even a learned spectator might not grasp. Such Carolingian vocabulary as I have found suggests that Carolingians sought splendour in their images, but admired skill in the craftsmanship of metal-workers or weavers. The image might shine, especially if it was reflecting a higher splendour. Moreover, there is at least one passage where a Carolingian author seems to go beyond this conceptual block. John the Scot, glossing Martianus Capella's account of the twelve gems in Juno's crown (i, 75), explains the nature of the twelve precious stones linked to the signs of the Zodiac. The stones shine with light: Astrites has a star walking in it, Smaragdus is greener than herbs and leaves, Eliotropios is splendid, Iacynthus is blue and of a wonderful and varied nature, shadowy or pure.[39] The stones are described in careful detail, though John was drawing on a lapidary tradition and had probably not seen many such jewels. The finest account of precious stones is in Bede's *Commentary on the Apocalypse*, (xxi, 19-20) where the colours and symbolism of the twelve foundation stones of the walls of the New Jerusalem are explained. Chalcedony shines like the flame of a candle, chrysolith shines like gold with burning sparks, beryl is like water struck by the brightness of the sun, amethyst shines pink, sometimes gently melting into little flames and its purple is not all fiery, but like red wine.[40]

To acknowledge that the eloquence of a description need not depend on knowledge of actual objects may be a start in exploring the nature of Carolingian pictorial style and finding Carolingian terms to complement and challenge our own descriptions and responses. The search for such challenges and stimuli, depending on close study of texts, manuscripts and meanings, has always distinguished the recipient of this volume. May these gleanings substitute for her necessary *titulus*. As Walahfrid's writing tablet remarked, 'I explain what I do not know, but I will not gainsay your question'.

[39] *Johannes Scottus glossae Martiani*, ed., E. Jeauneau, *Quatre Thèmes Erigéniens* (Montreal, 1978), pp. 159-62; ed. C. Lutz, *Iohannis Scotti annotationes in Marcianum* (Cambridge, MA, 1939), pp. 45-46. The descriptions all derive from Isidore, *Etymologiae*, 16, with additional material from Solinus.

[40] *PL* 93;197-203. There is an excellent study of Bede and his sources by P. Kitson, 'Lapidary Traditions in Anglo-Saxon England, II', *Anglo-Saxon England*, 12 (1983), pp. 73-123.

4

# Ruotger, the Life of Bruno and Cologne Cathedral Library[*]

## Henry Mayr-Harting

No single text gives clearer expression to the ideal of what historians have called the Ottonian Imperial Church System than Ruotger's Life of Bruno of Cologne (b. 925).[1] In highly charged and confrontational language, well removed from *sermo humilis*, the *Vita* of this youngest brother of Otto I describes his education; his efforts to secure peace in the kingdom as a whole and especially in Lotharingia by combining the offices of Duke of Lotharingia (954-65) and Archbishop of Cologne (953-65); his reform of monasteries and building works as at St. Pantaleon in the suburbs of Cologne; his pastoral conduct and his desire to establish good pastors in other Lotharingian sees; his death – at length in accordance with time-honoured hagiographical traditions; and his testament which perhaps shows the influence of Einhard's Life of Charlemagne.

The fact that Ruotger devotes so much energy to counteracting the views of those who considered that worldly rule and ecclesiastical office should not have been combined in the way that Bruno combined them, that above all he should not have turned himself into a military commander in order to secure peace in Lotharingia (which Ruotger justifies by the actual peace he achieved), shows that by no means all contemporaries shared the ideal which he was putting forward.[2] For if the Ottonian Church System means anything, it refers to rule

[*] It is a pleasure to thank Dr. Juan Cervello-Margaleff and his colleagues in the Diözesan- und Dombibliothek in Cologne for showing me a wonderful mixture of efficiency and warm-heartedness during my period of study there; Margaret Gibson, whose wise words, born of fine scholarship, were given without her knowing the destination of this essay; Conrad Leyser, who generously rang from Sheffield when I was in Cologne to give me vital help on Paterius; and Malcolm Parkes, superb palaeographer, whose advice, given after I had done some scouting in Cologne and before my main sojourn there, proved to be unbelievably prescient.

[1] *Ruotgeri vita Brunonis archiepiscopi Coloniensis*, ed. Irene Ott, '*MGH Script. Rerum Germ. in usum scholarum*' (Cologne, 1958): hereafter VB.

[2] See below, n. 10. For Ruotger's justification of Bruno's military activities, see above all VB, c. 23 (the beginning), pp. 23-24.

on behalf of the king by bishops and abbots in the regions and localities.[3] The whole notion that there was such a system has not passed without challenge, and some effective criticisms have been made of the idea that the Ottonian rulers developed a system of appointing specially groomed chaplains to bishoprics wherever they pleased and then transferring to them royal or comital rights of rule on a large scale.[4] But in this matter we must be careful that the baby does not go out with the bath water. The fact that there was no rational, bureaucratic system of episcopal appointments backed up by legally defined constitutional powers does not mean that there was no sense in which bishops were instruments of royal government. What Ruotger describes is a kind of rule exercised by the less formal but nonetheless real powers of a Holy Man. This was holiness not in the way that William Rufus's bishops conceived it when they told St. Anselm that he should continue to pray while they looked after church/king relationships (though that was part of it),[5] but in the way of one who could build expensively and give generously, who could inspire terror amongst the powerful as well as love amongst the poor, who could acquire treasures and saints' relics in impressive quantities, and who could command a large personal following of fighting men and ecclesiastics; in short, of one who could not only express supernatural power by his inner virtues but also ostensibly control it by his external actions in a manner understandable to a tenth-century aristocracy.[6]

In 1957 Hartmut Hoffmann published an important article about Ruotger's Life of Bruno, on which the present essay seeks to build.[7] It analysed very

[3] Leo Santifaller, *Zur Geschichte des ottonisch-salischen Reichskirchensystems* (Osterrei-chische Akademie der Wissenschaften, Vienna, 1964), the whole way the evidence of episcopal and abbatial powers are presented, may be taken to sum up the idea of such a system. F.M. Fischer, *Politiker um Otto den Grossen* (Berlin, 1938), chap. 3 has a good statement of Bruno's role, in a similar sense.

[4] Timothy Reuter, 'The *Imperial Church System* of the Ottonian and Salian Rulers: A Reconsideration', *Journal of Ecclesiastical History*, 33 (1982), pp. 347-74.

[5] Eadmer, *Historia novorum in Anglia*, ed. M. Rule (Rolls Series, London, 1884), i, p. 33. But Ruotger does refer to Bruno's private prayer, saying, in words derived from the Rule of St Benedict, that it was short but pure, VB, c. 9, p. 9, lines 18-19.

[6] Building: VB, c. 21, p. 22, lines 17-18; c. 43, p. 46, lines 23-24; c. 48, p. 51, lines 8-10 (St. Pantaleon). Giving to the poor: c. 8, p. 8, line 19 (*refugium egenis*); c. 43, p. 46, line 22; c. 46, p. 50, lines 6-7; c. 49, pp. 51-55 (testament). Terror: c. 12, p. 12, line 25; c. 20, p. 19, line 22; c. 37, p. 39, line 13. Relics: cc. 27-28, pp. 27-28; c. 31, pp. 31-32; c. 48, p. 51, lines 11-12. Following of fighting men: c. 37, p. 39, lines 7-9 (on how Ruotger had seen Henry of Trier, William of Mainz and Bruno of Cologne together, not only in reading and discussion, but also in the line of battle, i.e. as military commanders); c. 41, p. 43, lines 22-24 (Bruno's sending 'not lightly armed' forces of Lotharingians to Otto I for his Italian expedition of 961). Following of ecclesiastics: c. 37, p. 39, lines 15-25, and p. 39, n. 4. Ruotger's ideal is also expressed in other Ottonian *vitae*, e.g. of Udalric of Augsburg, Wolfgang of Regensburg (not an aristocrat), Bernward of Hildesheim; but of course Bruno was exceptional in his powers as a Holy Man because he was not only an *Adelsheiliger*, but actually a close member of the royal dynasty.

[7] Hartmut Hoffmann, 'Politik und Kultur im ottonischen Reichskirchensystem: zur Interpreta-tion der *Vita Brunonis* von Ruotger', *Rheinische Vierteljahrsblätter*, 22 (1957), pp. 31-55.

perceptively the structure of concepts on which the Life was based. Ruotger's arguments, as an arsenal, Hoffmann showed, were directed principally against those who attacked the mixture of secular and religious and ecclesiastical functions. With profuse citation of St. Paul, very politically interpreted, Ruotger stressed the needs of the church which Bruno's position and activities served; the *pax ecclesiae* is associated with the Pauline unity of spirit (Ephesians 4:3), which in turn is connected to the unity of the *Reich*. Dissension is the tempest of dissension in the church, which is how the rebellion of 953 against Otto I is described.[8] Hoffmann shows how Ruotger expanded his argument on a series of almost dialectical opposites (*Auseinanderklaffen*),[9] in which *dissensio in ecclesia* was opposed to *sinceritas religionis*, the *officium pastoris* to the *mercenarii vitium*, the *sapientia sagacium* to those *bonarum artium ignari*. No doubt with an eye on the ecclesiasticism of Mainz, where the principal opposition to Bruno of Cologne was concentrated,[10] Ruotger never loses sight of the church in his arguments; disturbers of the *Reich*, whom Bruno helps to quash, are 'wolves who seek to devastate the church of God'.[11] Not only does Ruotger love opposites, he also favours the sort of contrast which one might call Pauline paradox, such as the connection of the *cura internorum* and the *cura externorum* in Bruno, his *humilitas* and *mansuetudo* on the one side and his *nobilitas* on the other, his living a gregarious life amongst many people *as if* he were a solitary.[12]

Perhaps the most powerful point which Hoffmann made was that Ruotger stresses always the vital connection between Bruno's education, especially in the liberal arts, and his capacity to rule. When he applies to Bruno the famous phrase of St. Peter, 'a royal priesthood', he associates it with Bruno's knowl-

[8]  Ibid., p. 35; VB, c. 16, pp. 14-15.

[9]  The word is used by him at p. 46.

[10]  This is clear not only from the celebrated taunt of Archbishop William of Mainz against Bruno in 955 that he was both duke and bishop, made to Pope Agapetus II, 'Dux episcopi, episcopus ducis operam vindicat', Ph.Jaffé, *Biblotheca rerum Germanicarum* vol. iii, *Monumenta Moguntina* (Berlin, 1866), p. 349. It is also clear from the whole Mainz attitude to what ought to be the purity of episcopal office, exemplified in the letter of the priest Gerhard to William's predecessor, Archbishop Frederick (937-54), written at the beginning of the latter's pontificate. This letter gives a high religious view of episcopal functions, much of it explicitly derived from the letters of Pope Gregory the Great or from St. Boniface, and it speaks of how Ozias and Saul were punished for usurping priestly functions, see F. Lotter, *Der Brief des Priesters Gerhard an den Erzbischof Friedrich von Mainz* (Sigmaringen, 1975), p. 125. This last point seems to be answered specifically by Ruotger where he says that it was not new for wordly government to be carried out by the rulers (*rectoribus*) of the church, VB c. 23, p. 24, and see F. Lotter, *Die Vita Brunonis des Ruotger* (Bonn, 1958), p. 120. Ruotger is clearly answering criticisms emanating from Frederick of Mainz when, in justifying Bruno's military exploits by the peace which they brought to Lotharingia, he makes Otto I say to Bruno, 'some perverse men will say that battles do not belong to your ministry' (VB, c. 20, p. 20, lines 8-9). For the whole question of Bruno as a military commander, F. Prinz, *Klerus und Krieg im früheren Mittelalter* (Stuttgart, 1971), chapter 6.

[11]  Hoffmann, 'Politik und Kultur', pp. 35-39.

[12]  Ibid., pp. 45-49.

edge of the *artes* and his practice of the four cardinal virtues. The *artes* are the weapons of faith against the *spirituales nequitiae* who include opponents of the king and *Reich*; Ruotger formulates the cross between education and politics in Bruno with a Ciceronian paradox – when he was studying (and Hoffmann takes *otium* here to mean study of the classics) nobody seemed more engaged in business, when in business he never gave up study. Ruotger even gives his Life a humanistic streak by citing the playwright Terence to justify Bruno's involvement in wordly rule, 'humani nihil a me alienum' (nothing human is foreign to me).[13] At some stage in his career (it is not quite clear from the Life when ) Bruno held scholarly discussions amongst Latins and Greeks, which Otto I himself, no mean judge of such matters, often attended, from which the Greeks, whom he also used as his teachers, carried home amazed accounts of his learning. We shall see below that Ruotger must have thought from his knowledge of the Cologne manuscripts that there were easy opportunities to amaze, or *verblüffen*, the Greeks about their own learning, merely using marginalia of these manuscripts.[14]

Ruotger himself was schoolmaster of the monastery of St. Pantaleon, Cologne, which Bruno restored to monastic life not long before he died, and in which he placed as abbot one Christian from the Gorze-reform abbey of St. Maximin, Trier; he wrote before Bruno's successor, Archbishop Folcmar (965-69), died. These facts were established virtually beyond doubt by Irene Ott, editor of the Life of Bruno.[15] Whether Ruotger had lived in Cologne before the restoration of St. Pantaleon, or had come as an outsider only around 964, it is clear that he had a personal acquaintance with his subject, as well as full access to the Cologne traditions about him. I think we have to accept for a start that Bruno was deeply versed in the liberal arts, in other words in the classics. But what of patristic learning? For Bruno an answer is not easy, but the writings of Augustine of Hippo and Pope Gregory the Great are very apparent in the whole image of Bruno constructed by Ruotger, as I now hope to show with the help of still-surviving manuscripts available to him when he wrote in Cologne in the late 960s. It is not perhaps unimportant to appreciate how deeply the picture of this idealised Ottonian churchman is rooted in the traditions of the Carolingian Renaissance and its manuscripts at Cologne itself,

---

[13] Ibid., pp. 49-54. For the *otium/negotium* paradox, VB, c. 8, p. 8, lines 20-22; for the Terence citation, c. 40, p. 43, line 1.

[14] VB, c. 8, p. 8, lines 12-16. For Greek/Latin cultural exchanges in the west at this period, see Bernhard Bischoff, 'Das griechische Element in der abendländischen Bildung des Mittelalters', *Byzantinische Zeitschrift*, 44 (1951), pp. 27-55, (reprinted in his *Mittelalterliche Studien*, ii (Stuttgart, 1967), pp. 246-75), and for Cologne in particular, pp. 48-49, 40, n. 5, where a fragment of a tenth-century Greek grammar at St. Pantaleon, Cologne (Vienna, MS 114, fos. 13-15 v) is referred to. See also Walter Berschin, *Griechisch-Lateinisches Mittelalter* (Bern and Munich, 1980), esp. pp. 230-35. The evidence from these works would make me say that there is more here than the *puer/senex* topos of hagiography (which Lotter, *Vita Brunonis*, p. 33 rightly points out is present). See, on amazing the Greeks, n. 57 below.

[15] VB, pp. vii-x.

for it emphasises once again the broad cultural coherence of the Carolingian and Ottonian worlds, a theme on which Margaret Gibson has herself written with penetration.[16] Yet the patristic aspect is a near blank in Bruno/Ruotger studies, so far as I know. Irene Ott, in her admirable edition of 1958, identified scriptural quotations, classical allusions and echoes of the Rule of St. Benedict with verve, but with rare exceptions did not extend herself to the patristic influences. Hoffmann, quite legitimately, confined himself largely to analysing the internal structure of Ruotger's argument. Friedrich Lotter, who in his monograph on the Life made some excellent points about Ruotger's recourse to an earlier, miracle-less, tradition of early medieval hagiography,[17] was so smitten with the argument that Bruno and Ruotger were dominated by the monastic and political objectives of the Gorze monastic reform movement, that he looks for the principal parallels to the hagiographic concepts of Ruotger (and finds them) in the Life of John of Gorze.[18] This Life, written at Metz a good ten years later than Ruotger's, is seen by Lotter as deriving from the Gorze culture which was a paradigm for Ruotger. Such traces of Gregorian influence as he occasionally notes are therefore attributed to John of Gorze's own interest in Gregory rather than to the long-standing Cologne interest in that father.[19] The only direct patristic study of Ruotger known to me is that of Bernheim (1912) on the Augustinian ideas of peace in it, deriving primarily from *The City of God*, xix, where he points out that the verbal antithesis of *tranquillitas* and *perturbatio* is found in the *City of God* (xix, 13), as is the paradox between peace and the sword of justice (*City of God*), xix, 11-12), and he also recognises that peace is meant in the sense of unity of spirit.[20] But Bernheim concerns himself only with the text of Augustine, not at all with Cologne and its manuscripts, and besides, as Hoffmann in effect pointed out, some of his parallels are of only very generalised applicability.[21]

A word of explanation is required about the history of the Cologne manuscript collection and its present state; the story was well told by Kl. Löffler in 1923.[22] Whatever manuscripts were at Cologne previously, the effective history of the cathedral library begins with Archbishop Hildebald (before 787 to 819), who had been archchaplain at Charlemagne's court. He had a number of manuscripts made for the cathedral, most of which (but certainly not all)

---

[16] Margaret Gibson, 'The Continuity of Learning, *c.* 850-1050', *Viator*, 6 (1975), pp. 1-13.

[17] Lotter, *Vita Brunonis*, pp. 38-41, 129-30, and for Bruno's practical virtues, pp. 55-60.

[18] Ibid., pp. 51-52, 55, 65-78 (esp. 70-71), 78-90.

[19] Ibid., esp. pp. 51-52, 55, 70. On the especial interest in Gregory at Cologne, even in the period of St. Boniface, see Henry Mayr-Harting, *Ottonian Manuscript Illumination*, ii (London, 1991), p. 118.

[20] E. Bernheim, 'Die augustinische Geschichtsanschauung in Ruotger's Biographie des Erzbischofs Bruno von Köln', *Zeitschrift für Rechtsgeschichte* (Kan. Abt. 2), 33 (1912), pp. 299-335, esp. pp. 309, 313-16, 320-23; VB, c. 2, p. 4, lines 10-12.

[21] Hoffmann, 'Politik und Kultur', pp. 33-34.

[22] Kl. Löffler, *Kölnische Bibliotheksgeschichte im Umriss* (Cologne, 1923).

have an entry written in capitals, saying: CODEX SANCTI PETRI SUB PIO PATRE HILDEBALDO SCRIPTUS.[23] Most of these were doubtless written at Cologne in the scriptorium which Hildebald himself developed; in fact Bernhard Bischoff identified a Cologne hand of this period which had written in at least eight manuscripts, four of them containing the Hildebald inscription.[24] However, not all the manuscripts with this inscription were home-produced, for as Bischoff showed in another famous piece of palaeographical detective work, the three volumes of Augustine's *Enarrationes in Psalmos* were written by ten named nuns of the royal nunnery of Chelles – for Cologne at Hildebald's command.[25] The momentum of Hildebald's direction of the scriptorium lasted throughout the rest of the ninth century, as can be seen from inscriptions in their books relating to other ninth-century bishops at least up to the time of Archbishop Willibert (870-89).[26] Under Hildebald's successor, Hadebald (819-41), in 833 a (surviving) catalogue of the library was drawn up, containing 115 works in 175 volumes; of these early manuscripts only something over 40 volumes still survive in the Dombibliothek.[27] Losses occurred partly by the excessive ease with which the canons lent or sold their manuscripts down the centuries, particularly after printed editions meant that they had cheaper texts of the works in question. The philologist Johann Georg Graevius, for instance, could find nothing interesting for him in the Cologne monastic libraries in 1657, but acquired by loan or purchase many valuable classical manuscripts of the cathedral, which after his death passed to the Kurfürstliche Bibliothek in Düsseldorf. Later the librarian there sold them to Johann Jakob Zamboni, ambassador of the Landgraf of Hessen-Darmstadt to London, from whom Edward Harley acquired several of them in 1724-25.[28]

Here we have the main reason why the surviving manuscripts at Cologne itself, patchy as they may be on the patristic background of Ruotger, show

---

[23] Ibid., p. 1, and see Bernhard Bischoff, 'die Kölner Nonnenhandschriften und das Skriptorium von Chelles', in his *Mittelalterliche Studien*, ii (Stuttgart, 1966), p. 17. For Hildebald at Charlemagne's court, see J. Fleckenstein, *Die Hofkapelle der deutschen Könige*, i, *Grundlegung: die karolingische Hofkapelle* (Stuttgart, 1959), esp. pp. 49-52. L.W. Jones, *The Script of Cologne from Hildebald to Hermann* (Cambridge, MA, 1932), made manuscripts with such inscriptions, under Hildebald and his successors, the basis of his study, unfortunately including some which the archbishops had obtained from elsewhere, as Bernhard Bischoff showed (see next note).

[24] *The Epinal, Erfurt, Werden and Corpus Glossaries*, ed. Bernhard Bischoff, Mildred Budny, Geoffrey Harlow, M.B. Parkes and J.D. Pheifer, *Early English Texts in Facsimile* (Copenhagen, 1988), pp. 18-19.

[25] Bernhard Bischoff, 'Die Kölner Nonnenhandschriften', in his *Mittelalterliche Studien*, i (1966), pp. 16-34.

[26] Jones, *The Script of Cologne*, catalogue, pp. 29-73, nos. 3, 4, 6, 8, 9, 10, 12, 18, 19, 20, 25.

[27] Anton Decker, 'Die Hildebold'sche Manuskriptensammlung des Kölner Domes', in A. Chambalu, et al., *Festschrift der dreiundvierzigsten Versammlung deutscher Philologen und Schulmänner dargeboten v.d. höheren Lehranstalten Kölns* (Bonn, 1895), pp. 215-51; text at pp. 224-28. See also Rosamond McKitterick, *The Carolingians and the Written Word* (Cambridge, 1989), within a fine discussion on the organisation of Carolingian Library catalogues, pp. 191-92.

[28] Löffler, *Kölnische Bibliotheksgeschichte*, p. 26.

virtually nothing of his undoubtedly important classical background (though some of the Harleian manuscripts are probably a little later than Ruotger's time). Probably a worse cause of losses, however, was the removal of the cathedral manuscripts, first to various repositories during the French Revolutionary wars of the 1790s, and then, after the early nineteenth-century secularisation and the Peace of Luneville (1815), to the ducal museum of Westphalia in Darmstadt, from which only in 1866 after the peace between Hesse and Prussia were 193 manuscripts returned to Cologne.[29] These were the manuscripts catalogued by Philipp Jaffé and Wilhelm Wattenbach in their publication of 1874.[30]

The vast majority of these 193 manuscripts clearly always belonged to cathedral library and not to a conglomerate collection of various Cologne libraries. In the sixteenth century the library of the monastery of St. Pantaleon (a relevant case since Ruotger was schoolmaster and probably a monk of St. Pantaleon) was regarded as an entirely separate entity, to judge by the stated use of its manuscripts in Cologne printed editions (e.g. the Homilies of Bede and Maximus of Turin) of the 1530s. If we ask what subsequently happened to its library, the answer is certainly not that it ever merged with that of the cathedral; rather, its manuscripts were extensively sold by the monks themselves at the turn of the seventeenth and eighteenth centuries, as the two Maurists, Martène and Durand, reported in 1718, probably to finance the expensive building works and sumptuous architectural fittings of Abbot Konrad Kochen (1687-1717).[31] It is surely the cathedral library rather than that of St. Pantaleon which is relevant to Ruotger, as it was of course for Bruno. In the first place, when Ruotger was writing in the late 960s, only a few years after Bruno's re-establishment of St. Pantaleon, its library (and Ruotger makes no mention of an endowment of books to it)[32] can hardly have yet been built up significantly. Second, in the tenth century, whatever the case later after rivalries between churches developed, the teaching and library resources of Cologne must be regarded as a common pool; an early eleventh-century loan list of the cathedral library shows this well enough, where Abbot Elias of St. Martin and St. Pantaleon, Evezo the schoolmaster of St. Kunibert, and the abbess of St. Ursula appear amongst the borrowers, the last with a copy of Terence (shades of Hrotswitha of Gandersheim).[33] Third, it cannot be supposed that Archbishop Folcmar (965-69), for whom the Life of Bruno was written and to whom it is addressed,[34] said to Ruotger, sitting only a mile away

[29] Ibid., pp. 3-5.
[30] *Ecclesiae metropolitanae Coloniensis codices manuscripti*, ed. Ph. Jaffé and W. Wattenbach (Berlin, 1974).
[31] Löffler, pp. 6, 17-26, 28.
[32] VB, cc. 27, 48.
[33] Löffler, p. 3.
[34] VB, p. 1, lines 3-6, cf. VB, cl. 46, pp. 49-50.

at St. Pantaleon with its still exiguous collection of books, that he might write the Life but might not use the resources of the cathedral library to help him.

What I have been able to do in the time so far available to me amongst the manuscripts amounts only to a beginning, so I have founded my study primarily on manuscripts of agreed Cologne origin, which are at Cologne now and have obviously never left Cologne except for the half century when they were at Darmstadt. The essence of my problem, however, is not the palaeographical one of establishing which manuscripts originated in a Cologne scriptorium, but the historical one of establishing which manuscripts were at Cologne, wherever they came from, and were available to Bruno and even more to Ruotger. For this reason, corrections and annotations in the margins by Cologne scribes have been of vital importance, even if the manuscripts themselves in some cases certainly or possibly came from elsewhere to Cologne. Such annotations may also shed valuable light on the actual main interest of those using the manuscripts. We are all bound to be influenced by previous annotations in a book which we read, particularly when these highlight certain elements of the subject matter: it will be seen that this was a factor in the way that Ruotger wrote his Life of Bruno.

Ruotger asserts that Bruno regarded the poet Prudentius as the basis of his education because of his catholic faith and purpose and his pre-eminence in eloquence and truth.[35] Ruotger's own picture of Bruno as a scholar, however, is clearly founded on Augustine of Hippo's *De doctrina christiana*, the masterly treatises on what should be the Christian attitude to the learning of antiquity. Where there was truth, Augustine maintained, a Christian should not jib at its use because it had been associated with paganism; as Peter Brown has said in a brilliant discussion of this treatise, Augustine at a stroke 'secularised' much of classical literature and indeed the habits of a whole society; he was the great seculariser of the pagan past.[36] 'We should not think', said Augustine, 'that literature was forbidden because Mercury is said to be its inventor; . . . rather every good and true Christian should understand that wherever he may find truth, it is his Lord's.' This is like Ruotger's saying that Bruno studied the historians, orators, poets and philosophers (evidently of antiquity) and that wherever he found a master of quick intelligence he humbly offered himself as his pupil.[37] After all, truth and logic were not created by men; men simply pointed out God-created truths. The Egyptians, said Augustine in a famous analogy, had not only idols and superstition, but also gold and silver ornaments and other useful things which the Israelites took with them secretly when they fled. Just so when Christians separated themselves from pagan

---

[35] VB, c. 4, p. 5, lines 12-21.

[36] Peter Brown, *Augustine of Hippo* (London, 1967). Chapter 23 is a masterly discussion of this book; the particular phrase cited is at p. 266.

[37] *Aurelii Augustini De doctrina christiana*, ed. J. Martin, *CCSL*, 32 (Turnhout, 1962), II, xviii, p. 53. I have used, with some modifications, the translation of D.W. Robertson Jr, *Saint Augustine, On Christian Doctrine* (New York, 1958), p. 54. VB, c. 5, p. 7, lines 15-18.

society, they should take their treasures with them, their liberal arts or disciplines useful to truth, their precepts useful to morals, their human institutions which could be seized and turned to Christian uses. In just this way Bruno did not read the comedies and tragedies for their scurrilous jokes and buffooneries; what mattered was not the content but the style, 'the authority in the composition of the words'.[38] For as with Augustine – and this is a theme strongly emphasised by Ruotger – it was important not only to grasp the truth but also to teach it with all possible eloquence. Truth, for Augustine, had its own autonomy, regardless of purpose, however much he also thought it was necessary to understand words, numbers and nature in order to interpret the Bible; and thus when Hoffmann finds that *nobile otium* is a phrase used by Ruotger to imply that classical education had its own autonomy, he is in fact articulating an idea central to the *De doctrina christiana*.[39] Even the love of contrasts and paradoxes, which Ruotger shows in the exposition of his subject, is justified in the first book of Augustine's work, where he says that the medicine of Wisdom is applied to our human wounds, healing some by contraries and some by similar things.[40]

We can take Ruotger's study of the *De doctrina christiana* further than this. Cologne MS 74 is a manuscript of this work, agreed on all sides to be from the scriptorium of Archbishop Hildebald (pre-787), and never to have left Cologne (except for its nineteenth-century period at Darmstadt).[41] It is written with great clarity, the text is beautifully laid out on pages by no means unthumbed and it has a rather agreeable, vertical format for study; in short a perfect piece of Carolingian Renaissance work. It is not entirely studded with marginalia but has some forty, which are variously NOTA signs of a typically Cologne, monogrammic kind, scriptural attributions, or notes of subject matter. Some of them may be in the hand of the scribe of the text and virtually all are roughly contemporary with the manuscript. A study of them leaves little doubt that it must have been this very manuscript which Ruotger used (and which it is likely that Bruno had read before him); one can see the ways in which these marginalia must have helped to focus his mind on the text. Ruotger may well have heard Bruno say that he wished to die only so that he might be with Christ ('dissolvi vellet, tantum ut cum Christo esset'), but if so his mind may have been focused on it by the passage of St. Paul to the Philippians (I: 23-24), of which it is an adaptation ('compellor autem ex duobus, concupiscentiam habens dissolui, et esse cum Christo') one of the few

---

[38] *De doctrina christiana*, II, xl, pp. 73-74, and D.W. Robertson, p. 75; VB, c. 8, p. 9, lines 3-7.

[39] On truth and eloquence, esp. *De doctrina christiana*, IV, ii, p. 117; on the autonomy of truth, by implication, ibid., II, xxxii-v, pp. 67-69, and on the interpretation of the Bible, e.g., ibid., II, xxxi, p. 65 ('sed disputationis disciplina ad omnia genera quaestionum, quae in litteris sanctis sunt, penetranda et dissolvenda, plurimum valet'); Hoffmann, 'Politik und Kultur', p. 52.

[40] *De doctrina christiana*, I, xiv, p. 13, and D.W. Robertson, pp. 14-15. See also Augustine's *City of God*, xi, 18.

[41] Jones, *The Script of Cologne*, pp. 49-51; *The Epinal, etc. Glossaries*, p. 18.

scriptural attributions made in the margin of the Cologne MS, AD Philp (fo. 52 v).[42] Hoffmann has shown that Bruno's care for the *respublica* leads Ruotger into another argument from St. Paul, justifying Bruno's *vita activa* even to the point of taking the field of battle to suppress disturbers of the peace, namely that he provided for honest things not only in the sight of God but also in the sight of men. The correct reference for this citation is not Romans 12:17 as Irene Ott (followed by Hoffmann) gives it, but II Corinthians, 8:21, from which it is used near the end of the *De doctrina christiana*.[43] Here Augustine is making the point that a teacher should not only teach truthfully and eloquently but should also set a good example in life to those he expects to obey him, a point implied also by Ruotger where he refers to Bruno, the *tutor et doctor*, achieving peace in Lotharingia, and also where he refers to the devil spreading the virus of hate amongst the works of the pious teacher (*pii doctoris*).[44] Against the passage in the margin of the Augustine manuscript is a NOTA sign, NOTA *cum studio totum hoc* (fo. 110).

Another NOTA sign, NOTA *quia utilis adtenendum*, appears (fo. 75 v) against a passage about the relation of eloquence and wisdom, where Augustine says how desirable eloquence is to accompany wisdom and how necessary wisdom is along with eloquence. This is another point emphasised by Ruotger, of Bruno himself and particularly of his protegé (for the short time he could hold his see there), Bishop Rathier of Liège, who it was thought would be of profit at Liège, 'propter abundantem doctrinam et eloquentiam copiosam, qua inter sapientissimos florere visus est' (on account of his rich doctrine and flow of eloquence for which he was held in high repute amongst the wisest men).[45] Again, Augustine explained how serpents could have good or bad meanings in scripture, and here in the margin is written in capitals the word *serpens* (fo. 64); Ruotger was impressed by the unfavourable connotations.[46] Augustine says something about civil wars in the Africa of his own day, very much in passing in order to make a point about how to speak eloquently, where in the Cologne manuscript (fo. 106 v) the original glossator wrote (though it was later crossed out), 'quomodo prohibuerit bellus (sic) cybile' *(sic)*. The war of which Augustine speaks was not only between citizens, but also between relatives, brothers, even parents and sons ('verum etiam propingui, fratres, postremo parentes et filii lapidibus inter se in duas partes divisi'). Ruotger, doubtless drawn to this passage by the note, refers to Bruno's father, King Henry I, bringing peace to a kingdom which he had found troubled by continual incursions from outside and serious dissensions within, between citizens and

[42] VB, c. 30, p. 30, lines 18-19; *De doctrina christiana*, III, ii, p. 78.

[43] VB, c. 20, p. 21, lines 23-24 (where II Corinthians 8:21 is also cited in the margin); VB, c. 33, p. 34, lines 19-22 (where only Romans 12:17 is?); VB, c. 37, p. 39, lines 8-9 (ditto); Hoffmann, 'Politik und Kultur, p. 37; *De doctrina christiana*, IV, xxviii, p. 164.

[44] VB. c. 23, p. 24, line 3, and c. 24, p. 24, line 26.

[45] VB, c. 38, p. 40, lines 7-16; *De doctrina christiana*, IV, ii, p. 117.

[46] VB, c. 10, p. 11, line 6; c. 22, p. 23, lines 7-9; *De doctrina christiana*, III, xxv, p. 98.

also relations (*inter cives etiam et cognatos*).[47] We give one last example from this manuscript. Where Augustine expounds an analogy to eloquence without wisdom or truth, by saying, 'just as he whose body is beautiful while his mind is deformed is more to be pitied than he whose body is also deformed, in the same way those who speak false things eloquently are more to be pitied than if they had said the same things awkwardly', the Cologne glossator writes enthusiastically in the margin, *Comparatio mirabilis* (fo. 111). This seems to me the only explanation for the odd use of the word *deforme* by Ruotger, when he says of Bruno, as a teacher in the court circle of Otto I, that any deformity practically in the whole world was brought to light by his studies ('quicquid deforme per totum pene mundum esset, in studiis liquidius appareret');[48] in other words, taking Augustine's 'wonderful comparison', those attractively spoken falsehoods came to light which were like a deformity of mind not showing in the body.

As already mentioned, Bernheim argued (convincingly if in a rather genera-lised way) that Ruotger conceived of the peace for which Bruno struggled as the peace necessary for the pilgrims of the heavenly city as they made their journey through this life towards their heavenly fatherland, according to Augustine's *City of God*. Both Ruotger and Bruno before him, he thought, were good Augustinians. Cologne MS 75 is an indubitably ninth-century manuscript of the first ten books of the *City of God* which L.W. Jones assigned on the flimsy grounds of a few Tironian notes to the scriptorium of Archbishop Gunther of Cologne (850, deposed 863, replaced 870).[49] The grounds proved to be non-existent when Bernhard Bischoff was able to identify it as a St. Amand manuscript.[50] It has a series of marginal glosses in it which are also certainly St. Amand glosses, mostly appreciative notes of subject matter and occasionally making further explanations; these glosses have the appearance of belonging to the original (similar ink colour, for instance), and they are incorporated, in a very un-Cologne way, with a rather florid bracket like a *F* without its lower horizontal.[51]

Nonetheless there are good grounds for thinking that it reached Cologne soon after it was written, long before the time of Bruno or Ruotger. In general, Rosamond McKitterick has shown how important and prolific St. Amand was in this mid ninth-century period as an exporter of manuscripts to other

---

[47] VB, c. 3, p. 4, lines 15-18; *De doctrina christiana*, IV, xxiv, p. 159.
[48] VB, c. 5, p. 6, lines 22-26; *De doctrina christiana*, IV, xxviii, p. 165.
[49] Jones, *The Script of Cologne*, pp. 5, 63.
[50] *The Epinal . . . Glossaries*, p. 18, n. 65.
[51] An example is illustrated in Jones, *The Script of Cologne*, plate lxxxii.

churches.[52] More particularly, besides the St. Amand glossators, at least two
other hands of roughly contemporary date have made corrections in the
margin, and while I think that both these are Cologne hands, the smaller and
firmer almost certainly is. Here we come to the fact that while Jones's grounds
for assigning the manuscript to Archbishop Gunther's scriptorium were non-
existent, his instincts to place it in Gunther's Cologne were much sounder. For
when I saw the hand which wrote the first and fourth quires of Cologne MS 39
of Ambrose on St. Paul to the Romans, a book inscribed as *Liber Guntarii* and
almost incontestably from the Cologne scriptorium, I recognised it instantly as
the hand of this smaller glossator. I express myself in this autobiographical
manner because in my experience the true identifications of hand are not those
which one hypothetically posits for oneself and then spends hours in anxious
comparison of the hands; they are those which hit one immediately and
unexpectedly, like the envelope of a letter addressed in familiar writing, even
before one has had time to compare the letter forms (which are not in any case
always the best guide to an identification). Both specimens of this hand have
the same duct and 'aspect', the same compactness, almost compression, the
same slope to the right, the same extreme regularity of the minims, the same
unusually small loop under the *g*.[53] I was not looking in this manuscript to find
a particular handwriting, but to see what use might have been made of it
considering the importance of St. Paul to Ruotger's picture of Bruno, something borne out by Poppo's famous dream in which Bruno was defended at the
Judgement Seat by the advocacy of St. Paul for pursuit of 'inane philosophy'.[54]
The answer to my question was that virtually no use of it had been made, nor
did it show any signs of significant thumbing, for the Carolingians had
Augustine and Gregory much more in their sights than they had Ambrose or
Jerome; but in discovering this negative answer, it seems that I had identified
as a ninth-century Cologne hand one of the correctors of the *City of God*
manuscript.

Once again, if one compares Ruotger's text with the marginal comments in this
manuscript one can catch him composing some of the *tesserae* of his picture of

[52] Rosamond McKitterick, 'Charles the Bald (823-877) and his Library: The Patronage of
Learning', *Eng. Hist. Rev.*, 95 (1980), pp. 42-43, and see ibid., p. 42, n. 3 for the writings of A.
Boutemy on St. Amand's style of illumination. For import of St. Amand liturgical books into
Cologne in the ninth century, see Anton von Euw, *Das Buch der vier Evangelien*: *Kölns
karolingische Evangelienbücher* (Cologne, 1989), catalogue nos. 1 and 5, pp. 41-42, 47-49.
[53] For a good example of the hand in MS 75 see fo. 176: 'Qualiter intelligendum sit deus
deorum'. In Jones, *The Script of Cologne*, this hand can be seen in the margin of his plate lxxxi,
having written *theatrices et*, but Jones skilfully avoided illustrating Hand A, as he called it, of MS
39! For this MS, see Jones, pp. 60-61.
[54] *Thietmari Merseburgensis episcopi chronicon*, ed. Robert Holtzmann, '*MGH Scriptores rer.
germ. in usum scholarum*', new series, 9 (Berlin, 1955), ii, c. 16, pp. 56-58.

Bruno from the marginalia surely of this very manuscript. To take the most relevant ones:

> O divites qui timidi de vestra estis opulentia, demonstrantem vobis Agustinum aut gazofilatium intendite, ubi vestras recondatis opes, ubi fur at tinea accessum habere nesciat
>
> (fo. 9 v, *re* i, c. 10)

The *gazofilatium* here, the treasure house to which thief and worm alike have no access, surely prompted Ruotger's *gazophilacium* of the heart which Bruno had constantly at the ready.[55] For at this point Augustine cites Matthew 6:21, 'where your treasure (*thesaurus*) is, there will you heart be'.

> Comedi sunt qui privatorum hominum acta dictis actis gestu cantabant atque stupra virginum et amores meretricum in fabulis exprimebant. Tragoedi sunt qui antiquae iesta vel facinora sceleratorum regum luctuoso carmine spectante populo concinebant
>
> (fo. 28 v, *re* i, c. 8).

Not a very complimentary account of ancient comedies and tragedies; comedies are about the defilements of virgins and the loves of harlots, tragedies about the crimes of wicked kings. But it matches well what Ruotger says about the scurrilities and buffooneries in comedies and tragedies which caused others to shake with laughter but which Bruno read seriously for their Latin style.[56]

> palatum graeci . . . [blurred here] appellant et nonnulli latini palatum caelum vocaverunt
>
> (fo. 127, *re* vii, c. 8).

Compare Ruotger's rather odd phrase about how the poet, Prudentius, pleased the vault of Bruno's heart (*palato cordis eius*) so that he breathed in not only the knowledge of his external words but also the marrow and nectar of his inner sense.[57]

> pietas dei cultus dei quam Greci eusebiam vocant
>
> (fo. 178 v, *re* x, c. 1)

---

[55] VB, c. 5, p. 7, lines 10-11. For the text of The City of God, I have used, *Sancti Aurelii Augustini De civitate dei*, ed. B. Dombart and A. Kalb (with amendments), *CCSL*, and 48 (Turnhout, 1955).

[56] VB, c. 8, p. 9, lines 3-7.

[57] VB, c. 4, p. 5, line 18.

Compare Ruotger's 'de religione primo et cultu dei, quod Greci theosebian dicunt', etc.[58]

vide quid significet lex dei in arca posita

(fo. 191 v, *re* x, c. 17)

and Ruotger's . . . *bibliothecam suam* (meaning Bruno's actual library, but often the books of the Bible, the *lex dei*, were regarded as an actual library, as in the Cologne library list of 833 where they are itemised) *sicut arcam dominicam circumduxit*, etc.[59]

de hoc quod dicit psalmista, deus cordis mei et pars mea dominus, intellegitur ut prius homo interius mundetur et post exterius, sicut in evangelio dicitur, mandate prius quae intus sunt, et quae foris sunt munda erunt vobis,

Matth 23:26 (fo. 197 v, *re* x, c. 25).

This corresponds well to various passages in Ruotger representing the interior/exterior idea, particularly that on Bruno as a tireless fighter in the army of God, *intus et foris*, battling against wicked men and disturbers of the peace with his powers of mind rather than body.[60]

*Gazophilacium, Comoedi* and *Tragoedi, Palatum*, and *Arca* are all words dealt with by Isidore of Seville in his *Etymologies*, of which the cathedral library had an early copy (now disappeared),[61] but it is far more likely that they figure in Ruotger because they all appear in the marginalia of MS 75 than because he had been studying Isidore (though he could well have looked them up in the *Etymologies*). *Eusebia* or *Theosebian* is not treated by Isidore; the *intus et foris* antithesis is clearly not owed to him; and when Isidore deals with tragedies and comedies he does not inject the contempt into his definitions which Augustine, the St. Amand glossator and Ruotger all do.[62] As to *gazophilacium*, just the kind of Greek-sounding word which Ruotger liked (rather in the way of 'Baron Corvo'), Isidore gives only a literal definition without moral overtones. In fact at the point where the marginal note comes in

[58] VB, c. 21, p. 22, lines 23-24. One notes what easy pickings Ruotger must have thought that the margins of these texts provided, leaving aside the texts themselves, if he was trying to conceive how one might *verblüffen* the Greeks with their own learning, Cf VB, c. 8, p. 8, lines 12-16. There are several other references to Greek terms and ideas both in MS 75 and in MS 74, e.g. Plato's division of the study of wisdom into three parts, moral, natural and irrational (MS 75, fo. 145 v); or what the Greek term for demons meant (MS 75, fo. 174 v); or that the Greek term *climax* means *gradatio* in Latin rhetorical terminology (MS 74, fo. 77 r).

[59] VB, c. 8, p. 9, lines 8-14. For the treatment of the biblical books in the 833 library list, see Decker, p. 224.

[60] Especially VB, c. 26, p. 26, lines 14-21.

[61] 833 list, no. 63, Decker, p. 226.

[62] *Isidori Hispalensis episcopi etymologiarum sive originum libri XX*, ed. W.M. Lindsay, 2 vols, (Oxford, 1911), VIII, vii, 5-6.

MS 75, Augustine in his text uses not this word but *thesaurus*.[63] Ruotger presumably follows here the St. Amand gloss together with the Augustine text. Of course, as Conrad Leyser has pointed out to me, Ruotger could easily have had this word from various sources, not least Ezechiel or Gregory's *Homilies on Ezechiel*, a copy of which was in the Cologne library by 833, but taking the package of half dozen glosses from MS 75 as a whole, that manuscript seems its likeliest source.

There are numerous other marginalia in MS 75 not cited here, but they are not so numerous (at most one or two to a page and many pages without any) that those we have used fail to stand out in the manuscript. It is a pity that the second volume of this two-volume *City of God* is another of the casualties of the Cologne library's vicissitudinous history, for it means we can say nothing of Ruotger's use of it in his writing about earthly peace, one of Augustine's great themes in Book XIX. It is obvious, however, that he imbibed some large lessons from the book; it does not follow that because he used marginal notes as a short cut he was therefore uninterested in the broad themes of the work. He also derived from it some details, which in his picture of Bruno are rather like the flowers, the vases and the jewellery depicted in a fifteenth-century religious painting.

Turning to Pope Gregory the Great, the early efforts to assemble good texts of his writings at Cologne are striking: by 833 the cathedral library had virtually all his then known works. Unfortunately the copies of the *Moralia in Job* and the *Homilies on Ezechiel* have disappeared; so also has the *Dialogues* from which Ruotger took at least one important citation (that at Bruno's tomb, visitors *signa non querunt, vitam adtendunt* etc.), relating to the fact that his Life of Bruno deliberately omitted any miraculous element.[64] While Ruotger's observation, in connection with Bruno's moving a community of canons from the church of S. Maria im Kapitol to the church of St. Andrew, that men are not chosen on account of a place, but a place is chosen by God for the sake of men, looks as if it must derive from Gregory's *Responsiones* to Augustine, 'non enim pro locis res, sed pro bonis rebus loca amanda sunt' (things are not loved for places but places for good things).[65]

On the other hand, a very fine manuscript of some 250 of Gregory's Letters, listed in 833, survives as Cologne MS 92. It has the Hildebald inscription and is agreed on all sides to be from the Cologne scriptorium of the middle-Hildebald period, *c.* 800 or very early ninth-century.[66] The text is laid out spaciously in two columns, written in very clear minuscule, on leaves of fair size (now 355 x 250 mm) and good quality parchment, the letters being numbered in a

[63] Ibid., XX, ix, 1; *De civitate dei*, i, 10, c. 47, p. 11.
[64] As pointed out by Lotter, *Vita Brunonis*, p. 39, n. 80.
[65] *Bedae historia ecclesiastica gentis Anglorum*, ed. C. Plummer (Oxford, 1896), i, c. 27, responsio 2, vol. i, p. 49.
[66] Jones, *The Script of Cologne*, pp. 44-46; *The Epinal . . . Glossaries*, p. 18.

continuous series, each with its rubric in a mixture of uncials and minuscule naming the addressee. A table of contents, with numbers and addressees, occupies fos. I v-4 r, and a *capitulare* with brief comments and the *argumenta* of the letters in turn, fos. 169 v-180 v (lacking treatment of the last thirty or so letters). The whole book is a joy to use and would on its own give testimony to the high place which Cologne occupied in Charlemagne's business – and Alcuin's – of producing manuscripts which were effective instruments of study. Cologne MS 93 is a manuscript of the same letters, with an inscription referring it to Archbishop Hadebald (819-41); as it is not listed in 833, it must date from 833-41. It is obviously a copy of MS 92; except for noting that it illustrates the desire at Cologne to accumulate Gregory manuscripts, we can leave it out of our calculations. Cologne MS 94 cannot be excluded; it is a very interesting collection of letters, but representing a different tradition of selection and arrangement from that of MS 92. The book is about the same size as MS 92 and is also clearly written, but there is no table of contents (there probably never was), the letters are not numbered, and there are no *capitula*. Thus the manuscript can hardly have been written at Cologne, since it is clearly later than the Hildebald manuscript; nobody at Cologne with that model in front of them would have laid out a manuscript of other letters so much less usefully.[67] Our question becomes, therefore, whether Cologne MS 94 had arrived at Cologne by Ruotger's time; there seem to me very strong grounds for answering in the affirmative.

First, I cannot agree with the lateness of the Jaffé-Wattenbach dating, i.e. tenth to eleventh centuries; this manuscript could not possibly be as late as the eleventh century. It often shows scant regard for word division, and that applies even to the marginalia, e.g., 'quia sunt culpae in quibus culpa est' etc. (156), and there are even ligatures, or virtual ligatures, between *s* at the end of one word and the letter at the beginning of the next, e.g. *corpus lavare* (fo. 129 v, col. A, second line from bottom) or *asserens locum* (fo. 130 r, col. A, sixth line from bottom). This implies the ninth century rather than the tenth, and there are also letter forms far more likely to be ninth- than tenth-century, e.g. the minuscule *a* open at the top like an *u*, e.g. *iuxta* (fo. 129 v, col. A, line 7).[68] The initial S at the beginning of the collection (fo. 4 v) has a rather geometrical

---

[67] *Gregorii I papae registrum epistolarum*, ed. L.M. Hartmann, (*MGH*, Berlin, repr. 1957, 2 vols), hereafter Epp. Gregorii. MS 92 belongs to Group C + P; MS 94 to Group Q + P (vol 2, pp. viii-xix).

[68] I accept the general points made in her very helpful paper by Johanne Autenrieth, 'Probleme der Lokalisierung und Datierung von spätkarolingische Schriften (10 und 11 Jahrhundert)', *Codicologica*, 4 (1976), pp. 67-74, that it is not easy to make general rules for dating and localisation in what is palaeographically one cultural (Carolingian) period from C9 to C11, and that manuscripts of certain date and place are needed as fixed points for dating others, while the testimony of a learned and literary culture, as at Einsiedeln, may help to date manuscripts. Nonetheless there do appear to be certain criteria of word spacing and letter forms which are useful as broad guides to dating as between the ninth and tenth centuries.

interlace panel in the middle and interlace tail-ends which curl over at the sides, all of which put one in mind of the St. Amand style at the time of the Second Bible of Charles the Bald (*c.* 870).[69] Hence my preferred date for this manuscript would be *c.* 870-900. Second, it is clear that Cologne remained interested to build up its library throughout the ninth century and into the tenth, at least; in particular it would have had every reason to acquire MS 94 as soon as it was on offer. A librarian would have been able to take the first twelve letters of MS 94 and see that not one of them was already in MS 92. It took me less than two hours to establish this, and, because of the excellent lay-out of MS 92, I had little extra advantage from the indices of the *Monumenta* edition.[70] That would surely have been enough to tell him that he wanted the book. Third, at least two scribes have written in the margins of MS 94, both roughly contemporary with the text scribe, and although I cannot speak with the same degree of assurance as in the case of MS 75, they look to me like Cologne hands, particularly the larger of the two whose contributions are the more interesting for my purposes. Their comments are incorporated in the typically Cologne way of a monogrammic NOTA sign in various designs. A good example of the larger hand is *Quod non sit precium pro sepultura exigendum* (fo. 23 v), and the two hands may well be compared at fos. 149 v – 150 r. The nearest hand to the larger which I have encountered is that of a scribe who has added responses and versicles to MS 137 (especially fo. 52), a sacramentary of the time of Archbishop Willibert (870-89) or Archbishop Hermann (890-923).[71] Each has the same erratic sense of direction in the strokes, the same pronounced upward tendency from left to right, the same slight tremble, very much the same kind of minuscule *e* made in two pen movements, similar plain abbreviations and similar *g* with the lower loop often

descending very low. I do not feel confident in pronouncing these as the same hand, but the comparison in the style of writing does seem to point us towards

[69] See, for instance, Anton von Euw, *Das Buch der vier Evangelien*, p. 38, abb. 26, from a St. Amand Gospel book at the Schnütgen Museum; also manuscripts of the second half of the ninth century from Rheims and ? Trier or Cologne, ibid., p. 50, abb. 39, 40, and p. 52, abb. 42. See also Rosamond McKitterick, 'Carolingian Book Production: Some Problems', *The Library*, 12 (1990), esp. pp. 14-29. For the initials of the Second Bible of Charles the Bald, see A. Boutemy, 'Quel fut le foyer du style franco-saxon?', *Congrès archéologique et historique de Belgique*, 83 (Tournai, 1949), pp. 749-73, and J. Hubert, J. Porcher, W.F. Volbach, *Carolingian Art* (London, 1970), pp. 62-68.

[70] The first twelve letters of MS 94 are the first twelve in Book VIII of the Register.

[71] Prayers for the Emperor Arnulph (ob. 899) and Archbishop Hermann, as if still alive, were added at the end of the MS on fo. 182 r, which gives a *terminus ad quem* in the 890s; but these additions are probably not much later than the main body of the MS., because fo. 182 is integral to the last quire, being doubled with fo. 179 which in its turn is still an integral part of the main manuscript.

where and when we should look for the glossator with the larger hand in MS 94.

There is an important fourth ground for arguing that Cologne MS 94 was at Cologne by the tenth century. Berlin MS.theol.322 from the monastery of St. Liudger, Werden, is a ninth-century manuscript of Gregory's Letters, very close to Cologne MS 94 in selection, arrangement, and text. Ewald, who dated Cologne 94 to the tenth century, suggested with force that *Cologne* was copied from a better version of the *Berlin* text and that *Berlin* was then corrected from *Cologne*. The marginal comments of *Berlin* reappear in *Cologne*, although a considerable number of new ones are added in *Cologne*. Now on fo. 127 of *Berlin*, after the Letters, there is a list of Werden abbots, followed on fo. 127 v by a list of Cologne archbishops. Both lists, said Ewald, were begun 'soon after the ninth century' and were subsequently continued by later hands. The likely reason for the list of archbishops in the Berlin manuscript is that at Werden, only some forty miles from Cologne on the Ruhr, the book used to correct the Berlin manuscript was associated by the tenth century with Cologne.[71a]

The contrast between the interest taken in Gregory's Letters at Cologne *c*. 800 and *c*. 900, on the evidence of the margins of MS 92 and MS 94 respectively, could hardly be greater. The margins of MS 92 are nearly empty except for some thirty to forty *NOTA* signs, of a very distinctive monogrammic sort and certainly contemporary with the manuscript, sparsely distributed amongst the 165 folios, or 330 pages, of the text. Sparsely, that is, except for a plethora of sixteen for one letter occupying fos. 145 r-146 v, a letter to Quirichus and other Iberian bishops about the return to the catholic fold of Nestorian heretics, who denied that the human Christ partook of the divine Christ. This letter obviously had a surpassing interest to the notator, with its strong assertions of the divinity of Christ, all pointedly noted. Some examples are:

> [Mary is called] the handmaid of the Lord because the Word was before all time, the only begotten son equal to the father; she is called mother also, because he became man in her womb, of her flesh, by the Holy Ghost . . . . The flesh was not first conceived in the womb of the virgin, divinity coming afterwards to the flesh, but as soon as the Word came in the womb, the Word, with its own nature preserved, was made flesh . . . All we sinful men first existed and afterwards were sanctified by the anointment of the Holy Spirit. But [Christ] was God, existing from eternity, conceived as man in time in the womb of the virgin by the Holy Spirit, and there as he was conceived, anointed by the same Spirit. He was not first conceived and afterwards anointed, etc.[72]

[71A]   Paul Ewald, 'Studien zur Ausgabe des Registers Gregors I', *Neues Archiv*, 3 (1878), pp. 488-89; cf Dag Norberg, *In Registrum Gregorii Magni*, 2 (Uppsala Universitets Arsskrift, no. 7, 1939), p. 69. Bernhard Bischoff, *Latin Palaeography*, trans. Dáibhí O Cróinín and David Ganz (Cambridge, 1990), p. 94, note 84, suggests that Cologne MS 106 (C9, Alcuin and Bede etc) may have come from Werden.

[72]   *Epp. Gregorii*, xi, 52, vol. 2, pp. 325-27.

Nobody could ask for a clearer statement than this of catholic orthodoxy, not only against the Nestorians of the sixth century, but also against the Adoptionist heresy which Charlemagne, Alcuin and the whole Carolingian church so strenuously tried to counter in the 790s, the Spanish heresy which denied the divinity of Christ, maintaining that Christ was not the true Son of God but was born man and then became the adopted Son of God. One does not think of Gregory, rather than Augustine or Marius Victorinus, being deployed by the Carolingians in the front line of patristic learning against the Adoptionists, but it seems that at Cologne he was.[73] Hildebald himself, as a leading churchman of the 790s, had certainly been involved in the Adoptionist Controversy, receiving around 794 a letter from Charlemagne (clearly drafted by Alcuin) stressing the divinity of Christ.[74]

With the marginal notes of MS 94 we move away from this trinitarian and christological world much more into the world of Ruotger, with his admiration for useful knowledge, action and practical virtues, a world to which Gregory's Letters as a whole are much more naturally attuned. So much is this so, that the reader may accuse me of irrelevance to my theme in the previous paragraph, though it is perhaps germane to Ruotger to perceive the profound, long, and multi-strata history of Gregory's reception into Cologne which lay behind him. Characteristic in MS 94 is the *NOTA* monogram followed by a note of subject matter, or the *NOTA* (or Chi-Rho monogram) on its own, or note of subject matter on its own. These draw attention to such subjects as the burials and reverence due to martyrs (fo. 30), that bishops should not be elected from another church (fo. 32), the lives of solitaries (fos. 42 v-43), appeal to Rome (*NOTA quid dicat de episcopis*, fo. 80 v), sick bishops not to be deposed (fo. 110), the pallium not to be paid for (fo. 178 v). These and many other passages like them did not provide Ruotger with direct quotations, with the language of his work, but taken together they could have given, and probably did give, him much of his subject matter. For if one wanted to focus the mind on how to construct an image of an archbishop of Cologne; and what he actually did or was supposed to have done in that capacity – and that is what a good proportion of the Life of Bruno is about; if one wanted to select the right sort of topics to deal with out of perhaps a mass of traditions, tales and information, these notes and the texts into which they led would have been the ideal way of doing it. The reverence due to martyrs was highly relevant to what Ruotger had to say about Bruno's refoundation of the monastery of St.

---

[73] For the Carolingian counter to Adoptionism, see, for instance, Wilhelm Heil, 'Der Adoptianismus, Alcuin und Spanien', in *Karl der Grosse*, 2, ed. B. Bischoff (Düsseldorf, 1965), pp. 95-155; Donald Bullough, 'Alcuin and the Kingdom of Heaven', in *Carolingian Essays*, ed. Uta-Renate Blumenthal (Washington, DC., 1983), pp. 49-56. See also P. Hadot, 'Marius Victorinus et Alcuin', *Archives d'histoire doctorinale*, 29 (1954), pp. 5-19.

[74] *Epistolae Alcuini*, in *MGH epistolarum*, iii, *karolini aevi*, ii, ed. E. Dümmler (Berlin, 1895), p. 530. '*Numquid magnum est, sic haec*' (the seven gifts of the Holy Spirit) '*in Christo mansisse dicantur, in quo omnis plenitudo divinitatis inhabitare cognoscitur*' . . . and more similarly.

Pantaleon.[75] That bishops should not be elected from another church was a matter to which strong feelings probably attached in Cologne, since Bruno's predecessor and four successors all belonged to the Cologne clergy, which may help to explain why Ruotger stresses the desire and harmonious agreement of the church to elect Bruno (who had not belonged previously) and his education at Utrecht, a church historically associated with Cologne.[76] Appeal to Rome and the pallium are both subjects which figure with importance in Ruotger, for Cologne based its position amidst the metropolitan rivalries of the Ottonian church quite as much as any other church on papal support.[77] Ruotger is explicit in stating that Bruno received the pallium with the unusual privilege, but customary to Cologne, that he might wear it whenever he chose, adding, against the charges made by Archbishop William of Mainz in his letter of 955 to Pope Agapetus II, that he received it for his great virtue and wisdom, i.e. not because of any payment made.[78] Ruotger used the title *universalis pontifex* for the pope, the very title which Gregory eschewed for himself in criticising the use of it by John, patriarch of Constantinople,[79] but it is of interest that a marginal note in MS 94 (fo. 165 v) has, *quid dicat de Johanne qui se universale dixit*. As for solitaries, Ruotger does not repeat what Gregory had said in his famous letter to the recluse Secundinus, where MS 94 marks with a *NOTA* the passage about how the weakness of human nature prevents anyone from praying the whole time, and how anyone who tries is in danger of having an idle mind and offering an opening to the devil, but he does recount Bruno's veneration for this way of life and his attempt to make suitable provision for it, in effect arranging for solitaries to be supervised in ones or twos by various monasteries of good repute. The spirit is the same; the idea that it is a good way of life but one which needs careful regulation.[80]

The whole background of Cologne interest in Gregory during the early ninth century is impressive. The library list of 833 refers to his forty *Homilies on the*

[75] VB, c. 27, pp. 27-28; c. 31, pp. 31-32, for the relics of martyrs, acquired by Bruno, more generally.

[76] VB, c. 4, p. 5, lines 1-4; c. 11, p. 11, lines 17-21. For Archbishop Wicfrid (924-53), see W. Neuss and F.W. Oediger, *Das Bistum Köln von den Anfängen bis zum Ende des 12 Jahrhunderts* (Cologne, 1964), p. 164. For Archbishop Folcmar (965-69), VB, c. 46, p. 49, lines 34-36. For Archbishop Gero (970-76), see *Die Miniaturen des Gerocodex*, ed. Adolph Schmidt (Leipzig, 1924), pp. 34-37. For Archbishop Warin (976-85) I can find no evidence of whether or not he belonged to the Cologne clergy before his elevation, but since he is not mentioned as a royal chaplain in Fleckenstein's work on the *Hofkapelle*, I imagine he did. For Archbishop Everger (985-99), see Thietmar of Merseburg, ii, c. 4, p. 100, from which it would appear that as *custos* of the cathedral in 976, he played no creditable part in the death of Archbishop Gero. On Utrecht and Cologne, see *The Greatest Englishman*, ed. Timothy Reuter (Exeter, 1980), pp. 74, 84, 91, n. 63.

[77] Mayr-Harting, *Ottonian Manuscript Illumination*, ii, pp. 122-23.

[78] VB, c. 27, pp. 27-28.

[79] VB, c. 27, p. 27, line 18, cf. Mayr-Harting, *Ottonian Manuscript Illumination*, ii, p. 122.

[80] *Epp. Gregorii*, ix, 147, vol. 2, pp. 142-49; VB, c. 33, p. 34, lines 5-19.

*Gospels* in three volumes.[81] Cologne MS 86 must fit into this picture, a book of about the same size as the Hildebald manuscript of the Letters (MS 92) and with the same clear lay-out in two columns, the same sort of rubrics and numbered list of contents. There was a time when Bernhard Bischoff gave a warning against regarding any manuscript which lacked the Hildebald inscription (and MS 86 lacks it) as being a Cologne manuscript of that period; but his own findings forced him to change his view during his later years, since a major Cologne hand of the period, which he identified, appeared in several manuscripts without the inscription.[82] Neither he nor L.W. Jones dealt with MS 86. I cannot be positive in identifying any hand of this manuscript as Hildebaldian, though when I compare its fo. 92, for instance, with MS 54, fo. 159 v as illustrated in Jones, plate VII, the latter having the Hildebald inscription, I feel that I am looking at the same hand. It is the ornament on some of the capital letters, however, characteristic of the early period of Hildebald, for instance the *h* s at fos. 4 v and 124 v, with trident terminals, cross-banding, and decorative 'eyes', which convinces me that when palaeographical succour arrives this manuscript will prove securely to be not only Hildebaldian, but early Hildebald.[83] As to the three volumes mentioned in 833, I cannot fully explain this, but that MS 86 is now a composite volume of sermons previously not all bound in one is strongly suggested by the fact that it is actually missing nine quires (i.e. xv to xxiii), or sermons 23-34). This early manuscript at Cologne would explain why in a Cologne homiliary of Hildebald's time (MS 171), where only eight out of thirty seven sermons are attributed to a named author, as many as four attributions are Gregorian, all four sermons being (or having been) in our manuscript.[84]

Even more striking is the case of Paterius's *Liber Testimoniorum*, extracts from Gregory's writings. Paterius was a notary of Gregory who found that the pope in the course of commenting on Job had commented also on so many other parts of the Bible that he drew these comments, or testimonies, and comments from Gregory's other writings, together in the order of the biblical books, to form a quasi-systematic commentary on the whole Bible (though

---

[81] Decker, p. 226, no. 51, and p. 239.

[82] References in n. 23 and 24 above.

[83] MS 54 has the Hildebald inscription and is generally agreed to be early Hildebald. So is MS 51 to which the initial ornament of MS 86 is very similar, e.g., Jones, *The Script of Cologne*, plates xvii, 1 and xxi, 1, and MS 41, ibid., plate xii, 2. There are of course no illustrations of MS 86 in Jones, and since I lacked all photographic facilities when I was in Cologne, I cannot supply illustrations either. Nor are my drawings good enough for reproduction. But I am confident that anyone who made the comparison in the manuscripts would be struck by the similarity of style. Several initials in MS 103, another agreed early Hildebald manuscript, have similar cross-bandings in the double lines of initials, e.g. at fos. 23 v, 24.

[84] MS 171 (Jones, *The Script of Cologne*, pp. 57-58), for Christmas (MS 86, fos. 30 v-32 r); for Lent, fos. 52 v-54 v (where the second half is omitted, suggesting MS 171 was for use in church while MS 86 was a full master copy, this sermon fos. 64 v-68 v); for Easter; and for the octave of Easter; both now missing from MS 86 but listed in the table of contents there.

Paterius's work did not reach beyond the Song of Songs).[85] Cologne MS 82 is a manuscript of Paterius (fos. 2-53 r) and Eucherius's *Membra domini* (fos. 53 v-87 r), which dates from Hildebald's time, probably early, as Bischoff showed.[86] But the Cologne scholars must quickly have become aware of its poor organisation and numerous *lacunae*, which they made shift to remedy in the acquisition of MS 97 with its clear lay-out and full text up to the Song of Songs.[87] One must assume that MS 97 is not a product of the Cologne scriptorium rather than an acquisition from outside, but it is clear that it was at Cologne early, by 833 in fact. How else can one explain the 833 catalogue entry no. 94, *Eucherii volumen I Paterii volumnina II*, than by positing that MS 82 represented the Eucherius and one copy of Paterius, while MS 97 represented the other copy, or volume, of Paterius?[88] Here I have to take issue with those writers on Paterius who, following Jaffé-Wattenbach, have dated MS 97 to the tenth century.[89] Its frequent lack of word spacing, its use of the ampersand when one word ends in *e* and the next beings with *t*, its very open *g*s like **3**s, its ligatures, its initial letters with their bird, fish and trinitarian ornament, would all place it in the first half of the ninth century.[90] Above all it has two *NOTA* signs unmistakeably in the same hand as that which made the *NOTA* signs beside Gregory's letter to Bishop Quirichus in MS 92, and that is certainly a Cologne annotator. The identification hits one ⤻ immediately, even though it is but a single monogram, whose open *a*, ⚂ incidentally, implies an early date.

---

[85] For a good account of Paterius, see Paul Meyvaert, 'The Enigma of Gregory the Great's *Dialogues*: A Response to Francis Clark', *Journ. of Eccl. Hist.*, 39 (1988), pp. 335-81, esp. pp. 352-58.

[86] *The Epinal . . . Glossaries*, p. 18.

[87] MS 82 numbers sections of text consecutively, whereas MS 97 exhibits the classic organisation by biblical books; MS 82 ends, except for one further paragraph, with the texts on Leviticus, whereas MS 97 goes up to the Song of Songs. After 'Dum de persecution . . . distribuit', MS 97, fo. 41, has, in mixture of red capitals and uncials, *Incipiunt capitula libri Exodi* and lists the Exodus chapters, according to its normal practice; whereas MS 82, fo. 32 v, continues with the third section of Exodus without a 'by your leave', *Dum de divinis mysteriis*, which is on fo. 43 of MS 97. I have traced the many other similar lacunae in MS 82. Independently of all this one should note that quire 4 of MS 82 is missing.

[88] Decker, p. 227, no. 94, cf. p. 249, where, quite impossibly, he calls the hand of MS 97 eleventh century.

[89] E.g., A. Wilmart, 'Le recueil Grégorien de Paterius et les fragments wisigothiques de Paris', *Revue Bénédictine*, 39 (1927), p. 86; R. Etaix, 'Le *Liber testimoniorum* de Paterius', *Revue des sciences religieuses*, 32 (1958), p. 67, n. 6. References by the kindness of Conrad Leyser.

[90] A good example of a *g* (one of many comes in the passage we cite below from fo. 106 v, line 17, where the name of Gedeon begins with a large miniscule *g*. I cannot find in my notes an example of the ampersand between words, but I am certain that I have seen it in this manuscript. For a fish initial (and this is Trinitarian), with a duck's head finial, fo. 172 v. For pure Trinitarianism, fo. 198 v has a lovely *O* initial with cusped ornament inside, and inside that a Celtic interlaced trefoil. I discuss Trinitarian initials from the period of the Adoptionist Controversy in my paper, 'Charlemagne as a Patron of Art', *The Church and the Arts*, ed. Diana Wood, Studies in Church History (Oxford, 1992), pp. 70-71.

Moreover, the first of these *NOTAS* (fo. 106 v) is placed against a comment about Gideon and the Book of Judges, which, extraordinarily, has exactly the same christological interest as the letter to Quirichus. Gideon coming to battle, says Gregory, signifies the advent of our saviour. The name of Gideon itself means *circumiens in utero*, and what is that but that almighty God, redeeming us in his full divinity and assuming humanity in the womb, became incarnate in the womb but was not enclosed by it, because he was within the womb through the substance of our infirmity, but outside the world by the power of his majesty.[91] Once again we see that early reception of Gregory at Cologne within the context of christological preoccupations under Charlemagne. The identity of subject matter gives extra force to the identification of the annotator's hand. Might the annotator have been Hildebald himself, studying in the midst of his external business, as Ruotger insisted that Bruno had done?

There are not many marginal annotations in the manuscripts of the homilies and of Paterius which we have been discussing, and hence the method of studying Ruotger's patristic sources and intellectual framework which we have applied to other manuscripts is not directly applicable here. Nor have I yet been able to study Paterius in sufficient detail to tell whether the whole slant of Ruotger's Gregorianism suggests the significant mediation of Paterius.[92] It is quite possible, for Paterius became common property in the greater Carolingian libraries: anyone in the tenth century who felt that he knew all the writings of Gregory, as John of Gorze was said to have felt, might easily have derived the sensation from a study of Paterius's well organized and impressive extracts.[93] Even so, one of the reason for stepping back momentarily from Ruotger in order to consider the general picture of Gregory's writing at Cologne, as we have done, is that Ruotger would seem to be more a Gregorian than he was an Augustinian. One work whose whole structure and purpose he had undoubtedly grasped was Gregory's *Regula pastoralis*, the famous treatise on how to rule as a bishop (though not necessarily only as a bishop).

In the *Regula pastoralis* Gregory stresses that he who rules, the *rector*, as both he and Ruotger sometimes call him, should strike a good balance between the necessities of the active life or external works, and the inner life of the soul without which he would freeze amidst his outer works. Inwardly (*intus*) he is rapt in contemplation; outwardly (*foris*) he is pressed by the business of carnal men. The contrast of *otium* and *negotium*, or study and business, in Bruno's life is part of this, but Ruotger also explicitly has the *intus*

---

[91] Text, as from Paterius, *PL* 79:787A.

[92] It is possible that Hamburg, MS Theol. 1523, said to be tenth-century and from St Pantaleon, Cologne (see R. Etaix, as in n. 88, p. 67, n. 6) would help here. I have not yet been able to examine it.

[93] *Vita Johannis Gorziensis auctore Johanne abbate S. Arnulfi, MGH SS*, ii, p. 360: 'in his primum moralia beati Gregorii ordine quam sepissime percurrens, pene cunctas ex eo continentias sententiarum ita memoriae commendavit'. On Paterius in Carolingian libraries, see Wilmart, 'Le recueil Grégorien de Paterius'.

*et foris* contrast: inwardly and outwardly, he says, Bruno is a tireless fighter for the Lord.[94] The *rector* cannot avoid secular business (*secularia negotia*) 'out of compassion', says Gregory, but he should not court it, otherwise it drags him down from the heights (*de coelestibus*) and plunges him into the depths; something Ruotger obviously bore in mind when he wrote that Bruno was never preoccupied by secular business, to which not his own desire but the needs of the people drew him; he was intent above all on religion and study.[95] Both Gregory and Ruotger, following him, believed that an effective *rector* should know how to inspire terror.[96] A large part of Gregory's book is taken up with advice on how to admonish or correct various contrasting sorts of people, the taciturn and the talkative, for instance, the poor and the rich, the sowers of discord and the peacemakers. One chapter is entitled: 'Quomodo admonendi humiles et elati'. Just so, Ruotger has it that towards the *humiles*, none was more humble than Bruno; towards the wicked or *elatos*, none was tougher.[97] Ruotger was keen to show that Bruno had something of the finesse in admonition which Gregory advocated. It can be necessary, says Gregory, to temper the reproof of sin with great moderation (*magno moderamine*). Bruno tried moderation in his admonition, it seems, and only used terror when it failed, for Ruotger writes of the *indomita barbaries* of the Lotharingians which despised the *blandimenta* of fatherly exhortation and scarcely felt the *terrorem potestatis*. The idea here derives from Gregory's views on admonition; the verbal contrast between *blandimenta* and *terror* also comes from the *Regula pastoralis*, but from another context.[98] On the other hand Gregory warned against seeking human approval, and Ruotger, following suit, was anxious to say of how little account Bruno held it.[99] Gregory said that the peaceful themselves were to be admonished not to desist from words of correction for fear of disturbing the temporal peace; likewise Ruotger has Otto I say to Bruno, as a reason for involving himself (though a bishop) in the rule of Lotharingia even to the point of battle, 'I know, my brother, that nobody will persuade your prudence that it is none of your business how much perverse men glory in damaging the good'.[100] It is doubtless true that Ruotger was

[94] *Reg. past.*, ii, 5, *PL* 77:33B: 'qui intus in contemplationem rapitur, foris infirmantium negotiis urgetur; intus dei arcana considerat, foris onera carnalium portat'. VB, c. 25, p. 26, lines 15-17. The reader will have noticed that I referred to the *intus/foris* contrast above in connection with Augustine, who strongly influenced Gregory on this theme, see Cuthbert Butler, *Western Mysticism* (London, 1926), part ii, chapters 1 and 2. I suppose a cumulative effect on Ruotger.
[95] *Reg. Past.*, ii, 7, *PL* 77:41A; VB, c. 29, pp. 29-30. Cf. VB, c. 14, p. 13, lines 19-20, that Bruno's intention was to fortify the church *in secularibus* and adorn it *in spiritualibus*.
[96] *Reg. past.*, ii, 6, *PL* 77:34C-D; VB, c. 12, p. 12, line 25, and c. 37, p. 39, line 13.
[97] *Reg. past.*, iii, 17, *PL* 77:77D; VB, c. 30 p. 31, lines 15-16.
[98] *Reg. past.*, ii, 10, *PL* 77:46A; VB, c. 37, p. 39, lines 10-14; *Reg. Past.*, ii, 3, *PL* 77:28D: 'blandimenta mundi respecto intimo terrore despiciat, terrores autem considerato internae dulcedinis blandimento contemnat'.
[99] Ibid., ii, 8, *PL* 77:42B-C; VB, c. 9, p. 9, lines 20-23.
[100] Ibid., iii, 22, *PL* 77:91C; VB, c. 20, p. 20, lines 4-8.

familiar with the Augustinian peace of the *City of God*, but Gregory knew all about the *pax ecclesiae* and how it was harmed by dissension, and Ruotger would scarcely have needed to look further than the *Regula pastoralis* for everything he had to say about peace.[101]

It is slightly surprising that Gregory's *Regula pastoralis* has hardly been brought into the discussion of Ruotger's work; actually, amidst the weighty discussion of its *hagiographische Grundschema*, I have not myself managed to find a single reference to it in anything that I have read on the subject.[102] Yet my argument would be that Ruotger's most important aim in writing was to show that, whatever anyone might say about Bruno's political involvements, he was a model bishop according to the image projected by Gregory in this work. All his use of other patristic writings was subservient to this principal aim. It may be true, as Timothy Reuter says, that Bruno's following of ecclesiastics was analogous to the followings of fighting men which kings and aristocrats had; but at the same time as perhaps glorying in his large 'connection', Bruno insisted that his episcopal protegés should be men who knew what was the *pastoris officium*.[103] Indeed, Ruotger's whole language of religion and virtue was the language of the *Regula pastoralis*, made up of words such as *patientia*, *moderatio* and *moderamen*, *sinceritas*, *humilitas*, *tranquillitas*, *mansuetudo* and *stabilitas*.

One needs no Cologne manuscript, I suggest, in order to show that Ruotger knew Gregory's treatise. Nonetheless, there is a Cologne manuscript which can carry a little further forward the understanding of Ruotger's use of it, Cologne MS 89. This manuscript, which is certainly from the first half of the ninth century and thus early enough to be the manuscript listed as *Pastorales libri quattuor* in the library list 833, is an ugly duckling. Its particular disagreeable quality is the extremely uneven cut of its folios, which led Decker to

---

[101]The phrase *pax ecclesiae* seems not to be used in the *Reg. past.* itself, though the idea is implicit in several passages, e.g., the harm to the church of evil-acting priests, *Reg. past.* i, 2, *PL* 77:16A, and the whole discussion of disturbers of the temporal peace in *Reg. past.*, iii, 22. But R.A. Markus, 'The Sacred and the Secular: From Augustine to Gregory the Great', *Journ. Theol. Stud.*, 36 (1985), pp. 84-96, shows how fundamental to and pervasive in Gregory's thinking this idea was, and at p. 93 cites a passage from the *Moralia* which uses the actual phrase *pax ecclesiae* (*Moralia*, xix, 9, 16, *PL* 76:106B) – reference by the kindness of Conrad Leyser.

[102]Except for Hoffmann, 'Politik und Kultur', p. 36, note 29, where he mentions Gregory's use of the phrase *regale sacerdotium* in *Reg. past.*, ii, 3. His point is that the phrase had always, before Ruotger used it of Bruno, been applied to lay rulers, and that Gregory constitutes no precedent in applying it specifically to priests, because he wrote allegorically. But Ruotger uses the phrase allegorically in exactly the same way as Gregory (see below, n. 107). I do not say this to deny the extra significance of actual royal blood in Bruno's case (see K.J. Leyser, *Rule and Conflict in an Early Medieval Society: Ottonian Saxony* (London, 1979), pp. 17, 86-87), but to mark Ruotger's dependence on Gregory's thought. The phrase *hagiographische Grundschema* is that of F. Lotter, 'Das Bild Brunos von Köln in der *Vita* des Ruotger', *Jahrbuch des kölnischen Geschichtsvereins*, 40 (1966), pp. 19-50.

[103]Reuter, 'The *Imperial Church System*', p. 355; VB, c. 37, p. 39, lines 20-21.

describe it (wrongly) as damaged.[104] It was never made to look beautiful, in that sense, but most of its leaves are of good thick parchment, the handwritting is clear, and the Roman numerals which mark the chapter divisions in the margin sometimes have the ornament of narrowing lines receding from them in the style of quire numbers in certain ninth-century Cologne manuscripts.[105] The thinner leaves show that at various stages it has been quite well used. It cannot at present be shown to have been a Cologne product, and it is theoretically possible that it was not the manuscript of 833, rather than another which may since have been lost. Here, however, its unattractive appearance turns to our argumental advantage, since it seems hardly likely that, if it had not been written at Cologne, a Cologne librarian would jump at the opportunity to acquire it, amidst all his opportunities to acquire this basic text, a long time after it was produced. It is probable therefore, as Decker thought, that this is the manuscript which was already in the cathedral library in 833.

The feature of MS 89 most relevant to Ruotger, indeed which makes me think that he used this very manuscript when he wrote, is that the scriptural books from which quotations came are identified in the margins by a contemporary hand with unusual clarity and comprehensiveness. The *Regula pastoralis* is heavily studded with scriptural quotations, as is the Life of Bruno. They are not, of course, consistently the same ones, for as we have seen Ruotger had other sources to draw on, including – it would be churlish to deny it – his own direct knowledge of the Bible. Moreover, he seems to have taken to heart Augustine's view in the *De doctrina christiana* that it was good to quote the words of Scripture, but even more important to understand them, and sometimes he shows his understanding by taking a verse contiguous to that quoted by Gregory and of similar purport rather than by using Gregory's own citation. Nonetheless, of Ruotger's four quotations from Proverbs, for instance, two are in the *Regula pastoralis* and are marked as such in the margins of MS 89 (fos. 57 v, 65 r).[106] Gregory uses the phrase from St. Peter's first epistle (I Pet. 2:9), which Ruotger takes over, the royal priesthood (*regale sacerdotium*), following Gregory's meaning at this point very closely when he says that in Bruno, priestly religion and royal fortitude were both strong. Gregory refers the phrase to the desirable combination in priests of interior nobility and external power of a kingly sort.[107] In the margin of MS 89 here (fo. 16) is written *in epistola Petri Apostoli*. The quotation from St. James (fo. 54), 'sit omnis homo velox ad audiendum tardus autem ad loquendum' must surely be the source of Ruotger's phrase *ingenii velocitate*.[108] Ruotger alludes to Exodus 28, 35 when describing Bruno's entry into his see, which Gregory uses

[104]Decker, p. 226, no. 56, and p. 240.

[105]Jones, *The Script of Cologne*, pp. 44, 50, 75 (no. 63), 76 (no. 98).

[106]Proverbs 20:21, *Hereditas ad quam festinavit*; VB, c. 18, p. 16, lines 23-24; Proverbs 16:18, *Ante ruinam exaltatur cor*; VB, c. 35, p. 36, line 2.

[107]*Reg. past.*, ii, 3, *PL* 77:29, VB, c. 20, p. 19 lines 20-21.

[108]Ibid., c. 5, p. 7, line 18.

and which is marked with red letters in a frame, *in exodo* (MS 89, fo. 17 v).[109] He also refers, in a phrase which would be unintelligible without the *Regula pastoralis*, to some bishops of Bruno's following as being like the blue curtains (*cortine iacinctine*) adorning the interiors of the Lord's house. This alludes to Exodus 26:1. Gregory discusses hyacinth blue, one of the colours of the humeral veil worn by the priests of the Temple (Exodus 28:8) in order to use it as an allegory of priestly virtue: 'hyacinth is added, brilliant with the colour of the skies, that by every matter which the priest penetrates with his understanding, he may not stoop to the base favours of earth, but rise up to the love of heavenly things'.[110] In the margin here (fo. 15 v) is also *in exodo* and the word *iacinthus*.

To study the manuscripts at Cologne, fraction as they are of what was once there, begins to feel almost like entering the workshop, a Carolingian workshop, of the Ottonian Ruotger.[111] Its great instruments were the fathers, Augustine and Gregory, in whose terms Ruotger articulated the ideals of Ottonian churchmanship, while its finer tools were the marginalia in the manuscripts of their works belonging to Cologne. In Ruotger's time it was, as has been shown, not only a patristic but also a classical library; and even now, apart from the manuscripts of classical literature which have been dispersed or lost altogether, there remain at Cologne early manuscripts concerned with the *artes*, of Boethius, Priscian, Martianus Capella, etc., which I have not yet had opportunity to study but which would certainly repay attention.[112] They may help to point up the reality of Bruno's knowledge of the *artes* and what lay behind Ruotger's stress on it. The manuscript of Vitruvius, now in the British Library (MS Harley 2767), which was produced in another scriptorium but belonged to Cologne cathedral around Ruotger's time, shows the Cologne disposition of that period to turn knowledge relevantly towards contemporary preoccupations and social needs. A page of this manuscript (fo. 145 v) contains a remarkable drawing of a cross and, next to it written in dark ink, the words *Goderamnus prepositus*, which have generally been taken to refer to the person of that name who was provost of the monastery of St. Pantaleon,

---

[109]Ibid., c. 21, p. 22, lines 8-9.

[110]*Reg. past.*, ii, 3, *PL* 77:29A-B. I have used the excellent translation here of Henry Davis, *St. Gregory the Great: Pastoral Care*, Ancient Christian Writers, no. 11 (New York, 1950), p. 50. VB. c. 37, p. 39, lines 23-24.

[111] A remarkable awareness of the debt owed by the Ottonian 'renaissance' of study to the age of Charlemagne (as Josef Fleckenstein has convincingly argued) is shown in a poem composed by Bruno of Cologne himself, praising Otto I for presiding, in his rule, over a revival of Carolingian learning, after dark times and the pressure of barbarian attacks. See Josef Fleckenstein, 'Bruns Dedikationsgedicht als Zeugnis der karolingischen *Renovatio* unter Otto d. Gr.', *Deutsches Archiv für Erforschung des Mittelalters*, 11 (1954-55), pp. 219-26.

[112]E.g., MSS 185, 186 (Boethius on arithmetic), 193, 194 (Martianus Capella), 200 (Priscian). Whether or not these are Cologne products is not yet for the most part clear. The Priscian, a huge manuscript, came from Prüm (*The Epinal . . . Glossaries*, p. 18, n. 65), but could have been at Cologne in the tenth century.

Cologne, before he became abbot of St. Michael, Hildesheim, in 996. It appears that St. Pantaleon was borrowing a cathedral book.[113] Whether the wonderful church of St. Pantaleon, whose building was initiated by Bruno in the 960s and presumably continued over the next decades, was influenced by the architectural principles or practical advice of Vitruvius, I am not qualified to say. But in terms of the assumed relevance of a piece of classical learning to a building project, if only in sharpening architectural awareness (and the opening book of Vitruvius stresses the need for architects to be persons of 'philosophy'), one could not have neater illustration of the relation between *otium*, or study, and *negotium*, or business, as both Ruotger and Bruno conceived it. The fathers, too, seem normally to have been held in early medieval Cologne to have something to say to the world beyond that of the library and the theologians. A manuscript of Jerome on the Minor Prophets (Cologne MS 53), written under Archbishop Everger (985-99), has mono-grammic NOTA signs in the margin against passages which speak of the relevance of prophecies to one's own times (fo. 4 v), of Saul being made king not by the will of God but by the error of the people (fo. 42 v), of the inevitability if a bishop sins that so will his people (fo. 229 r), and of the necessity that a wife should fear her husband (fo. 236 v). These are four of only some fourteen NOTA signs altogether. Few people, at Cologne, it seems, believed in the *nobile otium* without wanting to see it applied to the world of affairs.

[113] For Goderamnus, see *Thangmari vita Bernwardi episcopi Hildesheimensis*, *MGH SS*, iv, c. 50, p. 779. For B.L., MS Harley 2767, see especially Bernhard Bischoff, 'Die Uberlieferung des technischen Literatur', in his *Mittelalterliche Studien*, iii, (Stuttgart, 1981), pp. 277-97, esp. pp. 281-82.

# 5

# A Glossed Manuscript of Priscian's Institutio, Vatican, MS Reg. Lat. 1578

Colette Jeudy

A series of recent studies[1] have traced the importance and the diffusion of Priscian's little manual entitled *Institutio de nomine et pronomine et verbo* in the schools of the early middle ages.[2] The manuscript in the Vatican Library, MS Reginensis latinus 1578, has been of interest to me for some time.[3] This article will examine the marginal and interlinear glosses that accompany the text of the *Institutio* in the manuscript and which reflect the way grammar was taught in the eleventh century.

The manuscript is composed of several distinct parts of which only the first interests us here. Fos. 1-46, measuring 220 x 148 mm, were copied during the first half of the eleventh century, probably in the south of France, near the Pyrenees, according to Professor Bischoff. The textual composition of this first part of the manuscript corresponds with the pedagogical method of the eleventh century. As in preceding centuries, the *Ars minor* of Donatus is placed at the beginning, but only in the form of Remi d'Auxerre's commentary

[1] C. Jeudy, 'L'*Institutio de nomine et verbo* de Priscien: manuscrits et commentaires médié-vaux, *Revue d'histoire des textes*, 2 (1972), pp. 73-144 (catalogue of 69 manuscripts). M. Passalacqua, *I codici di Prisciano* (Rome, 1978) (Sussidi eruditi, 29) adds four manuscripts from the fifteenth century: no. 204, pp. 91-92; no. 354, p. 155; no. 364, pp. 158-159; and no. 601, pp. 285-286. Cf. also C. Jeudy, '*Complément à un catalogue récent des manuscrits de Priscien*', *Scriptorium*, 36 (1982), pp. 319, 322 and 324 and '*Nouveau complément . . .* ', *Scriptorium*, 38 (1984), p. 147; G. Ballaira, *Per il catalogo dei codici di Prisciano* (Torino, 1982), pp. 39-40, no. 13+, pp. 54-55, no. 29+; and pp. 60-61, no. 34+.

[2] H. Keil, ed., *Grammatici latini*, 3 (Leipzig, 1859, reprinted, Hildesheim, 1961), pp. 441-56. The critical edition of M. Passalacqua, *Prisciani Caesariensis opuscula*. Vol. 2 is now in press in Rome in the collection *Sussidi eruditi*.

[3] For details of the content and history of the manuscript, cf. C. Jeudy, 'L'*Institutio . . .* ', pp. 134-35, M. Passalacqua, *I codici . . .* , pp. 318-19, no. 664 and E. Pellegrin, *Manuscrits classiques latins de la Bibliothèque Vaticane*, ii, 1 (Paris, 1978), pp. 304-6 (Documents, études et répertoires publiés par l'institut de recherche et d'histoire des textes). The manuscript comes from the collection of Paul and Alexandre Petau.

which has been substituted for it.[4] It is not surprising to find Prisician's little *Institutio* at the end as a natural complement to Remi's commentary on the fundamental treatise of Donatus. Although it usually follows the *Ars Donati* immediately, it is separated from Remi's commentary in this instance by a series of poems that often travel together in the manuscript tradition: the distichs of the Pseudo-Cato, the *Carmina* 30-33 of Eugenius of Toledo (*De philomela*),[5] followed by the *Carmina* 6, 2 and 7 of Eugenius,[6] which were taken to be the fifth book of Cato, the *Epitaphium filii Catonis* (*Anthologia latina* 487a), and finally, on fo. 26r-v a poem on Samson[7] and three epitaphs: that of Pope Damasus,[8] that of Alcuin[9] and that of King Dagobert I.[10]

The title of Prisician's manual begins on the last line of fo. 26 v and overflows onto fo. 27: *Incipit liber Prisciani Gramatici de nomine et pronomine et verbo et participiis*. In most manuscripts the participle is never mentioned and the title refers only to the three essential parts of the discourse, sometimes omitting the first *et*. The participle, however, figures in four other manuscripts:

. . . *ac participio* (Paris, B.N., lat. 14087, fo. 99 v; early ninth century; Corbie)

. . . *et participio* (Paris, B.N., lat. 8672, fo. 92; tenth century; France)

. . . *et participio et verbalibus nominibus* (Leyden, Bibliotheek der Rijksuniversiteit, MS BPL 67, fo. 208; second half of the ninth century; perhaps from western Germany. Paris, B.N. lat. 7498, fo. 81; mid ninth century; France. The MS has been compared to books from St. Amand).

---

[4] The text is imperfect at the beginning, cf. W. Fox, ed., *Remigii Autissiodorensis in artem Donati minorem commentum* (Leipzig, 1902), p. 30: 'ipse prope quasi dicas . . .'

[5] Cf. L. Holtz, *Donat et la tradition de l'enseignement grammatical: étude et édition critique* (Paris, 1981), pp. 341, 347-48. (Documents, études et répertoires publiés par l'institut de recherche et d'histoire des textes).

[6] Concerning this series of poems following the *Distichs* of Pseudo-Cato and the pedagogical and moral use of the poetry of Eugenius of Toledo in grammar classes, cf. Y.-F. Riou, 'Quelques aspects de la tradition manuscrite des *Carmina* d'Eugène de Tolède . . . ', *Revue d'histoire des textes*, 2 (1972) pp. 26-33.

[7] This poem of sixteen lines, entitled *De Samsone fortissimo* appears in the same context on fos. 68 v-69 of Paris, B.N., MS lat. 8318 (tenth century), on fo. 42 of Paris, B.N., MS, lat. 9344 (eleventh century) and on fos. 10 v-11 of Vatican, MS Reg. lat. 251 (first half of the ninth century). Cf. also D. Schaller and E. Könsgen, *Initia carminum latinorum saeculo undecimo antiquiorum*, (Göttingen, 1977), no. 8361 (MS 8318 is unknown to these authors).

[8] D. Schaller . . . , *Initia* . . . , no 13255.

[9] Alcuin, *Carmen* 123 (*MGH Poetae*, i, p. 350; cf. ii, 656). Cf., D. Schaller . . . , *Initia* . . . , no. 6688. Add Vatican, MS Reg. lat. 2078, fo. 122 (first quarter of the ninth century, from Rheims according to B. Bischoff). The epitaph is inserted between the *Carmina* XV and XVI of Hibernicus exul, which are preceded by the *Distichs* of Ps.-Cato and followed on fos. 149 v-150 by the *Carmina* 6, 2 and 7 of Eugenius of Toledo, the pseudo Book V of the *Distichs*.

[10] Edited by A. Duchesne, *Historiae Francorum scriptores*, i (Paris, 1636), p. 590 after a manuscript belonging to Alexandre Petau, probably this one, which moreover is the only one currently known.

The Vatican manuscript is the only one where the participle is mentioned in the plural at the end of the title.

From fo. 27 on, the text of the *Institutio* is accompanied by contemporary marginal and interlinear glosses that are especially abundant in the *De nomine* up to fo. 30 v. They virtually frame the text on fo. 27; thereafter they are distributed irregularly; for the pronoun there are only two glosses and for the verb only three. The following is a transcription of the most significant glosses:[11]

[fo. 27]

*Omnia* (443, 3) Quare omnia et non cuncta vel universa posuit? Respondetur: Omnia et cuncta hoc inter se differunt, quod cuncta omnia sunt, si modo cuncta etsi simul faciunt, aliter omnia dicuntur cuncta. Si vero cuncta proferret, greca praetermitteret. Ergo maluit omnia ponere, ut dixerat, lingua suum perficeret tractatum.

*Declinatio* (443, 3) in sensu, flexio in superficie, casus in utroque. Ideo non dixit quinque flexionibus declinantur, ne superficies antecederet sensum. Et ideo non dixit quinque declinationibus declinantur, ne omitteret superficiem. Quando dixit quinque declinationibus flectuntur, apprehendit omnia sensu et superficie. Cum dicit quinque deffinitionem numeri facit, quidam dicebant. VII. esse declinationes, quidam. IIIIor., quidam autem. VI. propter. VI. varietates casuum. Priscianus autem medium locum tenens nec. III. neque. IIIIor. neque. VI., sed quinque voluit esse declinationes propter. V. litteras vocales.

*In ae dyptongon* (443, 5). Ideo dicit in ae quia antiquitus genitivus prime declinationis terminabatur in as, ut haec familias huius familias, unde remansit in usu pater familias, sicut legimus in Evangelio.[12]

*Poetae* (443, 6) Poites grece, latine qualitas. Inde poetae dicuntur a quadam qualitate. Antiqui enim in forali habitu conversi, quaedam scripta excogitabant, quibusdam pedibus et numeris ligata, de quibus gesta suorum deorum scriberent unde obtinuit ut poeta excogitator vocaretur. Vel poesis grece, latine fictio. Inde poeta facit carminum, videlicet qui carmina et versus componit.

*In i productam* (443, 6): Ideo dixit in i productam, ne videatur esse correpta, sicut in adverbio.

*In is brevem* (443, 7): Ideo dixit in his correptam, ut sit differentia inter nomina et pronomina his et ab his, quae semper longae sunt. Sciendum est autem quod nomina .III. declinationis semper in genitivo singulari breviantur praeter unum, quod est naturaliter longum, ut haec vis huius vis, significat potestas.

---

[11] I have reproduced the *lemma*, indicating in parentheses the page and the line in the Keil edition. Only the citations are identified in the notes.

[12] Cf. Matthew 20: 1; 21: 33; Luke 12:39; 14:21.

*In us productam* (443, 8). Ideo dixit in us productam, ne videatur esse correpta, sicuti eius nominativus, ut hic *senatus*. Senatus compositum est a senibus et natu nomine indeclinabile. Erat autem locus Romae apud antiquos, ubi cotidie conveniebant .CXX^ti. senes tractantes de re publica, id est de romano imperio. Romanum enim imperium semper publicas res vocabatur. Vocabatur enim senatus et ipse locus et ipsa multitudo senum.

*In ei divisas* (443, 9): Ideo dixit in ei divisas ne videantur esse coniunctae, sicut in secunda declinatione, ut Tydeus Tydei, Orpheus Orphei, Oyleus Oylei, si hoc in propriis vel grecis nominibus invenitur. Sciendum est autem omnia nomina quintae declinationis feminini generis esse, praeter duo: dies et meridies. Sed secundum quosdam quinta declinatio exceptio est primae declinationis. Sciendum est autem quod *dies* in singulari numero communis generis est, quamvis dicamus abusive : hic dies. In pluralitate vero masculini, ut hi dies. Inde componitur *meridies*, id est media dies, quem omnes gentes aequalem habent, mane autem et vespere non sic.

*Scriba* (443, 14) : id est translator legis vel scriptor.

[fo. 27 v]
*Toreuma* (443, 21) toreumata ornamenta in modum bullarum quae fiunt in stillicidiis, quibus antiquorum nobilium pueri utebantur, ut per haec panderetur, quia eadem infirmitas consilio indigeret. Nam bolim consilium dicunt Greci.

*Vt* δ ... *hic,* τοῦ ... *huius* (443, 25) : Articuli sunt Grecorum, quod nos dicimus hic, illi dicunt ὅ et quod nos dicimus huius, illi dicunt τοῦ

*Thucydides* (444, 1) proprium nomen oratoris a loco vel patre.

*Euripides* (444, 1) ab Eurypo castello pro scilicet canalibus, ubi aqua currit.

*Ariobarzanes* (444, 3) : barbara, ut hic proprium montis.

*ut hic Orontes* (444, 4) : nomen fluvii

[fo. 28]
*Oleaster* (444, 11) olea agrestis.

*Apiaster* (444, 11) species apis et locus ubi apes nutriuntur.

*Sequester* (444, 12 et 14) medius inter duos lites dirimens,
*Sequester* divisor.

*Tuber* (444, 17) tufera species boleti, qui fertur ex tonitruo nasci, et species arboris.

*Gener* (444, 17) qui assumitur ad augendum genus.

*Cancer* (444, 18) signum caeleste vel vulnus sive piscis uel serpens.

*Treviri* (444, 20) aliquis ex gente Treverorum.

*Ir . . . indeclinabile* (444, 23) Quare dixit ir indeclinabile, cum legamus Iris et Irem ? Sciendum est si de arcu nubium dicitur, declinabile est, si de medietate palmae, indeclinabile.

*Saturatus* (444, 24) omnium rerum, satiatus tantum cibi.

*Fur* (444, 25) a furvo noctis tempore.

*Luxus* (444, 29) quicquid in inmensum procedit, luxus dicitur, unde et luxa membra dicuntur, inde luxuria, id est in corporalibus.

*magistratus* (444, 31) multitudo magistrorum.


[fo. 28 v]
[*quaestus*] (444, 35) adquisitio, lucrum pecuniarum.

*Rictus* (444, 35) nimia oris apertio, sunt vox leonum.

*Musta* (444, 36) Quare facit ? quia non est fixum et femininum facit in a et non est quartae sed secundae.

*Portus* (445, 2) quod ibi adportentur naves.

*Arcitus* (445, 2) repulsus. *Arceo* repello.

Vultus (445, 3) id est voluntas.


[fo. 29]
*Tyrus . . . Cyprus* (445, 17) : Greci dicunt Tyros, Cypros et sunt nomina insulae.

*Arctus* (445, 17) septentrio.

*Pylus* (445, 18). Pilus proprium nomen est feminae, quae usum lentis adinvenit. Virgilius: *Pylus iacet curam spernabere lentis.*[13]

*Cupressus* (445, 18) arbor odorifera.

---

[13] Cf. *Verg. Georg.*, i, 228.

*Manus* (445, 21) a munere, quod illi munus manus dicitur, eo quod his compleatur madimus.

*Ligus* (445, 29) homo de Liguria.

*epycoenon* (445, 31) epy super, cenon commune.


[fo. 29 v]
*Pus* (445, 28) ut illud Origenis: *Positis in purem fratribus. Pus* quando putredinem significat, indeclinabile est, quando vero custodiam significat, tunc declinatur.[14]

*Senectus* (445, 39) multitudo senum, senecta vero ipsa aetas.

*Palladium* (446, 4) : Pallas Minerva, inde Palladium ipsius effigies.

*Orator* (446, 8) vir bonus dicendi peritus.[15]

*Civitas* (446, 8) : cives dicuntur quod simul coeuntes vivant, civitas vero quod plurimorum vitas consciscat et contineat moenia, urbs civitas habitatores sunt.

*Caput* (446, 8) quod sit cavum.

*Monile* (446, 10) ornamenta mulierum.

*Consul* (446, 14) consilium dando.

*Titan* (446, 14) id est sol.

*Sinciput* (446, 14) id est prior pars capitis, sicut occiput posterior.


[fo. 30]
*Bostar* (446, 16) ubi cremabantur corpora vel vestigium bovis vel tortor.

*Locuples* (446, 34) ex loco et pleno compositum est, dives locis et possessionibus plenus. Hinc Flaccus dicit : *In loculete plenus defensis pinguis umbris*.[16] Priscianus vero: '*Incolitur populis locupletibus arma direntis*.[17]

*Spes* (446, 34) res invisibilis per patientiam exspectabilis, *fides* vero argumentum rerum non apparentium.


[14] Cf. *Virg. Maro, Epit.*, 11, 3, G. Polara, ed., p. 150, 15-18.
[15] *Cato ad fil.*, frg. 14; *Cic. de orat.*, ii, 85; *Quint. Inst.*, i, 2, 3; ii, 16, 11; iii, 7, 25 etc.
[16] *Pers.*, 3, 74.
[17] *Prisc., Periheg.*, 841.

[fo. 30 v]
*Neapolis* (446, 38) : nee novem, polis civitas, Neapolis urbs super novem civitates.

*Dos* (447, 2) quod dabitur nubentibus, quod invicem accipiebant, quasi do ite.

*Praes* (447, 6) : praes est qui praesidet; praes calcator uvarum; praes, rus, ager fertilis.

*Fraus* (447, 7) quasi fracta fides.

[fo. 32]
*Tertiae* . . . (449, 9) Tertia, prima et secunda persona singula habent pronomina, tertiam vero sex voces diverse indicant. Respondetur quod prima et secunda persona ideo non egent diversis vocibus, quod semper sunt inter se praesentes et demonstrativae. Tertia vero persona modo demonstrativa est, ut hic, iste, modo relativa, ut is ipse, modo praesens iuxta ut iste, modo absens vel longe posita, ut ille.

*Vestras* (449, 10) Cur nostras et vestras a plurali tantum numero diriventur? Respondetur quod patriam seu gentem significant. Patria autem vel gens unius possessio esse non potest, sed semper multorum. Itaque nostras dicimus, qui est ex nostra patria vel quam multi possident, hoc est tam mea quam meorum civium.

[fo. 33]
*Analogia* (450, 12) dicitur proportionalitas seu qualitas declinationum vel iuxta Marcianum *cumracionabilitas*.[18]

[fo. 34]
*Illud autem notandum est* (451, 17-18) Quod exponit, hoc est: omnia verba praeter anomale corripiunt primam et secundam personam praeteriti subiunctivi et de ipsis anomalis pluraque licet auctoritas variet.

The glosses with grammatical content on fo. 27 are very close to the marginal commentary in two other manuscripts: Orleans, B.M., MS 295 (248 bis), p. 43 and Oxford, Bodleian Library, Auct. T. II. 20 (Madan 20624) fo. 41 v. The first was copied in the third quarter of the ninth century at Rheims, the second probably at Fleury in the first half of the tenth century; the glosses are contemporary. For the purposes of the present essay, we will give the explanations of four words.

The first, *Pilus* (445, 18) refers to a verse from the *Georgics* by Virgil: 'Nec Pelusiacae curam aspernabere lentis' (i, 228). There is probably a confusion between Pylos (Pylus) the city in Messenia, the country of Nestor, and

---

[18] Cf. Iohannes Scottus, *Annotationes in Marcianum*, 114, 19, C.E. Lutz, ed. (Cambridge, MA, 1939), p. 78, lines 11-13.

Pelusium the port in Lower Egypt. The gloss is more comprehensible when one refers to the commentary of Servius on the verse of Virgil: 'Pelusium unum est de septem ostiis Nili, ubi primum lens inventa dicitur, vel ubi optima lens nascitur' (ed. by G. Thilo and H. Hagen, *Servii grammatici in Vergili Georgicon librum commentarius*, iii, 1, (Leipzig, 1902), p. 58). Other glossed manuscripts have usually interpreted *pilus* as the name of a tree from which one fashioned the javelins of Roman soldiers (*pilum*).

The explanation of the second word *pus* (445, 28) is borrowed directly from Virgilius Maro the grammarian (*Epitom*. xi, 3,2) with the citation attributed to Origen: '*Pus* in Latinitate filosophica custodia dicitur, sicut Originis ait: *possitis in pure fratribus ille solus evasit*, hoc est *in carcere*, corpus ergo a corona circumdandi et a custodia dicitur' (ed. by G. Polara, with Italian translation, *Virgilio Marone grammatico: epitomi ed epistole* (Naples, 1979), p. 150-53). The other glossed manuscripts, with regard to this second meaning of the word *pus*, resort to the biblical citation of Jeremiah in the prison of Abdemelech: '*Extraxit eum de pure*, id est de custodia . . .' (cf. *Ier.* 38:13).

For the third word, *locuples* (446, 34), the glossator first gives the etymology attested in Isidore (*Etym.* x, 155) which in turn relies on the *De republica* of Cicero (ii, 16). Then he cites two verses borrowed by turns from the third satire of Persius:

'In locuplete penu defensis pinguibus Umbris' (3,74) and from the *Periegesis* of Priscian:[19]

'Incolitur populis locupletibus alma diremptis' (v. 841. ed. by P. Van de Woestijne (Bruges, 1953), p. 85; *Poetae latini minores*, (Leipzig, 1883), p. 308).

Almost the same gloss with the two verses occurs on fo. 47 of MS Auct. T. II. 20 in the Bodleian Library. For Persius, the two manuscripts have *plenus* instead of *penu*.

No explicit citation accompanies the fourth gloss, but the last synonym for *analogia* (450, 12) is not without interest. The first two are common in the grammatical tradition: *proportionalitas* or *proportio* and *qualitas declinationum* and recall Book III of Martianus Capella on grammar (*De nuptiis Philologiae et Mercurii*, iii, 114, 12 and 114,19. The third, on the other hand, despite the affirmations of the glossator, does not figure in the works of Martianus Capella. The word *corrationalitas* or *corrationabilitas* is in fact used for the first time by Augustine in the *De musica*, in c. 17 of Book VI, paragraph 57 (*Deus creator omnium*):

'Unde corrationalitas (ita enim malui analogiam vocare) . . .' (*PL* 32:1192; edited and translated by G. Finaert and H.J. Thonnard, *Oeuvres de saint*

[19] Fifty manuscripts remain of the *Periegesis* of Priscian, of which eighteen are datable earlier than the twelfth century. Cf. M. Passalacqua, *I codici . . .* , pp. 382-85 and G. Ballaira, *Per un catalogo . . .* , pp. 121-201.

*Augustin, 1ère série: Opuscules, vii. Dialogues philosophiques, IV: La musique* (Paris, 1947), pp. 474-75 [Bibliothèque augustinienne]).

The gloss refers to the discussion of this word by John Scot in his *Glossae in Martianum Capellam*:

'Analogia ἀνά praepositio, λόγος ratio, inde componitur analogia, id est corrationabilitas secundum Augustinum vero, et secundum alios proportio' (114, 19, ed. by C.E. Lutz, *Iohannis Scotti Annotationes in Marcianum* (Cambridge MA, 1939), p. 78 lines 11-13, 21). The word is found in several forms in his works: *corrationabilis, corrationabiliter, corrationabilitas.*[20] Certainly, as Père Folliet remarked to me, the adverb *corrationaliter* is also present in the *Adversus Arium* of Marius Victorinus (i, 13, 21), contemporary with Augustine.[21] But John Scot refers directly to Augustine whom he knows well, and Book VI of the *De musica* was particularly wide-spread in the early middle ages. The gloss thus reflects a discussion concerning the exact translation of the Greek word *analogia*. Contrary to current usage, John Scot, relying on Augustine, proposes the synonym *corrationabilitas*, which indeed seems to have disappeared thereafter in medieval texts. A slightly deformed echo of that discussion is found, however, in the eleventh-century gloss. It also appears in the left margin on fo. 89 v of another manuscript of the *Institutio*, MS lat. 7503 in the Bibliothèque Nationale, copied in France, perhaps at Fleury in the first half of the ninth century.

These few examples indicate that there is still much to glean from the marginal glosses of grammatical manuscripts that will help our knowledge of the evolution of the Latin language and the transmission of culture.

---

[20] Cf. *Periphyseon*, IV = *PL* 122:783-85 (*corrationalis*) and 789 (*corrationabiliter*); transl. Pseudo-Denys III, 2 = *PL* 122:1122 B (*corrationabilem*); *Expositiones in Ierarchiam coelestem*, J. Barbet, ed. (Turnhout, 1975), p. 18 = i, 623 (*corrationabilem*); p. 60 = iii, 157 (*iuxta analogiam, id est corrationabilitatem*); p. 143 = ix, 343; p. 153 = x, 67; p. 172 = xiii, 229-30 (*corrationabiliter*); p. 76 = iv, 432 and 435 (*corrationabilium*).

[21] Marius Victorinus, *Adversus Arium*, i, 21: *PL* 8:1043A, edition and French translation by P. Henry and P. Hadot, *Marius Victorinus: traités théologiques sur la Trinité*, 1 (Paris, 1960), p. 216, line 29 (Sources chrétiennes, 68): 'Duo ergo et isti, ex alio alius, ex filio spiritus sanctus, sicut ex Deo filius et conrationaliter et spiritus ex patre'.

# 6

# Peter Damian, Consanguinity and Church Property[*]

## D.L. d'Avray

Nearly all or perhaps all societies have a consanguinity prohibition (rules against marrying relatives), but some more than others. At one extreme we have Roman Egypt, where it appears to have been acceptable for a brother and sister to marry each other.[1] Near the other extreme was medieval Europe, especially in the period from the eleventh-century reform to the Fourth Lateran Council, when it was thought unacceptable to marry if the couple had a common great-great-great-great-grandparent, or, by a slightly different system of reckoning, even a great-great-great-great-great-grand-parent.[2] It is argued by Christopher Brooke, in his remarkable recent study of medieval attitudes to marriage,[3] that 'for us the crucial moment comes when St. Peter Damian in the early 1060s,[4] writing to interpret the rules for his colleagues among the papal reformers (who included Pope Alexander II and Hildebrand, the future Gregory VII), revised the system of counting so as greatly to extend the area of prohibition'.[5] Brooke thinks that the man is significant:

[*] The first words of the first footnote of Margaret Gibson's first book are 'Peter Damian', so he is an appropriate subject for an essay written in her honour.

[1] 'Brother-Sister Marriage in Roman Egypt', *Comparative Studies in Society and History*, xxii (1980), pp. 303-54.

[2] On these two systems of reckoning, contrast two letters of Peter Damian, the first of which goes for five 'greats-' and the second for four: see K. Reindel, ed., *Die Briefe des Petrus Damiani, MGH, Die Briefe der deutchen Kaiserzeit*, IV, i, no. 1-40; (München, 1983), letter 19 (1046), pp. 179-99, and letter 36 (*c.* 1050), pp. 339-45. To make sense of this second letter it seems to me that one must adopt the reading *nos* rather than *non* on p. 341, line 7.

[3] Christopher Brooke, *The Medieval Idea of Marriage* (Oxford, 1989). It is a book which seems more original the more one thinks about it: note especially the way in which artistic and literary representations are used.

[4] Brooke presumably either did not notice, or disagrees with, Reindel's justification for dating Letter 19 to the beginning of 1046, rather than to 1063: *Die Briefe*, p. 179.

[5] Brooke, *Medieval Idea*, p. 135. Other scholars suggest that the 'maximising' method of counting degrees had been current long before Peter Damian, in which case his intervention did not so much transform the status quo as lead to its firm definition in the face of a challenge. See A. Esmein, *Le Marriage en droit canonique* 2 vols. (Paris, 1891), i, pp. 348-350 and 353-54, and Constance B. Bouchard, 'Consanguinity and Noble Marriages in the Tenth and Eleventh

for Peter Damian had a quite exceptional horror of human sexuality, and even among the great ascetics of his age stood out for his reluctance to accept the married state as within God's providence. He viewed marriage as a doubtful legal cover to sin, and rejoiced in any device which discouraged men on whom the divine image had been stamped from engaging in anything so degrading. It was an extraordinary chance that placed so near the centre of the church's government in the 1060s a man with so virulent a hatred of sexual union, and so powerful a sense that avoidance of incest . . . should and must be extended to include every person conceivably connected by any human tie.[6]

Some support is lent to this interpretation by the last part of Peter Damian's crucial letter about consanguinity (no. 19), and above all by the following sentence:

Chastity is indeed a certain special virtue, which from the very beginning of the world was held in honour among the worshippers of God, and as the ages proceeded, always grew little by little, but now, when the judgement of God is imminent, when it were fitting that men be persuaded to cut off altogether the pleasures of the flesh, they are even gratuitously provoked to contract incestuous marriages.[7]

Nevertheless, it might be a mistake to press this passage too hard, or to regard Brooke's interpretation as more complete than he himself does (he points out that this is 'a region both deep and obscure, and simple or single explanations will not do; the whole question needs much fuller examination').[8] It seems most unlikely that Peter Damian imagined that anyone would actually refrain from marriage altogether because they could not find a partner outside the forbidden degrees (a point to which we must return).

Furthermore the principal rationale which Peter puts forward for his views on consanguinity assigns a positive value to marriage. The following passage has a bearing on the whole question of the consanguinity prohibition in the medieval church:

For the law of matrimony is put together, under the discipline of the church, with so

Centuries', *Speculum*, 56 (1981), pp. 268-87, *passim* (this article is of major importance). However, Bouchard's findings are compatible with the view that Peter Damian's influence led to a drastic tightening up of what had been a slack attitude on the part of the official church in the preceding period: a view powerfully represented by Pierre Daudet, *L'etablissement de la compétence de l'église en matière de divorce et de consanguinité (France xe-xiie siècles)* (Etudes sur l'Histoire de la Juridiction Matrimoniale; Paris, 1941), pp. 80, 129 (pp. 97-99 are also relevant). It may be that in the period before Peter Damian's intervention the aristocracy had been making a genuine effort to obey the consanguinity prohibition, without much pressure from 'the church', and that the influence of Peter Damian ensured that the church tried much harder to reinforce this self-imposed discipline, while beating off a reinterpretation of it by secular jurists, which would have diluted it.

[6]  Brooke, *Medieval Idea*, pp. 135-36.
[7]  This may be an echo of I Corinthians 7:29: 'This, therefore, I say, brethren: The time is short. It remaineth that they also who have wives be as if they had none'.
[8]  Brooke, *Medieval Idea*, p. 135.

carefully designed an educative intent (*tanta magisterii arte*), for the following reason: that the bond of mutual charity among men might be ineluctably maintained, viz., that so far as the order of inheritance (*successionis*) is extended, the love of and care for our neighbour (*vicarious amor proximi*) is supplied from the very necessity of blood relationship (*ipsa germanitatis necessitudine*). However, when [kinship] terms are no longer found and the clan (*genus cognationis*) now ceases to be, the law of matrimony steps in forthwith, and calls it [love of neighbour?] back when it is already going off quite far away as if in flight, and reconstitutes among new people the laws of an ancient love (*antiquae dilectionis . . . iura*). Nor is it strange if love should be provided for (*charitati consulitur*) in the procreation of men (*hominibus*) since God the founder of all things seems to have procured that same thing in creating them also. For when, at the very start of nature's beginnings, out of each kind of living creature (*singulis animantibus*) he created not single specimens but many . . . then he founded man, not as many, but as one, and drew out of his side a rib, from which woman might be formed.

For why, when almighty God created a plurality out of other kinds of living creatures, was he content to make a single man, from whom indeed – as if matter were lacking to the potter – he also wished to propagate the female sex: why, if not to commend charity to men and to bind them together in the unity of brotherly love, so that, while they were being consistent with their own origin,[9] people who are judged from the body to be one should in no way recoil with hostile minds (*quatinus propriae origini congreuntes nequaquam diversi resilirent mente, qui unum probarentur ex corpore*). Therefore Paul too says [Eph. 4:4]: *One body, one spirit, just as you are called in one hope of your calling.* However, when blood relationship (*affinitas generis*) has become distant and lost to view (*elongata discedit*), through the vice of human perversity the flame of love (*amoris*) grows cold, as if the kindling wood has been taken away.[10]

(Peter Damian then moves off on to the analogy between the six degrees of relationship and the six ages of the world and of man's life.)[11]

It is a simple idea: God meant humans to be united by mutual charity, so he made sure they were united by common descent. When blood relationship becomes too remote, it ceases to perform this function of promoting charity between humans, and at this point marriage takes over.[12]

This is not the only place where Peter Damian writes eloquently about marriage. His sermon on St. Vitalis gives a rather positive view of it:[13]

For if it is asked what the virtue of St. Vitalis was like before the flight [i.e.,

---

[9] Or: 'converging in respect of their own origin'?

[10] Reindel, ed., *Die Briefe*, p. 184.

[11] 'Enimvere quia sex aetatibus et mundi tempus evolvitur et humanitatis vita finitur, ipsa naturae vis praebet, ut usque ad sextum propinquitatis gradum germanus amor in humanis visceribus sapiat, et quodammodo odorem inter se genuinae sotietatis emittat.' Reindel, ed., *Die Briefe*, pp. 184-85. See his n. 18 for comparison with Augustine and Isidore.

[12] Peter Damian also uses the following striking image: 'Ubi autem manus consanguinitatis, quae captum ad se trahebat, deficit, ilico matrimonii uncus, que fugiens revocetur, occurrit'. Ibid., p. 185.

[13] A note by Reindel directed my attention to this sermon: Ibid., p. 184, n. 15.

persecution and martyrdom], with what energy and discipline the good *paterfamilias* ruled his household, with what a religious and holy order of living he brought up his children, let his wife, blessed Valeria, tell us, questioned together with her two sons, 'so that in the mouth of two or three witnesses every word may stand' (Matthew 18).' For she, hearing of the death of her most blessed spouse Vitalis, did not fear greedy invaders (*pervasores*) [threatening] her possesions, did not seek the protection of some powerful man, did not try eagerly, in the manner of widows, to gather together in a safe place her possessions which were scattered around everywhere, but went with wonderful fervour from the town of Milan right up to Ravenna to offer the service of a funeral, keeping the faith of most chaste marriage. The difficulty of so long a journey did not deter her, fear of losing property could not keep her back, the love of her relatives and fellow citizens in the town of Milan did not hold her, the most terrible fury of the imperial governor (*consularis . . . furor*) did not drive her away from the boundaries of Ravenna. Her noble spirit was indeed utterly intent on going to the place where she knew that her most blessed husband, now trampled down by death, had preceded her . . . (col. 588) . . . Therefore we should not doubt that every day she begged him, her most blessed husband, with a special and intimate kind of devotion, that by his most holy prayers she might be worthy to attain the palm of martyrdom, so that indeed those whom here the marriage-bed of mutual charity had bound together unstained, an equal triumph, too, should join in the glory of heavenly blessedness, and, since they were two in one flesh, they should also become united in respect of the crown.[14]

Later on in the sermon Peter tells the city of Ravenna that since it has the body of St. Vitalis, in a mystical sense, hers, too, is not lacking to it. 'For if St. Valeria was, as Scripture bears witness, in one flesh (*in carne una*) with her husband (Gen. 2), it necessarily follows that there should be one sepulture (*sepultura*) of one flesh.'[15]

It may therefore be doubted whether an aversion to the idea of the union of the flesh in marriage on Peter Damian's part can be the whole explanation for his intervention in the history of the consanguinity prohibition (nor does Brooke, if read attentively, go so far as to suggest that it is the whole explanation).[16] What, then, of the theory proposed by Jack Goody (from which Brooke is almost explicitly dissenting) that the function of the prohibition was to channel property towards the church? The figure of Peter Damian

[14] *PL* 144:587-88.
[15] *PL* 144:590.
[16] Even a scholar who has stressed with resounding emphasis Peter Damian's hostility to the world and the flesh (R. Bultot, *Christianisme et valeurs humaines. A. – La doctrine du mépris du monde*, IV, I *Pierre Damien* (Louvain and Paris, 1963), especially chapters 1 and 9) shows that Peter could not easily cross the line to an outright condemnation of flesh and marriage (see ibid., p. 22 and n. 14, p. 107 and n. 264).

is not given such high relief in Goody's account;[17] for him, the medieval consanguinity prohibition's breadth would require explanation even if Peter Damian's opponents had won the day. Nevertheless, a discussion of Peter Damian's Letter 19 is a good peg on which to hang some reflections about Goody's thesis, if only because the letter is a stimulus to thought about the rationality of the medieval church's attitude, and indeed the logic of Goody's argument. It is important for Goody's argument that the prohibition lacked a half-way convincing rationale. It does indeed go far beyond anything in the Bible. This is what lends *prima facie* plausibility to his hunch that collective institutional interest (in the acquisition of property) was at work, even if not at a crude conscious level.

Goody's theory that the function of the consanguinity prohibition was to increase the wealth of the church has an interesting and non-obvious starting point: the observation that the northern and southern sides of the mediterranean have rather similar social structures when set against those of sub-Saharan society, but that the strict consanguinity prohibition on the Christian, European side, north of the Mediterranean, differentiates it both from the southern Arab side and from the ancient civilizations of the Mediterranean.[18] Goody believes that the influence of the Christian church, and its underlying need to acquire property, can explain this exception to the general rule:

> If the church introduced and encouraged procedures for acquiring land and other property for itself, did it also discourage, at least in consequence if not always in intention, those practices that might provide a family heir for the property of a dead man or woman? If so, this would provide some explanation for the dramatic shift from close to distant marriage, as well as for the abandonment of adoption, widow inheritance, concubinage, divorce and remarriage, and other strategies of heirship available to the Romans, to the Anglo-Saxons, the Irish, as well as to the rest of the Mediterranean and probably to most of Europe.[19]

In fact the consanguinity prohibition requires more explaining than the

---

[17] In Goody's opinion, Peter Damian 'opted for the Germano-canonical system of wider, inclusive computation, partly for a political reason, to refute the claims of the secular jurisdiction based on Roman law and sustained by the lawyers of Ravenna' J. Goody, *The Development of the Family and Marriage in Europe* (Cambridge, 1983), P. 136. I can think of no way of testing Goody's speculation about motive; he supports it with a not hopelessly incorrect reference which, when I ran it to earth in Daudet, *L'Etablissement* (Goody refers to an earlier volume by the same author, but gets the page number right) does not provide the extra data one expects. Neither my reservations about this minor point nor my disagreement with a wider thesis of the book should obscure its extraordinary richness, both in learning and in stimulating ideas.

[18] Goody, *Development*, chap. 2, especially p. 32.

[19] Ibid., p. 46

medieval church's opposition to concubinage and divorce,[20] for the rules of monogamy and indissolubility (unlike the consanguinity rules) could be explained as an obvious reading of famous New Testament texts.[21] Where the authority of sacred texts provide an obvious rationale, an explanation in terms of property interests is like a fifth wheel on a waggon. Not so with consanguinity.

Yet a conscious or unconscious desire on the part of the church to discourage practices that might provide a family heir, an implicit hope that some ecclesiastical institutions might take the place of such an heir, does not provide the explanation for the shift from close to ever more distant marriage. As has already been suggested, it does not seem probable that any substantial body of people would have actually refrained from marrying because of the consanguinity prohibition. One supposes that in some cases they ignored the rules, and that in others they simply did not know who was related to them within the remoter of the forbidden degrees. Rather surprisingly, it appears that it was not at all unusual for nobles of the tenth and eleventh centuries to look for a spouse outside the extended family clan.[22] There seems something a little absurd about the idea of large numbers of medieval people remaining unmarried because they could not find a non-consanguineous partner; nor, I think, is Goody suggesting anything of the kind.

A less obvious, but simple and crucial consideration, is that *the consanguinity prohibition could not have reduced the number of heirs related by blood.* The number of a person's relatives and potential heirs does not decrease because they marry outside the clan. It might even increase, if in-laws have any claim. Exogamy does not diminish the set of family heirs and endogamy does not increase it; and if the consanguinity prohibition does not reduce the number of heirs, why should it channel land towards the church?

To the foregoing argument, the following rejoinder can be anticipated. To marry relatives (endogamy=in-marriage) does not decrease the number of relatives and potential heirs, but it does mean that some blood relatives

---

[20] I do not propose to discuss here Goody's implication that adoption and widow inheritance ceased to be important, but it does require critical scrutiny. On adoption in the middle ages see John Boswell, *The Kindness of Strangers: The Abandonment of Children in Western Europe from Late Antiquity to the Renaissance* (London, 1988), p. 224 and n. 155. I would take a lot of convincing that the remarriage of widows was inhibited on a significant scale by the church in the middle ages.

[21] For a discussion of the texts, see Brooke, *Medieval Idea*, pp. 43-46, 48-49.

[22] 'In the tenth and eleventh centuries, the nobles' attempt to find spouses for their children who were not related to them within the seven forbidden degrees (or six in practice) helped lead to marriages between men and women of different strata within the nobility. Though consanguinity was surely never as important an issue for the French nobility as it was for the ecclesiastics developing a theory of marriage, it made impossible a number of marriages that other considerations made highly desirable . . . . Nobles frequently had to chose spouses for their children from distant geographical areas, or else marry them to those who were not strictly their equals.' Bouchard, 'Consanguinity', p. 286.

become in-laws as well. Claims to inherit are thus reinforced. Could not the church have been subliminally aware of this, and have banned endogamy accordingly (since such reinforcement of claims to inherit might keep land away from the church). After all, if a potential heir were both blood-relative *and* a relative in-law, it would be that much harder to exclude him and give land to the church.

This argument or rejoinder has the advantage of making abstract logical sense, even though it would imply some sophisticated anthropological thinking (worthy of a Cambridge social scientist) on the part of medieval churchmen. Nevertheless it runs into problems when we start to look again at texts. Indeed, it seems to be falsified by the letter of Peter Damian with which we began.

For Peter Damian (and not only he) defines consanguinity in such a way as to reinforce and put the spotlight on the inheritance rights of extended family members: exactly what they should not be doing if the theory is to work.[23] Here it is necessary to look closely at another passage from Letter 19:[24]

> But so that what we say may be able more easily to reach its conclusion (*exitum*), let us compare the sacred canons with the same secular laws. For the council of Meaux contains the following statement. It says that: 'concerning affinity of blood through the degrees of relationship by blood, it was resolved to maintain observance (*placuit . . . observare*) up to the seventh generation. For it is laid down by legal decrees that the inheritance of goods extends the succession of heirs up to the seventh degree; for they would not succeed to it, unless it was due to them from the continuance of blood relationship.'[25] Therefore according to this edict, giving the synod's decision, when somebody has the right to inherit, they also have a family relationship . . . .[26]

The point need not be laboured: the incest prohibition draws attention to precisely the same inheritance claims that Goody's theory would have them undermine.

The influential canonist, Burchard of Worms,[27] quotes virtually the same words from the same putative council,[28] and the text was also taken up by Gratian's *Decretum*, where it is attributed to 'Gregorius Papa in Concilio

---

[23] Goody appears to sense that this poses a problem for his theory – see *Development*, middle paragraph on p. 145 – but so far as I can see the tension is not satisfactorily resolved.

[24] Reindel, ed., *Die Briefe*, p. 185.

[25] 'Nam et haereditas rerum per legales diffinitiones sanccitur usque ad septimum gradum praetendere heredum successionem; non enim succederent, nisi eis de propagine cognationis deberetur.' *Die Briefe*, ed. Reindel, p. 185.

[26] 'Secundum hoc igitur sententiae synodalis edictum, cui competit ius haereditatis, competit etiam propinquitas generis.' Ibid. He continues: 'Neque enim, ut dicitur, in haereditatem succederent, nisi ad cognationis propaginem pertinerent'.

[27] On Burchard, see Willibald M. Plöchl, *Geschichte des Kirchenrechts*, i (Munich, 1960), p. 450 (note his remark that 'Über die Abfassungszeit herrscht keine Einigung. Die Annahmen schwanken zwischen 1007 und 1022'.)

[28] *Decretorum Libri XX*, VII, c. 16, in *PL* 140:782. The difference is just a textual variant.

Meldensi', though no one knows where it really comes from.[29] Whatever its origin, its influence cannot be ignored. If the consanguinity prohibition did have the function which has been attributed to it, then Burchard of Worms, Peter Damian, and Gratian were subverting it with consummate skill.

We have considered two interpretations of the consanguinity prohibition, the first of which is at least incomplete (without pretending otherwise) while the second looks like a brilliant mistake. There are problems with other recent explanations also. James Brundage has suggested that:

> Ecclesiastical authorities demanded that families desist from intermarrying with members of their own clans in part, at least . . . to break up the concentrations of landholdings that supported the economic and political power of the feudal nobility . . . . Although clear and explicit evidence for their rationale is difficult to come by, popes, bishops, church councils, and canonists seem to have reckoned that if blocs of feudal property were dispersed among large numbers of holders it would be possible for the church to free itself from the power of the grand noble clans whose power rested squarely on the control of extensive landed estates. A policy of exogamy was well-calculated to achieve these goals, and church reformers used the canon law on consanguinity to pursue them with vigor and tenacity.[30]

Whether large concentrations of lay feudal property were more of a threat to the church than the same amount of property dispersed among a larger number of smaller feudal lords would be hard to prove; nor does it seem intrinsically plausible except on the questionable assumption that there was a sort of Cold War going on between the church (in the sense of the higher clergy) and the nobility, in which the former attempted to divide and rule.[31] One could equally well argue that larger power blocks were more conducive to public order than a plethora of independent castellans. It has been pointed out that 'Gregory VII himself berated Abbot Hugh of Cluny for welcoming Duke Hugh I of Burgundy . . . as a monk in 1079, saying that the duke's conversion, which Gregory might have expected to welcome, was a disaster that had left a

---

[29] Reindel, ed., *Die Briefe*, p. 185, n. 19 (with further references).

[30] James A. Brundage, *Law, Sex, and Christian Society in Medieval Europe* (Chicago and London, 1987), p. 193. This book is indispensable for anyone working on marriage in the middle ages, because of the astonishing range of manuscript material and secondary literature on which it draws.

[31] Note the closing words of the conclusion of a major recent study: 'But the monks of the eleventh and twelfth centuries and the nobles who supported them should be seen as representing a sustained effort, which has not been duplicated since, to make spiritual issues the chief priority of the rules of secular society'. Constance Brittain Bouchard, *Sword, Miter, and Cloister: Nobility and the Church in Burgundy, 980-1198* (Ithaca and London, 1987), p. 254.

hundred thousand Christians without a protector'.[32] Arguments in either direction are too theoretical to amount to much – hypothesis cannot exist without empirical nourishment.

Another hypothesis, proposed by David Herlihy in an otherwise admirable study, seems even more speculative than those of Brundage and Goody.[33] Herlihy argues that 'One reason for this policy may have been the concentration of women in the households of the rich and powerful, to the deprivation of other sectors of society. The church's insistence on exogamy must have forced a freer, wider circulation of women through society. The poorer, less powerful male improved his chance of finding a mate'.[34] It is an attractive thought but is there any evidence that the church was concerned to promote a freer, wider circulation of women throughout society?

The problem remains a problem. In these circumstances we should perhaps ask ourselves whether naïveté might not be a better guide than sophistication, and look again at an explanation for which there is textual evidence and which a recent interpretation of medieval social structure renders more plausible. The explanation is the one set out by Peter Damian himself: that the incest prohibition promoted social harmony by creating alliances between different clans. The idea was available in an old, authoritative and influential text, Augustine's *City of God*.[35] In the ninth century, Augustine's reasoning is borrowed with acknowledgement by Jonas of Orleans.[36] Even the reduction of the consanguinity prohibition from seven to four degrees in 1215 could be explained within the same framework of concepts.[37] We would be rash simply to assume that Peter Damian could not have taken this reasoning seriously, and there does seem to have been a direct causal link between Peter's convictions and papal policy and law. It may even be that Peter had a better understanding of his own society's structure than the historians discussed

---

[32] Ibid., p. 128.

[33] Note however an interesting negative argument against Goody's theory: 'Were the Church's leaders unified enough, conscious enough, and shrewd enough to devise and implement this rather devious strategy of aggrandizement? It is not at all clear that the Church would have profited materially be preventing the wealthy from having heirs. Almost always, a young person entering the religious life brought with him or her some property as a kind of dowry; many of these recruits were the younger sons and daughters of the wealthy. In this way the Church stood as much to gain by facilitating as by obstructing marriages and procreation among the affluent . . . .' D. Herlihy, *Medieval Households* (Cambridge, MA, 1985), p. 13.

[34] Ibid., p. 61. (Monogamy would tend to prevent the rich and powerful from monopolising women, but that is a different question.)

[35] Augustine, *De civitate Dei*, XV, c. xvi.

[36] *De institutione laicali* II, c. viii, *PL* 106:183.

[37] For an interesting explanation of this kind see the remarks of the Sienese Dominican Ambrogio Sansedoni, in Siena, Comunale, MS T. iv. 7, fos. 13 v – 14 r: passage beginning ' . . . nihil est in mundo . . . ' and ending ' . . . ad quartum gradum.' (I hope to discuss the passage elsewhere.) See also now D. Waley, *Siena and the Sienese in the thirteenth century* (Cambridge, 1991), p. 143 and n. 61, for a fascinating suggestion about marriage alliances between previously hostile families in Siena.

above. It is worth reflecting on Peter's explanations in the light of Jacques Heer's original synthesis on the family clan in the middle ages.[38] Many of the individual pieces of the jigsaw he puts together have long been familiar, but the balance and emphasis of the final picture was and still is new. He suggests that the extended family clan was a fundamental element in medieval society, and his evidence seems especially strong for Italy in the central and later middle ages. If we put the clan near the centre of our picture of medieval society, or even of the society with which Peter Damian was familiar, then his reasoning begins to look quite 'relevant' to his world (however it may have been with St Augustine and the world of late antiquity). In the last analysis, our interpretation of the reformed papacy's policy on consanguinity depends on our view of the rationality of Peter's convictions. 'And rational belief does not mean true belief. It means belief that is in harmony with the evidence and in harmony with other major beliefs.'[39] If the passages translated above pass this test, we do not need to fall back on theories about his psyche or hidden institutional interests; in fact it is hard to see how these theories can be maintained. This negative conclusion is more certain than the positive suggestion – that the prohibition was designed to promote friendship between clans – which I have not devised, so much as revived from the thought of Peter and other medieval writers, and which modern scholars have too readily dismissed.

[38] J. Heers, *Le Clan familial au Moyen Age. Etude sur les structures politiques et sociales des milieux urbains* (Paris, 1974). The book is principally concerned with the central and late middle ages. For the very early middle ages, the importance of clans has been challenged by Alexander Callander Murray, *Germanic Kinship Structure: Studies in Law and Society in Antiquity and the Early Middle Ages*, Studies and Texts, 65 (Toronto, 1983). However, he may not be addressing the same question as Heers (whose study he does not mention). The 'clans' whose existence A.C. Murray denies are not necessarily the same kind of thing as the less formal structures that Heers writes about, which might well not leave much trace on the kind of evidence that Murray examines. A good authority on Merovingian history, Richard Geberding, tells me that he has found evidence of clans of the sort Heers describes. Another study which needs to be pondered before Heers's model is applied to the early middle ages is Constance B. Bouchard, 'Family Structure and Family Consciousness among the Aristocracy in the Ninth to Eleventh Centuries', in *Francia*, 14 (1986), pp. 639-58, at pp. 647-48. She does not discuss Heers's model of the clan either, and any incompatibility between their views may be apparent rather than real. For instance, it may be that clans – defined in a loose non-technical sense as largish groups of real or soi-disant relatives, with some sense of solidarity and the capacity to act together for some purposes – were especially a feature of Italian society and/or urban society (in which case they would not be so important in northern Europe in the early middle ages).

[39] R. Bartlett, *Trial by Fire and Water: The Medieval Judicial Ordeal* (Oxford, 1986), pp. 161-62. (Bartlett writes in the context of the important debate about 'rationality' among philosophers and anthropologists.)

# 7

## The Temptation of St. Hugh of Grenoble

### Alexander Murray

Every schoolboy – every student at least, who has written essays for the contributors to this volume – knows that it all began with Gregory VII. Gregory VII, more conspicuously than anyone else of his time, turned Catholics into Papists, by exalting Roman church authority. The same man turned them also into Protestants, by rousing lay evangelism against bad priests. Hence both great themes of ecclesiastical history in the next four centuries, the 'descending' and 'ascending' principles of authority, trace their ancestry to Gregory, the medieval Abraham with free and slave lines of posterity. No wonder Caspar could call him 'the great initiator, who stands on his own'.[1] No wonder every student has heard of him – if for no other reason than that his otherwise serene tutors still take up, in print and out of print, and as if nine centuries had not passed, the disputes which Gregory occasioned in his own generation.

A peculiarity of history, as of all matters human, is that it changes under our gaze. The first picture may be quite correct. It is usually based on 'facts'. But there are other facts behind these and, as we gaze, the recessive become the dominant, changing the image. The Gregorian Reform is an example. From one angle there was no such thing. It is not just that the word *reformare* or its cognates are not known ever to have passed Gregory's lips.[2] Some perfectly respectable contemporaries – including at times Gregory himself – thought things were getting *worse* in his time, in preparation for the end of the world;

---

[1]   E. Caspar, 'Gregor VII. in seinen Briefen', *Historische Zeitschrift*, 130 (1924), p. 30.
[2]   G.B. Ladner, 'Two Gregorian Letters: On the Sources and Nature of Gregory VII's Reform Ideology', *Studi Gregoriani*, ed. G.B. Borino, v (Rome 1956), p. 221, says 'actually, the term *reformare* occurs less frequently in Gregory's letters than other renewal terms'. It is a pity that neither there nor in his *The Idea of Reform* (Cambridge, MA, 1959), did Dr. Ladner indicate where he found Gregory using the term *reformare* or its cognates, since I have not done so. The letters are in Gregory's Register [ed. E. Caspar, *MGH Epist. sel.*, 2 (Berlin, 1920-23), p. 702] and the non-registered letters now edited by H.E.J. Cowdrey, *The Epistolae Vagantes of Pope Gregory VII* (Oxford, 1972). Negative assertions are rash, so I have limited mine to those letters known to have been dictated by Gregory personally.

while if contemporary impressions are a guide it was in 1002, exactly, that Rodulf Glaber dated what he chose to see as a general ecclesiastical 'innovation'.[3] Even allowing a movement *we* might call 'reform' in the latter half of the century, a look at its local manifestations – Lanfranc's England is just one example – puts in question what Gregory personally had to do with it. 'S'il n'existait pas', we could say of him, 'il faudrait l'inventer'.

Now of a 'great initiator' that is a paradox; and paradox is, in fact, a feature of the whole movement. Meant to exalt the clergy in general and the Roman clergy in particular the reform found its most conspicuous support among laity and outside Rome; its most conspicuous opposition among clergy, and inside Rome. The irony was not missed. 'Clement was not clement, nor Urban, urban', people remarked in 1090 when the French ex-monk Urban II (the name meant 'Roman') was barred from Rome by the Italian bishop, Wibert; 'pulsus urbe, ab orbe suscipitur', wrote St. Bernard of Pope Innocent II, French-backed rival of an old Roman cardinal.[4] Social as well as political paradoxes abound; for instance, that a movement promoting authority in a male elite depended so critically, and often, on military support from a woman, Countess Matilda.

The familiar picture of Gregory and his reform becomes, then, more subtle as we explore it. Familiar images turn inside-out. Now at the heart of all the images is one more important than all these others. It is that of Gregory as a man of adamantine faith. Faith, after all, was the moving force of the whole movement, or was meant to be: faith in both senses, of Catholic doctrine and personal devotion. Whether we think the movement was really his or not, Gregory himself was apparently moved by such faith, and conscious of its imperatives in his main public acts.

Take an example: the letter that marks, if anything does, the conception of the crusading movement. In the early 1070s the Seljuks had invaded eastern Christendom and threatened to destroy it; and in December 1074 Gregory wrote to Henry IV, suggesting what to do. The paradox this time was that it was to be Henry IV, of all people, who was to be left in charge of the western church, while the pope went off with the army. The great initiator goes on:

> What spurs me above all to this enterprise is that the Byzantine church, which dissents from us concerning the Holy Spirit, is awaiting a settlement from the apostolic see. Most of the Armenians, too, err from the Catholic faith and indeed nearly all easterners are waiting to see how the faith of St. Peter will adjudicate between their divers doctrines.

---

[3]   C. Erdmann, 'Endkaiserglaube und Kreuzzugsgedanke im 11. Jahrhundert', *Zeitschrift für Kirchengeschichte*, 51 (1932), 384-414, esp. pp. 385-86, 403-14. Rodulfus Glaber, *Historiae*, iii, c. 4, para. 13, ed. J. France (Oxford, 1989), pp. 114-16.

[4]   J. Haller, *Das Papsttum*, ii (Stuttgart, 1951), p. 435. Bernard, *Epistolae* 124,2 [*PL* 182: 268].

And Gregory goes on to quote the Gospel, in the clear conviction that he represents St. Peter on earth, as St. Peter represented Christ.[5]

Examples of such acts of faith (in both senses) abound in Gregory's letters and in others' accounts of him. They confirm the 'image'. Now the aim of this essay is not to challenge the image. Rather, it is to examine it, in the hope of adding a dimension otherwise scarcely visible. I shall do so by examining a single incident. Its hero was not in fact Gregory but another of the 'reformers'. But that is no sooner said than I wonder. Which *was* the hero? Let the reader decide.

The reformer in question was Hugh of Châteauneuf, bishop of Grenoble. Hugh was one of those unco-operative medieval churchmen who devoted themselves so thoroughly to communicating with their own contemporaries that they largely forgot later historians. If it had not been for a pope, who saw to it that a proper Life of Hugh was written when memories were fresh, we would know little about Hugh beyond a few preambles of charters. Little, that is, in terms of quantity; for the little leaves no doubt about quality. Here is a description, given in the *Vita Prima* of St. Bernard of Clairvaux, of Bernard's visit to Hugh at Grenoble in 1125. The humour of the scene only amplifies its witness to Hugh's reputation.

> Bishop Hugh welcomed Bernard with reverence, prostrating himself on the ground before his visitor. The colour left Bernard's face. That such a famous man, of senior years and conspicuous sanctity, should thus lie prostrate at his feet! So the abbot, in his turn, got down on the ground and would receive the kiss of peace in no other posture, alleging that his own humility would otherwise be confounded by the veneration of so celebrated a man.[6]

Geoffrey, who wrote this, had access to Bernard's thoughts and no cause to exaggerate. So we must believe him when he goes on to say that Hugh at once won a place in Bernard's affection, as vice-versa; they were like Solomon and the queen of Sheba, he says, whose regard for each other was even higher after

---

[5] *Registrum*, ii, 31; ed. Caspar, pp. 165-168; the quoted words are on pp. 166. 32-167.5.

[6] *Vita prima*, iii, c.2; *PL* 185,305; the references that follow are to cols. 305-6. Hugh's care for future historians was confined to the matter of diocesan claims, as shown by his cartularies: J. Marion, ed., *Cartulaires de l'église cathédrale de Grenoble, dits cartulaires de St. Hugues*. Documents inédits sur l'hist. de France. I Série. Hist. politique (Paris, 1869), Cart. A, No. 23 (p.49): 'posterorum noticie trado'; *cf.* Albert Du Boys, *Vie de Saint Hugues* (Grenoble, 1837), p. 446: 'noscat posteritas . . . '.

their meeting than their mere reputations had made it before. 'Those two sons of splendour', Geoffrey concludes, 'became that day a single heart and soul'.

Now one half of that soul was a writer of books, and much written about; the other, not. That it was the active bishop, not the monk, whose portrait so nearly escaped historical record – and relied for it on a mention in the other's biography – should not surprise us. We are used to paradoxes. But it was anyway only a near-escape. For a portrait of Hugh does survive, one instigated (as it happens) partly by Bernard, though it makes no reciprocal mention of him. What it does, is extend tenfold what we would otherwise know of St. Bernard's 'other half'.[7]

The portrait in question was made in response to a letter of Pope Innocent II, who wrote as president of a small council held in Pisa in 1134, nine years after the meeting just described. Among acts of the council had been to canonise the bishop of Grenoble, lately dead; and it now called for the required Life and Miracles. This was to reverse the order soon to become normal: the Life would be demanded first. But the council, which included Bernard and others acquainted with the late bishop, knew enough about him to act at once and justify it afterwards. The procedure of papal canonisation was young enough, and the Innocent's own position uncertain enough, to admit that strategic improvisation.

Like the canonisation, the Life must be completed soon. As the making of a saint became more formal a higher premium was placed on, *inter alia*, the historicity of claims made for him. Hugh had died only two years before. But he had then been over eighty and in the previous few years had been steadily losing his memory. No one alive had known him when young. Few had known him in full possession of his powers. So only a few people were in a position to write a Life. The successful choice of author may have been due to Bernard, or equally to Chancellor Aimeric, the grey eminence behind Innocent's appointment four years earlier. For it was a pen-friend of both who was chosen: Guigo, prior of the Grande Chartreuse, the house to which Hugh had been godfather and guardian. He had known Hugh and was a proven writer, of – besides letters – the first Carthusian customary, and of a book of Meditations. So it was to Guigo that the request went. Innocent asked him to write 'what

---

[7]  Sources on Hugh are conveniently listed by B. Bligny in the introduction to M.-A. Chomel's translation of Guigo's Life: *Guigues le Chartreux, vie de Saint Hugues, évêque de Grenoble, l'ami des moines* (Cahiers de l'Alpe, Grenoble, 1984; repr. as *Analecta Cartusiana*, 112:3, Salzburg, 1986), pp. 5-23, esp. 21-23, with secondary bibliography on p. 71. I thank Dr. James Hogg, creator and general editor the *Analecta Cartusiana*, for acquainting me with this publication. The Bollandist edition of the Life is reprinted in *PL* 153.761-84, from *Acta sanctorum* 1 April (1675) pp. 36-48.

you know' of Hugh's pious life and 'coruscating' posthumous miracles 'so that the clergy may read and the laity hear'.[8]

We read the Life long after the clergy who first did so. We shall be studying an episode on which it is our only source, and to which it gives barely a dozen dozen lines; an episode of an intrinsically elusive nature and which happened, if it happened, three years before the author was born. Now the leading modern authority on Hugh's episcopacy has a modest view of our source. It is in no sense objective biography but hagiography, a typically Christian genre, obeying precise rules 'differing little from one Life to another'.[9] These are slender credentials for a source from which we are asking a lot. Their improvement is a necessary preliminary. The rest of the first part of this essay – there are four parts – will accordingly ask: 'How could he have known?' and 'Can we trust him?' This typical hagiographer will be shown to have been untypical in ways entirely to our advantage. The second part will show the same in respect of the area of our quarry, the mind.

How did Guigo know? Between Hugh and Guigo there was a big difference in ages. When he wrote the Life, in 1132-33, Guigo was barely fifty, younger than Hugh had been at the earliest date – 1106 – when the two men could have met. As a very old man, furthermore, Hugh had lost 'that part of the memory which contains the forms of things spatial and temporal'.[10] But between 1106 and Hugh's loss of memory Guigo had had many opportunities for 'oral history'. He had joined the Chartreuse in 1106, at about twenty-three. Three years later he was head of the community and thus likely to meet high functionaries with business at the Chartreuse. The latter's cartulary mentions Hugh and Guigo in the same documents around 1112 and again in 1129. The Life refers to many undatable conversations.

These conversations, furthermore, covered spiritual subjects, and included events well before 1106. 'One day we were talking together', Guigo will write in the Life; and, the topic that time being a recalcitrant count, Hugh reveals to Guigo that he, Hugh, has been praying 'most earnestly' for the count's

---

[8] The role of Aimeric in the schism of 1130 was analysed by H.-W. Klewitz, 'Das Ende des Reformpapsttums', *Deutsches Archiv für Erforschung des Mittelalters*, 3 (1939), pp. 379-412; repr. in Klewitz' *Reformpapsttum und Kardinalkolleg* (Darmstadt, 1957), pp. 209-59 esp. pp. 224, 228 and 242-55; and by H. Bloch, *Monte Cassino in the Middle Ages* (Rome, 1986), 2, pp. 944-60. Aimeric and Guigo: *Lettres des premiers Chartreux*, i, *S. Bruno – Guigues – S. Anthelme* [Sources chrétiennes, 88. Série des Textes Monastiques d'Occident, No. 10] (Paris, 1962), pp. 184-95. Innocent II's letter to Guigo, in *PL* 153. 761A-2A. Guigo and his writings: J. Leclercq, F. Vandenbroucke, L. Bouyer, *La spiritualité du moyen âge* [Hist. de la spiritualité chrétienne, ii] (Paris, 1961), pp. 189-202; H. Leyser, 'Hugh the Carthusian', in H. Mayr-Harting, ed., *St. Hugh of Lincoln* (Oxford, 1987), pp. 15-18. A longer and more recent treatment is that by G. Mursell, *The Theology of the Carthusian Life in the Writings of St. Bruno and Guigo I*, Analecta Cartusiana, 127 (Salzburg, 1988).

[9] Bligny, *Vie*, p. 6; and more generally pp. 5-8, 23.

[10] *Vita s. Hugonis episcopi gratianopolitani, auctore Guigone priore carthusiensi*, c. 6 para. 26 [*PL* 153: 779D-80A]. Further references to this work are cited simply as *Vita*.

salvation.[11] That is typical of many. Some conversations touched on topics clearly datable before 1106. The outline of Hugh's childhood almost certainly came from Hugh himself (an unlikely alternative is his father, who died as an aged Chartreuse *conversus* a few years after Guigo's arrival). This took Guigo's knowledge back to Hugh's birth in *c.* 1052, and indeed earlier, since we learn of the death of his father's first wife and of other children.[12] Guigo would have remembered these conversations: among his qualities picked out for special praise in the earliest in-house description of the priors was that Guigo was *memoria tenax.*[13]

Guigo also shared many friends with Hugh, some of whom had known Hugh for as long or longer. One was Airaud of Portes (a Carthusian house fifty miles north of Grenoble above Lyons), later archbishop of Lyons, who claimed to have known Hugh for thirty years, and contributed reminiscences to the Life. Another was Walter, a Carthusian formerly on the bishop's staff at Grenoble, who recalled, long afterwards, details about sacramental confession he had made to Hugh.[14] One reason he had delayed to write the Life until the pope demanded it, despite many requests from friends, was that interested parties, like these and others, knew it all anyway.[15] But it was to Guigo that the requests came. That suggests that Guigo was, of all survivors who had known Hugh, the one whose knowledge was most intimate.

The second question about Guigo's credentials is whether we can trust him. Two features of the Life speak for its veracity. The first is its attitude to miracles, the main problem-area of hagiography. Innocent II had asked Guigo for a 'Life *and Miracles*'. There is no sign, in the Life or anywhere else, that a book of miracles was written. It has usually been assumed Guigo did not write one, and the only disagreements have been why. The seventeenth-century Bollandist editor assumed it was because Guigo was too old and ill.[16] But he

[11] Ibid., c. 4 para. 17 [*PL* 153: 774AB].
[12] Ibid., c. 1 paras. 2-3 [*PL* 153: 763C-5A]. That Hugh's father was a *conversus*, and the approximate date of his death, can be learned from the 'Notice sur Odillon' printed (from a MS in the Grande Chartreuse) by Du Boys, *Vie*, p. 448, a notice which otherwise appears to be taken from Guigo's Life. The Life says that Odilo (Hugh's father) had been eighteen years as a Carthusian when he died, so that he must have entered the order in or after 1092. Hugh's mother had married Odilo after the death of his first wife and had borne him at least three sons who reached adulthood. Hugh was born about 1052-53, so Odilo's first wife must have died before that date.
[13] Ed. A. Wilmart, 'La chronique des premiers Chartreux', *Revue Mabillon*, 16 (1926), pp. 77-142; c. v, para. 1 [p. 126]: 'litteris secularibus et divinis admodum eruditus, acer ingenio, memoria tenax, facundia admirabilis'.
[14] Airaud: *Vita*, Prol. para. 1 [*PL* 153: 763A]; c. 4 para. 15 [*PL* 153: 772B-D], and L. Le Vasseur, *Ephemerides ordinis Cartusiensis* (Montreuil-sur-mer 1890), i, pp. 3-6. Walter: *Vita*, c. 3 para. 14 [*PL* 153: 771D]. Another friend's reminiscence (from Vinay): *Vita*, c. 5 para. 22 [*PL* 153: 777C].
[15] *Vita*, Prol. [*PL* 153: 763A]: 'erga eos quidem quos prae longa familiaritate vel convictu latere non poteram'.
[16] *Monitum*, para. 4 [*PL* 153: 761-2].

had been too old and ill to start it, according to him, so that cannot be the only reason. Another suggestion has been the canonisation had happened already so that the main stimulus for a miracle-collection had gone.[17] That, too, may be a reason. But there is a more important one. Guigo belonged to a self-conscious minority of hagiographers who were reserved about the miracles most others thought were necessary. The tradition, which still awaits its monograph, went back at least to Gregory the Great. More recently it had been fed by what has been called 'Carolingian rationalism' and its legacy in Ottonian writers, always in conspicuously 'reformist' circles. It is found in other Carthusian writing in the twelfth century and would continue, in one context or another, to the end of the middle ages.[18]

Guigo firmly embraced this tradition. Twice in the Life he says physical miracles are much inferior to virtues, – like Hugh's chastity, or lifelong devotion to God.[19] And he practised what he preached. Miraculous traits in the Life are limited to three, two of them prophetic dreams – by Hugh's mother before his birth (as she 'used to say'), and by Hugh himself, about the foundation of the Chartreuse.[20] The only 'miracle' even implied is that Hugh's body remained uncorrupt for four hot days despite the press of crowds.[21] What is more remarkable is that Guigo's narrative remained uncorrupt despite the same pressure. He describes the crowds at Hugh's tomb with their 'burning faith' as they kissed his feet and carried off things he had touched 'pro reliquiis', or brought sick infants to touch his body – all a perfect culture for

[17] H.E.J. Cowdrey, 'Hugh of Avalon, Carthusian and Bishop', in M.G. Sargent, ed., *De cella in saeculum* (Cambridge, 1989), pp. 41-57, p. 48. I take this opportunity of thanking Dr. Cowdrey for commenting on a draft of this essay to its great advantage.

[18] Professor Bligny mistakenly reads as unique the tendency in Guigo to depreciate physical miracles (*Vie*, p. 6: 'on chercherait en vain chez le autres hagiographes'). A guide to its background in Gregory the Great can be found in F. Lotter's study of Ruotger's *Life of Archbishop Bruno of Cologne* (see Dr. Mayr-Harting's contribution this volume, on p. 37 and n. 17). A strong expression of it is in the last chapters of the *Vita altera Bonifatii* attributed to Radbod, bishop of Utrecht (899-917) [ed. W. Levison, *MGH, SS separatim editi*, No. 57 (Hanover-Leipzig, 1905) 1, pp. 74-78. Further tenth-century examples can be traced through L. Zoepf, *Das Heiligen-Leben im 10, Hahrhundert* (Leipzig-Berlin 1908), p. 250 ['Wunderkraft – Ablehnung']. Nearer to the time of Hugh of Châteauneuf the theme is found in Poppo of Trier's recommendation of the cult of Simeon the hermit [*PL* 141: 1369B-70A], and Gilbert Crispin's *Life of Herluin* ed. A.S. Abulafia and G.R. Evans, *The Works of Gilbert Crispin* (London and Oxford, 1986), para. 35, p. 192. For Peter the Venerable's failure to record Carthusian miracles: *De miraculis*, ii, c.27 [ed. D. Bouthillier, [*CCCM*, lxxxiii] (Turnhout, 1988), 152. 1-7]. Long after Guigo Innocent III was to react against the tendency, which only regained official ascendency under John XXII; see A. Vauchez *La sainteté en occident aux derniers siècles du moyen âge* (Rome-Paris, 1981), pp. 43, 589-91.

[19] *Vita*, c. 4 para. 15 [*PL* 153: 773A]; c. 6 para. 32 [*PL* 153: 782D-3B].

[20] Ibid., c. 1 para. 3 *PL* 153: [764D-5A]; c. 3 para. 11 [*PL* 153: 769D-70A].

[21] Ibid., c. 6 para. 33 [*PL* 153: 784A].

miracle, and still fecund at the time of writing. There is still no hint either of any actual miracle, or that any will follow.[22]

The second buttress supporting Guigo's veracity is that he lays special stress on this virtue, otherwise a remarkably late arrival in the repertoire.[23] Here again Guigo was being a Carthusian. 'Love in the heart, truth on the lips, chastity in the body', in that order, St. Hugh of Lincoln would name as the necessaries for Heaven.[24] Guigo had put truth before chastity half a century earlier. Of the two paramount virtues he ascribes to Odilo of Châteauneuf, Hugh's father, chastity, though rare at the time, comes only second; the first being Odilo's *veriloquium*, and 'a natural candour, which made him shun lies, more than very many persons in religious orders'.[25] Guigo lays the same emphasis on Hugh's own *veriloquium*, to illustrate which he tells single incident, from his own experience. At a council of magnates a count whom Hugh had excommunicated charged Hugh with mendacity, and Hugh publicly challenged him: could he give a single instance? The accuser blushed and said no. 'That single example', Guigo concludes, 'is surely enough'.[26]

It is also enough to show where Guigo placed *veriloquium* in his own moral theory. His narrative style accords with this. Guigo may drastically compress Hugh's politico-economic exertions, as witnessed in charters; but compression was not *sup*pression. All historians pick their own emphases. When Guigo has to speak of unedifying subjects he does so, but says no more than he has to (and praises Hugh for the same restraint).[27] Thus when he describes the various corruptions of the Grenoble clergy before Hugh's time his assertions are brief and factual. Where we can check these, they tally with other evidence, as in respect of the dispersal of episcopal property.[28] Rarely, for a

[22] Ibid., c. 6 para. 34 [*PL* 153: 784BC]. Comparable Lives on the pattern of the new, reforming bishop are those of St. Antelm of Bellay (1107/8-1178), ed. J. Picard, *Vie de St. Antelme, évêque de Bellay, Chartreux* Collection de recherches et d'etudes cartusiennes, i (Bellay, 1978); see esp. para. 38 (p. 32) for the importance of miracles; and of the three Latin bishops considered in this regard by P. Toubert, *Les structures du Latium médiéval* (2 vols., Rome, 1973), pp. 807-29, esp. 823-25. None of these authors is as reserved towards miracle as Guigo.

[23] The late arrival of mendacity in lists of sins: M.W. Bloomfield, *The Seven Deadly Sins* (East Lansing, MI, 1952), pp. 86-87.

[24] *Magna vita s. Hugonis Lincolniensis*, iv, c. 9, ed. D.L. Douie and D.H. Farmer. Oxford Medieval Texts (Oxford, 1985), vol. II, p. 46. Hugh's strictness in this regard is elaborated further on in the same chapter ([p. 48) while Hugh's corresponding reservation about the miraculous is shown for instance in Bk. V, c. 18 [vol. II, p. 216].

[25] *Vita*, c. 1 para. 2 [*PL* 153: 764AB].

[26] Ibid., c. 4 para. 16 [*PL* 153: 773C-4A].

[27] Ibid., c. 4 para. 16 [*PL* 153: 773B].

[28] Ibid., c. 2 para. 9 [*PL* 153: 768B]; c. 1 para. 2 [*PL* 153: 764AB]; *cf.* the author's moderation about Count Guigo, c. 4 para. 16 [*PL* 153: 773C]. B. Bligny, *L'église et les ordres religieux dans le royaume de Bourgogne aux xi^e et xii^e siècles* (Paris, 1960), p. 71, thinks Guigo may have exaggerated clerical abuse. Dispersal of property: *Vita*, c. 2 para. 9 [*PL* 153: 768B]; *cf.* Bligny, *L'église*, pp. 114-9, 136-7; and Bligny, *Histoire du diocèse de Grenoble*, Hist. des diocèses de la France, 12 (Paris, 1979), pp. 43-44, 49.

hagiographer with strong spiritual preoccupations, Guigo uses enough precise numbers to afford an outline chronology of Hugh's life.[29]

Whatever the 'typical' features of his Life, Guigo was well-placed to know the truth, and set much store by telling it. So he is unusually trustworthy. This applies especially in a field not well-covered by other historical sources of the time: the mind.

So Innocent II had to do without Hugh's miracles. Historians must share his disappointment. More would have been heard of him now if some solid miracles had been put in the Life. For biographers shared with artists the task of preserving a saint's memory, and artists – in this like God himself, according to theologians – used physical miracles as visible signs of the invisible. The custody of Hugh's memory was left too much to Carthusians – the same who gave Peter the Venerable no miracles for his collection *De miraculis* – for artists to have much more than tenuous dreams to work on. Not surprisingly, therefore, 'devotional pictures of St. Hugo are rare' – in the words of a diligent seeker of them.[30] That was a price paid for Guigo's reserve on miracles.

It is a small price, for it buys two things. One was strict veracity. The other, contrasting with a taste for external miracles, was Guigo's preoccupation with *in*ternal portraiture. He tells us about Hugh's mind. This was in Guigo's character. In that first Age of Discovery, of pilgrimages and crusades, Guigo led explorations *in*wards. 'Some may go to Jerusalem', he had written a few years earlier, in meditations for his brethren, 'but let *your* pilgrimage be towards humility and patience.' Again: 'see, how little you know yourself: there is no region as remote to you as yourself, or as unknown; nor any of which you so readily believe the bearer of false tales'. There is more like this.[31] Transferred to biography this interest is as much a 'godsend' to the historian as miracle would have been to an artist. It makes a rare adit to the thoughts and feelings of a Gregorian 'reformer', who might otherwise survive as many do as a montage, at most, of charter-preambles.

---

[29] The more saintly an author, the fewer the dates: W. von den Steinen, 'Heilige als Hagiographen', *Historische Zeitschrift*, 143 (1930), pp. 229-56, reprinted in the same author's *Menschen im Mittelalter* (Bern-Munich, 1968), pp. 7-31.

[30] J. Jameson, *Legends of the Monastic Orders as Represented in the Fine Arts* (London, 1850), p. 144. The pictures were rarer than she thought for her one example is of St. Hugh of Lincoln. On the confusion of the two Hughs see F. Werner, 'Hugo von Grenoble' in E. Kirschbaum and W. Braunfels, ed., *Lexikon der christlichen Ikonographie*, vol. 6 (Rome, 1974), pp. 552-53 (on p. 553). Werner identifies sixteenth-century representations of St. Hugh of Grenoble. H. Roder, *Saints and their Attributes* (London, 1955), p. 307, mentions more themes associated with our St. Hugh but without references. Hugh's miraculous metamorphosis of partridges into turtles (viewed as fish, and therefore edible on days of abstinence from meat) is not in Guigo's Life. The fortunes of St. Bruno and the miracle of the dead professor, and of St. Hugh and the swan, can be followed through the same works of reference.

[31] *Meditationes*, nos. 262, 303. Ed. par un Chartreux. Sources chrétiennes, no. 308. Série des Textes Monastiques d'Occident, no. 51 (Paris, 1983), pp. 184, 202.

Guigo's interest in the mind is especially important in Hugh's case. For Hugh's religion had a strong intellectual dimension, and our assessment of his 'temptation' depends on an understanding of this. His was to start with a religion 'of the book'.[32] As a youth Hugh had been moved (Guigo says) by 'an extraordinary devotion to letters', and had wandered off from his native Dauphiné to 'foreign regions' to study. Carthusian tradition suggests the main foreign region there was Rheims, and that Hugh sat there at the feet of the then cathedral schoolmaster, Bruno.[33] St. Bruno had died in 1101, too early to have counted among the monastic intellectuals of Hugh's old age; but there were still disciples of his at the Chartreuse, notably Prior Guigo himself and that Airaud, *litteris conspicuus*, who would probably have been asked to write the Life if Guigo had not. Their religion, too, was 'of the book', and they cherished a telling story about Hugh, which went into Guigo's Life. At Hugh's consecration in 1080 the Countess Matilda had given the young bishop the pastoral staff he later used as bishop. Nothing distinctive about that, apparently, at the height of the 'Investiture Contest' (and a woman too). But Hugh's consecration was distinctive, for all that. For what other lay magnate would have given the young bishop, as well as his staff, two *books*: St. Ambrose's *De officiis ministrorum* and St. Augustine's enormous *Enarrationes in psalmos*. But then Matilda's religion, too, was 'of the book'.[34]

Hugh lived up to this gift. He became in his own way a man of letters. If the Cartularies of St. Hugh, kept now in Grenoble, do bear a few examples of Hugh's calligraphy, it is apparently inexpert; and the matter is at best doubtful.[35] But Guigo insists that Hugh, if he did not write his own letters and charters, supervised their writing and dictated many personally 'especially' – as if this were rare – 'when he thought the subject important'.[36] Hugh also organised a scriptorium for the copying of books, he says, and held, at table and elsewhere, regular readings by a *lector* for himself and his staff.[37]

The intellectual dimension of Hugh's religion appears in a second way. In Guigo's Life he is a born contemplative. His 'other half', St. Bernard, was a

---

[32] An expression from the classic essay by W. Liebeschütz, 'Wesen und Grenzen des karolingischen Rationalismus', *Archiv für Kulturgeschichte* 333 (1950-51), pp. 17-44.

[33] *Vita*, c. 1 para. 4 [*PL* 153: 765A]. The tradition is in the anonymous fourteenth-century *Historia brevis ordinis Cartusii* printed by U. Martène and E. Durand, *Veterum scriptorum . . . amplissima collectio*, vi (Paris, 1729), pp. 150-215, on p. 154AB. Traps in this text: Wilmart, 'La chronique des premiers Chartreux' (as in n. 13 above), p. 79. Bruno was schoolmaster *c.* 1056-76.

[34] *Vita*, c. 2 para. 8 [*PL* 153: 768A]: 'additis psalmorum secundum B. Augustinum Explanationibus'. Airaud was 'litteris et puritate conspicuus', c. 4 para. 15 [772B]. Matilda as scholar: J.W. Thompson, *The Literacy of the Laity in the Middle Ages* (University of California, 1915), pp. 69-70.

[35] The abbé Barthélemy, canon of Grenoble, reported by Du Boys, *Vie*, p. 445. Contrast Marion, *Cartulaires* (as in n. 6), pp. xliv-xlv, who records no trace of Hugh's hand.

[36] *Vita*, c.5 para. 22 [*PL* 153: 777A]; *cf.* Marion, p. xlv, for charters 'sicut ipsemet dictaverat' etc.

[37] *Vita*, c. 3 para. 14 [*PL* 153: 771BC].

monk often drawn into the world; Hugh was the opposite, his episcopate – if we trust Guigo – a long, unfulfilled love affair with monasticism – unfulfilled in that he was forever being dragged back to a bishop's duty. I shall return to Hugh's initial resistance to episcopal office. When he had accepted it was less than two years before he had persuaded his friend Seguin, abbot of La Chaise-Dieu, a Cluniac-influenced house a hundred miles west of Grenoble, to accept him – a bishop! – as a monk. He stayed about a year, loved it, and only went back to Grenoble because the news got slowly but surely to Gregory VII, who ordered him back.[38] Less than two years after *that* – everything suggests with Hugh's prior connivance – Master Bruno came and began his austere hermitage just thirteen miles away at the Chartreuse. Hugh was given a cell there. (He shared it – in Bruno's time cells were double – with William, later abbot of St. Theoffrey, who told Guigo what Hugh was like in those days). From then on Hugh was forever at the Chartreuse, meditating and praying with the others so that, this time, it was Bruno who told him to go back to Grenoble and behave like a bishop.[39]

These particular sojourns must have been before 1090, for Bruno was still head of the Chartreuse. At latest they were before Bruno's death in 1101, since he still wielded moral authority from Calabria in his last years. Guigo must have learned it from his elders at a time when Hugh perhaps came less, and priors (now looking young to Hugh) had less authority. But Hugh's monastic leanings survived. In the late 1120s he petitioned Pope Honorius II – he wrote first, later rode to Rome – for release from his office; his plea, infirmity, but his aim, still, *vacare Deo*, an expression implying monastic retreat. He failed again. Honorius replied that the sick man's authority and example did more good to his diocese than would the bustling activity of most healthy men. Then Hugh's failing memory came to his aid. In 1130 Innocent II came to Valence and released the old bishop, replacing him with a man now long his aide-de-camp, Hugh II, himself a Carthusian. As Hugh of Châteauneuf finally sickened towards death in Grenoble, appropriately, he would have none but monks, largely *conversi*, to nurse him.[40] This cannot be mere biographer's colouring. The other half of St. Bernard was himself all but a monk.

Whatever reasons Guigo may have had for dwelling on this fact, for us it throws light on Hugh's mind, and in particular on his approach to his pastoral office. Hugh became convinced, during his stay at La Chaise-Dieu in 1080-81, that the world was potentially a huge monastery. Guigo clearly sympathised with this view but there is no reason to doubt that he had it from Hugh's own words:

[38] Ibid., c. 3 para. 10 [*PL* 153: 768D-9A]. The tenacity of old historiographical traditions, even into the nineteenth century, is shown by Du Boys' paraphrase of Gregory's letter to Hugh at La Chaise-Dieu (*Vie*, p. 58). Du Boys invented the letter. But for Gregory's philosophy on the issue, calling on the abbot of Cluny to disgorge a duke of Burgundy, see his *Registrum*, vi, 17, pp. 423-24.

[39] *Vita*, c. 3 para 12 [*PL* 153: 770AB].

[40] *Vita*, c. 5 para. 24 [*PL* 153: 778C-9C]; c..5 para. 25 [779BC]; c. 6 para. 27 [780AB].

Hugh gained as much from his year of monastic endeavour as many do after a lifetime. He missed the cloister; but had in its place an ever-watchful conscience [*circumspectio*], controlling not just his bodily affections but the very thoughts of his heart. He missed the abbot; but now took his orders from Justice, from whose obedience neither favour nor opposition could sway him. Finally he missed the brethren, whose affectionate company he had so much valued; but now he had the entire church, whose fortunes, good or bad, he felt in the very depths of his own being.[41]

Too weak to stifle his monastic yearnings, the effect was strong enough to guide Hugh as bishop.

For the formula just quoted serves as a key to Hugh's episcopate. It largely resolves the puzzling contrast between the Hugh of the charters and the Hugh of the Life.[42] Obedience to Justice – the substitute-abbot – and a feeling for the church – the substitute-community – made Hugh socially 'amphibious'. In politics Hugh stood up to great magnates, battling locally for the derelict rights of his bishopric – for years, for instance, against the great Guido, archbishop of Vienne (later Calixtus II); and battling in the universal church against king and antipope. In 1112 he had been a moving force behind the excommunication at Vienne of the Emperor Henry V, while in 1130 he was *the* force behind that of Pierleone-Anacletus II, Innocent II's rival, and a former friend and patron.[43] The lion was also a lamb. When first bishop Hugh had had to be restrained from selling all his horses to help feed the poor – restrained by Bruno (on the grounds that foot travel would demean the bishop's office and be impractical among the mountains); and later Hugh did, in a famine, sell church treasure for the same purpose, inspiring further generosity from local nobles. Repeated examples underline both the twin, contrasting qualities Hugh drew from his monastic experience. His circle of devotees, both in life and after death, was drawn from a corresponding variety of social classes.[44]

We are studying a mind. Hugh also studied it. His substitute for the Benedictine rule, after La Chaise-Dieu, was *circumspectio*, an inner surveillance of his own conscience. This too left its stamp on his episcopate. He was among a small group of bishops – Lanfranc and Anselm of Canterbury were among others – to have pioneered the practice of regular lay confession, long

---

[41] Ibid., c. 3 para. 10 [*PL* 153: 769AB].

[42] Cf. Bligny, *Vie*, esp. p. 12.

[43] *Vita*, c. 5 para. 25 [*PL* 153: 779AB]. The 'venerationes et obsequia' shown by Pierleone senior probably included hospitality to Hugh in 1080 as well as political support in the crisis of 1111-12. Hugh's disputes with Guido of Vienne (among other local powers) are recorded in Marion, *Cartulaires*, Cart. A, narrated by Du Boys, chaps. 3-8, and described analytically and concisely by Bligny, *L'Église*, pp. 71-73, 104-11, 340-41; and *Diocèse*, pp. 50-52.

[44] Chalice, and example to nobles: *Vita*, c. 5 para. 19 [*PL* 153: 775B]. Horse, and delight in servile work: c. 3 para. 12 [770BC]. Appeal to all classes: c.5 para. 21 [777A] (alive); c.6 para. 33 [784B] (dead); etc.

before it is known to have been generally practised.[45] While turning 'the eye of his heart' regularly on his own conduct, Hugh urged the same on his parishioners, teaching them both *to* confess, and what to confess. More than one of Guigo's anecdotes show Hugh as confessor. An episcopal secretary, later a Carthusian, recalled confessing to Hugh and becoming aware in the course of the session that the confessor was weeping because the penitent felt the confessor's tears as they dropped on his hair.[46] Another story tells how visitors from beyond the diocese would travel far to confess to Hugh and be heard; and yet another, of a sermon Hugh gave which induced a woman publicly to confess to poisoning her husband – after which so many others in the congregation wishes to make their confessions that the numbers far exceeded Hugh's capacity to hear them.[47] It is as if he were a thirteenth-century friar in the pages of Salimbene of Parma.

Each medieval 'saint' has his physiognomy. I have summarised Hugh's. None of its elements – his literate, contemplative instincts, his combination of strength and tenderness, and his interest in the motions of the heart – was unique. Taken together, nevertheless, they stamp him with a character, distinct enough to explain both his stature among the mass of contemporaries, and the strength of his bonds with the handful of like-minded colleagues. The summary has had a purpose: to put in context the theme in Guigo's Life which gives this essay its title, and to which it is now time to turn.

In his early twenties Hugh of Châteauneuf had been made a canon of Valence. As a noble youth with a taste for books he might expect as much. Income from the post may have come to relieve his privations as a student. Although a canonry there and then did not involve the wearing of clerical dress it introduced its holder to church affairs; as such it occasioned the encounter which, in the end, was to bring Hugh to public attention.[48]

---

[45] The word *circumspectio* as applied to the heart, as well as bodily movements, *Vita*, c. 3 para. 10 [*PL* 153: 769B]; and in a similar sense in c. 5 para. 23 [778A] and c. 4 para. 15 [774D]. *Mentis oculos*: c. 3 para. 10 [768D]; *sensus vigilantia*: c. 4 para. 15 [772B] (referring to Jer. 9:21); *ocula cordis*: c. 4 para. 17 [774C]. The history of confession: B. Poschmann, *Penance and the Anointing of the Sick* (Freiburg-London, 1964).

[46] *Vita*, c. 3 para. 14 [*PL* 153: 771D].

[47] Ibid., c. 4 para. 15 [*PL* 153: 773B]; c. 5 para. 22 [777BC].

[48] For the date of canonry see Du Boys, *Vie*, 48-49, who dates Hugh's appointment to a canonry after his return from Rheims. The imperfect *erat* makes an earlier date more likely. The appointment may, indeed, have been procured for Hugh in his absence to relieve the privations which Guigo associates with his studies, *Vita*, c. 1 para. 4 [*PL* 153: 765A]. Lay dress: c.2 para. 5 [766B]. Hugh of Die in Valence: Gregory VII, *Registrum*, vi, 27 [p. 439, 30-35] (20 March 1079) instructing the monks of Déols to send a representative to Hugh of Die in Valence on 19 May. *Cf.* P.R. Gaussin, 'Hugues de Die et l'episcopat franco-bourguignon (1075-1085)', *Cahiers d'histoire*, 13 (1968), pp. 77-98; p. 87; and Bligny, *L'Église*, p. 70.

There is reason to date the encounter to 19 May 1079, or a day around then. It was with another Hugh (the nobility of the Dauphiné confined themselves to a confusingly small number of names), the bishop of Die, on the Drôme, the famous papal legate – or infamous, to some, for his high-handed depositions of simoniac prelates. The legate (whom I shall call 'Hugh Senior': he must have been about forty) was impressed by Hugh of Châteauneuf's 'good looks, tall stature, polite speech and modest manner', and by his noble birth and education. So he joined young Hugh to the personal staff who accompanied him on his legatine rounds. It was in this capacity that Hugh of Châteauneuf attended a provincial council at Avignon in February 1080, and there, 'barely twenty-seven years old', he got an invitation from the Grenoble chapter to fill their vacancy as bishop.[49]

Hugh's reaction was shock. He

was at once struck by fear, to the very depths of his being.[50]

He loudly protested that his 'age, level of knowledge, and above all his moral inadequacy' were unmatched to an office so holy. Its acceptance by a man so unsuitable would endanger such a man's salvation. Hugh Senior, on the other hand, was only too pleased that a church as apparently intractable as Grenoble should have chosen his own lieutenant as bishop. With back-up from other wise heads at the council he used his rhetoric to persuade young Hugh to accept. At a time when the most unsuitable people were clamouring for high church office, for wrong reasons which it was precisely the purpose of the reform movement to eradicate, Hugh of Châteauneuf's humility – the legate pointed out – was admirable. He should not, however, be afraid of the post, but should put his trust in God, who would look after him. By the legate's and others' persuasion young Hugh was slowly brought round.[51]

Now Hugh was a layman; so the bishop of Die quickly gave him the necessary ordination as priest. Next he must be consecrated bishop. Wormund, archbishop of Vienne and metropolitan of Grenoble, was the proper authority; but he had lost favour with the Gregorians as a simoniac. So it was agreed that Hugh of Châteauneuf should join two other bishops-elect, whom the legate had picked up on his tour of Provence, and go to Rome where all three could be consecrated by the pope.

The events that follow are datable certainly to the year 1080 and more

[49] *Vita*, c. 1 para. 4 [*PL* 153: 765BC], and c. 2 para. 5 [765CD]
[50] Ibid., c. 2 para. 5 [*PL* 153: 766A].
[51] Ibid., c. 2 para. 5 [*PL* 153: 766AB].

probably than not to the few weeks spanning the end of March and the early part of April.[52] Guigo writes:

> While staying there and waiting for the day for his consecration, Hugh was victim to an extremely grave attack of the Old Enemy – raw and inexpert as Hugh was in these things, and at the very first stage in his holy service.[53]

Guigo must have heard all this from an elderly Hugh whose memory could sweep easily over the forty years between his youth and extreme age. He goes on:

> this temptation never left him, night or day. Now stronger, now milder, it lasted right up to the illness which brought him to the sickbed on which he later died.

Guigo puts Hugh's temptation in its tradition: of St. Paul, buffeted to prevent his becoming elated; of Joshua, tested; most important of all, of Jesus, victorious here as elsewhere.

Suffering so severely, Hugh of Châteauneuf renewed his earlier refusal:

> Thus unexpectedly attacked by the Ancient Enemy, as I say, he reflected that the Lord might be indignant with him for yielding to the electors' wish, with whatever reluctance. So now he resolved to refuse the election by all means available, and never on any condition to go through with the consecration.[54]

Hugh of Die had to be told:

> At once he went to the legate and informed him, with tears and sighs from the depths of his heart, both of this wholesome decision (as it seemed to him) and of the temptation.[55]

The legate repeated his earlier argument. It had a little effect but did not

---

[52] Gaussin, 'Hugues de Die', p. 80; C.-J. Hefele and H. Leclercq, *Histoire des conciles*, 5, pt. i (Paris, 1912), pp. 267, 282. The Lenten council in Rome was called for 7 March 1080. But the Life (c. 2 para. 6 [*PL* 153: 766C]: 'opperiens diem'; and para. 8 [767D] after the consecration: 'toto illo quo ibidem demoratus est tempore') suggests that the Hugh of Châteauneuf, for his part, stayed some weeks in Rome, though not beyond late June when Gregory left for Ceprano. On 26 March (*Registrum*, vii, 16 [pp. 489-90]) and 17 April (vii, 20 [pp. 495-96]) Gregory wrote two letters in apparent connivance with Hugh of Die. The latter (vii, 20) in particular betrays a connection with persons then or later in Hugh of Grenoble's circle: it has as principal aim the protection of Master Bruno of Rheims from the sanctions of his simoniac archbishop, who is to be consigned in exile to La Chaise-Dieu, whose abbot Seguin had accompanied the two Hughs to Rome; Bligny, *Vie*, p. 14.

[53] *Vita*, c. 2 para. 6 [*PL* 153: 766C]: 'ubi dum, consecrationis statutum opperiens diem, commoraretur, in ipsis quodammodo divinae servitutis initiis, et in primis sacrae militiae tirociniis, gravissimam hostis antiqui impugnationem, rudis et talium inexpertus, incurrit'.

[54] Ibid., c. 2 para. 7 [*PL* 153: 767AB].

[55] Ibid., c. 2 para. 7 [*PL* 153: 767B].

change young Hugh's resolve. But they were in Rome now, not Avignon. Hugh of Die knew there was a better counsellor at hand and said young Hugh must go to him: Gregory VII. Young Hugh must go to the pope and tell him 'everything' as 'vicar of Christ'.[56]

There follows the only surviving account, brief though it is, of a pastoral interview with Gregory VII:

> What the pope said, and the affection he showed him, fed Hugh with such consolation that the temptation which had previously driven him almost to despair all at once became a source of joy and hope.

Later, the consecration duly went ahead, and Pope Gregory showed special regard for young Hugh throughout the rest of his stay in Rome.[57]

The biography – it is oblique autobiography – nevertheless adds that the new bishop's problem, though much relieved, did not disappear. Twice more the Life refers to the 'temptation'. Guigo pairs it with Hugh's bodily illnesses – head-aches and stomach-ache – as one of the two types of 'buffet' sent to save Hugh from elation. The second time he mentions the temptation is in chapter 5, when Hugh is approaching his last illness. Guigo says that at this point, as the physical problem got worse, the other problem, the temptation, finally vanished, such 'that not even a trace of it remained'.[58]

Now what was the 'temptation'? More often than not it is referred to thus, with no explanation. The Life seems hesitant to say more, as if, even as a temptation, its substance was too dreadful even to mention. It must indeed have been to buffet Hugh as it did and drive him 'nearly to desperation'. Let us begin by ascertaining what it was not. Here and there in the Life Guigo mentions temptations that Hugh did *not* suffer from. Thus in chapter 4 we learn that Hugh's strict life had rendered him virtually *insensibilem* to sexual temptation. A moment later we are told that gluttony was put beyond his reach by chronic stomach ailments.[59] In the usual run of first-rank temptations that leaves vainglory. It is declared both expressly, and implicitly by the monastic tenor of Hugh's life, that he saw wordly glory as something to flee from, not seek.[60]

We do not, however, have to rely just on negative evidence. We saw earlier that Guigo's style in speaking of evil was one of discreet brevity. In one place he says what the temptation was, with just this discreet brevity. It is when Hugh was first tempted in Rome in the Spring of 1080. Guigo first refers to the 'temptation' *tout court*. Then he sets it in the tradition of tempted saints,

[56] Ibid., c. 2 para. 7 [*PL* 153: 767B]: 'et quidquid ejus angebat animum (utpote Christi vicario) totum revelare suasit'.

[57] Ibid., c. 2 para. 7 [*PL* 153: 767B].

[58] Ibid., c. 3 para. 13 [*PL* 153: 770D-1A]; c. 6 para. 26 [779C].

[59] Ibid., c. 4 para. 18 [*PL* 153: 774C-75A].

[60] Ibid., c. 2 para. 5 [*PL* 153: 766B].

culminating in the three temptations of Jesus. In St. Luke's Gospel (4: 1-13) these end with Satan's suggestion that Jesus throw himself from the Temple in the trust that he will be borne up by angels. Guigo chooses the version of Matthew (4:9). The crowning temptation here is Satan's promise that, in return for worship of himself, Satan, Jesus will be granted lordship of the world. Guigo goes on:

> And just as Satan had the incredible presumption to suggest idolatry to the Lord himself, so his snakish machination suggested blasphemy to the Lord's servant, namely that he should think something unworthy of God, or of things pertaining to God.[61]

> [. . . 'Sic et ejus servo suggerebat viperea machinatione blasphemiam, scilicet ut de Deo, vel de his quae ad Deum pertinent, aliquid cogitaret indignum'.]

*Scilicet*, in that phrase, makes the words after it a definition of the word before, *blasphemia*. *Blasphemia* in Greek means literally 'evil speaking'. Moralists of the thirteenth and fourteenth centuries would generally understand the word thus, as the *speaking* of things inappropriate to or unworthy of God.[62] But there is a specifically monastic tradition, going back to the *Vitae patrum*, of understanding the term to indicate mere wrong *thinking* about God. When so used it is often in compounds like *blasphemia cordis* or *spiritus blasphemiae*. Understood thus, as in Guigo's phrase of Hugh, the meaning of *blasphemia* approaches that of *haeresia*, and if their use as synonyms is relatively rare, this is as much due to a difference in the contexts in which they were employed, as to an intrinsic difference in their meaning: namely (in this case) 'ut de Deo, vel de his quae ad Deum pertinent, aliquid cogitaret indignum'.

Students of classical inscriptions commonly expand a fragmentary word, even a letter, through knowledge of analogous cases. An employment of the same method here points, first, back to the case of Otloh of St. Emmeram, a Regensburg monk who had died while Hugh was a boy, *c.* 1070. Shortly before his death he wrote a book called *Liber de tentationibus cuiusdam monachi*, in which described the personal crisis he had himself confronted soon after becoming a novice, in 1032, and began reading the Bible. To Otloh, too, the Devil had suggested *cogitationes* unworthy of God. One was the idea that the Bible was the false invention of priests. This led to others, culminating in the ultimate thought: that God did not exist.[63] Otloh was appalled by these thoughts, the more so because he imagined no one else had ever had them; so that he kept them to himself, rendering the crisis worse for want of older

---

[61] Ibid., c. 2 para. 6 [*PL* 153: 767A]. The end of the corresponding account in Luke might have been thought more appropriate to Hugh: the Devil left him 'usque ad tempus' ('for a season').

[62] For this and what follows: E.D. Craun, '*Inordinatio locutio*: Blasphemy in Pastoral Literature, 1200-1500', *Traditio* 39 (1983), pp. 135-62, esp. pp. 146-47, n. 33.

[63] *PL* 146:29-58. (Extracts, but textually more reliable, in *MGH, SS*, 11, pp. 378-93). No God: *PL* 146: 32B-33B.

counsel. After describing what we would today wish to call a nervous break-
down, some of it passed in the abbey infirmary, Otloh eventually settled to
become a distinguished monastic scholar. When he himself approached the age
of sixty Otloh wrote an account of his youthful temptations so that other
novices should be able to confront these temptations if they came, rather than
suffer in isolation as he had done.[64]

Documentation on this subject only grows to significant volume in the
thirteenth century. To pursue analogous cases from then on would exceed the
limits of this essay. But it will be useful to indicate one area where they are
found, both because the term *blasphemia* recurs, and because there is now no
mistaking its more representative character. I refer to the in-house literature of
friars, and cite one example. A Franciscan novice-master, who lectured to
novices in two convents throughout the 1230s and '40s would single out the
'spirit of blasphemy' and 'hesitation about the Catholic faith' as in a very small
handful of 'very bitter' temptations against which novices should be especially
on their guard.[65]

None of this – and there is more – is certain proof that Hugh of Châteauneuf
and Grenoble was tempted to religious doubt. Yet it renders possible that
interpretation of the few lines the discreet Guigo devotes to the subject, and
accounts for features in those lines that would otherwise be anomalous. No
other reading suggests itself as readily. So let us, if provisionally, assume this
interpretation and ask how it fits a more general historical context.

In matters of learning the relation of quantity to quality is perennially
debated: whether 'more' means 'better' or 'worse'. However the debate goes,
'more' nearly always means 'different'. Let us apply this idea to the eleventh
and twelfth centuries, each being understood (by historian's licence) approxi-
mately. The twelfth century had more learning than the eleventh: more books
and a bigger fraction of the population who could read them. In some respects,
of course, its learning was also demonstrably better. More important to us is
that it was different. Because Christian scholars in the eleventh century were
few, they stood in a different relationship both to their fellow men, and to their
books.

Look at the fellow men first. The writer of the Fleury miracle-book, around

[64] *PL* 146:51A. Literature: H. Schauwecker, *Othloh von St. Emmeram*, Studien und Mitteilungen zur Geschichte des Benedkiktinerordens und seiner Zweige, Band 74, (Munich, 1965).

[65] David of Augsburg, O.F.M., *De exterioris et interioris hominis compositione*, ed. Collegium
s. Bonaventurae (Quaracchi, 1899), p. 180 [= *Formula novitiorum* ii, 5, ed. M. de la Bigne,
*Maxima biblioteca veterum patrum* (Lyons, 1677), vol. 25, p. 902B]. For a Dominican novice so
afflicted: Etienne de Bourbon, *Anecdotes historiques*, ed. A. Lecoy de la Marche (Paris, 1877),
para. 226, pp. 195-96. References to recent literature on religious scepticism, a different if related
matter, can be found with wholesome counsel in S. Reynolds, 'Social Mentalities and the Case of
Medieval Scepticism', *Transactions of the Royal Historical Society*, 41 (1991), pp. 21-41.

1038, had no hesitation in describing his local country-folk as 'semi-pagan',[66] and while there was doubtless variation in degree, there is every reason to believe his aspersion would have applied to much of western Europe. Where did the intellectual stand in relation to this world? Let me borrow a theory from the Norman historian Lucien Musset, conceived by him to explain the speedy conversion to Christianity of those Vikings who settled in Christian countries. Their own religion, he observed, was strongly topographic: the sacred was attached to mountains, rivers and so on. The result was the migration weakened religious self-confidence and exposed them to whatever religion, be it still semi-pagan, they found in their new host-society.[67] In the eleventh century an intellectual was in an analogous position. He was a migrant, leaving one world for another, often, like any migrant (and like Hugh of Châteauneuf)[68], at the cost of personal privation; as Gregory VII would have put it, he left Custom, for Truth.[69] For he was starting now to *read* about his religion – which meant (as if his own religion did not pose enough problems of its own), other religions too, like those classical doctrines which had thrown, in a famous but still mysterious episode, Vilgard of Ravenna and his friends off their heads at the beginning of the century.[70] Some of the shock that upset Otloh – and Hugh if the present hypothesis is right – could be accounted for in this way.

There was also a difference in the world into which the migrant arrived. R.I. Moore has argued that western Christendom would become in the course of the twelfth century a 'persecuting society'.[71] It was placed to be so because the religion 'of the Book' had by then come of age. The migrant entered a New World well past its pioneer age. Early scholasticism had produced a set of answers to the main questions new readers were likely to raise; answers which, for all their inadequacies (food for philosophy and theology from that day to this), could comfort the not too zealous contemporary, as they have antago-nised his modern equivalent, with the illusion that scholasticism was a system which explained everything. The settlers of a century before had lacked that comfort. They were in some measure the persecut*ed*, – as witnessed by those unflattering popular legends about isolated scholars like Gerbert of Aurillac and Abbo of Fleury; and as embodied, at a more radical level, in the profoundly ambivalent relationship of Gregory VII with heresy, even in his

---

[66] *Miracula s. Benedicti*, v, c. xii, ed., E. de Certain. Société pour l'histoire de France, 54 (Paris, 1858), p. 210.

[67] L. Musset, 'La pénétration chrétienne dans l'Europe du nord et son influence sur la civilisation scandinave', in *La conversione al cristianesimo nell'Europa dell'alto medioevo*. Setti-mane di studio sul alto medioevo, 14 (Spoleto 1967), pp. 263-326, esp. pp. 264-65.

[68] See n. 48.

[69] Tertullian would also have put it that way. *Cf.* Ladner, 'Letters' (as in n. 2), pp. 225, 232-33.

[70] Rodulfus Glaber, *Historiae* (as in n.3), ii, c. xii para. 23, pp. 92-3.

[71] *The Formation of a Persecuting Society Power and Deviance in Western Europe, 950-1250* (Oxford, 1987).

own time (as when one of his own supporters was burned as a heretic by a crowd in northern France).[72] The born Christian of that pre-scholastic age, in a word, was more exposed than his successors to the raw problems that confront the intelligence as it begins to read and think about its religion, in a learned tradition heavy, as Latin literature was, with past attempts to solve religious problems. If St. Hugh did have a crisis of faith, in the spring of 1080 and later, considerations on these lines would help explain it.

They would explain more. There are two potential heroes in my story. Let me return to the interview with Gregory VII. Hugh's temptation had proved too much for the legate, lion of the French church. But the legate did know where help was to be found, and he was right. Guigo reveals – he must have treasured Hugh's own reminiscence – how Gregory spoke on that occasion. He taught young Hugh about the positive values of temptation, a sign of God's favour and the Devil's envy; and Gregory spoke 'as one lacking neither knowledge nor experience in these matters' ['utpote in rebus his nec rudis nec inexpertus'].[73]

Are we to understand, then, that Gregory VII, corrector of the peoples, was *expertus* in the temptation 'ut de Deo, vel de his quae ad Deum pertinent, aliquid cogitaret indignum'? Perhaps his knowledge was hearsay: he could have talked about such things with his German ally William, abbot of Hirsau; for William had been a young monk in St. Emmeram in Otloh's time, and the two had often exchanged views, perhaps also on this.[74] That, however, would be to rule out Gregory's own experience, for which we have no grounds. Guigo's phrase can once more be read best with the help of analogues. There is one to hand in the crusade-letter quoted at the beginning of this essay, with its call for 'St. Peter's faith' to rally the erring millions of the east. At first glance, it is true, the letter does not read at first as if its author had ever doubted. But it mentions St. Peter. *He* had had doubts (Matt. 14: 30-31). Why should his representative be immune? And might not his doubts be cured in the same way? Gregory answers these questions for us. The letter in question goes on, after the passage quoted above:

> For the time has now come for the fulfilment of that which our pious Redeemer deigned to tell and command the prince of the Apostles: 'Peter, I have prayed for thee, *that thy faith fail not; and when thou art converted, strengthen thy brethren*'.[75]

[72] *Registrum*, iv, 20, ed. E. Caspar, p. 328.22-34.

[73] *Vita*, c. 2 para. 7 [*PL* 153: 767C].

[74] Schauwecker, pp. 226-29; B. Bischoff, 'Literarisches und künstlerisches Leben in St. Emmeram (Regensburg) während des frühen und hohen Mittelalters', in the same author's *Mittelalterliche Studien*, 2 (Stuttgart, 1967), pp. 77-115, pp. 94-95.

[75] *Registrum*, iv, 20, ed. Caspar, p. 328.22-34.

That quotation, from Luke 22:32, was a favourite of Gregory's, as if he, like Peter, knew he need of help 'ut non deficiat fides'.[76]

The same point is made by a second analogue. It is a letter Gregory wrote expressly to 'strengthen' one of his brethren. In what is probably Gregory's best-known letter there is a passage which remains – it is one last paradox – one of his least-known. The exordium appears to describe, with what Guigo would have called the 'eye of his heart', the feelings of a writer *nec rudis nec inexpertus* in the experience of doubt. The letter in question is the elaborate, often copied statement of papalist theory sent to Bishop Hermann of Metz in March 1081.[77] From Hermann's day to our own many pairs of eyes have read that letter. Hungry for the feast of church political doctrine that distinguishes the letter most eyes will speed over its first, non-political paragraph. This alludes to the letter's occasion. Hermann had doubted. What he had doubted was Gregory's authority to excommunicate an emperor. Hermann was a political waverer. Gregory's reply starts by considering doubt as such. He tells the bishop about the positive value of the hesitation he has just experienced. God's grace towards his elect, the pope says, is such that he will not let his chosen ones go far astray. God makes their hesitations an occasion for greater strength. Doubt is like a soldier's fear in battle:

> For fear has opposite effects in different hearts. In a coward's heart it turns into terror, so that he flees more shamefully than the rest. But in a brave man's, it strikes fire, so that he rushes forward more courageously, excelling his neighbour in valour.[78]

These lines were written less than twelve months after the Hugh of Grenoble had spoken with Gregory VII. Their interview was private. But might not Gregory not have spoken to the young man in similar terms, about deeper doubts – and given the church a saint, and the Carthusian Order, by doing so?

---

[76] Ibid., p. 646.

[77] *Registrum*, viii, 21, pp. 544-63; occasioned by a dilemma described by F.R. Erkens, *Die Trierer Kirchenprovinz im Investiturstreit* (Vienna, 1987), 45-55.

[78] *Registrum*, viii, 21, p. 547, lines 10-12.

# 8

## The Necessity for Two Peters of Blois

### R.W. Southern

In the letter-collection of Peter of Blois there are many letters which throw light on the writer's development as a scholar, author and man of affairs. Among them there are two which illuminate his struggle between a desire for literary fame and his call to a life of serious religious dedication. But though the general theme is clear, the two letters have received two widely differing interpretations. The purpose of this essay is to examine these interpretations, and to show that only one of them is consistent with the facts. If this is correct, it has some important consequences for the literary history of the second half of the twelfth century. But before coming to this wider problem, it is necessary to examine the contents and occasion for the two letters which are the source of the problem.[1] In the printed edition, and in all the manuscripts in which they both appear, the two letters in question, *Epp.* 76 and 77, follow one another in reverse chronological order. The earlier of the two (*Ep.* 77) appeared in the earliest collection of his letters, which the writer made in 1184, and it reappears with considerable changes and additions to the text in all the later editions of the collection for which the writer was himself responsible. The later of the two letters (*Ep.* 76) first appears in the fourth edition of the letter-collection, which the author made in about 1198, and so far as I know its text never varied.

A late appearance of any letter in the sequence of the writer's editions of his letter-collection is not necessarily an indication of a later date of the particular letter. But this is the normal reason for a letter's late appearance, and in this case (as we shall see) there can be no doubt that *Ep.* 76 was written about ten or more years after *Ep.* 77.

We may be sure that, in placing them together, the author wished them to be understood in relation to each other. Why he should have put them in reverse chronological order is more open to speculation, but (for reasons which will become apparent as we proceed) he may have wished the reader to understand

---

[1]  For the texts of the two letters, see Migne, *PL*, 207, cols. 231-39. For an account of the various editions of the letter-collection made by the author, see R.W. Southern, *Medieval Humanism and Other Studies* (Oxford, 1970), pp. 113-23, 129-32.

the attitude expressed in the later letter before approaching the very different outlook of the earlier one. We cannot of course be sure of this, but there is a great deal of evidence in his later works that his change of attitude was very important to him, and there are many symptoms of it in his writings. However, whatever the precise intention of the chronological inversion, the conjunction of the two letters is an essential part of their message. The thread which holds them together is their contrasting attitude towards the person to whom they are addressed, and the piquancy of the situation arises from the addressee having the same name as the writer: he too is Master Peter of Blois.

In all discussions of the letters before 1963, it was – perhaps too readily, but also I think rightly – supposed that the Peter of Blois to whom they were addressed was a real and different person from the writer. But in 1963 Professor Bezzola suggested that the addressee in both letters was the writer himself, and that the two letters were exercises in self-portraiture. The second of these statements is true whether or not the addressee is the same person as the writer, but it is true in a contrary sense: in Bezzola's view, the writer is arguing about two different threads in his own character; but, on the view which I shall put forward, he is displaying a real change in his outlook which has caused a change in his attitude towards the recipient of the letter, who (if we take the account he gives of himself in the two letters at their face value) had been his master, and whom he had at first admired, and from whom he had increasingly dissociated himself.

Bezzola in 1963 put forward his view of the two letters very tentatively. But in 1976 Professor Dronke took up Bezzola's suggestion and developed it with great assurance and skill in introducing a valuable and widely ranging edition of a considerable body of late twelfth-century poetry, which he attributed to the letter-writer.[2] I shall hope to show quite conclusively that the view expressed by Bezzola and developed by Dronke is mistaken. But I may add at once that I think the value of Dronke's editions and explanations of the poems is enhanced rather than diminished by what I believe to be the true situation, which – to put it briefly – is that only very few of the poems which he lists were written by the letter-writer. There is a lot of ground to cover before we can get to that conclusion.

The first step is to prove that two Peters of Blois existed, and that one of them wrote to the other the letters with which we are concerned. This is not in

---

[2] See R.R. Bezzola, *Les origines et la formation de la littérature courtoise en occident (500-1200)*, 3 (Paris 1963), *Bibliothèque de l'école des hautes études*, vol. 319, pp.41-42. Peter Dronke's account of the question is in his 'Peter of Blois and Poetry at the Court of Henry II', *Mediaeval Studies*, 37 (1975), pp. 185-235, where he develops Bezzola's view with confidence and with widely ranging consequences both for the letter-writer's poetic production and personality and for the courtly environment in which he lived. Dronke's paper is divided into two parts: first, a series of texts, with translations and comments; second, an appendix containing 'a tentative bibliography of the poetry of Peter of Blois'. The pieces in the appendix are listed alphabetically and numbered, and it is to these numbers that I refer in what follows.

fact very difficult but the evidence must be taken step by step, and these steps are worth taking because several important issues depend on disentangling the various threads. In particular, the character of the letter-writer, his intellectual horizons and development, the aims and nature of his letter-collection, as well as the character of another considerable author with the same name but with very different interests and abilities, will all emerge from the inquiry. Indeed there are so many issues involved in this apparently simple task of analysing two letters in a well-known letter-collection that it will be impossible to do more here than touch on the major issues in this brief account of the problem.

To understand the problem it is necessary first to understand the development of the letter-collection in which the two letters appear. In the study which I have mentioned above, I have distinguished five main stages in the growth of the collection during the lifetime of its author, and I shall here repeat only those facts which are relevant to the present problem. In its earliest form the letter-collection was made by the author himself in 1184. At this stage the collection contained only the earlier of the two letters, *Ep.* 77, in which the writer described himself as archdeacon of Bath. Since he had obtained this position in 1182, we can without much doubt date the letter 1182-4. We may also notice that he describes the recipient as 'his dearest master'. These are details which deserve to be taken seriously, because one of the writer's aims in making his collection was to teach budding letter-writers to take great care in the details of correct nomenclature.

Bezzola and Dronke argue that the two letters are pure make-believe, and in support of this view Dronke mentions doubts that have been raised in the past about the genuineness of many of the letters. Yet the fiction which is now suggested is quite different from the falsifications detected by earlier critics. All previous doubts about the historicity of some of Peter of Blois's letters have arisen either from accepting as genuine letters which were not in the collections formed by the author himself in his lifetime, or from a failure to recognise the author's practice of altering the texts of earlier letters in the later recensions of his collection. The purposes of these additions were either to add quotations from the Bible or the classics in order to give the doctrines which he wished to inculcate greater weight, or to modify or omit doctrines or opinions of which he no longer approved. For example, in later life he turned against the study of Roman law, against King Henry II and against service in the royal administration. These changes of mind are all reflected in later modifications in the texts of his letters on these subjects. To get back to the original text it is necessary to remove these alterations. Even when these alterations have been identified and stripped off, we may still not have the letter in the form in which it was dispatched, and in some cases it is possible that a letter may never have been dispatched. These considerations apply to nearly all letter-collections at all times: the only important fact for our present inquiry is that there is no letter in any of the collections made by Peter himself and circulated in his lifetime which can plausibly be regarded as fictitious. Even with all the additional rhetoric and changes of emphasis in later recensions, the reality of the events described in the letters remains unimpaired. There is no sign anywhere, so far as I have been able to discover, of any invention of persons or events. The reason for this is that the aim of the later accretions was not to invent events, but to interpret or modify their doctrine.[3]

By contrast, if the Peter of Blois to whom *Epp.* 76 and 77 are addressed is interpreted as simply a mirror-image of the writer himself and an excuse for an introspective view of his own personality, we have not only an otherwise wholly unexampled fantasy, but also much detail on our hands which contradicts all that we know of his family, his career and the development of his interests. These detailed contradictions will emerge as we proceed. In outline it may be said that nothing that we know about his own family bears any relation to the tale of disaster affecting the family of the recipient of these two letters; and nothing that we know about the letter-writer in his later years bears any relation to what he tells us about the continuing studies of his namesake to whom these letters are addressed. Moreover, there is irrefragible evidence for the existence of another Peter of Blois with characteristics similar to those described in the two letters. I shall return to this last point presently. For the moment, the reasons I have given may suffice to establish a provisional basis for the historicity of the person and situation described in the two letters, which now requires further investigation.

We may begin with the earlier of the two letters, *Ep.* 77. Since it appears in the first edition of the letter-collection of 1184, and since the writer describes himself as archdeacon of Bath, a position which he obtained in 1182, the letter can be dated with reasonable certainty between these two years.[4] At this time the writer's position in the ecclesiastical hierarchy as an archdeacon was not very high, but his standing among men at the centre of Angevin affairs, including the king himself, was brilliant. Since joining the household of Richard, archbishop of Canterbury, in 1174, he had written two works of edification for the king, and he was engaged on the composition of a serious panegyric on Henry II's reign. Moreover, he was well known at the papal court. He had been present at the Lateran Council of 1179, and had written in the pope's name – though whether on the pope's initiative or his own we do not

---

[3]  The nearest approach to a fictitious letter is the recension of his treatise *De Hierosolymitana peregrinatione* which is addressed to different dignitaries of the English church in different manuscripts. (For one pair of addressees, see *PL* 207: 1057.) This call for a crusade had originally been part of a larger work, which Peter took to pieces after the death of Henry II on 6 July 1189. But, though it had not originally been written as a letter, it is quite likely that he circulated it to officials in various dioceses in an attempt to stir up enthusiasm for the crusade. For an account of the circumstances in which this work was written and adapted to form a letter, see my essay, 'Peter of Blois and the Third Crusade', in *Studies in Medieval History Presented to R.H.C. Davis*, ed. H. Mayr-Harting and R.I. Moore (London, 1985), pp. 208, 213, 217.

[4]  Although the title 'archdeacon' is sometimes added unwarrantably in the late MSS, the best manuscripts are punctilious in reproducing the original addresses, and their consensus can confidently be accepted.

know – an instruction in the Christian religion for the sultan of Iconium. He had probably just been offered, and had refused, the minor bishopric of Rochester, which had been vacant between July and October 1182. Life had never looked brighter for him and after a long struggle he was very pleased with himself.[5]

*Ep*. 77 fully expresses his self-satisfaction. Its main point was to stake out the writer's claim to have reached an eminence comparable to that of his namesake and 'dearest master'. Since one important purpose of the letter-collection was to teach correct modes of address, the writer did not use such titles carelessly, and we may take it that his namesake had in fact been his master, perhaps in his home town of Blois before he went further afield to study at Tours under Bernard Silvestris. Alternatively, the recipient of the letter may himself have been a master in Tours under Bernard Silvestris. At all events, when the letter-writer wrote *Ep*. 77, he felt that he had reached a plateau from which he could address his former master as an equal:

> If [he wrote] a man of inferior life or humbler fame were to share our name, we would have to earn more honour to make up for the deficiency. But the honour which I add to our common name by accumulating revenues and enjoying the familiarity of magnates and by my writings, you too enlarge in similar or even more elegant ways. Our name and writings are diffused throughout the world so that neither flood nor fire can destroy them.

This is the self-satisfied theme of the whole letter. A notable feature of the boasting lies in its assurance that *writing* is the road to fame both for himself and his namesake, and also for those who were immortalised in their writings – particularly in his own. He unashamedly portrays his namesake and himself seeking glory by leaving writings which will last for ever.

From this happy scene we turn to the later of the two letters, *Ep*. 76. The difference of mood and attitude to his namesake is very conspicuous. It reflects the mood of all that he wrote after his return to England from the Third Crusade in 1192: old, ill, without a patron, without any important employment, turning his mind increasingly to a life of religion, especially to the ideals of the Cistercian and Carthusian Orders. In this letter he says that he had already sent his namesake several other letters with a similar message of admonition, but since he did not include them in his letter-collection we may take it that they added nothing to the facts which he wished the reader to know. Nevertheless, his namesake is represented as having answered one of these letters, reiterating his intention of continuing his chosen studies and deriding the letter-writer's addiction to the Bible. It was this reply which had inspired the full-scale denunciation of his former master's chosen studies contained in the later of the two letters to him, *Ep*. 76.

The message of this new letter was that he now looked on himself as having

---

[5]  *PL* 207: 238A.

diverged from his namesake in almost every respect. While his former tutor – ignoring all the advice given him in intermediate letters – had continued to relate the fables and loves of Hercules and Jove and other pagan deities, to study the philosophers and canon law, and to deride theology, the letter-writer had taken on the task of cultivating the truths of religion and of forming others in virtue. This new stance led to the criticisms of his master with which the second letter was filled:

> Quid tibi ad vanitates et insanias falsas? Quid tibi ad deorum gentilium fabulosos amores, qui debueras esse organum veritatis? . . . Et quae insania est de Hercule et Jove canere fabulosa, et a Deo qui est via, veritas et vita, recedere? . . . In fabulis paganorum, in philosophorum studiis, tandem in iure civili dies tuos usque in senium expendisti et, contra omnium te diligentium voluntatem, sacram theologiae paginam damnabiliter horruisti . . . Quid tibi ad Jovem et ad Herculem? . . . Ego quidem nugis et cantibus venereis quandoque operam dedi, sed per gratiam eius qui me segregavit ab utero matris meae reieci haec omnia a primo limine iuventutis . . . Omitte penitus cantus inutiles et aniles fabulas et naenias pueriles! Illud mihi maxime vertitur in stuporem unde tibi materia cantandi possit erumpere quem inter anxietates innumeras video constitutum . . . Hoc unum precor ut, omissis inanibus scribas quae theologicam sapiant gravitatem, quae ad honestatem fructificent et aedificent ad salutem.[6]

These sentences come from all parts of *Ep.* 76 and illustrate the passionate vigour and consistency of the expostulation to his old master. He continued to express all his old admiration for his master's learning and eloquence, but he wholly deprecated the levity which kept him in his former courses and led to his continuing to call the Bible 'insipid and infantile'.

This remonstrance was the main theme of the letter. A secondary theme was the blindness to reality which led his namesake to persist in his old ways despite the manifold disasters which had befallen his family. His elder brother, John, his younger brother, Gerard, and his nephew, Nicholas, had all died; and his other brother, Haimo, was in prison. How (the writer asks) in the midst of such disasters could his namesake continue his inanities?

There is ample evidence that the letter-writer himself had followed the course he recommends. Increasingly his works show evidence of the study of theology, and of giving his mind to serious theological and religious problems. He had turned from his admiration of Henry II, and his acceptance of the aims of secular government, to a close attachment to the ideals of Cistercian and Carthusian monasticism. As for his family, we know that he had only one brother, William, who was a monk, and several sisters, whose sons were rather

---

[6] *PL* 207: 232B-C, 233A, 234A-B, 237A-B. For *aniles fabulas*, see I Tim. 4:7; for *naenias pueriles*, Horace, *Ep.* i, 1, 62; for the disasters to his namesake's family, see below and p. 111.

troublesome, and that he himself was the sole heir to his father's property.[7]

It is only by ignoring all that we know of the letter-writer's family and the well-known works of his later life, and by attributing to him writings displaying interests quite different from any for which we have evidence in his known works, that it is possible to argue that – far from having abandoned the kind of conduct and its associated writings which he ascribes to his namesake – the letter-writer had secretly continued to write poetry which circulated without his name, but to which (in the guise of his *alter ego*) he now puts forward a kind of clandestine claim.

Besides, despite Dronke's doubts, there certainly was another contemporary Peter of Blois with interests and personality which fit the account given in the two letters *Epp*. 77 and 76.

## Characteristics of the 'Other' Peter of Blois

In establishing the identity of the 'other' Peter of Blois, it is first necessary to take into account an initially confusing fact: they were both canons of Chartres. Yet, on examination, this initial similarity, far from uniting them, emphasises their difference.

To deal first with the letter-writer, it had been one of his earliest ambitions to become a canon of Chartres and he believed that, after his return from Sicily in 1169, he had had a promise of a canonry from the bishop of Chartres, who was also at this time archbishop of Sens.[8] To his chagrin, this promise had not been kept and he had had reluctantly to go to England to make his career. Several years later, however, John of Salisbury, who was bishop of Chartres from 1176 to 1179, gave him a canonry at Chartres and the letter-writer wrote to thank him for it in effusive terms.[9] In a later letter, he wrote again to defend himself against the accusation of using his influence with various lay

---

[7]  For the changes of the letter-writer's attitudes to the royal court and to the religious life I must provisionally refer the reader to what I have written on this subject in *Medieval Humanism and Other Studies*, pp. 107-24, and in *Studies in Medieval History Presented to R.H.C. Davis*, ed. H. Mayr-Harting and R.I. Moore (London, 1985), pp. 207-219. For the letter-writer's brother William, see *Ep*. 90; for one of his nephews, *Ep*. 12; and for a brief account of his family the following extract from an unpublished letter (which, with many other unpublished letters, will soon appear in E. Revell, *The Later Letters of Peter of Blois*, in *Auctores Britannici medii aevi*): 'Pater meus in territorio Blesensi nihil patrimoniale habuit, sed acquisivit industria sua unde omnes filias suas honorifice maritavit, singulique in earum maritagio assignans de possessionibus suis quantum potuit et velle debuit et prout ipsum decuit. Me omnium bonorum suorum quae superant publice et solemniter heredem constituit'. Erfurt, Amplonian MS F.70, fo. 190, for which (pending the appearance of E. Revell's edition of these letters) see R.W. Southern, 'Some New Letters of Peter of Blois', *English Historical Review* (London, 1938), pp. 412-24.

[8]  In *Ep*. 128, to William, archbishop of Sens (1168-76), who also continued to act as bishop of Chartres (1166-76), Peter writes of his great desire for a prebend at Chartres which the archbishop had promised, but failed to give him. *Ep*. 72 has more on the same subject.

[9]  See *Ep* 70, to John of Salisbury, who was then bishop of Chartres, in which Peter calls himself *canonicus tuus* and expresses his sense of obligation in effusive terms.

magnates in an attempt to get the deanery of Chartres.[10] In this attempt he failed; and there is no sign that he ever had a residential position at Chartres or that his canonry carried with it any significant function or emolument. He remained to the end of his life just one non-resident canon of Chartres among the large body of seventy-six canons.

The situation of the other Peter of Blois with regard to Chartres was quite different. He was not only a canon but also active in diocesan administration and, for some time at least, as archdeacon of Dreux, one of the four archdeacons of the diocese.[11] And he hated it. We know about his feelings on this subject because he wrote a *Speculum iuris canonici* with a preface in which he describes his situation at Chartres and his feelings about it.[12] In this preface, he represents himself as a new Prometheus chained to the Caucasian mountain, keeping his free mind fixed on the stars while an eagle tears at his entrails. And what was the rock to which he was punitively chained? It was the cathedral of Chartres. The stars among which his free mind moves as he attempts to alleviate the burden of his office at Chartres are the pagan myths of antiquity; and, as a further cure for the tedium of his official life at Chartres, he has written the work on canon law, of which this account of his position forms part of the preface.

It is at once obvious that the position, interests and outlook of the writer of this preface bear no relation to those held or expressed by the letter-writer in any of his vastly voluminous works. But they are entirely in keeping with the description of his namesake given in *Ep.* 76, in which the letter-writer deplores

---

[10] See *Ep.* 130, also to John of Salisbury as bishop of Chartres. Peter defends himself against this charge.

[11] A Peter of Blois witnesses several charters as a member of the chapter of Chartres. On some occasions this may be the letter-writer, but certainly not the one in which he is called archdeacon of Dreux. (See *Collection de cartulaires chartrains*, ed. R. Merlet and M. Jusselin in *Archives d'Eure-et-Loir*, 2 vols. 1906-9, p. 53.) I owe this reference to Prof. Elizabeth Revell.

[12] *Petri Blesensis Speculum iuris canonici*, ed. T.A. Reimarus, (Berlin, 1837), p. 1. On this work, see S. Kuttner, *Repertorium der Kanonistik (1140-1234), Studi e testi*, 71 (Città del Vaticano, 1937), p. 220, where it is dated about 1180, but chiefly on 'biographical grounds', which seem to be non-existent. So far as internal evidence goes, any date between about 1175 and 1190 would be possible. I quote here the words in the preface in which the author describes his position at Chartres:

Prometheus in Caucasi montis cacumine religatus, quamvis iecur eius a vulture perhenniter roderetur, inter haec tamen supplicia ad astrorum circuitus excubabat. Animi enim libertatem carcer corporeus non inclusit. Ut igitur utar simplicitate bucolica qua dicitur, 'urbem quam dicunt Romam, Melibee, putavi stultus ego, huic nostre similem'; et infra, 'sic magnis componere parva solebam', me quidem Prometheo, Carnotum Caucaso, vulturi muneris iniuncti solicitudinem audeo comparare. A domestico enim revocatus exilio, a scolasticis semotus deliciis, Carnotensemque detrusus in carcerem, vitam consumpsissem penitus ociosam nisi torporem quibusdam operi(bu)s exercuissem. Assidua igitur lectione, voluminibus legum et canonum revolutis, varias inter canones rebellionum insidias apprehendi, diligentiam scrutabundus adhibui ut inter illam canonum repugnantiam quarundem distinctionum remedio pacis federa reformarem.

his namesake's addiction to pagan myths, philosophical studies and Roman Law, and begs him to turn (as the letter-writer himself had done) to theology and the study of the Bible. The contrast between the witty, brilliant, rebellious canon of Chartres, who sought relief from business in pagan myths, in the study of law and in erotic poetry, on the one hand, and the letter-writer, who in all his known works displays a deep commitment to the conventional ideals of his time – the crusade, orderly government with due recognition of the rights of clerical and secular interests, a thorough immersion in biblical language and imagery and a growing commitment to Cistercian and Carthusian religious ideals – is brilliantly illuminated in the contrast between the whole body of the letter-writer's voluminous works and the preface of the *Speculum iuris canonici* written by his namesake.

So far as I can judge, the contents of the *Speculum* have the same imprint of a mind widely different from that of the letter-writer. It would need a lawyer to judge its qualities accurately, but it does not need a lawyer to see that it is a work stamped with great lucidity and individuality of style, exhibiting at least as much knowledge of Roman as of Canon law, and remarkable for its paucity of quotations from the Bible. In looking through the work, I have noticed only one biblical quotation: 'Sit sermo vester, Est, Est; Non, Non' (Matthew 5:37).[13] No doubt a diligent search would reveal others, but the brevity of this one is characteristic of the writer and provides a strong contrast to the style of the letter-writer. This contrast, combined with the allusions in the preface to pagan myths and his hatred of the ecclesiastical business which chained him to the cathedral of Chartres, confirms the picture of him drawn by the letter-writer in *Ep.* 76.

One further point can be added. The letter-writer's appeal to his former master to change his way of life was partly based on the disasters which had befallen the other Peter of Blois's family: his elder brother, John, his younger brother, Gerard, and his nephew, Nicholas, had all died, and his other brother, Haimo, was in prison. These details, as I have already pointed out, are totally unlike anything we know of the letter-writer's family.[14]

In addition, therefore, to the contrast between the minds, interests and writings of the two Peters of Blois, the details about their respective families provide further evidence for distinguishing between the two men. We could of course have wished for more, but there is enough to establish, first, that there were two contemporary Peters of Blois whose interests and careers, despite some basic similarities, were demonstrably different; and, second, that the two

---

[13] *Speculum iuris canonici*, p. 66. It may also be noted that, on p. 63, he quotes the Golden Rule in a non-biblical form: 'Scriptum est enim, *Ne facias alii, quod tibi non vis fieri*'.

[14] For details, see above, pp. 6-7 and n. 7.

letters we have been considering can only be understood in the light of these differences.

## The Poetry of the Two Peters of Blois

It is necessary in the first place to understand the nature of these two letters, and to accept the real existence of the other Peter of Blois, in order to understand the writer of these letters and his aim in collecting them. But there is a further reason for distinguishing the two characters who have the same name: they both wrote poetry, and we must ask whether any, and how much, of their poetry has survived.

The essential evidence that the letter-writer was also a poet is found in several places in the letter-collection itself. Besides the statement in *Ep*. 76 quoted above, there is an early letter (*Ep*. 12), in which he asked his nephew to send him 'versus et ludicra quae feci Turonis'. Since it was at Tours that he had his earliest mature education in literature and letter-writing in the 1140s, we may presume that the 'versus et ludicra' belonged to that period of his life. Although he described these pieces as 'trifles', they were sufficiently important for him to wish to copy them and to promise to return them to his nephew when copied. So far as we know, they have not survived.

Then in *Ep*. 57, which first appears in the second edition of his letter-collection of 1189 and was probably written between 1184 and 1189, he provides the main evidence for his poetry. The letter was written in reply to a friend who, having become a monk, had asked him for some titillating reading to relieve his tedium. The essential passage runs thus:

> Quod autem amatoria iuventutis et adolescentiae nostrae ludicra postulas ad solatium tediorum, consiliosum non arbitror cum talia temptationes excitare soleant et fovere. Omissis ergo lascivioribus cantilenis, pauca quae maturiore stilo cecini tibi mitto si te forte relevent a tedio et edificent ad salutem.[15]

In the letter-collection of 1189, the poems attached to the letter consisted of only nine stanzas. They are always printed as a single poem, but they could equally well, or better, be regarded as a series of poetic *pensées* on the theme of turning from lascivious thoughts to more mature reflections. Entirely appropriate though they are to the theme of the letter, they are very meagre, and in the fourth edition of his letters of about 1198 Peter of Blois added four more

---

[15] *PL* 207:172C. In the first line, I have corrected the *vestrae* of the printed edition to *nostrae*, which has the support of all good MSS. The texts enclosed in this letter are the verses beginning *Olim militaveram*, *PL* 207: 1127-30.

poems, two on the corruptions of the clergy, one on the capture of Richard I by the duke of Austria, and one on the folly of court life. The poem on King Richard's captivity was certainly written in 1193 and the others are probably of a similar date. We can only suppose that, in making a new edition of his letters, Peter took the opportunity to fill out the meagre display of his poetic talent in the earlier edition by adding these recent examples of his serious poetry.[16]

In addition to these verses, which are preserved in recensions of the letter-collection made in the writer's life-time, there are a few other poems which were inserted in collections of the letters made in the fourteenth and fifteenth centuries. On the surface these later additions have very little authority, but it is clear that some late medieval collectors of the letters had access to the writer's literary remains and some of the additional *letters* which collectors added to the letter-collection are undoubtedly genuine. Whether this is true of any of the additional *poems* is much more doubtful, and I shall do no more than list them at the end of this essay.

Apart from these poems preserved in the letter-collection, three further poems are known which have the name of Peter of Blois attached to them in medieval manuscripts. Two of these are poems in praise of wine as against beer, found in a late medieval English manuscript. They consist of seventeen lines of rhymed hexameters in praise of wine by Peter of Blois, which are answered at similar length by a canon of Salisbury, Robert de Bellofago, in praise of beer. These are then followed by fifteen elegiac couplets in praise of wine by Peter and a roughly comparable number of verses in praise of beer by his opponent.[17]

Finally, there is a fragment of another poem independently preserved and attributed to the letter-writer in his life-time. It denounces the flatteries and rumours of court life. Only a few lines have survived in a polemical work written in or near Cologne in 1206. Dronke has for the first time made metrical sense of this fragment and rightly associates it in style – and, one can also add, in sentiment – with the poems attached to *Ep.* 57 in the edition of 1198. The full text has not come to light, but the attribution of the fragment by the contemporary German writer is very explicit; we may accept it as a unique

---

[16] The verses added in the later recension of the letter are the four (or five on Dronke's reckoning) poems beginning 'Qui habet aures audiet, In nova fert animus, Quis aquam tuo capiti, Quod amicus suggerit', in *PL* 207: 1127-36; in Dronke's list, nos. 35, 19, 38, 40; for an important text, and analysis of the last, see pp. 206-13 of his article.

[17] For the texts, see E. Braunholz, 'Die Streitgedichte Petrus von Blois und Robert von Beaufeu (de Bellofago) über dem Wert des Wein und Bier', *Zeitschrift für Romanische Philologie*, 47 (1927), pp. 30-38; with additions in A. Wilmart, 'Une suite au poème de Robert de Beaufeu pour l'éloge de la cervoise, *Rev. Bénédictine*, 50 (1938), pp. 136-40.

illustration of the wide circulation of some of the verses of the letter-writer during his lifetime.[18]

No other poems with medieval ascriptions, either to the letter-writer or to his namesake, have so far come to light. Despite this, a new age of conjectural attributions began in 1929. The initial impetus for this development probably came from Karl Strecker's edition of the poems of the most famous of late twelfth-century poets, Walter of Chatillon, which appeared in 1925. In this edition Strecker gave for the first time a reliable text of a survey of contemporary learning, which Walter of Chatillon had delivered as a sermon to the students of Bologna, probably in about 1174. In this survey Walter mentions no names of authors except in the sub-section of grammar in which he lists four outstanding writers of rhythmical verse: Stephen of Orleans, Peter of Blois, Berterus and Walter himself. No doubt his reason for mentioning names at all at this point was to stake out his own claim to fame as a poet, and of the four whom he mentions, it is only his own poetry that has survived in any quantity.[19]

The work leading up to Strecker's edition had one important consequence in stimulating interest in the poetical remains of Peter of Blois. Unfortunately, no one seems to have considered the possibility that the Peter of Blois to whom Walter of Chatillon was referring may have been the recipient of *Epp.* 76 and 77 rather than the letter-writer. Yet that is surely the first problem raised by this passage. When he wrote *Ep.* 77 in 1182-84, the letter-writer regarded his master and namesake as the better-known of the two Peters of Blois, and he may well have been the poet to whom Walter of Chatillon referred. Be that as it may, all the suggestions that have so far been made have had the letter-writer and not his namesake in mind. I shall now briefly review them with the alternative possibility in mind.

The earliest of the new suggestions came in the first volume of Hilka and Schumann's new edition of the *Carmina Burana*, published in 1930. In this volume the editors pointed out some striking similarities between the language and style of three poems in the *Carmina Burana* and those which Peter of Blois had added to *Ep.* 57. These three poems, beginning respectively with the words: 'In lacu miserie . . .'; 'Dum iuventus floruit . . .'; and 'Vitae perditae me legi subdideram . . .' have the same theme as the verses attached to the

[18] The fragment is quoted in a *Dialogus clerici et laici contra persecutores ecclesiarum* written in the neighbourhood of Cologne in about 1206. In the course of the debate, the *clericus* quotes Peter of Blois: 'Dictator ille egregius magister Petrus Blesensis archidiaconus dixit: Mide regis vicio/ aures gerunt asini /magni rerum domini, /quibus adulatio /palpat late patulas /auriculas /et humani bibulas /favoris, /ausi de se credere /quicquid potest fingere /vox adulatoris.'

For the dialogue in which these verses appear see G. Waitz, *Chronica regia Coloniensis, MGH, SS rerum Germanicarum in usum scholarum*, xciii (1880) p. 321. The only connection between the dialogue and the chronicle is that they were both written in the neighbourhood of Cologne. It may be noted as characteristic of the letter-writer that these lines are an echo of John of Salisbury's *Policraticus*, iii, c. 12 (in Webb's edition, i, pp. 213-15). For the verse form, see Dronke, no. 52.

[19] *Moralisch-satirische Gedichte Walters von Chatillon aus Deutschen, Englischen, Französischen und Italienischen HSS*, ed. Karl Strecker (Heidelberg, 1929), p. 41: for the date, see p. 37.

first edition of *Ep*. 57.[20] Despite their anonymity in the *Carmina Burana*, and the absence of any medieval attributions to Peter of Blois, these poems have a similarity of style, phraseology and subject-matter which makes the attribution to the letter-writer very attractive. The only oddity is that the letter-writer should not himself have added them to *Ep*. 57. Despite this, these additions fit so well into the pattern of the letter-writer's habits of thought and expression that they can be accepted without much hesitation.

The same cannot be said of the next suggestion which has been generally accepted. The suggestion was made in 1934 by F.J.E. Raby, with the support of Dom Wilmart and with a hint that there might be more to follow, that a poem long ago printed by H. Hagen from a Berne manuscript might very well also be the work of Peter of Blois. It was addressed to King Henry II and began:

> Post dubiam,
> post nugatoriam
> fortunae gloriam,
> post opes Siculas,
> convertor anxius . . .[21]

The poem is a plea for patronage from someone who had recently returned from Sicily. Since it was well known that Peter of Blois had returned from an ill-fated venture in Sicily in 1169, Raby ascribed it to him with some confidence. It too has very generally been added to the list of the letter-writer's poems, and it is accepted by Dronke.[22] But there is a fatal snag which has not, so far as I know, been generally noticed. In the course of the poem, the author mentions that Henry II's younger son had been named as king of Ireland, and this did not happen until 1177. But by this date Peter of Blois was firmly established in the household of the archbishop of Canterbury and in high favour with Henry II. So, attractive though the suggestion seems at first sight, the attribution to the letter-writer cannot stand, despite the similarity in style and general situation.[23]

This provides a warning which needs to be heeded in all these attributions. When a fashion of verse has gained favour, whether the rhythmical versification of the twelfth century, the metaphysical fashion of the seventeenth, or the romantic fashion of the early nineteenth, it is remarkable how quickly it can be successfully adopted by several authors. This has been insufficiently

---

[20] *Carmina Burana*, ed. Alfons Hilka and Otto Schumann (Heidelberg, 1930), 1, nos. 29, 30, 31; for notes and sources, see 2 (1930) pp. 42-49.

[21] For the text, see H. Hagen, *Carmina medii aevi* (Berne, 1877), pp. 183-86. For Raby's suggestion, see F.J.E. Raby, *A History of Secular Latin Poetry in the Middle Ages* (Oxford, 1934), ii, pp. 141-42.

[22] No. 31 in Dronke's list.

[23] The reference to the king of Ireland and its consequence for dating the poem was noticed by Dom Laporte in *Revue Mabillon*, 43 (1953), p. 5n., who suggested William of Blois as the author, certainly mistakenly.

taken into account in attributions to the letter-writing Peter of Blois even when the argument of style and content seems fairly strong.

Worse was to follow – this time from a source than which none could be more distinguished. In 1945, in the second volume of his catalogue of the *Reginenses* manuscripts in the Vatican Library, Dom Wilmart initiated a new phase in hypothetical attributions. In describing four *rythmi seu cantilenae delicatiore forma distinctae* in MS *Reginensis* 344, fo 36/r-v he tentatively attributed them also to Peter of Blois, the letter-writer. It will suffice for present purposes if I simply list the titles and first lines of the poems in question:

1. *De gestis Herculis*

beg. *Olim sudor Herculis / monstra late conferens . . . Carmina Burana*, ed. A. Hilka and O. Schumann (Heidelberg, 1941), vol. 2, no. 63; see also A. Wilmart, 'Le florilège mixte de Thomas Bekynton, *Mediaeval and Renaissance Studies*, i (London, 1940), p. 62. Dronke no. 27.

2. *De amica cuiusdam clerici*

beg. *Sevit aure spiritus / et arborum . . .*
(*Carmina Burana*, vol. 2, no. 83) Dronke no. 43.

3. *Hic monet contemnere divitias*

beg. *Divitie si affluant / nolite cor apponere . . .*
(ed. Wattenbach, *Anzeiger f. Kunde der deutscher Vorzeit*, 22 (1875), p. 120, and B. Hauréau, *Notices et extraits des manuscrits de la Bibliothèque Nationale*, vol. 29, ii, pp. 313-14.) Dronke omits.

4. *De virginis rapta virginitate . . .*

beg. *Dum prius inculta / colerem virgulta*
(*Carmina Burana*, no. 84.) Dronke omits.

Even these slight indications of subject matter make it clear that three of the four (nos. 1, 2, 4) are erotic poems with a leaning towards pagan fables. All three appear in the section *Liebeslieder* in the Hilka-Schumann edition of the *Carmina Burana*. Dronke claims nos. 1 and 2 for the letter-writer and ignores the other two. Yet, in the light of the description of the 'other' Peter of Blois's interests in his own preface to his work on canon law and in *Ep*. 76, it would be more reasonable to consider attributing nos. 1, 2, and 4 to the *recipient* of this letter, and only no. 3 to the letter-writer. Nos. 1, 2, and 4 have the wit, the knowledge of classical myths and the lubricity, which the letter-writer attributes to his old master and namesake, and which are partly displayed in the preface to the *Speculum iuris canonici*. No.3 has the serious purpose, which the letter-writer expresses abundantly in his letters. It is also possible, perhaps more likely, that none are to be attributed to either of the two Peters of Blois.

I have not the learning necessary for pursuing the question of attributions beyond this point. My only purposes in pursuing it thus far are, first, to point out the dangers of any attributions made only on stylistic grounds; second, to emphasise the need, in making any further attributions, to bear in mind the different characteristics of the two Peters of Blois as exhibited in their other writings, and as described in the letter-writer's *Epp*. 76 and 77; and, third, to suggest that Dronke's long list of poems which he claims as being 'probably' by the letter-writer, like Wilmart's short list of nearly sixty years ago, are valueless as indicators of authorship, despite the great contribution that Dronke's article makes to our understanding of these texts in themselves.

If the facts set out in this essay are accepted, no more progress can be made until the distinction between the two Peters of Blois is taken seriously as the basis of any further conjectures. I suggest that the only poems which can at present be fairly confidently attributed to the letter-writer are the following:

1. The poems attached to *Ep*. 57 in both its first and second recensions.
2. The poems in praise of wine, which are attributed to him and have a local context entirely consistent with what we know of his career and correspondents.
3. The fragment of the poem attributed to him in 1206 by the Cologne writer.
4. Probably also the three poems in *Carmina Burana* suggested by Hilka and Schumann in 1930, which are closely related in style and subject-matter to those attached to *Ep*. 57.

This conclusion does not of course diminish the importance or interest of Dronke's list of poems as expressions of a phase in the history of medieval learning and literature. Nor does it diminish the value of his editions, translations and comments on their subject matter. But, beyond the limits which I have indicated, his list cannot be used as evidence of the writings, interests or psychology of the letter-writer, and emphatically not (as Dronke supposes) for the interests and activities of the court of King Henry II.

*Appendix*

I add here references to additional verses found in late medieval manuscripts of Peter of Blois's letter-collection. Although they have no substantial authority, they may have been found among his literary remains:

1.  Oxford, Bodleian Library, MS Laud Misc. 650, fifteenth-century from Carthusians of Mainz, after *Ep*. 111, a poem beginning *Qui mea scripta leges*. Printed from this MS in Giles's edition of Peter of Blois's letters, but not in *PL*, nor in Dronke's list.

2.  London, BL, MS Harley 3672, fifteenth-century, a German MS from the diocese of Passau; after *Ep*. 15, with the rubric, 'Hec epistola continuatur cum praescripta et non habet rubricam nec etiam numerum epistolarum', a poem beginning:'Non te lusisse doleat,/ sed ludum non incidere . . . This poem is found in a thirteenth-century English MS, Bodl. 57. fo. 66 v. with the inscription, *Documenta clericorum Stefani de Lanketon*, and printed in F.M. Powicke, *Stephen Langton*, (Oxford, 1928), pp. 205-6. It is printed without author's name in *Carmina Burana*, no. 33. Dronke, no. 23, describes it as 'possibly Peter of Blois'.

# 9

# *Maio of Bari's Commentary on the Lord's Prayer**

## Donald Matthew

For many years historians have emphasised the part played by the royal court of Sicily in the cultural life of the twelfth-century kingdom.[1] Here it was possible for men of many different traditions to meet – Greek, Latin, Muslim and Hebrew, Lombard, French, Spanish and English. In this environment there was a demand for translations from works of several kinds and particularly from Greek or Arabic into Latin. The Norman kingdom has accordingly enjoyed an enviable reputation for cultural eclecticism. This impression of refinement in Sicily has been enhanced by modern appreciation of the buildings that survive from the period. The royal palace chapel in Palermo exemplifies this achievement best, with its Arabic-style painted roof and paving, its Greek mosaic wall-decoration and its Latin plan. Much less is known of the decoration provided for the living quarters of the royal palace and the royal pleasure pavilions, but enough is still visible to show in what lavish style the Norman kings entertained their court. To this the kings deliberately attracted men of learning and curiosity, some from quite distant lands. The intellectual quality of courtly society under William I was praised in the mid twelfth century by Henry Aristippus, archdeacon of Catania. He says of William I that his court was 'schola comitatus, cuius singula verba philosophica apophthegmata, cuius questiones inextricabiles, cuius solutiones nichil indiscussum, cuius studium nil reliquit intemptatum'[2] Both Roger II and William I deserved credit for stimulating the intellectual life at court, but they were not

* The Bibliothèque Nationale in Paris made this study possible by preparing a microfilm for me of B.N., MS Nouv. Acq. Latin, 1772. I should like to acknowledge here the help I received in France from Professor Serge Chassagne and from Mademoiselle M.F. Rose. While writing this paper I obtained valuable advice from Dr. A.I. Doyle, Professor R.A. Markus and Dr. Nigel Palmer. Without their generous responses to my enquiries I would not have been able to proceed very far.
[1] C.H. Haskins *Studies in the History of Medieval Science* (Cambridge, MA, 1924), pp. 141-42, 185-87. G. Sarton *Introduction to the History of Science* ii/1 (Baltimore, 1931) p. 119.
[2] V. Rose 'Die Lücke im Diogenes Laertius und der alte Ubersetzer' *Hermes Zeitschrift für classische Philologie* i (1866) pp. 367-97.

the only ones to patronise art or learning. Some works of translation, for example, were also commissioned by others, like Hugh, archbishop of Palermo, and by the royal chief minister under William I, Maio of Bari. Maio appears to have encouraged several young scholars. The Tuscan canonist Laborante, who was made a canon of Capua in Maio's time (probably under Archbishop Hugh's patronage) dedicated to Maio a treatise *De iustitia et iusto*.[3] He later became a cardinal and probably remained a friend of the kingdom at the papal curia. Maio and Hugh jointly commissioned from Henry Aristippus a translation of Diogenes Laertius's work on the ancient philosophers: *De vita et conversatione dogmataque philosophorum*.[4] Aristippus probably owed his appointment as archdeacon to Maio, who had been responsible for the political disgrace of the previous archdeacon, the chancellor Aschettin. After Maio's death, Aristippus briefly assumed his place in William I's counsels. Maio's importance for the culture of the royal court was properly stressed by Valentin Rose, who first published the prologues written by Aristippus for his two Platonic translations into Latin of the *Meno* and the *Phaedo*, but Maio's role as politician has rather effaced his intellectual reputation.[5] Maio began his career as a professional notary and, when he became a royal minister, inevitably brought with him from the mainland some of the characteristic interests of notaries in law and Latin composition. Unlike most of the men associated with the court who were translators, rather than authors in their own right, Maio did actually write an original work of some length himself. Probably because it was a work of piety, a commentary on the Lord's Prayer, little interest has been shown in it. Most scholars attracted to a study of the Norman court have stressed its strongly secular outlook and the evidence of its interest in the classical past. Yet it is surely not necessary to argue a case for examining this work. Any book written by such an important figure as Maio deserves attention, however out of character it may seem at first sight for the strong man of mid twelfth-century Sicily to be instructing his son about the meaning of his prayers.

Maio of Bari is best known to historians from the *Liber de regno*, the extraordinary chronicle of twelfth-century Sicily that presented Maio as the

---

[3]  *Laborantis cardinalis opuscula*, ed. A. Landgraf, Florilegium Patristicum, fasc. xxxii (Bonn, 1932). The *De iustitia et iusto* was printed on pp. 6-42. All the opuscula were printed from the twelfth-century manuscript in Rome at St. Peter's: chapter archive 110 C. Laborante was born at Pontormo (Florence) before 1130 and died in Rome *c.* 1191.

[4]  See Rose, n. 2 above.

[5]  The prologues to the Meno and Phaedo of Plato from the old translation were printed by Rose, *Diogenes Laertius*, pp. 386-89 and reprinted by Hartwig (see n. 12 below). The text of the Prologue to the Phaedo was supplied by the fifteenth-century manuscript at Corpus Christi College, Oxford, n. 243.

all-powerful minister of William who actually plotted to take his throne.[6] Although the chronicler had respect for Maio's undoubted abilities, he concentrated on presenting him as an upstart cordially detested by the baronage, not so much for his alleged disloyalty to the king, but for his own hostility to themselves and for the promotion of his own family and cronies to important offices in the kingdom. The chronicle claims that he was of low birth (*humili ortum genere*)[7] and reports that one of his political enemies jeered at him as a former oil-merchant (*dudum olei venditorem*).[8] The exact significance of this remark has been lost, but Maio's father was in fact Leo de Terza, chief royal justice in Bari) *regalis Bariensium protojudex*), which presumably gave Maio a good start in the legal profession. Aspersions cast on his social rank by the chronicler are further proof of how much Maio was disliked; they do not need to be true to be revealing. The hostility of the baronage to him arose because of the undoubted influence Maio exerted over King William I and the prominence of his family, friends and protégés in the government of the kingdom. In their hatred of Maio's manipulation of the state, his political opponents found no difficulty about interpreting his actual conduct as evidence of his unprincipled ambition. Although it is not possible to prove that Maio neither plotted

---

[6] *La Historia o Liber de regno Sicilie di Ugo Falcando*, ed. G.B. Siragusa, Fonti per la Storia d'Italia (Rome, 1897). According to this text Maio was 'monstrum utique nulla pestis immanior, nulla ad regni perniciem ac subversionem poterat efficacior inveniri'. Nevertheless the author immediately provided Maio with an impressive testimonial: 'nam ingenium illi promptum erat ad omnia; facundia non dispar ingenio; simulandi ac dissimulandi que vellet summa facilitas . . . dominandi quoque semel accensus desiderio, multa volvebat in animo, multis mentem fatigabat consiliis et continuis scelerum stimulis agebatur, sed estuantis animi tempestatem vultus serenitate celebat' (p. 8); he is also contrasted advantageously with Matthew of Salerno who aspired to take his place after his death: Matthew 'disposuerat admirati ritus et consuetudines imitari, omnibusque se prebens affabilem, eis maxime quos oderat arridebat ipsumque regem adulationibus iam ceperat demulcere, sciens ob id ipsum Maionem si maxime placuisse. Largitatem vero Maionis . . . imitari non poterat nec illi se, cum impeditionis esset lingue facundia similem exhibere' (p. 84). The passage omitted from the first quotation relates to Maio's lascivious interest in the matrons and virgins of the nobility and in the context was intended to besmirch Maio's reputation. If he was as successful as the chronicler indicates, even this could be interpreted to show that Maio was attractive to some women and helps to round off the character sketch. Maio was a man of many parts.

[7] *Liber de regno*, p. 7. Of his father, the judge Leo, the chronicle also says: 'oleum Bari vendere consueverat' (p. 17).

[8] *Liber*, p. 33. Roger de Marturano referred to him as 'notarius . . . dudum olei venditorem'. This could be interpreted to mean that Maio was, like his father, a small shop-keeper or ambulant salesman; anyway a man of very modest social origins. But something different may also be intended. Laborante in his treatise *De vera libertate*, addressed to Archbishop Hugh, makes passing reference not only to *unctione venditorum olei* but also to *olei venditrix*, where the sense requires not so much a literal meaning but a metaphorical one, such as flatterers, or possibly greedy favourites, or even venal judges, since they sell oiliness for gain. *Oleum* was used in classical Latin for more than the vegetable product; it was used as the equivalent of sweat or effort derived from the use of oil for sporting purposes. The Christian Fathers used *oleum* metaphorically to mean balm or comfort. The range of meanings was considerable and it would be quite unimaginative to suppose that nothing more than a vendor of olive oil was being belittled here.

to overthrow William I nor aspired to take his place, both charges seem far-fetched. William I was both lethargic and indifferent to public business, which left Maio to enjoy real power without incurring additional risks from attempted usurpation. This makes the chronicler's suspicions of the minister seem extravagant, but since the chronicler was a sharp observer of the royal court and kept his ears and eyes open, it is not legitimate to set aside his theory of Maio's treachery without advancing some plausible explanation for the detestation Maio inspired.

Maio's eminence was in two respects unusual and this could have contributed to his unpopularity. First, he rose in the royal secretariat from the relatively humble role of *scrinarius*. He seized his chances when they came to secure promotion in turn to the offices of vice-chancellor (at least by 1149) and then, shortly before Roger II's death, of the chancellorship itself, finally becoming great admiral early in William I's reign.[9] Working one's way up may strike modern readers as no more than proper and even conventional, but under the Norman monarchy this was probably unusual or frowned on. Most strikingly Stephen of Perche, chancellor and chief minister under William II, was brought in from France to direct the government because he was a kinsman of the queen-regent. Maio's predecessor as chancellor was also a foreigner, the English clerk, Robert of Selby, who is not known to have been promoted to high office after long service lower down. Roger II's great admiral, George of Antioch, was another alien. Moreover, it is worth noting that the speed with which Maio moved from being vice-chancellor to chancellor is in strong contrast to the fate of Matthew of Salerno. Chief notary by 1160, he was made vice-chancellor in 1169 but only promoted to the chancellorship itself in 1190. This was not because his promotion was blocked by a long-lived incumbent: the office had been deliberately left vacant. In these circumstances, there may have been a prejudice against appointment to high office for upstarts. Such an attitude would help to explain why the *Liber de regno* insisted so much on Maio's humble birth. A notary born to a royal judge lacked the distinction of noble connections.

The second reason for Sicilian hostility to both Maio of Bari and Matthew of Salerno was probably that Lombards from the southern mainland were not trusted. Before Roger II claimed the succession to the duchy of Apulia in 1127, he had been surrounded in Sicily with men of Norman descent and relied for his government of the island, and of Calabria, on Greeks and Muslims. His mother, Adelaide, who came from north Italy, had introduced her relations into the island and encouraged emigrés from Liguria to settle there, but opportunities for men from the Lombard south to enter Roger's service only occurred long after her death. Roger is said by the Salerno chronicler to have been interested in obtaining men from many lands to serve him.[10] Some of these were from France or England and as French-speakers they would have encountered little hostility from the native (Norman) baronage. George of Antioch, likewise, presumably found a welcome amongst the other Greeks in Roger's government. Southern Lombards from the mainland could not count on comparable support. Sicilians considered all Apulians to be feckless and disloyal (*inconstantissima gens*),[11] a view surely based on their bitter impressions of the many campaigns Roger had had to mount in Apulia, particularly, as it happened, to secure the submission of Bari. For Maio to arrive in Palermo and so soon to make himself indispensable to the royal government was an outrage. When the new king William I began to leave Maio in sole charge of his affairs, this provoked a political explosion in the island. Maio nevertheless retained the king's confidence, weathered the storm, managed the policy of reconciliation with the papacy and the withdrawal from a militarily untenable position in north Africa. His political competence in looking after the interests of state till his assassination in November 1160 cannot seriously be questioned. Maio was able and outshone his opponents. Such a man could only be toppled by the dagger.

It is a matter of considerable regret that Maio must be studied historically as a politician from a chronicle committed to blackening his character. Attempts to rehabilitate him have been made in modern times once it was no longer thought reprehensible in principle to challenge the political ascendancy of the nobility. Hartwig published an extended essay on Maio in 1883,[12] about the same time as Siragusa worked on his book about William I, which first came out in 1885.[13] Maio figured prominently in this. By the time Siragusa, then in his eighties, published the second edition of this work in 1929, Maio's example seemed to him even more appropriate to the age. In a sad and muted preface he openly professed his admiration for Mussolini and saw in the *Duce* a man of the same kind as Maio: 'any one who studies their lives and work will perceive obvious parallels, particularly in the way both men roses so high from humble backgrounds and in their determination to make the nation (*patria*) great, respected and feared'. Both men worked within the framework of monarchy without ostensibly overthrowing it. The association made between the two by

---

[10] Romuald of Salerno, *Chronicon*, ed. C.A. Garufi, *Rerum Italicarum Scriptores*, vii, 1 (Città di Castello, 1914-35), p. 233: 'Quamvis autem predictus rex sapiencia ingenio et plurima discretione polleret tamen sapientes viros diversorum ordinum et e diversis mundi partibus evocatos suo faciebat consilio interesse . . . novissime Maionem iuvenem de Baro oriundum virum utique faciendum satis providum et discretum primo scrinarium dehinc . . . '

[11] *Liber de regno* (n. 6 above), p. 14.

[12] O. Hartwig 'Re Guglielmo e il suo grande ammiraglio Maione di Bari', *Archivio Storico per le provincie Napoletane* viii (1883), pp. 397-485.

[13] G.B. Siragusa, *Il regno di Guglielmo I in Sicilia* (Palermo, 1885; second edition 1929). Siragusa felt that Hartwig's article, published earlier, had stolen his thunder and made his book look derivative. His comparison of Maio with Mussolini occurs in the Avvertenza to the second edition, pp. 11-13.

Siragusa may have damaged Maio's chances of a more acceptable assessment since Mussolini's fall. Miss Jamison, who enthusiastically claimed him as an institutional innovator, typically inflated the evidence and made his father not only an eminent city-judge, but the wealthy proprietor of vast oliveyards in the neighbourhood.[14] No upstart Maio here. The study of Maio has, however, had at its disposal for many years a treatise of some 10,000 words from which further insight could have been derived. Some attempt is made here to show the interest of Maio's own contribution to learning.

Maio's exposition of the Lord's Prayer (*Expositio orationis dominice*) was written for his son Stephen as he entered into manhood, sometime between 1154, when Maio became great admiral (*magnus ammiratus*) and his death in 1160. According to the Salerno chronicle Maio was still young himself when he became the last of Roger's new men to be brought into government about 1144.[15] By the time the commentary was written, his son Stephen was already himself an 'emir' (*ammiratus*) and this seems to make it more likely that the work was finished nearer to 1160 than to 1154. Despite the somewhat pompous insistence on both their government titles, the text casts little light on Maio the man of state.[16] This is not to say, however, that it is without interest on its own terms and it can also be used as evidence not merely for Maio's own contribution to the culture of the kingdom, but for what it reveals about that culture as a whole. The commentary has never been published complete. Though Hartwig made no comments on the work itself in his essay, he printed, in an appendix to it, the text of it as known to him from a manuscript then at Turin, which has since been totally destroyed.[17] This manuscript may itself have been as defective as the printed text and it certainly lacked both a long section in the middle as well as in the final sections. Professor Buchtal was the first scholar to notice in print the existence of another and much better manuscript of the commentary.[18] This is now in Paris, where it was acquired

---

[14] E.M. Jamison, *Admiral Eugenius of Sicily* (London, 1957), p. 260.

[15] See n. 10.

[16] Its more interesting 'political' statements refer to the Roman church: 'Our mother the church, whose head is Christ' and God's offer of salvation 'to those of us in danger on the sea in St. Peter's ship'. Maio was one of the royal negotiators at Benevento in 1156 who secured a settlement with the papacy on terms widely recognised in the twelfth century as exceptionally favourable to the monarchy. The *Liber* makes no mention whatever of these important services rendered by Maio. As a devout churchman Maio must have been concerned to obtain papal friendship for the Norman kingdom; it may also have helped him to get a more sympathetic response from the papacy than Roger II had ever done.

[17] See n. 12 above. The text was printed pp. 461-85.

[18] H. Buchtal, 'The Beginnings of Manuscript Illumination in Norman Sicily' *Studies in Italian History Presented to Miss E.M. Jamison*, Papers of the British School at Rome, xxiv (n.s. xi) (1956), pp. 78-85. Paris, B.N., MS Nouv. Acq. Lat. 1772 is described pp. 79-82.

by the Bibliothèque Nationale in May 1897 from the sale of manuscripts belonging to the late Baron Jérôme Pichon.[19]

This manuscript appears to be a copy intended for presentation, with a handsome title-page and some fine illuminated initials to the text, which is written in double columns in a good clear twelfth-century hand, said to show foreign influences, but certainly made in Palermo.[20] In this manuscript the text of the commentary is complete and shows how much had been lost in the Turin text. Hartwig's version can also be corrected from the Paris manuscript. In some places words or phrases had been carelessly omitted and there are minor errors of spelling. Since the Turin manuscript is no longer available for study it is not possible to establish whether the mistakes of the printed version are all due to the faulty transcription or to the editor. It remains a possibility that some of the differences in the two versions need to be explained on the assumption that the Turin manuscript was not copied from the Paris manuscript itself, but from some other text now lost.

More surprising than the quality of this early manuscript of the commentary is the very existence of three others now in Austria. One early fifteenth-century manuscript at the university of Graz came from the Chorherrenstift at Seckau;[21] the others, at the monasteries of Göttweig and Admont, may have been written for those monasteries and kept there ever since.[22] The Admont copy is precisely dated by the scribe, 2 June 1400 (day of St. Erasmus, confessor).[23] How these copies came to be made in the later middle ages and from what exemplar they were copied cannot be shown. The Paris manuscript bears a note which has been interpreted to mean that it was held in a conventual library at Naples in the thirteenth century.[24] The most likely explanation for the Austrian copies is that they were made from a text in Italy, at a time when the monastic reforms of the fourteenth century brought many German monks south to such places as Subiaco. Erasmus was revered as a

[19] *Catalogue de la bibliothèque de feu M. le Baron Jérôme Pichon* (Paris, 1897) p. 5 n 17; *Bibliothèque de l'Ecole des Chartes*, lix, (1898), p. 99. F. Avril and Y. Zaluska, *Manuscrits enluminés d'origine italienne VI<sup>e</sup>-XII<sup>e</sup> siècles* (Paris, 1980), n. 39.

[20] S. Harrison Thomson, *Latin Bookhands of the Later Middle Ages, 1100-1500* (Cambridge, 1969), n. 59 'One might hazard the suggestion that the scriptorium out of which this codex came had undergone some non-Italian influence.'

[21] *Die Handschriften Universitätsbibliothek Graz* ed. A. Kern (Leipzig, 1939; Vienna, 1956), MS No. 1344, fos. 1-19.

[22] *Katalog der Handschriften im Stift Göttweig*, (Ann Arbor, MI, 1981) MS 128, fos. 93-100; *Katalog der Handschriften im Stift Admont*, (Ann Arbor, MI, 1981) MS 198, fos. 195-204. [These are hand-written catalogues of the eighteenth century only 'published' as photocopies from microfilm at Ann Arbor.]

[23] Admont, MS 198 fo. 204 r: 'Explicit expositio patris nostri script' anno cccc° in die sancti Erasmi conf'' (*sic*).

[24] See n. 19, Avril: 'ex libris effacé lu aux rayons u.v., *Hic liber est sanctissimi .. de Ne(a)p(o)li,* xiii-xiv.' There are also notes in the margins of this manuscript to show that it was still read attentively in the fifteenth century.

saint in Campania, so a German visitor who read the commentary and thought
it worth copying could have added the date in local form. There are many
general and unanswerable questions that naturally arise in this connection.
How widely known in the middle ages was Maio's commentary? With five
known manuscripts, however, Maio's text must already be regarded as a
success with readers of quite different backgrounds. If any further arguments
were still considered necessary, this conclusion should surely allay any linger-
ing doubts about the need for closer study of the text.

Both the Paris and the Turin manuscripts bear the title *Expositio orationis
dominice edita a Maione magno ammirato ad Stephanum ammiratum filium
suum*, which is omitted from the Austrian manuscripts. When Maio wrote,
there were in existence a great number of commentaries on the Lord's Prayer.
Most of them were very much shorter than Maio's version, which is unusually
elaborate. Although there is no earlier commentary quite like his, Maio did
not undertake his task without making extensive use of earlier work, and
indeed claimed to have done research in many books for the writing of his
exposition. The title itself only claims for him an 'editorial' role (*edita a
Maione*). Some quite long sections of the work have been simply lifted from
Gregory the Great's *Moralia in Job*.[25] Gregory is courteously cited by Maio,
but it is not obvious till the passages are put side by side quite how much
plagiarism was involved. This naturally gives rise to the suspicion that other
passages may also have been copied from earlier writers without proper
acknowledgement. The act of selection and arrangement may require some
intellectual effort, but texts linked together by the editor's own comments
would constitute more of an achievement than a mere *florilegium*.

An author who has left such an impression of masterfulness in the historical
record does not seem likely to have been content to string together extracts
from the works of others, yet at first sight the commentary is disconcertingly
impersonal. There are no individual reminiscences or observations, nothing
about the author's own religious practice, not even conventional allusions to
his sins. Nor does Maio choose to put himself in the limelight. He claims to be
doing nothing more than hand on to his son the tradition he had received (*sicut
accepimus*) in order to build up Stephen's spiritual resources. Quoting from
sound authorities for this purpose is obviously appropriate. Even so, in the
context it would not have been out of place to explain why Maio thought that
an exposition of the Lord's Prayer would be more useful for his son's spiritual
progress than, for example, a treatise on the vices and their virtuous remedies.
Here perhaps Maio betrays how little of a pedagogue he was, particularly by
contrast to many earlier commentators – mostly monks or bishops engaged
full-time with educating the young and the ignorant or indeed training further
teachers. Augustine had made much of the fact that the Lords's Prayer in
Matthew contained seven petitions, which gave plenty of scope for exploring

[25] Gregorii Magni, *Moralia in Job*, ed. M. Adriaen, *CCSL* cxliii, 3 vols. (Turnhout, 1979-85).

the significance of the number seven in many commentaries. Maio has no real interest in this kind of number symbolism. His commentary was written to be read as an interesting text. He was fully committed to elucidating the meaning of each phrase by appropriate quotations from Scripture, and in the process of doing this Maio stumbled across certain difficulties, just as earlier writers had done. It is not strange that he tried to resolve them by reference to trustworthy authorities. Intended for his own son, rather than for the class-room or the pulpit, it did not need to be either as systematic, or as elementary as the earlier monastic efforts. This does not mean that it is altogether deficient in its articulation of the argument. Each of the chapters (or books) has a heading and the divisions are marked off in the Paris manuscript by fine initials. If this copy was, in fact, the one made for his son Stephen, its layout could have been supervised by Maio himself. (Thomson suggested that he could have even written it himself, but this seems unlikely.)[26] The individuality of the author nevertheless gradually begins to impress itself on the mind.

The texts of the chapters are all quite extensive compositions. Even the shortest of the chapters on the petitions of the prayer, that on *Adveniat regnum tuum*, runs to well over 600 words, though there are some shorter subsections, like that on *Sicut in celo* (*c.* 350 words) which concludes *Dimitte nobis* (*c.* 1300 words). The most elaborate of the subsections are, in fact, reserved for the opening invocation, where there are separate discussions of *Pater*, *Noster* and *Qui es in celis*. Taken together with the prologue (600 words), these early parts of the commentary constitute a quarter of the whole work, which alone makes it notably different from others. Most commentaries had simply concentrated on explaining the petitions themselves, from *Sanctificetur* on.

In order to define Maio's part as author/editor, it is necessary to identify the sources he used. Most of his texts are from the Bible and he is usually quite specific when quoting, though his prose also frequently echoes Scripture without actually citing it. God's words when given are accredited to him as having been spoken (*dixit*) by *dominus*, or *veritas*, even *lator et executor legis* and *medicus*. The prophets are quoted by name, Ezechiel, Isaiah and Jeremiah; *propheta* is invariably used to mean the author of the Psalms, though Maio occasionally refers also to the *psalmista* and to the *rex et propheta* (David). Maio's texts are, however, built into his own discourse and do not on their own provide a continuous sequence. The considerable number of quotations deployed in each section means that Maio's assembly of the text, even at this level, is a far from negligible achievement. In addition to Scripture, Maio names three other authorities, Ambrose, Augustine and Gregory, though no more than eight times in the whole text. When these passages have been identified, there appears to be left a comparatively small residue that was

[26] See n. 20: Thomson: 'Maio might have not only composed the *Expositio*, but might indeed have written it'. Maio more probably wrote in a notarial hand originally developed in south Italy, not in the kind of clear book-hand used in this manuscript.

entirely Maio's own composition. Even some of these passages could have been taken from other writers not yet identified, but this itself could make Maio's powers of organisation seem still more remarkable, as it would augment rather than detract from his achievement to show that he could juggle with more authorities than it seems on first sight.

His manner of procedure can conveniently be illustrated from the shortest of his chapters, *Adveniat*.[27] God's kingdom is described as both true and peaceful. Maio properly quotes from four verses of the psalm (71) interpreted by the Vulgate as showing how Christ would reign when his kingdom came. Maio explains that the last phrase (from verse 7), 'until the moon is no more', refers to the time when the rise and fall of the church will cease, or in more abstract terms, until what is perfected only in part is perfected completely. Maio now admits to some surprise (*in mirum me ducit*) that what is already everywhere can nevertheless come and go. Although there can be no doubt that God is everywhere and everywhere is already king, the fact that we pray for the coming of his kingdom appears to involve either asking for the coming about of what has not yet happened, or for something to come where it is not already. That God is everywhere is proved from Philippians (2:10) – to him every knee is bowed. It seems to me (*videtur michi*), Maio continues, that although God must reign everywhere, his grace is nevertheless not operative everywhere. This point he demonstrates from Scripture: the foolish virgins whom the Bridegroom denied, 'I do not know you' (Matthew 25:10); Paul's affirmation to the Corinthians that those who did not acknowledge him, God would not acknowledge (I Cor. 14:38); and John, 'the light shining in darkness which comprehended it not (1:11). For these reasons, Maio concludes quoting Jesus, first, 'My kingdom is not of this world' (John 18:36) and second, 'No man can serve two masters, God and Mammon' (Matthew 6:24). God's kingdom has now been set in contrast to that of the devil, with which no pact is possible (II Cor. 6:15-16, 14). But Jesus said, 'Where there is light, darkness flees away (John 14:30). This provides Maio with his explanation. Since there are actually two kingdoms, one of light and one of darkness, it is proper to ask for the coming of God's kingdom, because when this happens, it will cause the kingdom of darkness to fade away. Moreover when God's kingdom comes in that full sense, the king of peace who is in us *per potentiam* will indeed become king regnant in us through the grace promised *per filium*. Here Maio appears to be thinking of the Mass, where Christ broke bread and the Lamb is sacrificed to make peace between men and God ('Qui in cena panem simul iunxit et agnum, qui inexorabilem litem sedavit'). 'God used the stone which the builders had rejected at the head of the corner' (I Peter 2:7). The comment on this petition really finishes here, but Maio now reverts to the difficulty he had raised earlier about how God could come and go if he was anyway everywhere. He begins by quoting Ezechiel on the way the spirit moved from

---

[27] Hartwig, 'Re Guglielmo', see nn. 12 and 17 above, pp. 475-77.

within the middle of the (four) winged animals (1:12). Maio asks why the Holy Spirit, which existed before the world and is co-equal with the Father and the Son should be said to move about *(discurrere)*, since everything which moves proceeds to the place where it was not and leaves the place where it was, whereas the Spirit must anyway be already everywhere. This leads on to another problem: How can the Spirit be described as both mobile and stable (Wisdom 7: 2-23)? Here Maio invokes the help of Gregory the Great to provide an answer, but though he appears to be quoting one of the homilies on Ezechiel only from this juncture, in fact the whole of his afterthought, beginning with the reference to Ezechiel the prophet, is a more or less continuous quotation from it, as far as Gregory's quotation from Daniel. Gregory's paragraph does not conclude here, but Maio breaks off to end his chapter with it: 'tronus eius flamma ignis, rote eius ignis accensus'.[28] One third of Maio's whole chapter is, in fact, therefore no more than an extended passage from Gregory, with only the most misleading indication of Maio's real dependence on it. In the previous fifty lines of the printed version, which is all his own work, Maio has, however, quoted from the Psalms, from the Gospels (Matthew twice, John three times) and from one Petrine and three Pauline Epistles. There may on the one hand seem here to be little originality; on the other, Maio has deployed many sources in his own argument. For him plagiarism was not the easy option of a lazy writer.

Modern scholars who reprimand pupils for copying word for word cannot easily condone Maio's practice of quoting Gregory so extensively that at least one sixth of his whole text turns out to be taken from the great pope's work. Maio would certainly not have seen it as anyway blameworthy to use Gregory to this extent, even without formal footnoting and, for the most part, he does indicate his reliance on Gregory's authority. Even so, he does not quote simply to save himself trouble. Gregory's position as pope may have encouraged Maio to think of him as the most authoritative of the Latin fathers, though Maio only calls him *beatus* not pope. More likely still, Maio found Gregory's approach to the study of Scripture congenial and could, in fact, have learned how to set about it by reading Gregory's works. Not only did he mark passages for inclusion in the commentary; he assimilated Gregory's way of raising problems and trying to solve them. When copying out long sections of Gregory, Maio picked only what he wanted and only three of his chapters have very extensive passages, taken from the Homilies on Ezechiel or from the *Moralia*. Maio can quote both Ezechiel and Job without immediately reaching for Gregory's comments on them, but it is not surprising if Maio used Scriptural texts whose value had not only been perceived already by previous writers but for that reason also had been explained in passages that were themselves correspond-

---

[28] Gregorii Magni, *Homiliae in Hiezechihelem prophetam* ed. M. Adriaen, *CCSL*, cxlii (Turnhout, 1971), *Lib*. I Homilia, V 8, 9, 10 pp. 60-61.

ingly useful to Maio. One of these sentences taken by Maio from Gregory without acknowledgement gave him a fairly brief aside in his discussion of 'our daily bread', which is likened to that food provided for the ravens (Job 38:41), symbols of sinful men; but Gregory's exposition of this soon ceased to serve Maio and he breaks off to insist that 'we' are not ravens but rational men needing the food specially assigned to us by God.[29] Maio's longest extracts from Gregory were inserted into the next chapter, *Dimitte*, and the last, *Libera nos*. *Dimitte* is linked to the preceding *Panem* by the need to receive our daily bread with a clean heart, if it is not to turn to our damnation, so this brings him to the importance of humble and open confession of our sins, with an appropriate quotation from Job (31:33). It is this that causes him to bring in a passage of about 800 words from the *Moralia*, which provides most of the rest of the chapter.[30] Since confession is at issue here, Maio could have considered it fitting to leave a priest and bishop with the exposition. Only in the last few lines does Maio presume to add his mite to round off Gregory's message on the virtues of oral confession. Even so, he is not perfunctory about this. He gives three quotations from the Psalms, one from Ezechiel and one from Paul, none of them used by Gregory himself. Maio had learned from Gregory how to quote Scripture and here it is almost as though he were presuming to add some profitable texts that Gregory had regrettably overlooked.

Maio's greatest dependence on Gregory comes towards the end of the commentary where he refers to the belief that what is openly expressed in the New Testament had been prefigured in the Old.[31] Gregory's own illustrations of this were derived not only from his exposition of the passage in Ezechiel about the wheel in the middle of a wheel (1:16) but from the text on the two cherubim placed by Bezalel on the two ends of the mercy seat (Exodus 37: 7-8). This Augustine had first interpreted as meaning the Old and New Testaments; Gregory took over the idea. From here it is but a step for Maio to reach Job, the archetypal figure: 'qui mediatoris tipum eo verius tenuit, quo passionem illius non loquendo sed patiendo prophetavit'; a Gregorian concept itself. This leads him inevitably to the *Moralia*, where he found Gregory's interpretation of the sevenfold feast of Job's seven sons and their three sisters. Maio adopts Gregory's exposition of this as a reference to the seven gifts of grace: *sapientia*, *intellectus*, *consilium*, *fortitudo*, *scientia*, *pietas* and *timor* (all, ultimately from Isaiah 11:2-3) and the three sisters, Faith, Hope and Charity. From Gregory Maio also took the idea that in our prayers we should ask for each of these virtues. Gregory could have found in Augustine's commentary

---

[29] Paris, B.N., MS Nouv. Acq. Lat. 1772, fos. 26v-27; *Moralia Lib.* xxx, c. ix, 28-29, pp. 1510-11.

[30] Hartwig, pp. 479-82; *Moralia Lib.* xxii, c. xv, 30 – xvi, 38, pp. 1113-19.

[31] Paris, B.N., MS Nouv. Acq. Lat. 1772, fos. 43 v-44 v, 45-47; *Homiliae Lib.* I, *Homilia VI*, 12, p. 73 and see Augustine's Questions on Exodus for the interpretation of the two cherubim. This passage is already excerpted by Eugyppius in his *Thesaurus ex S. Augustini operibus* c. 121 (*PL* 62 : 737-38); *Moralia Lib.* I, c. xxxii, 44-xxxv, 49, pp. 48-51.

on the Sermon on the Mount a very precise link between each of the gifts of the Spirit and the seven petitions of the Lord's Prayer but he did not adopt them.[32] Maio took his own independent line when he suggested that all seven virtues may be prayed for at each petition: 'qualiter singula petitio septem simul virtutes induat et septem simul fratres cum tribus sororibus in mensa unica pascat'.[33]

If Maio's use of Gregory suggests that he knew how to find his way to the useful texts and select what he needed, it is probable that he came to Ambrose and Augustine less directly. There is no extensive quotation from either author, which makes it easier to believe that he took his citations of them from earlier compilations. Ambrose is invoked in connection with the text of Paul's epistle to the Romans, so, in fact, it was not an authentic work of Ambrose that is in question but the so-called Ambrosiaster commentaries on Paul, which were believed to be by Ambrose until the sixteenth century. Ambrose is used only to justify the description in Latin of Christ as *predestinatus* (Romans 1:4) where the truth of the matter really required *destinatus* in order to avoid any implication that Christ was the adopted Son of God and not God from the Beginning.[34] According to Maio, it was Origen who had raised this difficulty about the Latin texts. The phrase quoted by Maio is, however, word for word the same as that found in Hrabanus Maurus's Commentary on Romans, though the objections there are more vaguely attributed: *iuxta quosdam*.[35] That Hrabanus was nevertheless Maio's source, indirectly if not directly, is proved by the fact that in Hrabanus, this passage immediately follows a quotation from Origen on the spirit of sanctification and the resurrection of the dead. The name of Origen was therefore carelessly transferred from the preceding to the following quotation. Maio was not himself responsible for this; the same mistake had been made as early as the ninth century by Haimo, bishop of Halberstadt, though Maio probably did not know of Haimo's commentary.[36] Ambrose was brought into this discussion because of the problem created by the idea of Christ as the adopted Son of God, and Hrabanus many lines further on in his commentary had naturally quoted from Ambrose too. He did not, however, cite the same passage of Ambrose as Maio did and it is not possible to show exactly where Maio obtained the relevant material. But given the abundant evidence for the use of Ambrose by other

---

[32] For Augustine on the Lord's Prayer see his Commentary on the Sermon on the Mount, *Lib.* II, c. iv-xi (*PL* 34:1275-87).

[33] Paris, B.N., MS Nouv. Acq. Lat. 1772, fo. 47.

[34] Ambrosiaster, *Commentarius in Epistulas Paulinas* Pt. 1. *In Epistulam ad Romanos* ed. H.I. Vogels (Vienna, 1966) *CSEL* lxxxi, p. 16.

[35] Hrabanus Maurus, '[Notandum autem juxta quosdam quod] quamvis in Latinis exemplaribus praedestinatus soleat inveniri tamen secundum quod interpretationis veritas habet destinatus scriptum est non praedestinatus' *Commentary on Romans*, *PL* 111:1277.

[36] Haimo, bishop of Halberstadt (840-53): 'Origens dicit qui destinatus est filius Dei dicens destinari illum posse qui est praedestinari non est.' *PL*, 117:366.

scholars in the same context, it seems very unlikely that Maio had needed to look up the Pauline commentary itself. There could have been many places where Maio could find the basic texts already assembled. He was still able and willing to select what was required in his own work, but the evidence for his use of earlier books is incontrovertible.

There are three references to Augustine, all not surprisingly in connection with Maio's attempts to wrestle with the problem of understanding God's will.[37] How can God both will all men to be saved (II Peter 3:9) and divide men at the Last Day into those on the right who will go to eternal life and those on the left bound for everlasting torment? If He can do everything he wants, why cannot He save all men when He wants to? Augustine's opinion on the problem is then quoted and Maio tries to explain it. Not content with this, however, he goes on to offer further reflections of his own: 'mihi .. hec et alia occurrit ratio'. If piety and justice are both in God (as all men of reason agree – 'quod neminem rationem degentem preterit'), God's piety must be just, and His justice, pious. God's will must therefore be both just and pious. If it were not just, it would not be pious, and vice-versa. When God wills all men to be saved, He can only will those men to be saved who are justly saved. He could not will anyone to be saved, unless it was just for them to be saved – not however, Maio adds cautiously, that salvation depends on the works of justice done by men themselves, but only on the gift of His grace. Maio's quotation from Augustine here does not therefore indicate that Maio had any profound understanding of Augustine and he probably took the quotation (from the *Enchiridion*) out of some secondary work. Later in the text, Maio again refers to Augustine in connection with the same problem, but under the heading, temptation.[38] Maio summarises this teaching as: whatever happens is either because of God's direct action, or because He allows it to happen. Augustine illustrated what he meant by citing the case of King Hezekiah (II Kings 20:6) to whom God allowed an extra fifteen years of life. Maio renders this as *Augustinus quoque in Iezechiele*, which makes it doubtful whether Maio really understood the allusion. Again it seems safest to conclude that Maio took his quotation from Augustine indirectly. These instances of indirect lifting of quotations prompt some uneasiness about supposing that Maio read Gregory at length. Excerpts from Gregory's *Moralia* were no doubt common in anthologies and there may have been abridged versions to help.[39] Maio's extensive reliance on Gregory is, however, so different from the occasional use he found for Ambrose and Augustine, that is is probably unsound to argue from one case to another.

Considering when Maio wrote in Norman Sicily, it seems reasonable to expect his text to show some signs of the new scholastic studies that had

[37] Hartwig, 'Re Guglielmo', pp. 477-78.
[38] Ibid., p. 485.
[39] See n. 46 below.

developed in northern France since the early twelfth century. There were certainly men in the kingdom, perhaps particularly at the court itself, who had followed courses of study in the north. Admittedly, no schools of this kind appear ever to have been opened in the kingdom and there is better evidence for educated northerners seeking employment in the south than for southerners deliberately choosing to go north to improve their education. Despite this, northern visitors seem to have considered their own scholastic attainments superior to what they found in the south. Peter of Blois was very disdainful about the quality of local teachers in the south.[40] The most erudite of twelfth-century scholars, John of Salisbury, nowhere suggests that he encountered men of training comparable to his own, despite his extensive contacts in the kingdom with men of rank and culture.[41] The south contributed to west European thought by supplying texts and translations into Latin of books needed by northerners. If the kingdom felt the need of men educated in the northern schools, it took them fully-fledged and did not send off its own young men to learn what was required. Maio as an outsider in Norman Sicily was himself introduced there to provide the king with the expertise he had acquired in Lombard south Italy; it would be understandable if he kept his distance from French novelties or was proud of his own native traditions. He must have been brought up in Bari in the last days of its princely independence. He had built his career on the base provided by his own legal studies there. It seems unlikely that he was exposed at the right age to early scholasticism.

There are, of course, certain resemblances to be found in commentaries on the Lord's Prayer. Yvo of Chartres, for example, like Maio later, explored the implications of 'our' father by insisting that the *divites et nobiles* shared the same father as the *pauperes et ignobiles* and saw that they were all joined together in *oratio fraterna*.[42] Maio also filled out the notion in his own way, but he did not necessarily need the stimulus given by Yvo, or indeed of any other scholar to do this. Yvo had an idea similar to Maio's that when we say that God is in heaven, we are being encouraged to rise towards him. Yvo probably adapted this from Hrabanus Maurus, who specified that for this we need the wings of fasting and almsgiving.[43] This kind of labelling, so common and useful in didactic works, has no place in Maio. Maio could, however, have profited from the clear and sharp minds who had written on the Lord's Prayer shortly before him. Yvo took from Augustine the idea that in praying for the coming of God's kingdom, we pray that it comes to those who are still ignorant of it and for whom therefore the kingdom is in that sense absent. Maio could have found this passage useful and if he did not use it, it was probably because

---

[40] Peter of Blois, Letters: 10, 46, 66, 90. *PL* 207:27-32, 133-37, 195-210, 281-85.

[41] John of Salisbury, *Policraticus*, ed. C.C.J. Webb, (Oxford, 1909) ii, pp. 173, 271.

[42] Yvo of Chartres: Sermon XII, *De oratione dominica*, *PL*, 162:599-604; for Maio see n. 50 below.

[43] Hrabanus: *De clericorum institutione*, c. xvi, *De discretione orationis dominice*, *PL* 107:332-33.

he did not know it. The commentaries made in the next generation by Abelard and Hugh of Saint-Victor, which were written before Maio left for Palermo, cannot have had any influence at all on him. If he did not know Yvo, he had even less reason to know about the later theologians.

Maio was not, however, totally out of touch or sympathy with the scholastic developments of the twelfth century, at least as far as legal studies are concerned, which was anyway his own professional concern. The canonist Laborante, later cardinal, who was a canon of Capua in Maio's time, wrote for Maio a treatise on justice that is deeply marked by Laborante's studies in the northern schools, possibly under Gilbert de la Porrée.[44] Laborante addressed Maio in most respectful terms: 'vir illustris sapientiae luce virtutum nitore prefulgens' and underlines Maio's attainment of high office from humble beginnings: 'vestri dudum tanti dignatio culminis infimam lactentis humilitatem infantiae', which shows that Maio did not object to being reminded of his lowly past. Laborante and Maio shared some common interests. Maio owed his advancement essentially to his legal training. He must have been one of the earliest lawyers in twelfth-century Italy to obtain power from the exercise of political office and because he had no influential family to help him, Maio probably owed much to his professional abilities.

Nothing is really known about the way the law-schools of Italy, north or south, imparted their learning in the early twelfth century, but it is probable that they focused attention on texts and clusters of contradictory authorities in order to reach some consensus about the law. Arguing cases in the courts must have been an ordinary part of a lawyer's life and notaries in particular had to be able to draw up documents that would protect their clients' interests in litigation. Just as Maio had wrestled with the difficult text of the Lord's Prayer and the conflicting quotations from Scripture, so Laborante discussed difficult problems in connection with justice. Maio cannot have found the treatise difficult to read or to understand. Even the highly abstract language can be matched by passages in his own work, though Maio lacked Laborante's scholastic vocabulary. Laborante easily inserts scriptural references into his prose, though he also makes classical allusions and invokes the thought of Aristotle. Laborante seems altogether better versed than Maio in putting his ideas across; his language is more colourful. There is, however, no hint of the great northern scholar writing down for Maio's benefit, so that the treatise becomes evidence for Maio's assumed sophistication. Maio is presented as one willing to appreciate the nature of thinking about justice in the abstract. There is much here about the nature of goodness, reason, virtue, grace and necessity to interest a commentator on Scripture, though justice itself is defined from Aristotle: 'aequitas ius unicuique retribuens pro dignitate cuiusque'. It is not difficult to find points where Maio's interests overlapped with Laborante's. Writing for Maio may not therefore be a case of Laborante aiming to instruct

---

[44] See n. 3 above.

the royal minister in the ways of the Parisian intellectuals, so much as the young canonist, with a career still to make, offering his work because he knows that Maio will be interested in it.

There is one further piece of evidence that Maio was not completely cut off from the scholastic fashions of the day. When he reaches the point in the *expositio* of asking how God could both will all men to be saved and yet divide the just from the unjust, he says, perhaps with a glimmer of humour: 'Beatus autem Augustinus, fili karissime, corrigiam huius calciamenti sic solvere attemptavit', using here a current catchphrase from the schools to mean resolving a knotty problem. This phrase was used already by Bruno of Cologne in his commentary on the Psalms, a text probably known in south Italy. Intended originally, no doubt, to express the real humility of the teacher who was not worthy to undo his master's shoes, as the Biblical phrase implies, it had become instead a sign of the teacher's intellectual presumption when offering to resolve a seemingly impossible problem. Maio seems to be slightly sardonic when he shows his son how Augustine *attempted* to resolve the issue. The fact that he went on to make suggestions of his own about how it might be resolved also indicates how confident Maio himself had become of his intellectual acumen. He is not by nature a mere compiler of other men's great thoughts.[45]

The interest of lawyers in Scripture, and philosophy as well, in the lawbooks of twelfth-century Italy can be demonstrated from the collection of tracts and commentaries copied into British Library, MS Royal 11 B.xiv. Alongside the legal works attributed to Irnerius, Roger of Piacenza and Bulgarus, there is a small collection of extracts from the Fathers and older canonists which shows how extracts from the authorities were being gathered for purposes of easier citation. These extracts include pieces from Augustine and Gregory, particularly from the *Moralia*.[46] Such a collection could easily have been made in Maio's lifetime. He could even have compiled one for himself from his casual reading over many years. As royal *scrinarius*, at the beginning of his career in Palermo, Maio had been involved in a systematic attempt to check up on the privileges granted by earlier rulers of Sicily. Keeping registers with notarial regularity may have been one of the characteristics of his regime. Ignorant though we must be of the way Maio learned his craft, we have no justification for thinking that Maio was himself not well-educated according to the standards of his day and within the context of the kingdom. Roger II selected him for royal service alongside other distinguished foreigners. After the death of George of Antioch, there was no man in Sicily of comparable

---

[45] A.M. Landgraf, *Introduction à l'histoire de la littérature théologique de la scolastique naissante* (Montreal, 1973) p. 48. For the phrase in Bruno: 'Non sum dignus solvere corrigiam calceamenti eius questio quoque convenienter corrigia dicitur quia sicut corrigia nectit calceamentum sic et questio ligat illud unde fit' *PL* 152:918.

[46] British Library, MS Royal 11 B. xiv, fos. 105-113 v.

political ability and ingenuity. Some of his skills he must have owed as much to his education as to his native wit.

The Maio of the *Liber de regno* was a man of forceful character. This extensive text does not on the surface bear the marks of the great and fearsome minister. The politician may simply be judged as out of his depth, but it is not an abject performance and there proved to be readers for it over a long period. It is worth persevering to see if it is not possible to penetrate a little deeper into Maio's mind. There are not many laymen of his date who have left half as much evidence of themselves. In many respects he appears to keep his character out of the work better than many clerical writers, teachers or monks, had done. They resorted to colourful anecdotes or illustrations to hold the attention of their pupils. Maio's way of doing precisely this is more literal. With great frequency he appeals to his son to pay attention to what is being said. *Fili, bone fili, care fili*, and especially *fili karissime* and *fili mi*, occur together about eighty times in less than a hundred pages of text in the Paris version. There are therefore few pages without this reminder of the father's anxious concern for his son. At the time of Maio's murder, Stephen was old enough to be tortured in order to get damaging evidence of his father's treachery; by then he may have been a married man, even a father himself, but Maio made no exhortations as to his life or behaviour that would be relevant to the way he discharged the duties either of public office or of family obligation. The exposition is moreover so little interested even in the modes of prayer that it makes no reference to the right posture for prayer or in what place it might be recited or at what times, nor to any desirable mental preparation for it. Only the petition, 'give us our daily bread' may imply a daily recitation. The treatise must surely represent an attempt to supply Stephen with a work of devotion for his domestic use and must itself be an indication of Maio's lack of confidence that Stephen's spiritual needs would be adequately provided for by public prayer or clerical admonition. Maio acts as though, like the traditional *paterfamilias* of Roman and Lombard Italy, it was his personal duty to provide for the education of his son's spiritual life. This duty he takes so seriously that he does not even attempt to betray its spirit by slipping in advice about wordly conduct of any kind.

If daily domestic recitation was the norm in Norman Sicily, Maio's choice of the Lord's Prayer for his commentary on the Christian life would become intelligible. It might also have naturally given rise in some thoughtful minds to the asking of questions about some of its very puzzling features. In Maio's hands the commentary frankly recognises, as most previous extensive commentaries had also done, that every phrase, however familiar and revered, when thought about, actually provoked not merely wonder, but even bewilderment. Maio was prepared to confront these problems. He made no attempt to gloss over them, as the more perfunctory commentaries had done, by simply offering trite explanations of meaning. Had Maio read earlier commentaries like that of Paschasius Radbertus he could have acquired some of this open-mindedness from his reading, but it is equally possible that he had thought over the prayer for himself and only then begun to hunt for writings to help him understand the spiritual core of this baffling text. Impersonal though Maio's approach to the commentary may seem, it is certainly like no other.

One of the most original features of the commentary is the care given to expounding its opening sections, before the petitions themselves are reached. The prologue, which quotes Genesis, Psalms, Isaiah, Mark, Luke, Acts and four Pauline Letters in the space of less than 800 words is constructed out of Maio's concern to hand on the exposition of the prayer, as he had himself received it (*sicut accepimus*) for Stephen's spiritual benefit. He alludes both to his satisfaction with his son ('odor filii mei sicut odor agri pleni' – a favourite biblical quotation with Gregory the Great) and to the duties of the father to make known the paternal injunctions of the Father of All. Praying to God in the form of the Lord's Prayer would itself be an impertinence had we not been taught to do so by the Son whom God himself acknowledged and Who was himself bold enough to say that the Father is in Me and I in Him.[47] Maio's personal involvement as the father of his son with the Father-Son relationship in the Godhead could hardly be made more explicit, but it is confirmed by the emphasis is places on the vocative clause, *Pater noster qui es in celis*. Unlike most previous commentators, Maio takes each element separately – *Pater*, *noster* and the relative clause. The first chapter on *Pater* conventionally stresses that if we dare to invoke God as Father, it behoves us to behave like His sons.[48] With the honour we claim as sons, we must assume the burdens of sonship. Stephen is to be reassured because God helps us to bear the burdens put upon us. The chapter concludes, however, on a very different note. Maio argues that if we are sons, we must also be men and because we are men, we are rational; as rational beings, we must therefore act reasonably and not incline, for example, towards darkness rather than light, or prefer falsehood to truth. Echoes of Boethius are surely present. Much of the spirit of the passage could have been derived, perhaps indirectly, from Augustine's literal commentary on Genesis, where God's making men in his own image is interpreted to refer to his intellectual aspect and where the phrase *anima rationalis* provides a link with Maio.[49] Maio says that God has made men in His own

---

[47] Hartwig, 'Re Guglielmo', pp. 464-66. The opening words should be *Si labilia et caduca nostra*, as in the Parisian and Austrian manuscripts. Hartwig's transcription, rather than the Turin manuscript itself, was probably at fault here. *Labilia et caduca* may have been a current cliché. A school commentary on Terence's *Andria* glosses the word *proclive* as 'caducum et labile, non fixum' See F. Schlee *Scholia Terentiana* (Leipzig, 1893) p. 80.

[48] Hartwig, 'Re Guglielmo', pp. 466-69.

[49] Boethius, *Consolation of Philosophy*: 'et propria luce relicta tendit in externas ire tenebras' (C.1, Mus. 2, lines 2-3; Maio has: 'qui spreta luce tendit ad tenebras', Hartwig, 'Re Guglielmo', p. 468; Augustine: 'homo est animal mortale rationale', *De quantitate animae* c. xxv, *PL* 32:1062. In Book VI of the literal commentary on Genesis, Augustine argued that God made men in his own intellectual image. This passage also appeared in Eugyppius *Thesaurus* c. 51, *PL* 62: 656-61.

image and it is fitting for us to show our rationality when calling on God. We must aim not to be unworthy (*ut non sit degener*), if not as much as we should, at least as much as we can, and to have confidence in God's goodness.

In the section *Noster*,[50] Maio again, like others, calls attention to the fact that it is not 'my' father who is addressed, but our common Father. Maio's list of all those for whom we are instructed to pray is his own: friends, enemies, those of the household of faith, for pagans (*ethnicis*) and publicans, persecutors and detractors, for the perfect and the imperfect. This may just be regarded as a glancing allusion to contemporary Sicily, with its Muslim subjects and Maio's enemies. But Maio quickly moves on to interpret the inclusiveness of 'our' as involving a union of body and soul and of the inner and outer man. This leads him to introduce the two pairs, Martha and Mary, Leah and Rachel (probably a conscious reminiscence of Gregory's *Moralia*).[51] He concludes that Christ should be our example as the One who brought together what was opposed, reconciling action and contemplation. The effect of the section is therefore to move from a recognition of the complexities implied by *Noster* to an apparent polarisation between the active and contemplative life which can only be resolved in Christ.

Maio's sensitivity to the difficulties implied in the text are fully brought to the surface in the next chapter, where he puzzles about how God who is everywhere can be described as being in heaven.[52] This he believed was done for the purpose of inspiring us to take wing ourselves for the celestial regions and to emulate the saints. Maio says that since all men enjoy the same gift of humanity, we should labour to cultivate in ourselves those elements of humanity in order to be able to make as much progress as the saints had done and so that God's grace should be made real in us and not linger there *in potentia*.[53] Maio believed there were three steps to be taken to reach the heavenly heights. The first is the active life itself; the second is the contemplative life seen by Peter in the vision recorded in Acts (10:11); the third is the heaven described by Paul (II Cor 12:2-4). This extensive treatment of the prayer's first few words reveals a Maio who is far from being a scissors-and-paste compiler.

Some of the difficulties raised by Maio in connection with the petitions themselves have already been mentioned: the problem of predestination under *Sanctificetur*; the movement of the spirit in *Adveniat*; the power of God's will in *Fiat*; the nature of the daily food we ask for in *Panem*. A final example may be taken from *Ne inducas*,[54] because it raises another aspect of Maio's study, not hitherto discussed. Most other commentaries had had to grapple

---

[50] Hartwig, 'Re Guglielmo', pp. 469-70.

[51] *Moralia Lib*. VI, c. xxxvii, 61, pp. 330-31.

[52] Hartwig, 'Re Guglielmo', pp. 470-72.

[53] For the additional interest of this remark, see n. 66 below.

[54] Hartwig, 'Re Guglielmo', pp. 484-85, but there incomplete. It is necessary therefore to consult the Paris text, fos. 37-41 v.

with the conflicting biblical texts on temptation, where God is on the one hand said to tempt no man and on the other to have tempted Abraham.[55] Maio's resolution of this difficulty is neither clear nor very helpful, and again suggests that he had not found very satisfactory answers in the books he used. He distinguishes the temptations that are willed by God from those that are simply allowed by Him. He attempts to bring out its significance by saying that we must ask not to be tested beyond the limits of our endurance. God knows how far we can be stretched and does not will to test us further. Since God only tempts men as far as they are capable of bearing it, their successful endurance in fact serves to set others a good example. The devil, on the contrary, naturally tempts men who are ignorant to try to know what they do not know, that is tempts them to go beyond their proper limits. The most interesting observation in this chapter is, however, his noticing a textual point. Where the Vulgate renders the description of human life in Job (7:1), *Militia est vita hominis super terram*, Maio observes that in the old translation (*translatione veteri*) was replaced by *temptatio* which is in fact what Gregory has in the *Moralia*.[56] Though Maio could have noticed the different readings simply by comparing the texts available to him, he also made something more of the point by claiming that however much the two terms apparently differ outwardly, they agree in sense, since temptation is the fight against evil spirits and *militia* the combat (*exercitium*) against the enemy (*hostes*). And though other scholars also refer to the different readings in Job, Maio seems to be the only writer who actually explained it as being due to the old translations. This might be taken as an indication that in the Norman kingdom the old translation was still current or that the introduction of the new one was therefore still comparatively recent. But Maio goes further than this with his personal interpretation of the problem of temptation, for since human life is itself a perpetual state of temptation (constant combat with evil spirits), it seems rather odd to ask not to be led into temptation, for this would seem to be like asking not to be alive at all or to be left alive, but without what makes life what it is, which is both absurd and impossible. Only once he had raised this conundrum did Maio proceed in a more conventional way to make what he could of the conflicting biblical evidence.

Maio shows no other signs of being interested in textual criticism. Rather strangely he makes no reference to the fact that Matthew and Luke give significantly different versions of the petitions. Many scholars were put out to note that Luke gave only five where Matthew gave seven, a much more satisfactory number for them to ring the changes on. Maio moreover accepts without comment the Lucan text of the prayer for the fourth petition *panem nostrum cotidianum*, instead of retaining Matthew's *supersubstantialis*. He

---

[55] James 1: 13 and Genesis 22: 1.
[56] Hartwig, 'Re Guglielmo', pp. 484: 'legitur enim quod vita hominis militia est in hoc mundo et in hoc loco translationis veteri nequaquam militia vita hominis sed temptatio vocatur'.

alludes briefly to Matthew's reading, but only in such terms as suggest that he did not understand its significance.[57] Earlier writers who had discussed this textual point and explained it were therefore presumably unknown to him. This is important for the reason that it almost certainly means that Maio knew little Greek and could make no use of Greek scholarship. Carolingian scholars who thought *panis* in Latin was derived from the Greek *pan* (meaning 'all') would probably have struck even Maio as very ignorant, for he worked all his life with Greek speakers, but knowledge of such an elementary fact of Greek is hardly sufficient to suppose serious venture into Greek theology. Maio would not have commissioned a Latin translation of Diogenes Laertius had he been able to read the text in the original. He has been described as certainly of Greek origin by the most recent authoritative history of the kingdom.[58] His text actually shows less sign of a knowledge of Greek than that of the ninth-century German Paschasius.

This analysis of the text should be sufficient to demonstrate the quality and the merits of Maio's work for his son's spiritual progress. He says that he consulted many works to write it ('ex multa librorum volumine illius panis fracture auctoritate subnixo repperi') but it remains very unclear where Maio found what he needed. The books he used were older than the more up-to-date works studied by modern scholars and could probably only be found in the older monastic libraries of the kingdom. Maio would probably have had to borrow books from the monasteries of southern Italy, rather than from any in Sicily, though Catania itself might have been an exception, and he had connections there through Aristippus. But he was presumably himself responsible for getting both his father and his mother entered in the Venosa necrology and one of the first royal diplomas for which Maio is known to have been responsible as royal chancellor was issued for La Cava.[59] Maio probably had, therefore, good enough contacts in both these mainland monasteries for the kind of books he needed. His text, which shows him groping his way forward in understanding the Lord's Prayer, is not, however, the banal rehash of other men's work, nor does it show signs of having being drafted by a spiritual adviser ghosting for the great minister. Despite what it owes in places to

---

[57] Paschasius Radbertus, abbot of Corbie, in his *Expositio in evangelium Matthei*, PL 120:276-298 did deal with this problem.

[58] S. Tramontana in *Il Mezzogiorno dai Bizantini a Federico II* by A. Guillou and others (Turin, 1983), p. 619.

[59] His mother Kurala (*mater Madii magni ammirati ammiratorum*) was entered under 25 June and his father Leo (*pater ammirati ammiratorum*) for 8 September on the necrology from Venosa, now Cassino MS 450. King Roger's death was entered, but not those of Maio (1160) or King William (1166). This suggests that the entries were made before 1160 and that Maio was still alive and powerful when his parents died. '*Rerum Italicarum Scriptores*', ed. L.A. Muratori (Milan, 1725), vii pp. 948. For La Cava see P. Guillaume *Essai historique sur l'abbaye de Cava d'après des documents inédits* (Naples, 1877) App., p. xxxv.

Gregory, the commentary should be regarded substantially as evidence of Maio himself.

Turning from the text itself to assess its historical significance, two main questions seem to require attention. First, how does Maio's commentary compare with others available in his time, and second, what can Maio's composition tell us about the state of learning and culture in twelfth-century Sicily? A great number of commentaries on the Lord's Prayer had been written in Latin since Tertullian, yet Maio must have been dissatisfied with what was available in order to venture out and write his own. Moreover, his is an exceptionally long work and has few to rival it in this respect. As the work of a layman, written to stimulate lay piety, it is in a class on its own.[60] If he knew earlier commentaries, he could have judged them unsatisfactory because they had been written with a different kind of readership in mind. Judging from those now easily accessible for consultation (because they have been printed) most were remarkably short, summarising the spiritual meaning of the petitions in a few words. They often called attention to its formal structure, as seven petitions, probably in order to help the young remember them. Augustine may have been responsible for encouraging later generations to write variations on the ways the number seven could be used to open its meaning. Hrabanus Maurus already has the group of seven divided into one of three petitions for *eterna* and one of four, things *temporalia*;[61] later writers made much use of this analysis. Maio's commentary is not dominated by this kind of didacticism and his interests in matching sevens (petitions, virtues, vices) barely developed at all, until he comes to copy out Gregory in his summing up. Maio may not have been particularly interested in number symbolism, or disdained its use as more appropriate to the school-room than for his son, who was after all already a royal official. Maio's attitude could also explain why he had found so little use for the kind of scholastic work produced in France in the early twelfth century. The works that Maio's most resemble in style are those of the older monastic work, still represented in Maio's life-time by that of Archbishop Hugh of Rouen.[62] There is no reason to think that Maio had met Hugh, but there can be no doubt whatever that Maio knew men who knew Hugh. Maio would have found it much easier to write his commentary had he found an earlier outline text, on to which he could hang his own selection of biblical texts, snippets from his reading and his own reflections, but none of the printed versions appear to have been used in this way. If Maio ever saw Hugh's commentary, he could have gained an idea of what such a work could be like,

---

[60] The guide to these commentaries is M.W. Bloomfield, B.G. Guyot, D.R. Howard, T.B. Kabealo, *Incipits of Latin Works on the Virtues and Vices, 1100-1500 A.D.* (Cambridge, MA, 1979), nos. 8001-9261: incipits of works on the Pater Noster.

[61] Hrabanus, *PL* 107:332-33.

[62] Hugh of Amiens, first abbot of Reading and archbishop of Rouen: *Super fide catholica et oratione dominica*, *PL* 192:1330-34.

but it does seem unlikely that he had done so. Anyway, Hugh's text is much
shorter than Maio's and does not use the same quotations from Scripture. Had
Maio owed something to earlier monastic writers and to his monastic contemporaries who lent him books, it would still be interesting that Maio was not
satisfied, as other laymen of the time must have been, to leave his son's
spiritual development to the monks themselves. Perhaps in Sicily, Maio sensed
that his son could not draw upon the traditional spiritual resources of the
Lombard south which Maio had experienced in his own youth.[63]

The speculative element in this discussion of the first question has to be
regretted but can hardly be evaded. We have in Maio's commentary a work of
some importance that cannot easily be categorised, and about which certain
questions at least have to be posed. To help us resolve the second question,
there are fortunately some other texts to set beside Maio's as products of the
Sicilian court in his time, though even in this context it is again an exception.
Maio's personal care with the work may, however, be held up as another
example of the way learning in the southern kingdom depended on the gifts
and interests of unusual individuals. It was not the product of a school or
designed for scholastic use. Maio was a theological amateur who worked out
his own ideas. Unlike his scholastic contemporaries he did not expect to
encounter criticism from fellow scholars or prepare to combat them. Since
Maio was well-educated by the standards of his society and a man of considerable intellect, he saw no difficulty, or temerity, about reading the texts that
interested him and then composing his own commentary. The fact that he was
writing it specifically for one man for whose welfare he believed himself to be
responsible may have been an important factor in shaping the character of the
work. Making individual efforts for the culture and enlightenment of friends
and companions was characteristic of the way culture was diffused in the
kingdoms. However, the fact that at least five copies of the work are known to
have been made over as long a period of time as two hundred and fifty years
and as physically far apart as Sicily and Austria, indicates that Maio's achievements came to be appreciated beyond his narrow family circle. The interest of
it turned out to be less limited than he intended.

What impact the composition had in Maio's own time is nevertheless
incalculable. At first sight it seems difficult to place it in the context of the
brilliant court described by Aristippus and of which Maio was himself such a

[63] Laborante in his work *De vera libertate*, which he sent to Archbishop Hugh of Palermo,
probably without encouragement, denounces the inadequacy and corruption of the clergy. The
monasteries were not mentioned, but most of those in Sicily were of the Greek rite and rule. The
main Benedictine communities of the island at Catania and Lipari were, however, established in
episcopal sees, and the foundation of Monreale in 1174 as a monastery which almost immediately
obtained archiepiscopal status proves that such arrangements commanded public confidence in the
twelfth century. Until the agreement with the papacy in 1156, the Norman kings had found
difficulties about getting the bishops of the island consecrated and this may have had adverse
consequences for clerical discipline throughout the Latin church in the island.

conspicuous and generous member.[64] Yet what use to Maio was the translation of Diogenes Laertius which he commissioned? Why indeed should he
have wanted this insight into pagan philosophy when the commentary shows
him so immersed in the Bible and Gregory the Great? The commentary shows,
however, that Maio was also something of a philosopher himself: posing
questions about Scripture, invoking man's reason, probing the mysteries of
God's ways and God's will. If the cultivated intelligences at court discussed
scientific and moral problems there was no reason why they should not also
have debated religious, even strictly scriptural, ones too.[65] When Maio's own
work is considered as part of the court learning, it takes on another dimension.
Likewise it invites us to think of interpreting that courtly culture somewhat
differently. The courtly bishops who were well-educated and patrons of arts,
however worldly, would have been odd indeed if they had not been at all
concerned with religious and moral issues or eager to display their intellectual
accomplishments in courtly society. Nor when the pious Maio read the
translations of Plato made by his protégé, Aristippus, did he necessarily recoil
in horror from this evidence for pagan intellectual presumption. The *Meno* is
full of evidence about how seriously Athenians had taken the moral education
of their sons and how it could be supplied: if not from the Sophists (heaven
help them!), then from whom? The *Meno* concludes with the view that virtue is
placed in men by God and has somehow to be cultivated in us, even though it
cannot be taught formally.[66] Is Maio's work not precisely this: an attempt to
exhort and instruct by the device of the commentary, so that the innate virtue
planted in man by God should somehow be given its chance to grow? Passages
in the commentary that seem peculiar to Maio include the argument that as
men have been made in the (intellectual) image of God, we are as men morally
committed to try and realise our truly human potential, taking Christ and the
saints as our examples. Maio could well have learnt from the *Meno*, or had his
own ideas confirmed by this ancient authority, that it was his own (Christian)
duty to do at least as much for the moral education of his son as Plato showed
Athenian fathers had done for theirs. The *Phaedo*, likewise, which is a
discussion of the immortality of the soul, will have been understood by Maio as
a pious layman rather differently from the way either earlier or later Platonists
read it. There is even a precise passage of the Latin Phaedo that has a parallel
in Maio, where he expresses the idea that *militia* is really the same as *temptatio*:
'Etenim prelia et seditiones et pugnas nihil aliud prebet quam corpus et huius
concupiscentiae'.[67] There are no verbal echoes, but as Maio would himself
say, 'unum eundemque intellectum concorditer format'. When the archdeacon

[64] See n. 6 above for the generosity of Maio as compared with that of Matthew of Salerno, in the
*Liber*, despite its detestation of the minister.
[65] Theology is one of the disciplines mentioned by Aristippus as flourishing in Sicily: see the
prologue to the *Phaedo* as in n. 2 above.
[66] Meno as, for example, in the Loeb edition (ed. W.R.M. Lamb, 1962).
[67] See Rose, n. 2 above; compare *Phaedo*, 66 C (ed. H.N. Fowler, Loeb 1947).

of Catania made this translation, it was to satisfy the expectations of his Latinate contemporaries, not to foster a Hellenistic revival or indulge the temptation to learn about pagan philosophy for its own sake. Modern classical scholars interested in the revival of ancient learning from the twelfth century in the west have tended interpret the evidence for these translations without paying adequate attention to the context in which they were read and appreciated. At the time, Plato represented the inadequacy of human reasoning, only showing how far men could get before they realised their need for God's help. Again there seems to be no verbal echo of the *Phaedo* in Maio, but Maio does have one very odd phrase that could just have been inspired by a passage from it: 'quilibet homo non aliter natus est homo quam ceteri homines. Nemo hominum alio magis vel minus homo est . . . itaque pari dono humanitatis omnes equanimiter quademus . . . ' In the *Phaedo* Maio could have read that all souls were equal and all souls equally good.[68] The two ideas do not have to match completely for the main point to be established: with ideas like his the pious Maio would not have felt so out of his depth, or element, in the discussions of the court circle.

Aristippus praised the court for being the courtiers' school, where King William, Maio's lord, encouraged philosophical wit, discussion of intractable problems, and study of every kind. In Sicily there were libraries, philosophy, Greek literature, mechanics, optics, medicine, theology, mathematics, meteorology.[69] Aristippus left his mark as a philosophical wit in the pages of John of Salisbury's *Policraticus*.[70] His Platonic translations became familiar to later moralists, like his version of Diogenes Laertius. Why should he have not had comparable influence on the great minister who was his patron? More important still, why should Maio's own treatise not be used to open up for us the religious aspect of this secular court, just as the beautifully illuminated manuscript of his work now in Paris has opened our eyes to the development of this art in the kingdom?

[68] *Phaedo*: all souls are equal and all souls equally good: 94B; compare Maio: 'Nemo hominum alio magis vel minus homo est. Si itaque pari dono humanitatis omnes equanimiter gaudemus', Hartwig, 'Re Guglielmo', p. 471.

[69] Aristippus: see n. 5 above, Hartwig, 'Re Guglielmo', p. 463.

[70] John of Salisbury, *Policraticus*, see n. 41. Various quips of Aristippus quoted, 'indulgere vitiis a legendi studio temperare' (ii, p. 152) and, 'ut cum omnibus ait hominibus intrepida fabularer' (i, p. 366).

# 10

## The Vaticinia de Summis Pontificibus: A Question of Authority

### Marjorie Reeves

The age-long tension in the church between continuity and change is strikingly encapsulated in an early fourteenth-century set of prophecies which, in their enigmatic texts and pictures, sketched a drama deemed to be now nearing its climax. They rapidly captured the imagination of contemporaries and of succeeding generations. The *Vaticinia de summis pontificibus* in its earliest form is a series of fifteen 'prophecies', each consisting of a picture, a caption and a short text.[1] There can be no doubt that these were based on a series of Byzantine imperial prophecies, known as the Oracles of Leo the Wise, in which the pictures mostly represent emperors, each with its captions and text.[2] They were probably in circulation in the twelfth century and were collected *c.* 1180. In the western adaptation emperors become popes, although some early versions actually retain some imperial figures. The earliest known outside references to the *Vaticinia* come from Arnold of Villanova (*c.* 1304-

[1] For the pioneer work on these prophecies, see H. Grundmann, 'Die Papstprophetien des Mittelalters', *Archiv für Kulturgeschichte*, 19 (Berlin, 1929), pp. 77-159. See also A. Lattanzi, 'I Vaticinia Pontificum ed un codice monrealese del Sec. XIII-XIV', *Atti della Reale Accademia di scienze, lettere e arti di Palermo*, ser. 4, 3.2 (1943), pp. 757-92; M. Reeves, 'Some Popular Prophecies from the Fourteenth to the Seventeenth Centuries', *Popular Belief and Practice*, ed. G. Cuming, D. Baker (Cambridge, 1972), pp. 107-34; M. Fleming, 'Metaphors of Apocalypse and Revolution in Some Fourteenth-Century Pope Prophecies', *The High Middle Ages*, ed. P. Mayo (1983), pp. 405-18; R. Lerner, 'On the Origins of the Earliest Latin Pope Prophecies; A Reconsideration', *Fälschungen im Mittelalters*, *MGH Scriptores*, 33, v (Hanover, 1988), pp. 611-35. In the mid fourteenth century a second set of fifteen prophecies was produced. Later the two series were amalgamated, the second set being placed first. In this form they appeared in many manuscripts and printed editions in the Renaissance period.

[2] On the so-called Oracles of Leo the Wise, see C. Mango, 'The Legend of Leo the Wise', *Recueil des travaux de l'Institut d'études Byzantines*, 6 (1960), pp. 59-93. They can be read in Latin in the version by P. Lambecuis, *Imperatoris Leonis sapientis oracula* in G. Codinus, *Excerpta de antiquitatibus Constantinopitanis* (Venice, 1729), pp. 161-79. Editions of both the Leo Oracles and the earlier set of *Vaticinia* are in preparation and will, it is hoped, be published in concert.

145

6)[3], the Domincian chronicler, Francesco Pipini (1314-20)[4] and Hugo of Novocastro (1315).[5] Pipini knew a set of eight prophecies which began with the Orsini pope, Nicholas III (1277-80) and he named successive popes as far as Clement V (1305-14). Since in most versions the first picture associates the pope with bears, the early prophecies seem clearly to be *post eventum*. But the enigmatic character of both text and pictures in the middle part of the series makes it difficult to determine the point at which real prophecy beings, that is, the likely date of authorship. Broadly speaking, however, the series must have been adapted from the Byzantine source in the decade from 1295 to 1305.

Herbert Grundmann, in his pioneer work on the *Vaticinia*, suggested that they were produced by a group of Italian 'Spiritual' Franciscans, probably in the interregnum between Popes Benedict XI and Clement V, 1304-5.[6] This group, led by Fra Liberato and Fra Angelo Clareno, formed part of the 'Spiritual' element in the Order, dedicated to the uncompromising observance of St. Francis's Rule and Testament and inspired by an eschatological hope for the future.[7] They had already suffered persecution and had recently returned from the eastern Mediterranean whither they had fled from their oppressors. This latter circumstance supplies a major reason for imputing to them the authorship of the *Vaticinia*.

It is easy to build up a scenario around this hypothesis. In the summer of 1304 Fra Angelo, Fra Liberato and their followers were gathered in Perugia awaiting the outcome of what proved to be one of the most crucial papal elections in the later middle ages. It was to be a trial of strength between the pro- and anti-French parties in the consistory. While Napoleone degli Orsini, Nicholas of Prato and others were laying down the tortuous lines of the intrigues and bargainings which led to the election of Clement V, one can picture the little group of Spirituals ardently studying the prophecies, including the Leo Oracles which they had brought from Greece, seeking the signs to confirm their hope for the future. Seldom in history could the gap between hope and political reality have been wider. The Spirituals would see the situation in terms of *Heilsgeschichte* and the approaching crisis of all history; what actually transpired was the election of a Gascon pope and the removal of the papacy to Avignon.

[3]   See R. Lerner, 'On the Origins', pp. 629-30.
[4]   F. Pipini, *Chronicon*, Muratori, *Rerum Italicarum Scriptores*, old series, 9 (Milan, 1721), cols. 724, 726-8, 736, 741, 747, 751.
[5]   Hugo de Novocastro, *Tractatus de victoria Christi contra antichristum* (Nuremberg, 1471), unpag., c. xxviii.
[6]   For Grundmann's essay on the *Vaticinia*, see above, n.1.
[7]   Of the considerable literature on this group, in English the old study of D. Douie, *The Nature and Effect of the Heresy of the Fratricelli* (Manchester, 1932), is still very useful. In Italian the most recent work on Angelo Clareno is that of G. Polestà, especially 'Gli studi su Angelo Clareno: dal ritrovamente della raccolta epistolare alle recenti edizioni', *Rivista di storia e letteratura religiosa*, 24, 1 (1989), pp. 111-43.

This is one possible scenario. It presupposes a 'Spiritual Franciscan' purpose in producing the adaptation of the Leo Oracles. The intention, on this view, would be to juxtapose a series of real-life portraits denouncing deep-seated corruption in the papal office to a series of dream figures embodying a future angelic pope, or series of such. The expectation of a final crisis of tribulation and wickedness to be dramatically ended by an angelic period in the church can be traced back to the Abbot Joachim of Fiore's juxtaposition of the worst Antichrist and the Age of the Spirit. By the end of the thirteenth century his veiled prophecies of a new spiritual leader in the coming *ecclesia spiritualis* of the third *status* were already being crystallised into the expectation of a future angelic pope. One of the pseudo-Joachimist works, the *Oraculum Cyrilli* (*c.* 1280-90) appears to herald his coming under the figure of an *ursus mirabilis*, and there are several other indications that such a prophecy was circulating.[8]

This interpretation gives a radical and eschatological meaning to the work from the outset and locates it, if somewhat distantly, within the posterity of the Abbot Joachim whose name was later constantly associated with it. Two considerations support a Spiritual Franciscan authorship. First, the Oracles themselves – in spite of the enigmatic language which makes interpretation difficult – seem to carry a message of corruption, revolution and divine intervention to establish a holy regime. After an early sequence of violent pictures, with captions such as '*Principium malorum*', '*Sanguis*', '*Confusio*', '*Incisio*', '*Occisio*', the change or break occurs round about numbers 9, 10 or 11 (according to a slightly varying order in different versions), where an empty throne and an emperor swathed in grave-clothes with an angel hovering above, imply a crisis, while number 12, with the caption '*Pietas*', showing a half-naked man seated on a rock or sarcophagus and approached with reverence by a robed man, seems to depict the choice of a *nudus* or *pauper* to fill the vacant office. The final prophecies appear to mark the apotheosis of the saviour-emperor and his partner, the patriarch, with captions such as '*Innocentia*', '*Praehonoratio*', and '*Electio*'. Thus the Byzantine source seems extraordinarily well fitted to have expressed the eschatological outlook of the Spirituals, embodying, as it appears to do, a revolutionary change through divine intervention from corruption and violence to spiritual renewal. Secondly, the group associated with Liberato and Clareno had been in a unique position to have become acquainted with the Oracles during their sojourn in the east from which they returned in 1303.

These arguments seem to confirm Grundmann's attribution of authorship to a Spiritual Franciscan group and his dating of the work to *c.* 1304-5. But this whole hypothesis has been put in doubt by recent work on the *Vaticinia*,

---

[8] *Oraculum Cyrilli*, ed. P. Piur, in K. Burdach, *Vom Mittelalter zur Reformation*, ii (Berlin, 1928), Pt. iv, appendix, p. 292. See also Salimbene, *Cronica, MGH Scriptores*, xxxii, p. 492-93 and the references to Roger Bacon below at nn. 32, 33.

notably by Robert Lerner.[9] There are two main questions involved here. First, Lerner pointed to two of the earliest manuscripts which have an English provenance, one already in the library of Bury St. Edmunds' monastery by the middle of the fourteenth century. This is an anthology of prophecies put together by Henry of Kirkested at Bury St. Edmunds.[10] The *Vaticinia* on folios 88r to 95r are not in Henry's hand but in a regular and earlier Gothic hand. They are described as 'Prophetie Joachim abbatis de papis' and could either have been copied at Bury or acquired from elsewhere. This text has been tentatively dated *c.* 1320 or *c.* 1330 to 1340 at the very latest. The second manuscript, now in the Bodleian Library,[11] is a miscellany in a number of thirteenth-century and late thirteenth- to early fourteenth-century hands. The section which includes the *Vaticinia* on folios 140 r – 146 v has been dated to between 1277 and 1320. Lerner lists several characteristics which establish the English origins of this section which was certainly in the library of St. Augustine's, Canterbury by the late fifteenth century. Since, Lerner argues, these exhibit a 'pristine' text, they put in question the idea of a Spiritual Franciscan authorship located in Italy and, more generally, the claim that Joachimist 'overtones' were present in the original text of the *Vaticinia*.

This latter point seems to be supported by the fact that in these English examples the text and pictures of what are usually numbers 2/3 and 4/5 are elided, probably because of certain similarities in text. The first elision is of no great significance but the second involves the figure of Celestine V – assuming the series starts with Nicholas III – who should be fifth in the series. Now one of the marks of Franciscan Joachimism in the early fourteenth century was the belief that Celestine had been the prototype of the angelic pope to come. In five of the other early manuscripts this elision does not occur and the fifth portrait is consistently given as a figure (usually tonsured) holding a sickle and a rose and attended by an angel. It appears as a distinctively holy image, breaking a sequence of worldly and even violent figures in the first half of the series. The fact that in the two English examples this key application to Celestine V is blurred would seem to suggest that a Joachimist overtone was not here intended in the original adaptation. But the origins of this puzzle may, in fact, lie in the ambiguity of the source itself. In what is thought to be the original version of the Leo Oracles the counterpart of the Celestine picture is number 4, not 5. This shows a king with sickle and rose but no angel.[12] In one

---

[9]   For Lerner's article, see above, n. 1.

[10]   Now Cambridge, Corpus Christi College, MS 404, fos. 88 r-95 v. See Lerner's description, 'On the Origins', pp. 633-34.

[11]   Oxford, Bodleian Libr., Douce 88, fos. 140 r-146 v. See Lerner's description, 'On the Origins', p. 633.

[12]   This information is based on the as yet unpublished edition of the Leo Oracles which has been prepared by Dr. Basquin-Vereecken of Ghent.

version the caption '*Incisio*' seems to put the emphasis on the cutting sickle.[13] Thus the holy image may not belong to the Leo Oracles but rather to be the creation of western adaptors who added the angel. Some support for this suggestion is found in a third very early manuscript where instructions for pictures which were never executed give for the fifth one: '*Juvenis cum falce in dextera et rosa in sinistra*', but no angel. Confusingly, the two English examples which seem to miss the Celestine allusion by the elision of 4 and 5 do include the angel in their fourth picture. It seems impossible to determine at what point in a continuing process of adaptation the ambiguous fourth figure in the source was reshaped as the holy number five which became the standard symbol for Celestine V.

The argument for a Joachimist provenance for the pope prophecies, however, does not rest solely or even principally on the identification of Celestine V but rather on the whole direction given to the prophecies in the source itself, moving, as we have seen, from corruption and violence through revolution and divine intervention to an apotheosis of godly rule. Why should a western adaptation of these strange oracles be made in the first place? Was it a curious game for the exercise of ingenuity? Surely it was far more likely that the prophetic message of the Leo Oracles spoke from the beginning to those who believed that the final crisis of history was approaching. Without seeking to tie the authorship to a specific group of Franciscans, the most likely reason for the adaptation of the Leo Oracles seems to lie in the resonances of a 'Joachimist' message which could be detected there.

Lerner has also brought back to our attention the very early ascription of authorship to 'Rabanus Anglicus'.[14] The first reference to Rabanus is in the commentary of another prophetic work, the *Horoscopus*.[15] This, like the *Vaticinia*, deals with the popes from Nicholas III to a coming angelic pastor, but in astrological terms. Because it seems to allude to Benedict XI but not to Clement V, it has been dated to 1303-5. The commentary on it names Clement V but must have been written before 1308. It is in the latter that Joachim, Hildegard and 'Rabanus Anglicus' are cited as sources of revelation. The 'prophetic truth' here attributed to Rabanus is summarised by Lerner as 'the progress of the church as seen in the figures of the Roman popes from Nicholas III to the final pontiff'. This would seem to be a clear reference to the *Vaticinia*. The next reference occurs in the commentary to a third work of this genre, the *Liber de Flore*. This work, too, starts with a series of historical popes (from

---

[13] Oxford, Bodley, MS Barocci 170. Admittedly, this is a very late, sixteenth-century manuscript. In figure 4 (fo. 8 v) a turbaned ruler stand a holding a sickle in the right hand and a sprig of roses in the left. He is standing on a battle field of corpses and skulls. Dr. Basquin-Vereecken gives two versions of text 4 the first with the caption '*Confusio*' and the second with the caption '*Elatio*'. In her version '*Incisio*' is the caption for text five.

[14] Lerner, 'On the Origins', pp. 623-25.

[15] The *Horoscopus* and the *Liber de Flore* mentioned below were both the subject of a further study by Herbert Grundmann, 'Die Liber de Flore', *Historisches Jahrbuch*, 49 (1929), pp. 33-91.

Gregory IX [1227-41], not Nicholas III) but it has no pictures and its distinctive feature lies in the final descriptions of an angelic pope and three successors which give a more detailed programme of spiritual regeneration and introduce for the first time a holy partnership between the pope and a *rex generosus de posteritate Pipini*. Here there is a reference to Rabanus as describing two popes to come between Boniface VII and the first angelic pope. Grundmann dated the *Liber de Flore* to 1303-5 and its commentary to 1305-14. In the most recent study of Rabanus, Martha Fleming has shed new light on the question of exactly what Rabanus wrote by studying the evidence of a manuscript at Carpentras, in the Bibliothèque Inguimbertine.[16] This is a late sixteenth-century anthology of prophecies but after the title-page the first part consists of a late medieval copy of the *Vaticinia* which has been cut up and pasted into it. Since this copy contains the *Vaticinia* in the later arrangement, the prophecies which concern us occur in the second half.[17] Here there are four texts attributed to Rabanus which are comments on prophecies which were 11, 12, 13 and 14 in the original set of fifteen. These, which form variations on the original texts, mostly appear at the top, with the picture below, and again below the usual version of the text. This arrangement suggests a distinction between the texts attributed to Rabanus and the original versions. These same four texts are found in two late fourteenth-century manuscripts of the *Libellus* of Telesphorus of Cosenza where again they are ascribed to Rabanus.[18] It seems likely, then, that what Rabanus actually wrote was not the original text of the *Vaticinia* but commentaries on four of its angelic sequences only. Perhaps this was an attempt to reconcile the *Vaticinia* text with the angelic series in the *Liber de Flore*. However, the two much earlier attributions of the whole *Vaticinia* text to Rabanus remain. It is possible that Arnold of Villanova was the source of both of these.

What the later evidence does suggest is that Rabanus had a particular interest in the angelic sequence. It seems likely therefore that he belonged to a Joachimist milieu, perhaps more specifically to a Spiritual Franciscan group. The emphasis on his nationality might indicate an English Franciscan in an Italian group. But this does not necessarily mean that the *Vaticinia* were produced by Clareno and his group. Two arguments against this solution have been adduced by Lerner and others. Years ago Decima Douie expressed

[16] Carpentras, Bibl. Inguimbertine, MS 340. Professor Fleming's study, as yet unpublished, is entitled 'Rabanus the Englishman and the *Vaticinia de summis pontificibus*'. There is a brief description of this manuscript in Reeves 'Popular Prophecies', pp. 130-131.

[17] See above, n.1., for this later arrangement.

[18] As stated by Prof. Fleming. See Vatican, MS Reg. Lat. 580 and Paris, B.N., MS Lat. 3184. This section is headed 'De angelico pastore et eius bonitate . . . ' and can be also found in the printed ed. of Telesphorus's work, *Liber de magnis tribulationibus in proximo futuris* (Venice, 1516), fos. 25 r-27 r. See also M. Reeves, *The Influence of Prophecy in the Later Middle Ages* (Oxford, 1969), pp. 530-31.

doubts about Grundmann's attribution of authorship to the Clarenists,[19] while a recent scholar who has studied Clareno's thought questions the extent of his Joachimism and supports the view that in 1304-5 a radical critique of the papacy hardly accorded with the outlook and aspirations of this group.[20] Its members were at that moment seeking recognition from ecclesiastical authorship and Cardinal Napoleone Orsini was specifically Clareno's protector. 'Would a member of a persecuted band', asks Lerner, 'who knew that an Orsini Cardinal was one of his band's most needed patrons have invented and circulated a pamphlet that branded the Orsini as *Genus nequam*?'[21] It is true that in the original order the Leo Oracles do start with the prophecy featuring bears, so it could be that the western adaptor simply started with Nicholas II because the bear symbol could be matched to an Orsini pope more obviously than to any other. Thus the prominence given to the Orsini may have been almost accidental. Nevertheless Lerner puts a real question mark against the involvement of Clareno's group with the *Vaticinia*. But there were other Italian Spirituals who had returned from exile and probably knew some Greek.

It may not be possible on present evidence to identify the actual authorship. But the nub of the problem is whether from the outset the series was intended to carry a revolutionary and eschatological message which could be termed Joachimist and was of the type particularly associated with Spiritual Franciscans, or whether it was originally just a prophetic curiosity which was then 'taylored' to convey a Joachimist meaning.[22] The puzzle concerning the Celestine figure does indeed suggest a two-stage adaptation but the argument here is that the Joachimist case rests rather on the whole eschatological intention taken over from the Leo Oracles themselves. Lerner recognises that there are such overtones but suggests that at the turn of the thirteenth/ fourteenth century such eschatological hopes were not the monopoly of Joachimists. It is not clear what evidence might be cited for this general chiliastic expectation whether in England or elsewhere. It is true, as Randolph Daniel has shown, that the Franciscan Order at this time was characterised by its own sense of eschatological mission in the End Time, generated by the inspiration of St. Francis himself.[23] But the *Vaticinia* carry a much more specific message: the juxtaposition of a corrupt order in the church to a new and final spiritual order, brought about by divine intervention. This seems clearly to be derived from the distinctive programme of Joachimism in which tribulation issues in the *transitus* to the Age of the Spirit which Joachim placed at the end of the *saeculum*.

[19] D. Douie, *Nature and Effect*, p. 39, n. 5.

[20] G. Potestà, 'Angelo Clareno', pp. 120-22.

[21] Lerner, 'On the Origins', p. 617. *Genus nequam* are the opening words of the first prophecy. The picture shows a pope with little bears.

[22] Lerner's word, 'On the Origins', p. 618.

[23] E.R. Daniel, *The Franciscan Concept of Mission in the High Middle Ages* (Lexington, KY, 1975), pp. 26-34.

Where around the year 1300 would such a perspective be found? Much of the evidence concerning the production of prophecies in the later middle ages suggests that we should be looking for a group rather than an individual. Prophecies were, of course, frequently attached to a well-known name but appear so often to arise out of the eschatological anxieties and expectations of a particular order or group. The Dominicans supply a little evidence for such a perspective[24] and the heretical Dolcinists had their own programme for the future.[25] One might look to the Florensian Order itself but by this period there is no evidence within it of a radical attitude towards the papacy. Nevertheless, in connection with the English claim, it is worth noting that the Florensians had considerable lands and therefore connections in England. But until evidence of an alternative Joachimist milieu can be found, a group connected with the Spiritual Franciscans, their sympathisers, such as Arnold of Villanova, or disciples of Petrus Joannis Olivi, or tertiaries or other lay groups seem the most likely producers of the *Vaticinia*. But where? The use of the Byzantine source is perhaps the strongest argument for Italian provenance. Yet Arnold of Villanova's very early reference opens up the possibility of a Catalan origin. In the south of France were Franciscan houses and 'Beguin' groups amongst whom Joachimist ideas circulated. The most problematic candidate is England, its claim resting on the authorship of 'Rabanus Anglicus' and the two early manuscripts which Lerner regards as 'the remnants of what had been a very wide early English circulations of the *Vaticinia*'.

Were the English Franciscans really touched to any extent by Joachimism at this period? There is no known group of Franciscans in England harbouring these particular eschatological hopes around the turn of the century. Of course, Abbot Joachim was well-known by repute. All through the thirteenth century there are scattered English references to him, including attributed prophecies scribbled in manuscripts. But, as has been argued elsewhere,[26] in the first phase of knowledge about Joachim north of the Alps attention was almost entirely concentrated on his reputation as one who had received the gift of spiritual intelligence, as the prophet of Antichrist and, negatively, as one whose doctrine of the Trinity had been condemned. If the *Vaticinia* were indeed produced in England, it would be natural to look to the English Franciscans for possible authors. Miss Smalley showed that in the early fourteenth century several Franciscan writers referred to Joachim, using him as a prophetic authority on the End Time, but again – even in the case of Henry of Cossey who cites him extensively – there is no apparent awareness of Joachim's Third Age of the Spirit or the hope for an angelic regime at the end

---

[24] Reeves, *Influence*, pp. 161-64.
[25] Ibid., pp. 242-47.
[26] See M. Bloomfield, M. Reeves, 'The Penetration of Joachism into Northern Europe', *Speculum*, 29 (1954), pp. 775-93.

of the *saeculum*.[27] *Renovatio* appears nowhere in these references. In the fourteenth century, it is true, there was a considerable distribution of Joachimist works in English libraries, including both the genuine *Liber de concordia* and *Expositio in Apocalypsim* and the pseudo-Joachimist *Super Esaiam* and *De oneribus prophetarum*. Morton Bloomfield gathered together the evidence on this point.[28] It is not clear, however, how many of these were available in the late thirteenth or early fourteenth centuries when the *Vaticinia* appeared. Some must have been, for the English Franciscan, Adam Marsh, writing to Robert Grosseteste before 1253, refers to expositions of Joachim brought to him by a friar 'venientem de partibus transmontanis'.[29] Again, there is no mention here of a third *status* and Adam sees Joachim as a biblical exegete with a prophetic gift for interpreting the impending crisis of tribulation. A similar approach to Joachim is made by Roger Bacon who views him as one of the prophetic sources from whom 'greater certainty regarding the time of Antichrist' can be obtained.[30] But the collection of prophets whom he cites with Joachim suggests isolated prophecies flying around rather than a knowledge of Joachim's system or his works. Nevertheless, the Oxford Franciscans may already have possessed some of these works for both the *Liber de concordia* and the *Expositio* were apparently in their library by about 1400.[31]

We are probably looking for the wrong clue in trying to assess the availability of Joachimist writings. Significantly, the one positive piece of evidence to connect the Oxford Franciscans with the *Vaticinia* does not name Joachim at all. Roger Bacon, addressing the pope in 1267/8 refers to a prophecy which, he says, has been circulating for forty years concerning a holy pope to come who will carry out a programme which we recognises at once as that assigned to the angelic pope.[32] Again, in 1272, he repeats the same expectation that after the tribulation of Antichrist will come 'unus beatissimus papa qui omnes corruptiones tollet de studio et ecclesia . . . et renovetur mundus et intret plenitudo gentium et reliquiae Israel ad fidem convertantur'.[33] We recall that Salimbene echoed a similar prophecy which he specifically connected with Joachim.[34] It is, of course, not impossible that a prophecy of a holy pope unconnected with an eschatological programme was circulating independently of Joachimism, but Bacon's prophecy clearly stands in an eschatological context: the pope

---

[27] B. Smalley, 'John Russel, OFM', *Recherches de Théologie Ancienne et Médiévale*, 23 (1956), pp. 300-3; idem, 'Flaccianus De visionibus Sibulle', *Mélanges offerts à Etienne Gilson* (Toronto, Paris, 1959), pp. 552-54. For Henry of Cossey, see Reeves, *Influence*, pp. 86-87.

[28] M. Bloomfield, *Piers Plowman as a Fourteenth-Century Apocalypse* (New Brunswick, NJ, n.d.), pp. 158-60.

[29] *Monumenta Franciscana*, ed. J. Brewer, Rolls Series, (London, 1858) pp. 146-47.

[30] Roger Bacon, *Opus majus*, ed. J. Bridges (London, 1900), i, pp. 268-69.

[31] Bloomfield, *Piers Plowman*, p. 159.

[32] Roger Bacon, *Opus tertium*, ed. J. Brewer, Rolls Series, (London, 1859), *Opera inedita*, p. 86.

[33] Roger Bacon, *Compendium studii philosophiae*, Rolls Series, (London 1859), *Opera inedita*, p. 402.

[34] See above, n. 8.

must carry out the divinely ordained programme of *renovatio* in the End Time after Antichrist. For this no source presents itself other than Joachim's vision of a spiritualised papal leadership in the third *status* which was popularised in the figure of the angelic pope. Roger Bacon's references, together with the two early English manuscripts, constitute the most telling evidence in support of an English authorship for the *Vaticinia*. Although neither of the two manuscripts is associated with the Oxford Franciscans, these prophecies may have originated in this group, from which 'Rabanus Anglicus' might have come. But there is no record of his presence in Oxford. This seems the best case which can be made for an English provenance.

The third possible area in which the *Vaticinia* might have originated is the south of France and Catalonia. There was much coming and going between these two regions. Franciscan houses in the south of France had been centres of Joachimist interest. Olivi's influence had extended into Catalonia and there was easy intercourse between Catalonian religious centres and the Franciscan convents of Narbonne, Béziers and Carcassone.[35] Arnold of Villanova's very early knowledge of the *Horoscopus* points us to Catalonia and, more particularly, to Barcelona. Here there is clear evidence of Joachimist activity in the late thirteenth and early fourteenth centuries among First Order Franciscans and Tertiaries to whom the loose term 'Beguin' was applied, and these were explicitly linked with Arnold.[36] One of the problems in postulating an English provenance is the difficulty of accounting for the close association of the *Vaticinia* with the *Horoscopus* and the *Liber de Flore*, neither of which appear in England. By contrast, these are much more easily fitted into a south French/ Catalonian context. The *Horoscopus* was allegedly translated into Hebrew by one Dandalus of Lerida who could have been a member of the newly founded university there. Lerner suggests that Arnold acquired the *Horoscopus* in Lerida shortly after it had been produced and that he himself wrote the commentary on it which refers to Rabanaus.[37] In 1306 Arnold cited Hildegard, Cyril, Joachim and 'Horoscopus' as prophetic authorities in his *Expositio super Apocalypsim*.[38] In his unpublished commentary on Matthew 24 he is more explicit, referring to Cyril, Hildegard, Joachim and Rabanus.[39] The Spanish scholar Perarnau has identified a circle of Arnold's influential friends in Barcelona centred in the house of Pere Jutge.[40] At the time of Arnold's death in 1311 an inventory of his possessions in Jutge's house was made. This reveals the existence of a scriptorium in which Arnold's works were being produced. Perarnau also notes evidence of a Provençal group in Barcelona

[35] See H. Lee, M. Reeves, G. Silano, *Western Mediterranean Prophecy* (Toronto, 1989), pp. 53-55.

[36] Ibid., pp. 55-59.

[37] Lerner, 'On the Origins', pp. 629-30, nn. 44, 45.

[38] Lee, Reeves, Silano, *Western Mediterranean Prophecy*, pp. 40-41.

[39] Lerner, 'On the Origins', p. 629 and n. 44.

[40] Lee, Reeves, Silano, *Western Mediterranean Prophecy*, pp. 55-59.

labelled 'Beguin'. Furthermore, the inventory of Arnold's library shows that he had a copy of the *Horoscopus*, followed in the list by *Item Rabanus, unus quaternus*. Lerner takes this to be a copy of the *Vaticinia* but it could be a copy which included the Rabanus commentary,[41] leading Arnold to assign the authorship of the whole work to him. The concentration of prophetic interest among the Beguins of Barcelona is further attested by the group of documents studied by Perarnau. This suggests a very likely context for the production of the *Vaticinia* as well as the *Horoscopus*. The close connection with the south of France could also account for the pro-French slant in the *Liber de Flore*.[42] But at Arnold's death the scriptorium was closed and Arnold's books distributed among faithful disciples, while shortly afterwards the Catalonian groups of Beguins suffered a period of sharp persecution. These facts would account for the disappearance of manuscripts produced in this centre.

The south of France as a home for the *Vaticinia* should perhaps be considered separately, since the two most recently discovered early manuscripts are both French. A copy now in the municipal library at Lunel has been dated to the years 1315 to 1320 and on the evidence particularly of the pictures has been judged to be of south French provenance.[43] The other example was discovered at the end of a register of the reign of Philip the Fair, prepared for the chancellor, Pierre d'Etampes. Professor Elizabeth Brown who identified the *Vaticinia*, in a different hand from the register proper, suggested a date in Philip's last year, that is, before 29 November 1314.[44] The presence of the *Vaticinia* here is surprising, but might be explained by the fact that the 'documents divers' preceding them concern especially the conflict between Philip and the papacy. Were the *Vaticinia* seen as a propaganda weapon in this controversy? We should recall the significant point that the associated *Liber de Flore* was the first prophetic work to couple the angelic pope in a holy partnership with a French king described in terms which make him a second Charlemagne.[45] In the midst of the tough propaganda warfare between the French monarchy and the papacy there was a strain of eschatological vision which cannot be simply dismissed. Pierre Dubois in his *De recuperatione terre sancte* was arguing that the recovery of the Holy Land and the establishment of a universal peace could only be achieved through a transfer of the imperial title to the French royal house.[46] At the same time Ramon Lull, who shared a vision of the future with Arnold of Villanova, was canvassing his concept of a *rex bellator* and in person urging Philip the Fair to take up the prophetic role by

[41] Lerner, 'On the Origins', p. 630 and n. 45.

[42] See below, p. 156.

[43] Lunel, Bibl. de Louis Médard à Bibl. Municipale, MS 7, fos. 4 r-19 r, 22 v. It is fully described in the as yet unpublished edition of the *Vaticinia*.

[44] Paris, Arch. Nat., MS JJ 28, fos. 285 r-291 v. For a description of the MS, see *Catalogue des manuscrits conservés aux Archives Nationales* (Paris, 1892), no. 541.

[45] See Reeves, *Influence*, pp. 320-21, 404.

[46] P. Dubois, *De recuperatione terre sancte*, ed. C. Langlois (Paris, 1891), pp. 98-99.

launching a crusade.[47] Both the *Vaticinia* and the *Liber de Flore* could have sprung from the fertile Joachimist soil of south French Franciscanism in response to a scenario in which a great battle against evil and a great eschatological future were expected and in which the French monarchy was called to play a crucial part.

We thus have four candidates for the authorship of the *Vaticinia*. The group led by Liberato and Clareno was the most likely to have acquired the Leo Oracles, but the least likely to have launched an attack on an Orsini pope. An English provenance is supported by the 'pristine' text of two early manuscripts – although other early manuscripts have no English connections – and by the enigma of 'Rabanus Anglicus', while Roger Bacon's references to the rumour of the angelic pope supply an Oxford context for their production. But there is no evidence to answer the question as to how they could have acquired the Leo Oracles nor is there anything to connect the *Horoscopus* and the *Liber de Flore* with England, except the name of Rabanus. Catalonia and the south of France both supply the context of Franciscan and Beguin groups deeply concerned with a Joachimist future. Barcelona, in particular, had Arnold of Villanova's scriptorium, which produced prophetic works. Arnold himself supplies the connection with the *Horoscopus* and with Rabanus, while, travelling as he did between Italy and Catalonia, he himself could have been the carrier of the Leo Oracles. He was in Perugia in 1304 and in touch there with Clareno's group.[48] Yet the absence of any manuscript of the *Vaticinia* traceable to this source leaves the question open. On the other hand, two very early manuscripts do seem to have been produced in France, one at least in the south, while Ramon Lull, forming a link between Catalonia and the French court, was pressing an eschatological role on Philip the Fair. On balance, a group either in Barcelona or somewhere in the south of France seems the most likely source from which this best-seller of the later middle ages and Renaissance period emanated.

---

[47] J. Hillgarth, *Ramon Lull and Lullism in Fourteenth Century France* (Oxford, 1971), pp. 46-53, 58-63, 71-77, 107-13.
[48] Lerner, 'On the Origins', p. 630, n. 44.

# 11

## The Collectio Lanfranci and its Competitors

### Martin Brett

In 1604 Sir George More, the eldest son of Sir William More of Loseley in Surrey, gave Sir Thomas Bodley's new library at Oxford a parcel of twenty-three manuscripts and £40. The books were a mixed bag. Three seem to have come from Newark priory, and another from Waverley. Two more at least came ultimately from St. Albans.[1] No medieval home is known for the rest, including the composite volume which is now MS Bodley 561. The much later binding encloses at least seven distinct sections, written in several English hands at different times. Two versions of an early list of contents on the fly-leaves show that the miscellany had taken more or less its present form by c. 1200.[2]

My concern is solely with the first, and earliest, section, which occupies fos. 2-60. This was written in the earlier twelfth century, in long lines throughout. It is ruled for thirty-four lines (written above top line), with a single bounding line in each margin. The binding is very tight, and there are no catchwords or quire numbers to light one's path, so that the collation cannot be established in detail. In general however, fos. 1-32 seem to be a unit, followed by a gathering of four lacking the last leaf (fos. 33-34A), followed by another unit from fo. 35 to the end.[3] Though the whole section from fo. 1 to fo. 60 is physically very

---

[1] F. Madan and H.H.E. Craster, *Summary Catalogue of the Western Manuscripts in the Bodleian Library* (Oxford 1895-1953, repr. with some corrections 1980), i (1980), pp. 88-89; N.R. Ker, *Medieval Libraries of Great Britain*, Royal Historical Society Guides and Handbooks no. 3 (2nd. ed. 1964), pp. 133, 168, 194; A.G. Watson, *Medieval Libraries of Great Britain: Supplement* (1987), p. 60.

[2] F. Madan and H.H.E. Craster, *Summary Catalogue*, ii (1), no. 2345; MS Bodley 561, fos. i v, ii v. There is a brief account of fos. 6 v – 34 v by R.E. Reynolds in *Mediaeval Studies*, 41 (1979), pp. 300-1. Other parts of the manuscript have been discussed at length. See particularly R. Foreville and J. Leclercq, 'Un débat sur le sacerdoce des moines au XIIe siècle', *Studia Anselmiana*, 41 (1957), pp. 8-118, esp. 34ff for fos. 61-96 v.

[3] For the physical details of the book I am almost wholly dependent on the kindness of Professor A.G. Watson, who gave unsparingly of his time to examine the problem. He is not to be held responsible for the errors which I may have introduced into my account.

similar, it falls naturally into two parts, separated by a blank unnumbered leaf after fo. 34.

The first part, all in one hand, begins on fo. 2, with the beginning of the celebrated preface found at the beginning of copies of the *Decretum* and of the *Panormia* of Ivo of Chartres, and at least twice before a copy of the *Tripartita*, which has been attributed to him too. It also appears in some manuscripts of Ivo's letters. For which work the preface was intended, if indeed any, has been a perennial subject for debate.[4] While, however, the *Decretum* version ends with a list of the seventeen books of that collection, and the *Panormia* version with the appropriate eight, the end in MS Bodley 561 is quite distinct:

> Prima pars de fide et eius sacramento
> Secunda de baptismo
> Tercia de sacramentis
> Quarta de apostolica dignitate et Romane ecclesie
> Quinta de ecclesia et eius dignitate et causis
> Sexta de eligendis et ordinandis episcopis et eorum causis
> Septima de clericis et eorum causis
> Octava de abbatibus et monachis et eorum causis
> Nona de abbatissa et sanctimonialibus et eorum causis
> Decima de coniugiis
> Undecima de incesta copulatione
> Duodecima de diversis criminibus
> Terciadecima de penitentia

It is possible that this list is incomplete, for it breaks off abruptly well before the end of fo. 6 v, leaving the rest blank. The list of headings bears a loose relation to the titles of the first fifteen books of the *Decretum*, but a rather closer one to the first twenty-eight titles of the *Tripartita* B collection, an abbreviated and slightly re-arranged version of the *Decretum* which enjoyed a much wider success than its parent, though it remains unprinted.[5]

The collection which follows the preface in Bodley, MS 561 runs up to fo. 34 v; it seems to have been designed to receive a number of later additions, for there are substantial gaps and blank leaves left in the text. It is also incomplete. Though the sections announced in the preface are not clearly marked after the

---

[4]  For the literature on this long-standing debate see H. Fuhrmann, *Einfluss und Verbreitung der pseudo-isidorischen Fälschungen*, *MGH Schriften* 24 (Stuttgart, 1972-74), ii, pp. 543-49 and a paper by B. Brasington in the forthcoming *Proceedings of the Eighth International Congress of Medieval Canon Law. San Diego 1988*, ed. S. Chodorow. The preface precedes the *Tripartita* copies in Berlin, Deutsche Staatsbibliothek, MS lat. fo. 197 and Hamilton MS 345. The relation between the *Tripartita* and MS Bodley 561 is discussed below.

[5]  Compare *Tripartita* B's sections: De baptismo (I), De sacramentis (II), De primatu Romane ecclesie (VIII), De episcopis (IX), De clericis et eorum causis (X), De monachis (XI), De sanctimonialibus ((XII), De coniugiis (XV), De incesta copulatione (XVI), De penitentia (XXVIII). For the *Tripartita* in general see below.

beginning of Part III on fo. 12, the subject matter and lay-out show that the last one corresponds with Part VIII of the preface.

The immediate source for much of the material is easy to establish. Though many of the canons also appear in the *Decretum* of Burchard of Worms or Ivo's *Decretum*, all those that might derive from those sources are also found in the *Tripartita* B, and in an order much closer to that of the Bodley collection. Only in Part VI is there any substantial effort to re-arrange the materials of the source. The sequence is set out in the table at the end.

The *Tripartita* provided about half the material of the Bodley collection. Almost all the remainder comes from another source, the long form of the collection of Pseudo-Isidore. In spite of some earlier speculation, there is only the slightest evidence that this vast mid ninth-century collection was known in England before the Conquest.[6] Shortly after 1066 however it appears very widely; Zachary Brooke's classic demonstration that the centre of its diffusion was the surviving abbreviated copy bought by Archbishop Lanfranc from Bec has lost nothing of its force since he wrote.[7]

Since undisputed early examples of the work of the scriptorium of Bec are few, there seems no satisfactory means for determining whether the book Lanfranc bought had actually been written there, but it remains convenient to describe it as the Bec version. Apart from its omissions it has four particularities which set it aside from the bulk of the complete or abbreviated versions which thronged the libraries of eleventh-century Europe.

The first is its arrangement. Almost all the complete copies of the long form are constructed out of three elements: they begin with a preface in the name of 'Isidore mercator', the 'Canons of the Apostles' (ultimately from the collections of Dionysius Exiguus) and a long series of forged decretals of the earliest popes. The second and third elements are taken from an interpolated version of the seventh-century *Hispana* collection. The *Hispana* however began with a section of councils, followed by the decretals of popes from Silvester I to Gregory II, so that Pseudo-Isidore is a kind of sandwich, with forged decretals followed by largely genuine councils followed by a second series of decretals, some forged, some interpolated, many largely intact. The Bec abbreviation follows the natural course of bringing all the decretals into a single sequence, followed by the councils, headed by the 'Canons of the Apostles'.

It was suggested by Schafer Williams that the Bec manuscript was copied from two distinct exemplars, one for the decretals, one for the councils. He gave no evidence for the assertion in print, but he had an unrivalled familiarity with the manuscripts, and the claim has to be taken seriously.[8] It is lent some

---

[6] Fuhrmann, *Einfluss*, i, pp. 46-47, 229-32.

[7] Z.N. Brooke, *The English Church and the Papacy* (Cambridge, 1931) reprinted with new foreword by C.N.L. Brooke, Cambridge 1989.

[8] S. Williams, *Codices Pseudo-Isidorianae*, Monumenta iuris canonici, Series C, Subsidia 3 (1971), Excerpta no.1.

further weight by a clear distinction in the editorial processes at work in the two halves. While some of the decretals are omitted altogether and many substantially abbreviated, with some sections paraphrased or reduced to catenae of short extracts, the councils survive much more completely. The omissions involve only the elaborate prefatory matter to some of the councils, the abbreviations often little more than the lists of attesting bishops. It is clearly possible that much of the characteristic re-arrangement of the copy had been done earlier, not necessarily at Bec.

The second peculiarity of this version is that the councils of Nicaea, Ancyra, Neocaesarea, Gangres, Sardica, Antioch, Laodicea and Constantinople, in that order, are in the version of Dionysius as transmitted in the late eighth-century *Hadriana*, not that of the *Hispana*. This feature can scarcely be attributed to a redactor at Bec, for it is found in a small number of copies of Pseudo-Isidore from the earliest days of its circulation.[9]

The third distinguishing feature of the *Collectio* is the subdivision of the text. The canons of the councils have a natural internal unity, though the *Collectio* does have some idiosyncracies here. More strikingly, the chapters of the decretals conform neither to the subdivisions of the editions by Hinschius or Merlin nor to those described in some manuscripts of the A2 (short) version.[10] They are most easily understood as devised for the abbreviated text, rather than derived from a complete original. Where another collection follows these subdivisions one may suppose that the *Collectio* may be the source if no better criteria are available.

The fourth peculiarity of the Bec copy is the only one which may be associated directly with Lanfranc, for it adds the legislation of Nicholas II of 1059, documents concerning the submission of Berengar of Tours, and letters from Nicholas II and Alexander II to Lanfranc himself.

The version of Pseudo-Isidore used in the Bodley collection is clearly this Bec version. It cites no text which is not in the *Collectio Lanfranci*, occasion-

[9] J. Richter, 'Stufen pseudoisidorischer Verfälschung: Untersuchungen zum Konzilsteil der pseudoisidorischen Dekretalen', *Zeitschrift der Savigny-Stiftung für Rechtsgeschichte*, Kan. Abt., 64 (1978), pp. 1-72.

[10] *Isidori Mercatoris collectio decretalium* ed. J. Merlin (Cologne, 1530), reprinted in *PL* 130. Merlin worked from a late and idiosyncratic copy of Pseudo-Isidore. *Decretales Pseudo-isidorianae* ed. P. Hinschius (Leipzig, 1863), is based on a number of (not particularly well-chosen) earlier manuscripts for the forgeries. However, all the text printed in small type is taken from the earlier edition of the *Hispana*, not Pseudo-Isidore. His text of the councils and decretals from that source is therefore even more misleading than Merlin's edition. *Collectio canonum Remedio Curiensi episcopo perperam ascripta*, ed. H. John, *Monumenta iuris canonici*, Series B, Corpus collectionum, 2 (1976), pp. 128-29, 195-208; compare Fuhrmann, *Einfluss*, i, pp. 167-78.

ally employs exactly the catenae of the abbreviator,[11] and cites the councils in the same mixture of *Hispana* and *Hadriana* as the *Collectio*. Further, it cites the legislation of Nicholas II just as it occurs in the *Collectio*.[12] Often, though by no means always, the extracts begin and end at the same point as they do in the *Collectio*.[13]

Given the abundance of copies of the *Collectio* in circulation in England by the early twelfth century, the conclusion is scarcely surprising. If one considers the bulk of historical organisation of Pseudo-Isidore, even in this shortened form, with all its attendant inconveniences, it is more surprising perhaps that there should be so little evidence of other efforts to make it more attractive in use.

At Canterbury an effort was later made to produce an abbreviation of the *Collectio*, and to supplement it with a selection from the letters of Gregory I, who is very slightly represented in Pseudo-Isidore. This is if anything even more difficult to use than its parent, for it has only the slightest rubrics to the texts, far less than stood in the original, and there is no topical re-arrangement. It remains valuable, at least to us, as proof of a continuing interest in the *Collectio*, and also of a sense of its incompleteness.[14]

---

[11] For example, Bodley, MS 561, fo. 10 v: '*Ex decretis Urbani pape*. Omnes fideles per manus impositionem episcoporum Spiritum Sanctum post baptismum accipere debent, ut pleni Christiani inveniantur. De Spiritu Sancto accipimus ut spirituales efficiamur, quia animalis homo non percipit ea que Dei sunt. Quia cum Spiritus Sanctus infunditur, cor fidele ad prudentiam et constantiam dilatatur. De Spiritu Sancto accipimus, ut amore eterne glorie et ardore succensi, erigere a terrenis mentem ad superna et divina valeamus.' This is a re-arranged catena from *Decretales pseudo-isidorianae*, ed. Hinschius, p. 146, lines 23-31, which occurs in just the same form in Trinity College, Cambridge, MS B 16. 44 (James, no. 405), pp. 212-13.

[12] For the material from Nicholas II in the *Collectio* see now R. Schieffer, *Die Entstehung des päpstlichen Investiturverbots für den deutschen König*, Schriften der *MGH* 28 (Stuttgart, 1981), esp. pp. 64-67, 208-10.

[13] On fo. 24 Bodley cites c.1 of the council of Orleans (*Isidori Mercatoris collectio* ed. Merlin, *PL* 130, col. 409A, ed. Hinschius, p. 337a). Unlike either edition, Bodley and the *Collectio* both incorporate the *capitulatio* to the canon in their text.

[14] The Canterbury abbreviation of the *Collectio* survives in two copies, Durham Cathedral Library, MS B iv 18 and Lambeth Palace, MS 351. A substantial appendix of other canonical material was added the Lambeth copy, including a copy of the canons of Westminster (1125) and a series of extracts from Ivo's *Decretum*, Books I-VIII. Only the disorderly additions to Cambridge, Peterhouse, MS 74 provide any comparable evidence for continuous expansion of a *Collectio* manuscript. In conception the abbreviated *Collectio* is close to London, B.L., MS Cotton Vespasian A xv (twelfth century, later given to Cirencester), where an abbreviation of a Pseudo-Isidore distinct from the *Collectio* is followed by selections from Gregory I and the letters of St. Boniface. Another copy of the same collection with some interpolation is found in Göttweig, Stiftsbibliothek, MS 53 (56) (twelfth century, perhaps from Passau), fos. 8-107; compare J.F. Schulte, 'Die Rechtshandschriften der Stiftsbibliotheken von Göttweig, Heiligenkreuz, Kloster-neuburg, Melk, Schotten', *Sitzungsberichte der phil-hist. Classe der kais. Akademie der Wissens-chaften. Wien*, 57 (1868), pp. 560-69, M. Sdralek, *Die Streitschriften Altmanns von Passau und Wezilos von Mainz* Paderborn, 1890), pp. 64-65.

The only other example I have yet found of an intelligent effort to reorganise the *Collectio* according to subject matter is on a much smaller scale. In 1900 Felix Liebermann called attention to a short collection of canonical extracts in the *Textus Roffensis*, inserted after two secular law tracts of the first element of the book. The *Textus* appears to have taken its present form in *c.* 1125, very possibly under the direction of Bishop Ernulf, a former prior of Christ Church.[15] The texts deal exclusively with canonical procedure in cases involving the clergy.

Liebermann was able to identify all but one of the thirty texts in the collection in Pseudo-Isidore, and the last is in fact there too.[16] There can be little doubt that the Rochester texts were taken from the *Collectio* rather than a complete Pseudo-Isidore. With only one exception all are found in the *Collectio*, and all begin where a new section of the *Collectio* does; most also end at the same point, and there are a mass of small variants to link the texts.

The one exception is a passage from a spurious letter of Gregory I (JE+1334), which is found in the complete Pseudo-Isidore but not the original form of the *Collectio*. It seems likely that it had been added to the text from which Bishop Ernulf, or whoever else, excerpted his texts. More detailed study of the manuscripts may yet suggest which version this was.[17]

Seven texts in the first Bodley collection are not found either in the *Tripartita* B or the *Collectio Lanfranci*. The first, on fos. 8 v-9, occurs in the middle of a sequence from the *Tripartita*, after a series of Augustine excerpts, from 'Aug' in libro de bono perseverantie'.[18] It is followed at once by an extract from 'Aug' ad Vincentium Victorem'.[19] On fo. 17 v there is a short extract from the

---

[15] F. Liebermann, '*De accusatoribus* aus Pseudo-Isidor', *Deutsche Zeitschrift für Kirchenrecht*, no. 111 (1900), pp. 1-5. For the manuscript see *Textus Roffensis: Rochester Cathedral Library MS A. 3.5* [now Maidstone, Kent Archive Office DRc/ R1], ed. P. Sawyer (Early English Manuscripts in Facsimile, 7, 1957, 11, 1962), i, pp. 11-18, fos. 81 v-87. Sawyer shows that the passage is part of the original book (against Liebermann), and that it once stood near the beginning of the collection.

[16] Liebermann's excerpt no. 23 is from the *Canones apostolorum* (*Decretales Pseudo-isidorianae*, p. 28, cc. 25-26a).

[17] Liebermann's excerpt no. 25. A detailed study of the manuscripts of the *Collectio* is being made by Mark Philpott at Oxford, which may well resolve this problem among others.

[18] 'Absit ut causam parvulorum – in mortem secundam. Item. Neque enim fato cogitur – nascerentur elegerint. Item. Quid dicam quod parvulus – filios liberaret' (Augustine, *De dono perseverantiae* in *PL* 45, cols. 1011-12). 'Item. Ego autem dico parvulum – posse contendere' (abbreviated from Augustine, *De natura et gratia*, cc. 8-9 in *CSEL*, 60, pp. 238-39.

[19] 'Item ad Vincentium et Victorem. Noli credere, noli dicere – esse catholicus' (Augustine, *De natura et origine animae*, iii. 13 in *CSEL*, 60, p. 374). 'Item. Noli credere, noli dicere – sententiam suffragantur' (Ibid., iii. 9, *CSEL*, 60, p. 369.

spurious letter of Gregory I (JE +1848),[20] on fo. 25 an even shorter one from 'Ambr' in libro de mysteriis',[21] On fo. 27 v there is an extract 'Ex libro Rabani de institutione clericorum';[22] on fo. 29 canon 54 of the council of Laodicea is in the *Hispana* form, not the Dionysian of the *Collectio*.[23] The last two are substantial sections from the Rule of St. Benedict, which begin Part VIII on fo. 33.[24]

The Rule of St. Benedict was too widely available to offer much guidance on the origin of these excerpts. The others present a problem which I have not been able to solve, for no single intermediate source seems to provide them. Though they may help to identify the *Tripartita* or *Collectio* copy from which the compiler was working, they are too few to affect the judgement one makes of the whole collection.

The second part of the Bodley collection occupies fos. 35-60 v. It may be in another hand, but if so it closely resembles the first. Unlike the first part, the whole section lacks rubrics or directions to the rubricator, though substantial space has been left for their insertion. With that exception, no provision is made for the later insertion of other texts. Its sources are straightforward. It begins with the pseudo-Gelasian decree on the canonical and apocryphal scriptures, in the form found in the *Collectio Lanfranci*, though the text was transmitted by innumerable routes.[25] After that it is a more or less complete copy of the last and longest section of *Tripartita* B, xxix, cc. 8-283A.

The *Tripartita* collection is now known, in whole or in part, in some thirty manuscripts, which makes it one of the most widespread of the collections made in the century before Gratian, apart from the outstandingly successful *Panormia* of Ivo of Chartres. Since a high proportion of its texts were incorporated in Gratian's *Decretum*, its long term indirect influence was to be

---

[20] 'Vehementi tedio meroris afficimur – concupiscit. Sicut is qui – dubio repellendus' (*Gregorii I papae Registrum* ed. P. Ewald and L.M. Hartmann (*MGH Epistolae* 1891-99, Bk. IX, no. 218).

[21] 'In omnibus cupio sequi – rectius custodimus' (Ambrose, *De sacramentis* iii. 1. 5 in *CSEL*, 73, p. 40).

[22] 'Tres ordines sunt in ecclesia – servire studeant' (Hrabanus Maurus, *De institutione clericorum*, 1. 2 in *PL* 107, col. 297, slightly abbreviated).

[23] 'Non oportet ministros altaris – abire debere' (Pseudo-Isidore, ed. Merlin in *PL* 130, col. 290).

[24] 'Ex regula beati Benedicti. De ordinando abbate. In abbatis ordinatione – omnibus conservet. De quattuor generibus monachorum. Monachorum quattuor genera esse – disponendum veniamus' (*Regula*, cc. 64, 1 in *CSEL*, 65, pp. 148-51, 17-19).

[25] 'Post propheticas et evangelicas – esse damnata' (E. von Dobschütz, *Das Decretum gelasianum de libris recipiendis et non recipiendis*. Texte und Untersuchungen zur Geschichte der altchristlichen Literatur, 38.iv (1912), pp. 29-84). Bodley follows the Trinity manuscript of the *Collectio Lanfranci* (G 13 of the editor's apparatus) closely. It occurs in *Tripartita* A as i, 46, c. 1 with several differences from Bodley's text, and in Ivo, *Decretum*, iv, cc. 64-65 (from Burchard), but not in *Tripartita* B.

incalculable.[26] Two manuscripts containing most of the collection survive in England, and a third very possibly stood behind Paris, B.N., MS lat. 3858A, a French manuscript which includes the canons of the council of Westminster of 1125.[27] The Bodley text provides a fourth if partial witness to the collection's circulation in England.

The Bodley version however may well have a wider importance, for the genesis of the *Tripartita* is a considerable puzzle. The *Tripartita* A is a historically organised collection in two parts, one of decretals and the other of councils, both drawing heavily on Pseudo-Isidore. The design is similar to that of the *Collectio Lanfranci*, but it is independent of it and based on much wider reading. It took its present form after 1091, probably in northern France, and possibly at Chartres; at any rate it was exploited at length for Ivo's *Decretum*.[28] The *Tripartita* B collection reverses the relationship, for it is little more than a revised and slightly re-arranged abbreviation of the *Decretum*, a derivative rather than a source. The two elements must have had an independent life, at least for a while. However, no manuscript which contains the complete *Tripartita* A collection lacks some of the B text; many have all of it. After the two elements had been put together the whole text was revised, providing more elaborate rubrics, *capitulationes* to each section, and one or two added canons. This later version was that described by Theiner, Wasserschleben and Fournier,[29] and is the form in which the collection has long been discussed. The surviving copies are roughly equally divided between the earlier and later forms.

[26] P. Fournier and G. Le Bras, *Histoire des collections canoniques en occident depuis les fausses décrétales jusqu'au Décret de Gratien* (Paris 1931/2), ii, pp. 58-66, largely based on P. Fournier, 'Les collections canoniques attribuées à Yves de Chartres', *Bibliothèque de l'Ecole des Chartes*, 57 (1896), pp. 645-98; 58 (1897), pp. 26-77, 293-326, 410-44, 624-76. See further Fuhrmann, *Einfluss*, ii, pp. 542-54, iii, pp. 776-77, M. Brett, 'The Berkeley *Tripartita*', *Bulletin of Medieval Canon Law*, new series 16 (1986), pp. 89-91 and 'Urban II and the Collections Attributed to Ivo of Chartres', *Proceedings of the Eighth International Congress of Medieval Canon Law: San Diego 1988*, ed. S. Chodorow (forthcoming). A collaborative draft edition is in preparation. A more systematic list of the manuscripts, with bibliography, will shortly be published by Dr L. Fowler-Magerl.
[27] Brooke, *English Church*, pp. 242-43; the Paris MS was unknown to D. Whitelock, M. Brett and C.N.L. Brooke in *Councils and Synods I* (Oxford 1981), ii, pp. 733-41 but presents no striking variants from their text. No other copy of 1125 is known to survive outside English manuscripts.
[28] Fournier, 'Les collections' (1896), p. 677, (1897) pp. 73-77, 312-26; for some doubts on its authorship and date, Brett, 'Urban II and the Collections.'
[29] A. Theiner, *Disquisitiones criticae in praecipuas canonum et decretalium collectiones* (Rome, 1836), esp. pp. 154-61; H. Wasserschleben, *Beiträge zur Geschichte der vorgratianischen Kirchenrechtsquellen* (Leipzig, 1839), pp. 47-61; Fournier, 'Les collections' (1896), esp. pp. 684-98. Though he knew several Paris copies and Berlin, Deutsche Staatsbibliothek, MS lat. fol. 197, Theiner seems to have worked chiefly from Vatican, MS Reg. lat. 973, which is a twin to Paris, B.N. MS lat. 3858B, on which Fournier based his account. Wasserschleben certainly knew the Berlin copy, an eccentric version of the later form. To the list of manuscripts of either form in Brett, 'Urban II and the Collections' may also be added the later version in Gnesen, Bibl. Kapit., MS 25 and Vorau, Stiftsbibliothek, MS 350 (discovered by Professor R. Somerville); Berlin, Deutsche Statsbibliothek, MS Hamilton 345 belongs to the earlier family (see below).

Two fragmentary manuscripts which draw heavily on the B collection but show no acquaintance with the A text are already known, but at least one of them belongs to the second form, and can scarcely throw much light on the origins of the whole collection.[30] Both parts of the Bodley collection are certainly based on the earlier unrevised form, and its text has distinctive features which seem to take us back to the earliest stages of its formation. In general it is closest to the version found in Berlin, Staatsbibliothek, Hamilton MS 345 (later in Italy, but not I believe written there) and in Paris, B.N., MS lat. 4282 (from Troyes), both twelfth-century derivatives from a single exemplar with primitive characteristics. Like the Bodley text the Paris manuscript lacks B xxix, cc. 68-69, 93 and 122, and has added canons (also from the *Decretum*) after 153 and 195.[31] However, there are also important differences between the versions. On a number of occasions Bodley agrees with other texts of the earlier form in such a way as to suggest that its exemplar was one which goes back to a yet earlier stage of its transmission.

One last feature tends to the same conclusion, for Bodley ends, though in mid leaf, with xxix, c. 283A (*Decretum* xvi, c. 106a, omitted in the later form of the *Tripartita*). The last canon of the collection proper, c. 284, is one of only four in the whole *Tripartita* B which is not from the Decretum, and Fournier suggested that it was probably an early addition.[32] However, no other reported manuscript lacks it; all the remaining manuscripts of the earliest form so far described have not only c. 284 but a small trail of other canons which are not found in copies of the later form.[33] Though only a complete edition of the *Tripartita* would establish the point with certainty, it seems probable that the Bodley collection is a witness to the very origins of the *Tripartita* B; it may even be the first cogent manuscript evidence for the circulation of the B text without *Tripartita* A.

The Bodley collections therefore have a considerable interest in themselves as evidence of canonical activity in England soon after 1100; they show us an anonymous compiler seeking to re-arrange the inchoate materials of the *Collectio Lanfranci* on a thematic scaffold provided by a very early form of the *Tripartita*. They also have a wider interest, for they fit into a picture of

[30] Vienna, Osterr. Nationalbibliothek, MS 982 (theol. 355), fos. 116-33; the text is certainly from the second form. W. Stelzer, *Gelehrtes Recht in Osterreich*, Mitteilungen des Instituts für Osterreichische Geschichtsforschung, Ergänzungsband 26 (1982), pp. 29-32 notes the presence of *Tripartita* B, xxix, cc. 1-284 in Admont, Stiftsbibliothek MSS 43 and 48, two copies of his 'Collectio Admontensis'. His description suggests that this too represents the later form.

[31] The Hamilton copy has cc. 68 and 69, though it places 68 after 63. Bodley also lacks xxix, c. 32, which is found in both the Paris and Berlin copies. The added canons occur in a number of other representatives of the primitive form too.

[32] Fournier, 'Les collections' (1896), p. 698.

[33] Compare, for instance, H. Boeses, *Die lateinischen Handschriften der Sammlung Hamilton zu Berlin* (Wiesbaden, 1966), pp. 166-67 for the end of MS Hamilton 345.

England's participation in the legal revolution of the century which is in some ways unlike the portrait painted by Z.N. Brooke.

His *English Church and the Papacy* was, and remains, a notable achievement. He was the first scholar to place the legal learning of the English church at the centre of the discussion, and in a European context. Further, his identifications of English canonical manuscripts before Gratian were remarkably accurate and complete; subsequent work has refined his accounts here and there, and added a thin scatter of books to his list, but his map of the principal features of the landscape can still be used with great confidence.[34]

Around this enduring core of knowledge Brooke erected a general interpretation which has lasted less well. It was a clear and imaginatively satisfying account: Lanfranc introduced England to the study of the law of the church at large in the *Collectio Lanfranci*, a useful book if already a little antiquated. This was given a formal circulation which made it by far the most widespread law book of the English church until the later twelfth century. The determination of the English kings to remain masters in their own realm put strict limits on the extent to which their bishops could profit by the new canonical studies of the twelfth century, except for a brief failure of nerve under Stephen. Only after the murder of Becket was the English church exposed to the full force of the jurisdictional revolution directed by the papacy. The generation after 1171 was one of desperate effort to acquire the basic skills of this new world.

As he wrote, the study of papal decretals in the twelfth century was itself being transformed. Since then a long series of studies have altered our perspective remarkably. The death of Becket no longer marks such a turning point; so far were the Anglo-Norman canonists of the later twelfth century from being struggling tyros in a world of professionals that their works played a leading part in the formation of the major collections of decretals which culminated in the *Decretales* of Gregory IX. They now appear nearer the vanguard than the camp-followers.[35]

The contrast between a relative indifference to the pre-Gratian collections in England and close interest in the later decretals remains, but the straightforward political explanation of the change has lost much of its force. It could now be said that the problem has been reversed. If England had been as isolated from canonical study in the first half of the century as has sometimes been supposed by incautious readers of Brooke, the exceptional activity of the Anglo-Norman canonists in the second half of the century seems to spring from ill-prepared soil.

The elements of the argument which tended to establish this relative isolation have also begun to come under pressure, less by direct confrontation than by slow erosion. The barriers raised by the kings seem a good deal less formal and consistent than we once thought, royal hostility to ecclesiastical

---

[34] Brooke, *English Church* (1989), pp. xx-xxi.
[35] The most important new studies are listed in Brooke, *English Church* (1989), pp. xvi-xix.

jurisdiction a great deal more limited. We can now place the other pre-Gratian collections Brooke discovered in a firmer perspective. This reveals some interesting features that could not be known in 1931. Several of his copies prove to represent very early forms of the texts.[36] This is not perhaps surprising, when one remembers the vigorous correspondence of several of Henry I's bishops (all devoted royal servants) with Ivo of Chartres and Hildebert of Lavardin.[37]

Another kind of enquiry, represented by a number of dispersed studies, often apparently of modest application, is now beginning to dilute the unique significance we might attribute to the *Collectio Lanfranci*. If Brooke's survey of the principal manuscripts still stands with undiminished force, a rather different picture emerges from a study of works of less ambition. To deal with the subject adequately would require a detailed examination of the whole range of evidence; here I note only a few indications of what may be found.

A bare census of manuscripts has limitations as a guide to canonical reflection. The books represent a considerable investment but rarely give much hint of the way in which they were exploited. To judge by the absence of marginal notes or even wear on the leaves, some look as if they had barely been read at all. Though few works seem to have been written in England between 1066 and 1150 which directly address canonical issues, their testimony has a special significance. Here at least one can see which sources are being exploited, rather than merely collected.

One of the earliest to survive is the tract of Ernulf, prior of Christ Church, Canterbury, *De incestis coniugis*, addressed to Bishop Walkelin of Winchester, and therefore written some time before 1098.[38] Dr. Cramer's recent examination of the work shows that Ernulf may have used the *Collectio Lanfranci* for

---

[36] Ibid., p. xxi. The copy of Anselm of Lucca discovered by Brooke in Cambridge, Corpus Christi College, MS 269 has been shown to be an exceptionally early form by P. Landau, 'Erweiterte Fassungen der Kanonessammlung des Anselm von Lucca aus dem 12. Jahrhundert', *Sant'Anselmo, Mantova e la lotta per le investiture*', ed. P. Golinelli (Bologna, 1987), p. 326.

[37] For the relations between Ivo of Chartres and the English episcopate see most recently Lynn Barber, 'Ivo of Chartres and the Anglo-Norman Cultural Tradition', *Anglo-Norman Studies*, 13 (1991), pp. 15-33. For his letters to Bishop Walkelin of Winchester, Sampson of Worcester, Robert of Lincoln, Audoen of Evreux, Turgis of Avranches and Archbishop Thurstan of York see *PL* 162, nos. 38, 165, 212-13, 219, 242, 270, 278. Compare too the letters to Bishop Roger of Salisbury, William of Winchester, and Archbishop Thurstan of York to Hildebert in *PL* 171, cols. 219-20, 301-2, 307-10.

[38] *PL* 163, cols. 1457ff. See particularly the two studies by P. Cramer, 'Ernulf of Rochester and early Anglo-Norman Canon Law', *JEH*, 40 (1989), pp. 483-510, esp. 494-98, and 'Ernulf of Rochester and the Problem of Resemblance', *Anselm Studies*, 2 (1988), pp. 143-63.

two short texts, but turned elsewhere for much more.[39] He probably used Burchard's *Decretum*, though if so it was an unusual copy;[40] the citations from Augustine and Jerome are harder to identify.

Gilbert Crispin's two tracts, *De altaris sacramento*, probably written in the 1090s, and *De simoniacis*, perhaps a little later, can be shown to have used the *Collectio Lanfranci* clearly enough.[41] However he also quotes a canon of the eighth council of Toledo as if it were from the *Liber pastoralis* falsely attributed to St. Ambrose. This error first occurs in the rather earlier *Diversorum patrum sententie* (Collection in Seventy-four Titles), as far as is known, and no obvious alternative source presents itself.[42] Gilbert also cites the *Liber pastoralis* proper, once as a *Liber de observatione episcoporum*.[43] Since copies of this work were widespread, both in England and in Normandy, he may well have known it directly, but it is striking that his extended quotation in *De altaris sacramento* begins and ends exactly as it does in the *Decretum* of Ivo of Chartres (v.95).[44] Ivo's immediate source has not been identified, but it seems more likely that Gilbert and Ivo worked from shared materials than that Gilbert already knew the *Decretum*.[45]

[39] The quotations from the council of Elvira (*PL* 163, col. 1468) and Gregory II (ibid., col. 1472) are found in *Isidori Mercatoris collectio*, ed. Merlin in *PL* 130, cols. 420A, 1140C, and in the *Collectio Lanfranci*.

[40] *PL* 163, col. 1462 cites council of Mainz (813), c. 56 in a form much closer to Regino of Prüm ii, c. 198 (Burchard's source) than Burchard xvii, c. 9, but then refers globally to the legislation of the councils of 'Vermeria', Macon and Tribur, and quotes a letter of Pope Deusdedit, in a way which seems to refer directly to Burchard, *Decretum* xvii, cc. 10, 15, 16 and 44 (med.). The text of the letter of Deusdedit differs from that in Burchard, but it does not occur in Regino. For the transmission of the texts in Regino and Burchard see most recently J. Müller, *Untersuchungen zur Collectio Duodecim Partium*, Abhandlungen zur rechtswissenschaftlichen Grundlagenforschung, 73 (Munich, 1989), with abundant citation of the earlier authorities.

[41] *The Works of Gilbert Crispin, Abbot of Westminster* ed. A.S. Abulafia and G.R. Evans, British Academy, Auctores Britannici medii aevi, 8 (London, 1986), pp. xxxvii-xxxviii, 142-51. The edition of *De simoniacis* by W. Holtzmann in *Neues Archiv*, 50 (1935), pp. 246-70 is in some ways more convenient; it gives fuller references to the canonical sources.

[42] Ed. Evans, pp. 132-33, cc. 51-54; *Diversorum patrum sententie*, ed. J.T. Gilchrist, Monumenta iuris canonici, Series B. Corpus collectionum, i (1973), c. 136. I am grateful to Dr. Fowler-Magerl for confirming that the mis-attribution is not known earlier. It also appears in *Alger von Lüttichs Traktat de misericordia et iusticia*, ed. R. Kretzschmar, Quellen und Forschungen zum Recht im Mittelalter, 2 (1985), p. 341 (iii, c. 36), but Alger's text is shorter than Gilbert's. The Collection in Seventy-Four Titles is not known in an Anglo-Norman manuscript, and the passage does not occur in the dependent Collection in Four Books, which is. See J. Gilchrist, 'The Manuscripts of the Canonical Collection in Four Books', *Zeitschrift der Savigny-Stiftung für Rechtsgeschichte*, Kan. Abt., 69 (1983), pp. 64-120.

[43] Ed. Evans, pp. 133, 153.

[44] For the text, first known in ninth-century copies, and the manuscripts, see F.G. Nuvolone, 'Il sermo pastoralis pseudo-Ambrosiano . . . ; riflessioni', *Gerberto: scienza, storia e mito* (Atti del Gerberti symposium, 25-27 Luglio 1983), pp. 379-565. The citation in *De simoniacis* shows many echoes of the text beyond the extract in *De altaris sacramento*. A longer passage adequate to explain Gilbert's references is found in the Collection in Nine Books (Wolfenbüttel, Herzog-August Bibliothek MS Gud. 212, fos. 37 v-38) as iv, c. 38; for this collection see below n. 47.

[45] The date of the composition of the *Decretum* is usually placed c. 1095, but for a suggestion that it is later see Brett, 'Urban II and the Collections'.

Much further evidence on the sources being exploited a little later is found in Cambridge, Corpus Christi College, MS 442, an English manuscript of the early twelfth century of unknown provenance. It is a bewildering attempt to construct a new canonical collection. The rubrics are few and sometimes exceptionally unhelpful; quite what benefit the reader was supposed to derive from headings such as 'Utrum oporteat' is hard to tell.[46] If such faults may be blamed on an unintelligent scribe, the whole collection is so loosely articulated that it is difficult to discern any coherent pattern to it at all. Nevertheless the book repays study for the sources from which it worked. These are often obscured by the blundering of texts and inscriptions, and the use of drastic paraphrase, but it seems clear its most important source was a long version of Pseudo-Isidore which contained a great deal more than the *Collectio Lanfranci*.

This is may not be particularly remarkable, but some of the sources for the mass of supplementary material are certainly unexpected. They include the early tenth-century *Libri duo de synodalibus causis* of Regino of Prüm, the mid eleventh-century collection, named after the first manuscript to be identified at Sémur but more probably compiled in the neighbourhood of Rheims, and something very like the collection of *c*. 1100 from Flanders or northern France, best represented by the fragmentary manuscript Arras, B.M. 425.[47] Though manuscripts of Regino are not uncommon, none are known to survive from Anglo-Norman libraries. The Collection of 'Sémur' is a good deal rarer, and the Arras manuscript is unique. The connections of the Corpus collection seem to be rather with the Rhineland and northern France than with Normandy or the Paris basin.

[46] Corpus, MS 442, p. 108, preceding council of Gangres (vers. Dion.), c.4. It is apparently taken from the collection of Sémur (for which see the next note), iii, c. 110: 'Utrum oporteat oblationem accipere a presbitero habente uxorem'.

[47] In general see Fournier and Le Bras, *Histoire des collections*, i, pp. 244-68, ii, pp. 259-60, 285-96, and Fuhrmann, *Einfluss*, ii, pp. 435-41.

For passages apparently taken directly from Regino compare e.g. Corpus, MS 442, p. 25 with Regino of Prüm, *Libri duo de synodalibus causis* ed. F.G.A. Wasserschleben (Leipzig, 1840), Bk. I, cc. 253, 257, Bk. II, c. 93, Bk. I, cc. 112, 116b, Bk. II,; cc. 105, 109a, 124-25, 127. Much, but not all, of this reappears in Burchard, but in a sequence further from Regino's.

For the collection of Sémur see L. Fowler-Magerl, 'Vier französische und spanische vorgratianische Kanonessammlungen', *Aspekte europäischer Rechtsgeschichte: Festgabe für Helmut Coing zum 70. Geburtstag, (Ius commune*, Sonderheft 17, 1982), pp. 124-37. Compare e.g. Corpus, MS 442, pp. 63-4 with Sémur-en-Auxois, B.M., 13, fos. 28, 37 (covering i, cc. 190-91, 193-95, 197, ii, cc. 30-31, i, c. 196).

For the collection of Arras, B.M.m MS 425 (1005) and its relation to the Collection in Nine Books, formerly known only from Wolfenbüttel, Herzog-August Bibliothek, MS Gud. 212, see most fully L. Waelkens and D. van den Auweele, 'La collection de Thérouanne en IX livres à l'abbaye de St. Pierre-au-Mont-Blandin: le codex Gandavensis 235', *Sacris erudiri*, 24 (1980), pp. 139-53. There seems no adequate foundation for the belief of Fournier and Le Bras (*Histoire des collections*, ii, pp. 286-87) that the Collection in Nine Books itself (as opposed to its second appendix) owes anything to the *Tripartita*. Compare e.g. Corpus, MS 442, pp. 113-14 with Arras MS 425, fos. 37, 61 v-62, 2 v, 54 v, 41, 42, 62. Though the continuous sequences are short, they conform more closely to Arras than to its derivative, the Collection in Nine Books.

The collection as we have it cannot be earlier than *c.* 1100. Though the latest explicit citation is from Gregory VII,[48] a text attributed to Pseudo-Calixtus I, and best known from its appearance in the later form of the *Tripartita* A, is almost certainly twelfth-century text, one which Fournier attributed tentatively to Calixtus II.[49] More decisively, a sequence of texts attributed by the inscriptions to Gregory I, Hormisdas and Eusebius was taken from Ivo of Chartres' Letter 16 of 1094, for the 'Eusebius' citation continues without a break, 'Igitur, ut mihi videtur, in aliis est rigor iusticie, in aliis est intuitus misericordie', a paraphrase of Ivo's own commentary on the passage.[50] The surviving manuscript was written little if at all later than the materials were assembled.

The Corpus collection is in some ways the antithesis of the first part of the Bodley one: where Corpus is confused and diffuse, Bodley is orderly and compact; where Bodley is based on only two sources, Corpus ranges distractedly across a mass of material. Yet both in their different ways show an active curiosity about the canon law, and a readiness to seek materials beyond the limits of the *Collectio Lanfranci.*

We cannot form a just estimate of the character of the study of canon law in England before the reign of Henry II until much more has been done. As yet much of the evidence has not even been assembled. There is a great deal more to be extracted from the printed sources.[51] There is probably much more unrecognised in the manuscripts, for the canonical texts received short shrift from even the most devoted cataloguers of English libraries until very recently. The catalogue of the canonical manuscripts in the Vatican library has already revealed what riches may lie largely unnoticed, even in a collection which has been studied by generations of canonists.[52]

---

[48] Corpus, MS 442, p. 69: '*Decr' Greg.* Filios presbiterorum – conversati fuerint', c. 14 of Urban II's council at Melfi (1089), but often attributed to 'Gregory and Urban'; pp. 114-15, '*Greg' vii de temperamento excommunicationis.* Quoniam multos – non prohibemus' (council of Rome, Lent 1078, c. [16]); p. 118, '*Greg*'. Si quis prebendas – distribuat' (Rome, November 1078, c.); p. 123, '*Ex dec' Gg' pape cap.ii.* Quoniam investituras – subiacere' (Rome, November 1078, c. [13]); p. 127, '*Ex epistola Greg.* Quis dubite sacerdotes – ecclesia exclusit, Sic et Vigilius papa Theodorum augustum', a passage from *Reg.* viii, no. 21, but within the last phrase as in Ivo, *Decretum* v, c. 378 against the Register. On pp. 119-20 November 1078 c.[7], 'Decimas quas in usu pietatis – periculum incurrere', is entered without an inscription.

[49] See p. 98: '*Cap' Calixti pape v ex decr*'. Decanie, prebende , cetere – reus iudicetur'. Compare *Tripartita* A i, 14, c. 14, Fournier, 'Les collections' (1896), pp. 652n., 677n. It is probable, though not certain, that the Corpus collection knew the *Tripartita* directly. They share a number of texts, though none in sequences of significant length.

[50] Corpus, MS 442, p. 111; compare Ivo, Ep. 16 (*Yves de Chartres: correspondance*, ed. J. Leclercq (Paris, 1949), pp. 66-68).

[51] For example, the material used by the compiler of the *Leges Henrici primi*, ed. L.J. Downer (Oxford, 1972), appears to have come from many sources, though its formal origin may be identifiable with greater precision than has yet been attempted.

[52] *A Catalogue of the Canon and Roman Law manuscripts in the Vatican Library*, ed. S. Kuttner and R. Elze, Studi e Testi 322 (1986), 328 (1987), in progress.

Bodley MS 561 is not an important collection in itself, though its readings have some importance in the study of its sources. Yet on a larger view it has great value, for its stands as an example of a host of minor texts in which the origins of the later activity of the Anglo-Norman canonists may be found.

It has long been remarked that the most devoted royal servants among the bishops were also exceptionally active in diocesan government. In principle, an episcopate largely recruited from one of the most literate administrations of the century might be expected to value the skills and forms of the canonists in the conduct of diocesan affairs. There is no more than a superficial paradox in the suggestion that such servants of a masterful king were as active in one law as in the other.

The canons from *Tripartita* B in Oxford, Bodleian Library, MS Bodley 561, fos. 7-34, compared with Ivo, *Decretum* in *PL* 161, cols. 59-1022. Canons marked with an asterisk are much adapted in the Bodley version.

| Bodley 561 | *Tripartita* B | | Ivo, *Decretum* | |
|---|---|---|---|---|
| **Part I** | | | | |
| fo. 7 | I | 1 | I | 2a |
| | | | | |
| **Part II** | | | | |
| fo. 7 v | I | 2* | I | 156-59 |
| | I | 4 | I | 160b |
| | I | 5 | I | 160c |
| 8 | I | 7-8 | I | 162b, 170 |
| | I | 9 | I | 171 |
| 8 v | I | 10b | I | 178 |
| | I | 11 | I | 184b |
| | I | 12a | I | 191a |
| 9 | I | 13 | I | 208 |
| | I | 14a | I | 211a |
| 9 v | I | 15-16 | I | 244-45 |
| | I | 17 | I | 304 |
| | I | 18 | I | 305 |
| | I | 19 | I | 307 |
| 10 | I | 20a | I | 135a |
| | I | 21 | I | 136 |
| | I | 22 | I | 137 |
| 10 v | I | 23 | I | 149 + |
| | | | | |
| **Part III** | | | | |
| fo. 12 | II | 1 | II | 1b |
| | II | 2 | II | 25 |
| | II | 3 | IV | 26 |
| 12 v | II | 4 | II | 30 |
| | II | 6 | II | 56 |
| 13 | II | 8a | II | 85a |
| | II | 26a | II | 112a |
| | II | 27a | II | 113a |
| 14 | II | 13a | II | 97 |
| | II | 14b* | II | 99b |
| | II | 22* | II | 108 |
| | II | 23 | II | 109 |
| | II | 24 | II | 110 |
| 14 v | II | 5 | II | 31 |

Part IV

| | | | | |
|---|---|---|---|---|
| fo. 15 | VIII | 1 | IV | 238 |
| | VIII | 3 | V | 23 |
| | VIII | 4a | V | 24a |
| | VIII | 6 | V | 50 |
| 16 | VIII | 8 | V | 52 |
| | VIII | 7 | V | 51 |

Part V

| | | | | |
|---|---|---|---|---|
| fo. 19 | IX | 6 | V | 281 |
| | IX | 7 | V | 282 |
| | IX | 8 | V | 283-84 |
| | IX | 9 | V | 285 |
| | IX | 10 | V | 286 |
| 20 v | IX | 3 | V | 72b |
| 21 v | III | 9 | III | 11 |
| | III | 10 | III | 12 |
| | III | 11 | III | 13 |
| | III | 12 | III | 14 |
| | III | 13 | III | 113 |
| | III | 34* | III | 282 |
| 22 v | III | 22 | III | 180 |
| | III | 2 | III | 55 |
| | III | 3 | III | 56 |
| | III | 7 | III | 104 |
| 23 | III | 4* | III | 98a |
| | III | 5 | III | 98b |
| | III | 19-20 | III | 177-78 |
| 24 | III | 27 | III | 208a |
| 24 v | III | 15 | III | 123 |

Part VI

| | | | | |
|---|---|---|---|---|
| fo. 25 | III | 32 | III | 270 |
| | III | 33 | III | 273 |
| | VI | 1 | IV | 68 |
| | VII | 5a | IV | 204a |
| | VII | 6a | IV | 206a |
| | VII | 8b | IV | 208 |
| | VIII | 2 | V | 20 |
| | IV | 2 | IV | 14 |
| 25 v | V | 3a | IV | 33a |
| | V | 4 | IV | 45 |
| | V | 5 | IV | 53 |

Part VII

| fo. 27 | X | 1 | VI | 20 |
|--------|---|-----|-----|------|
| 28 | X | 2 | VI | 21 |
| | X | 3 | VI | 41 |
| | X | 4 | VI | 42a |
| | X | 12 | VI | 230 |
| | X | 17 | VI | 308 |
| 28 v | X | 18a | VI | 383a |
| | X | 19 | VI | 384 |
| | X | 51 | VI | 427 |
| 30 v | X | 9 | VI | 229 |
| 31 | X | 13 | VI | 231 |
| | X | 15 | VI | 236 |
| | X | 21 | VI | 386 |
| | X | 32a | VI | 397a |
| 31 v | X | 35 | VI | 400 |
| | X | 23 | VI | 388 |
| | X | 6 | VI | 252 |
| | X | 40a | VI | 405a |
| 32 | X | 42 | VI | 410 |
| | X | 45 | VI | 415 |
| | X | 47* | VI | 413 |

Part VIII

| fo. 33 | XIII | 3 | VII | 104 |
|--------|------|---|-----|-----|
| | XIII | 4 | VII | 114 |

+ The canon is found in manuscripts of the *Decretum* but not the edition; see. P. Landau, 'Das Dekret des Ivo von Chartres', *Zeitschrift der Savigny-Stiftung für Rechtsgeschichte*, Kan. Abt., 70 (1984), pp. 1-44, esp. 36.

# 12

# Two Letters Relating to Relics of St. Thomas
## of Canterbury

### Benedicta Ward

The relics of St. Thomas Becket were buried in haste in the crypt of Canterbury Cathedral on the night of his murder.[1] They were elevated with great
pomp to a shrine covered with gold and jewels on Tuesday, 7 July 1220, by
Stephen Langton archbishop of Canterbury and his assistant, Roger of Salisbury. They opened and examined the content of the coffin and, after abstract-
ing some fragments of bone for presentation to the pope, rewrapped the bones
and sealed them in a new oak coffin.[2]

The link between the cult of relics, that most visual and tactile of all
medieval ways of devotion, and the life of the mind is well exemplified in the
matter of the cult of Becket. Several men of learning were deeply involved in
the matter of the bones of the new martyr. John of Salisbury wrote an account
of Becket and ended on a note of admiration for the scenes at the tomb
containing his relics:

> There great miracles are wrought . . . in the place where he was at last buried,
> paralytics are cured, the blind see, the deaf hear, the dumb speak, the lame walk,
> lepers are cured..and (a thing unheard of from the days of our fathers) the dead are
> raised.[3]

Stephen Langton not only praised Becket in sermons and in teaching,[4] he
also masterminded the Translation and helped himself to some of the bones. It
seems, therefore, that the veneration of relics was not confined to a credulous
crowd of innocents nor to monks with an eye to the main chance; men of
learning and of sincere religion at all levels of society were as concerned with

---

[1] *Materials for the History of Thomas Becket*, ed. J.C. Robertson (Rolls Series, London, 1877),
iii, pp. 521ff. Herbert of Bosham, *Vita S. Thomae*.

[2] Ibid., ii, p. 249, Godfrey of Coventry.

[3] Ibid., ii. p. 322, John of Salisbury.

[4] Cf. B. Smalley. *The Becket Conflict and the Schools* (Oxford, 1973), pp. 204ff. for Stephen
Langton and Becket.

the veneration of the bones of the holy dead as they were with the elucidation of the holy page. A mixture of shrewd business senses, with home-orientated pride and devout trust in the prayers, presence and power of the saint of Canterbury motivated them all. There are two letters in the archives of Canterbury Cathedral Library which seem to show such a link at a more humble level, that of the average Canterbury boy studying in Paris in the thirteenth century, yet alert to anything that concerned the new cult of his home cathedral. They are about the same matter, the arrival in Paris in the late thirteenth century of some fragments of the bones of St. Thomas.

The first letter (Canterbury Cathedral Library, Eastry Correspondence, iv, 12) was sent by the abbot of St. Denis to the monk Robert of St. Augustine's in Canterbury, concerning some relics of Becket which had been offered to him, asking for verification of their authenticity:

> Viro religioso et honesto fratri Roberto dicto de sancto augustino monacho sancte trinitate cantuar. R. miseratione dei ecclesie beati dyon(isie) in Francia humilis abbas, salutem et sincerum in Domino caritatem. Noveritis nos a Huet serviente vestro ut dicit, recipisse quoddam os cum capillis de capite beati Thome martyris sicut vestre nobis directe littere asserebant existens in quodam parvo scrinio ligni rubei incluso in alio maiori scrinio de corio bullito et quod predictam os cum capillis, care, secure et reverenter reservare proponimus quusque de relatione literarum fuerit certa fides. valete. datum die Jovis ante Brandon.

The relics were said to have been sent to the abbot of St-Denis by the monk Robert of St. Augustine's; a monk of this name is mentioned in Serle's *List* as dying in 1291.[5] If, as seems probable, the abbot R. of St-Denis was Reginald Giffard, abbot of St-Denis 1287 to 1304, this letter would fall between 1287 and 1291. Giffard was an advocate of the canonisation of St. Louis and present at his Translation in 1285,[6] a man therefore especially likely to be interested in a gift of relics of the saint who had not only called upon St. Denis at his death but been the focus for the prayers of St. Louis, who visited his tomb with thank-offerings for Thomas's intercession for his son in 1179. It is probable that Robert of St. Augustine's was offering the abbot a private gift of relics and had described them in some detail in a previous letter.

A second letter (Canterbury Cathedral Library, Eastry Correspondence, iv, 2) seems to throw a little more light upon these relics brought to Paris by Huet which the abbot viewed with suspicion.

> Venerande religionis viro ac reverendissimo in Christo patri domino Henrico priori ecclesie Christi Cant. suus devotus J. Pikenot alumpnus scolaris Paris, si placet

[5] W.G. Searle, *Christ Church Canterbury: Lists of Deans, Priors and Monks of Christ Church Monastery*, Cambridge, Antiquarian Society, 34 (London, 1902.), 'Robert of St. Augustine's', p. 196.

[6] M. Felibien, *Histoire de l'abbaye royal de Saint-Denys en France* (Paris, 1706) pp. 256-61; *Gallia Christiana*, vii, cols. 396-97.

seipsum cum omni reverencia et honore. Sacrosanctam matrem ecclesiam Christi quasi proles nepharia nequiter contempnerem et erga vos quasi filius degenerans efficerer ingratus si ea que in predicta ecclesie prejudicium et gravamen et in vestram infamiam quamcumque oriuntur vobis celeriter non referarem. Quare sanctitate vestre significo quod pervenit as partes gallicanas quidem valetus nomine Huginet filius Henrici coci vestri qui deferebat abbati sancti Dyonisii ex parte domini Roberti de Sancto Augustino conmonachi vestri preciosas et sacrosanctissimas reliquias beati Thome Cantuariensis archiepiscopi, videlicet unam peciam de craneo capitis ipsius ad mesuram unius pollicis una cum quadam parte capillorum suorum, quas quidem reliquias cum predictus abbas in crastino cinerum recepisset admiratus est et hiis fides certam non adhibens ipsas vanas et transfatorias esse existimavit et prenominatus Huginet fore incarcerasset. Verumptamen fatebatur se reliquias supradictas reservaturum quousque per indicia variora vel per mandata spiritualia de premissis certificaretur, quoniam garcifer prenominatus litteras quas recepit a predicto domino R. in itinere amittebat. Unde domine abbas ipsum valletum remittebat ut literas certificatorias de premissis reportaret, unde prout existimo si prudenter et circumspecte procedetis reliquias prefaras de facili adquireretis, quoniam dominus abbas easdem (reliquias) predicto garcifer voluit retradisse. De premissis omnibus diligenti facta inquisitione certificatus sum per illos qui tali et tanto exennio faciendo interfuerunt (ver)umptamen reservatur vobis quedem ampulla vetustissima plena sanguine et quadam parte cordis gloriosi martiris supradicti, quam quidam ampullam predictus garcifer debuerat detulisse in Pykardiam et eam deputavit conservandam Thome Frere filio Thomae de Berkynge quondam servientis vestri. Renunciavit etiam valletus prenominatus quod predictus dominus R. in breve ad partes transmarinas accedet. Valet in Christo Jesu.

This letter was sent soon after the previous one and is from John Pikenot, a former schoolboy in Canterbury, now pursuing his studies in Paris. The Pikenots were a well-known family in Canterbury, for whom Pikenot Lane is named; Serle's *List*[7] mentions 'R. Pikenot' *c.* 1275 and a 'Rich. Pikenot' presumably the same man, who died in 1308; the list also contains the name 'John Pikenot' as a monk of Christ Church. In this letter John Pikenot was writing privately to Prior Henry Eastry (1285-1331) and in a style notably more inflated than that of the abbot in the previous letter. He expresses concern about some relics brought to Paris by Little Hugh, the son of the secular cook, Henry, employed in the cathedral monastery, which the boy claimed had been sent by his hand to the abbot of St-Denis from a monk Robert of St. Augustine's. There is no doubt that both letters are about the same event, which was well-known in Paris after the public offering of the relics by the boy to the abbot instead of the private presentation which had been intended. The manner of the gift and its bearer seems to have made Giffard suspicious, especially since Hugh brought no authenticating letters, saying he had lost them on the way. The abbot wrote immediately to Robert; his letter is dated the day following the presentation. It may be that the Canterbury men in Paris, intensely loyal to their own saint and church, at once attempted to corner these relics in order to send them home. While Giffard waited for the arrival of

---

[7] Searle, *Christ Church Canterbury*, 'R Pikenot', 'Rich Pikenot', 'John Pikenot', p. 169.

Robert himself to clarify matters,[8] John Pikenot, in collusion with Thomas of
Barking, another member of a well-known Canterbury family[9] and also a
faithful son of Canterbury, had taken another part of the relics into his own
keeping, wresting them by fair means or foul from the boy who claimed to be
taking them for Robert into Picardy. These included the valuable phial of the
'blood of Becket', already the most notable souvenir of the cult. Moreover, he
suggested to Prior Eastry a dubious ploy by which he should refuse to
authenticate the relics, and so ensure their return, so that thereafter they could
be treated as authentic relics of the martyr.

The question which was not asked is as revealing as those that were: a
private gift had become a contentious public matter and the abbot wanted to
be assured by a responsible person that he was indeed receiving genuine relics
from Canterbury; since the affair was public, he now needed public confirmation. John Pikenot assumed that if Prior Eastry withheld such confirmation,
the relics would not be accepted, but could still be made use of privately. The
question of how Dom Robert could possibly have acquired such relics privately
in the first place was not raised; the assumption was that for a public
acceptance of relics from one church by another, public affirmation was
needed, but that this need not at all affect the private status and authenticity of
the relics themselves. The questions for those concerned in this affair were not
about provenance or authenticity as we should understand it. John Pikenot's
studies may have been teaching him dialectic, Reginald Giffard, Prior Eastry
and Dom Robert may have been, like John of Salisbury and Stephen Langton,
sufficiently learned men within their own range, a selective reading of whose
works produces an effect of understanding across time. But this sense of
timeless familiarity is not the whole story. They were men of their age and this
difference of approach appears here as another and equally valid aspect of
their thought. Their objectivity is not their only trait when, as here, they were
totally absorbed and submerged in other and to us more alien ways of thought;
a salutary example, perhaps, of how alien so much in the area of medieval
learning is which seems at first to be immediately available.

---

[8]   The term '*Dominus R.*' might be taken to mean '*Dominus Rex*' but it seems more natural to
the sense to take it as referring to '*Dominus Robertus*', whose visit was pending.

[9]   Searle, *Christ Church Canterbury*, 'William of Barking', senior and junior, 'Robert of
Barking', pp. 174-75.

# 13

# A Contemporary Miniature of Thomas Becket

## Christopher de Hamel

I am not sure whether Margaret Gibson approves of Thomas Becket, but I suspect that if she had met him she would have regarded him as devious and intellectually shallow and as a social snob, all of which Margaret very certainly is not, and she would have fixed him with one of her pitying looks that make one wriggle miserably with the shameful realisation that one has not read every volume of the *Corpus Christianorum* and the *Patrologia Latina*. Becket was not well-read. To his credit, perhaps, he knew that he lacked the necessary scholastic training. When he became archbishop of Canterbury he surrounded himself with a team of *eruditi*, academic advisers and speech-writers among whom Master Herbert of Bosham was Becket's principal biblical tutor or (as Herbert himself called it) master of the holy page.[1]

Herbert was with the exiled archbishop during their two-year stay at Pontigny abbey, south-east of Sens, from December 1164. While they were there Thomas Becket made a special daily study of the Psalms and the Pauline Epistles under the guidance of Herbert, who recalled in his biography of Becket that the manuscripts which they used were seldom out of the archbishop's hands.[2] While they were at Pontigny, Thomas asked Herbert to undertake for him a special edition of Peter Lombard's Great Gloss on these two texts. In his preface to the edition, Herbert explained the circumstances at length.[3] The archaic Gloss by Anselm of Laon on these biblical books had been expanded by Herbert's former teacher Peter Lombard but the new versions had passed into circulation before their author had finished revising them, Herbert asserted, and soon afterwards Peter Lombard became bishop of Paris (1159) and died (1160). In fact, Peter Lombard's text is quite complete and usable and it remained popular for a hundred years or more, but it may

---

[1] B. Smalley *The Becket Conflict and the Schools: A Study in Intellectual Politics* (Oxford, 1873), esp. chap. 3, pp. 59-86.

[2] *Materials for the History of Thomas Becket, Archbishop of Canterbury*, ed. J.C. Robertson (RS, London, 1877), iii, p.379.

[3] M.R. James, *The Western Manuscripts in the Library of Trinity College, Cambridge: A Descriptive Catalogue*, i (Cambridge, 1900), pp. 189-91.

have seemed difficult to Thomas Becket. Herbert noted that critics might disagree with the need to rework the text yet again but that his justification was that Thomas Becket wanted it done, 'ita fieri voluit'. Herbert was asked to provide variant readings of the biblical text according to the usages of different churches and to supply cross-references to parallel passages. He divided the psalter into a series of *capitula* or *distinctiones*, as devised and laid out (he explained) when he was living with Thomas Becket. On the Routh principle, Herbert checked Peter Lombard's sources, and labelled them clearly. Sometimes, where Peter Lombard misattributed a quotation to an earlier authority, Herbert's revision includes a little drawing of that author pointing to the text and speaking phrases such as *Non ego* or *Ego non probo* , as if – how tactful and how characteristic of the twelfth century – it was not Herbert of Bosham who had dared correct the great Peter Lombard but the patristic author himself who had come back to look over his shoulder. Coloured inks and little drawings and sparkling expensive gold initials throughout are all part of the programme to make the text accessible. Thomas Becket could have understood it all at last. The Gloss was always something of a guide to instant erudition in patristic commentaries. The unique and even more visually clear version prepared by Herbert of Bosham for Thomas Becket conjures for us an intriguing image of the grand archbishop and his teacher busily hunched over the manuscript in frenzied tutorials at Pontigny.

In early 1168 Becket and his entourage were obliged to move on to Sens, and events accelerated rapidly, culminating finally with the return to England and the martyrdom in Canterbury cathedral in December 1170. Thomas Becket never finished his classes with his tutor and Herbert's special archiepiscopal version of Peter Lombard's Great Gloss was not among the books which Thomas Becket bequeathed to Christ Church.[4] On the contrary, Herbert of Bosham still owned it in the 1170s. He added dedications to William of Champagne as bishop of Sens 1168-76, but never gave the work to William either and the huge compilation in four folio volumes was bequeathed or given by Herbert himself to Christ Church where the big books were eventually shelved beside Becket's own manuscripts.[5] With the dispersal of the Christ

---

[4]  Idem, *The Ancient Libraries of Canterbury and Dover* (Cambridge, 1903), pp. 82-85, nos. 783-853 (this text is being re-edited by Margaret Gibson and Richard Sharpe); C. de Hamel, *Glossed Books of the Bible and the Origins of the Paris Booktrade* (Woodbridge, 1984), pp. 38-44. Becket's books included the standard *Psalterium secundum Longobardum* and *Epistole Pauli secundum Longobardum* (nos. 788 and 802). Quaritch catalogue 1147 (1991), item 94, comprises three leaves from a twelfth-century manuscript of Peter Lombard on the Pauline Epistles, now MS 639 in the Schøyen Collection in London; these leaves include the marginal marks of clusters of four dots added to many manuscripts at Christ Church in the early fifteenth century, and in view of the archaic page layout of the three leaves (cf. de Hamel, *Glossed Books*, p. 21) and the comparative rarity of this text at so early a date, it might be that we have a relic of Becket's copy. This was not a beautiful or clearly laid-out manuscript and, if Becket's, might have lead him into demanding a luxury version instead.

[5]  *Ancient Libraries*, p. 85. nos. 854-57, with Herbert's *Thomus* or life of Becket.

Church library in the sixteenth century, three of the four volumes found their way to Trinity College, Cambridge, and one came to the Bodleian Library.[6]

The preface quoted above occurs on fos. 1-3 of Trinity College, MS B.5.4. The first page opens with a large illuminated initial beside which is a standing figure of an archbishop wearing the pallium and giving orders to a smaller standing man holding a scroll. This second man is certainly Herbert of Bosham and, since the manuscript was his own, we must suppose it to be as accurate a portrait as is likely to exist in romanesque art. He appears as a layman with wavy brown hair coming down over his ears, with white bushy eyebrows and a white beard. Herbert was probably only in his fifties at this time, but was already called *senex* by a friend in 1173-76 and the white beard may have made him look older.[7] It is, however, the portrait of the archbishop which is of especial interest. M.R. James identified him as William of Champagne, bishop of Sens, and recorded the word *pontifex* written above his head. However, close inspection of this inscription along in the extreme upper margin, where it is rubbed and smudged and trimmed close, reveals further words before this, *Scs.Thom[.. ma]rt.& pontifex*, and this, therefore, is not William of Sens but Thomas Becket himself.[8] It may be compared with the miniature on fo. 71 of the manuscript beside the opening of Psalm 26, showing Christ with David in the same relationship, similarly with their names written above them, and Herbert of Bosham in his life of Thomas equates the saint with Christ and himself with his scriptural apologist.

There are no known contemporary portraits of Becket: the earliest acknow-ledged picture of the new saint in a manuscript is generally thought to be the famous scene of the martyrdom in the life and letters of Becket by John of Salisbury, B.L., Cotton MS Claudius B.II, datable to about 1185.[9] Recently

---

[6] The Psalms are (i) Trinity College, MS B.5.4 and (ii) Bodleian Library, MS Auct.E.inf.6; the Epistles are (i-ii) Trinity College, MS B.5.6-7. cf C.R. Dodwell, *The Canterbury School of Illumination, 1066-1200* (Cambridge, 1954), pp. 104-6; C. de Hamel, 'Manuscripts of Herbert of Bosham', *Manuscripts at Oxford: An Exhibition in Memory of Richard William Hunt (1908-1979)* (Oxford, 1980), pp. 38-41; idem, *Glossed Books*, chap. 4; [C.M. Kauffmann], *English Romanes-que Art*, ed. G. Zarnecki, J. Holt and T. Holland, exhib., Hayward Gallery (London, 1984), p. 124, no. 69.

[7] Smalley, *Becket Conflict*, p. 59.

[8] A careful identification of this figure with Becket was made by T. Borenius, 'Some Further Aspects of the Iconography of St. Thomas of Canterbury', *Archaeologia*, lxxxiii (1933, 2 ser., xxxiii), pp.172-73, fig.1, dating it to 'perhaps only twenty of thirty years after the archbishop's death'. I am grateful to Peter Kidd for his reference, rescuing me at the last moment from the embarrassment of mistakenly publishing the discovery as my own. There is a dedicatory miniature of William of Champagne, clean-shaven and looking nothing like the archbishop shown here, in Yale University, Beinecke MS 214, dated 1229 (fig.2 on p. 38 in W.B. Clark, 'Art and Historiography in two Thirteenth-Century Manuscripts from Northern France', *Gesta*, xvii (1978), pp. 37-48; cf. B.A. Shailor. *Catalogue of Medieval and Renaissance Manuscripts in the Beinecke Rare Book and Manuscript Library, Yale University*, i (New York, 1984), pp. 290-92).

[9] C.M. Kauffmann, *Romanesque Manuscripts, 1066-1190 A. Survey of Manuscripts Illumi-nated in the British Isles*, iii (London, 1975), p. 116, no. 93, with fig.257.

Thomas Becket, Cambridge, Trinity College,
MS B.5.4, fo. 1 r

Michael Gullick has recognised from its script that this manuscript was probably made in Cirencester rather than in Canterbury, as has long been supposed,[10] which perhaps weakens its evidential value for its depiction of Becket's appearance, but certainly from the 1180s onwards there are numerous representations of the martyr both from Canterbury and indeed from all over Europe.[11] The new miniature in Trinity College, MS B.5.4 cannot be later than 1176 since in that year William of Champagne was translated from Sens to Rheims.[12] The figure of Becket here is about 80 mm. high. Thomas is dressed in an orange cassock lined with blue, and he wears the blue and gold pallium he had received from Alexander III.[13] He holds a blue crosier surmounted by a gold knop with a white (presumably ivory) crook. He has brown tufty hair parted in the middle, and a short brown beard grizzled with

[10] A.G. Watson, *Supplement* to N.R. Ker, *Medieval Libraries of Great Britain* (London, 1987), p. 14 and n.2; M. Gullick, 'A Twelfth-Century Manuscript of the Letters of Thomas Becket', *English Manuscript Studies, 1100-1700*, ed, P. Beal and J. Griffiths, ii (Oxford, 1990), pp. 1-31.

[11] T. Borenius, *The Iconography of St. Thomas of Canterbury* (Oxford, 1929).

[12] Dodwell, pp. 105-6; P.R. Robinson, *Dated and Datable Manuscripts, c. 737-1600, in Cambridge Libraries* (Woodbridge, 1988), pp. 92-93, no.329.

[13] Herbert of Bosham makes the point of the pallium, noting that by the act of putting it on Thomas was elevated from a bishop into an archbishop, *Materials*, iv (1879), p. 281. It was afterwards preserved at Canterbury and performed miracles, ibid., ii (1876), p. 54.

white. The beard is a feature of the early portraits and occurs in pictures of the saint in the Canterbury stained glass.

If this was one of the actual manuscripts ordered by Becket and which he and Herbert of Bosham studied together at Pontigny, how are we to explain the presence of a preface which refers to Thomas unambiguously as saint and martyr?

There is no doubt that these big volumes are indeed Herbert's unique working copies. They contain corrections and cancellations and alterations and were doubtless being constantly improved and changed by their owner in the years before he finally gave them to Canterbury. The collation of the seven-leaf first gathering of Trinity College, MS B.5.4 is given by James as 'i$^8$ (wants 1?)' but is actually more complicated and a diagram of the structure of the first two gatherings will show it more clearly:

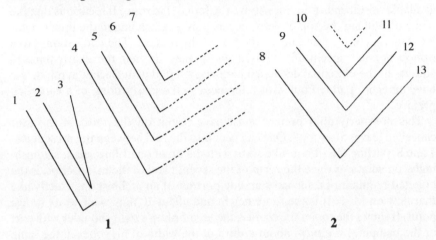

The text, as it is now, is continuous from fo. 1 through to fo. 10, and then two leaves are lacking with the opening of Psalm 1. Folios 1-3 are inserts. The first gathering originally consisted of 8 leaves., of which v-viii were cancelled, leaving narrow stubs after the present fo. 7. The manuscript must originally have opened on what is now fo. 4. This is the first prologue to the Psalms, 'David filius iesse . . . ', followed by the second prologue on fo. 4 v and the third prologue on fo. 6 v and the epistle of St. Jerome to Sophronius, ending at the top of fo. 7 v. Then there was a three-line heading in red and blue, now erased and over-written but of which the word *psalmorum* is still decipherable. The text on some of the leaves which followed fo. 7 may have included Herbert's list of *distinctiones* on the Psalms, joining up presumably with the text at the top of the present fo. 8. When the manuscript was in this form, Becket died. Herbert was left with an enormously expensive commissioned book intended for the specific use of a patron who would now never take delivery of it. He clearly made one (unsuccessful) attempt to capitalise on the fact that the work was assembled for a saint and he hastily changed the dedication from Thomas Becket into one addressed to his old and rich friend

William of Champagne, gushingly emphasising that this was the book ordered by St. Thomas himself. William did not rise to the bait and Herbert gave up, and he presented the volumes, still not quite finished, to Canterbury.

The change of dedication was done as follows. Four leaves were cut out after fo. 7, and a signature number 'I' was added at the foot what now became the last leaf of the gathering. The heading on fo. 7 v was scraped off and a new and longer heading written over the erasure and into the margin explaining now that these are the *distinctiones* which Herbert arranged and wrote when in exile with the blessed martyr Thomas. Three leaves were added at the beginning with a new preface recounting how the book was ordered by the now true and glorious martyr of Christ, Archbishop Thomas of Canterbury. The text was not quite long enough to fill the three leaves and so the script in the second column of fo. 3 v had to be stretched out in order to pad out the space available; it still ends four lines above the foot of the page. It is curious that the name of William, bishop of Sens, occurs only as a heading in the upper right-hand margin of fo. 1 and not in the text of the preface. The dedication is to a bishop but not specifically to William. It may be that the neatly-phrased address to the episcopal dedicatee here was drafted with Becket in mind. We have an echo, padded out with references to the martyrdom, of a cancelled preface.

This pre-martyrdom preface must have begun on the third of the four cancelled leaves after fo. 7. One can peer into the fold between the present fos. 7 and 8, parting the ribbon-like stubs with the tip of one's fingernail: astonishingly, on what was once the recto of the seventh leaf of the manuscript, is the bisected remnant of a second standing portrait of an archbishop, exactly like that now on fo. 1. It is the same height and about 10 mm. wide at its widest point. It shows the top of the crosier, the archibishop's right shoulder with part of the pallium, his elbow, about a third of the width of his robes in the same colours as on fo. 1, and his right foot. There is every reason to believe that this was Thomas Becket and that it prefixed Herbert's original dedicatory preface. It was surely painted in Becket's lifetime, perhaps at Pontigny. Although most of it was cut away by Herbert himself in the 1170s, it represents the only strictly contemporary picture of Thomas Becket.

Trinity College, MS B.5.4 thus gives us two new images of Becket. The second picture is a copy of the first, and the first may well have been seen and approved by the archbishop himself. The fact that references to Becket as martyr are all subsequent insertions into the book broadens the dating of the manuscript to before 1170, perhaps in part as early as about 1165, and it may be that a good part of the book production was indeed carried out at Pontigny Abbey and that Becket himself actually handled it in his attempt to master the Great Gloss. Margaret Gibson might well not approve of Thomas Becket's learning, but I hope she will give him credit for trying.

# 14

## Aspects of John of Salisbury's Historia Pontificalis

### Christopher Brooke

Modern students of John of Salisbury have placed very high among his qualities the capacity to portray men and events. His *Historia Pontificalis* is perhaps the most popular of his works today. It was not so in former times. Only one copy, and that incomplete, survives from the middle ages, and traces of its influence are few; even if we supposed that a great deal of what John wrote is missing (which is not very probable), it is hard to believe that John thought well enough of it to finish and polish and circulate it. It is too obviously a fragment.

Yet it is full of surprises; and a few of these are the theme of this essay. I take for granted the solid ground established by R.L. Poole in his edition, the ripe fruit of his later years, and I assume that Marjorie Chibnall's splendid text and translation, now readily available in Oxford Medieval Texts, is in my reader's hands.[1] In the introduction to *HP* and in her paper in *The World of John of Salisbury*, she has set securely the lines of our interpretation of John as a historian.[2] She shows, for example, how his introduction is a topos, but a very individual one, setting his own interpretation on the historian's task.[3] He opens with a hasty history of history, from the Books of Chronicles through St. Luke to Cassiodorus, Bede and Hugh of St. Victor (to whom he attributes a chronicle quite unknown and perhaps imagined). 'My aim' he says, 'like that of other chroniclers before me, shall be to profit my contemporaries and future generations' – and, like the best historians of his day, it may be said, he really

---

[1]  *Ioannis Saresberiensis historiae pontificalis quae supersunt*, ed. R.L. Poole (Oxford, 1927); *The Historia Pontificalis of John of Salisbury*, ed. and trans. M. Chibnall (Nelson's Medieval Texts, 1956; corr. repr., Oxford Medieval Texts, 1986). My debt to Marjorie Chibnall's edition – henceforth *HP* – will be very obvious; much of what I have to say is based on her introduction and on her study 'John of Salisbury as Historian' – henceforth Chibnall (1984) – in *The World of John of Salisbury*, ed. M. Wilks (Studies in Church History, Subsidia, 3, Oxford, 1984, otherwise referred to as *The World of JS*), pp. 169-77; and she kindly consented to my making many quotations from *HP*.

[2]  Chibnall (1984)

[3]  Ibid., pp. 169-70.

set out to interest and entertain and tell a story, and succeeded. 'In what I am going to relate', furthermore, 'I shall, by the help of God, write nothing but what I myself have seen and heard and know to be true, or have on good authority from the testimony or writings of reliable men.'[4] He does indeed show the benefit of his wide reading; his substance 'might have been found in a monastic chronicle' – the monastic influence, as Marjorie Chibnall has pointed out, is clearer here than elsewhere in his writings.[5] Above all, by analysing his account of the case of the Empress Matilda and the discussion in the papal curia of her claim to the English throne, she brings out his strengths and weaknesses – 'showing how he sometimes telescoped events and subordinated the causes of a dispute to the outcome, yet always helped to illuminate'.[6] Thus he attributed to his arch-enemy, Arnulf, bishop of Lisieux, the argument that the empress was illegitimate since her mother had been a nun and should not have married – an argument damaging to Arnulf in the 1160s when the empress's son was king of England; and he puts into the mouth of the empress's advocate, Ulger, bishop of Angers, a thundering rejection of the argument – even though we have an eye-witness account of Ulger's defence in 1139 from Gilbert Foliot, who tells us the good bishop made no answer to the charge.[7] John was marvellously well informed on many of the incidents he describes, and is so determined to have it both ways, to enjoy himself at his characters' expense – or in relating their virtues – that he produces an appearance of fair-mindedness not always so visible in his letters. Sometimes it is an illusion; often not. It achieves an exceptional subtlety in his treatment of St. Bernard and Gilbert of La Porrée. He owed Bernard patronage and savoured his sanctity; he had sat at Gilbert's feet and greatly admired him. But he is determined to poke fun at them as well as expounding the pros and cons of their dispute according to his lights.

> Various opinions are held of the abbot himself, some saying one thing and some another, because he attacked the two men most famous for their learning – Peter Abelard and this same Gilbert – and pursued them with such zeal that he secured the condemnation of Peter and only just failed to have the other condemned. For my

[4] *HP*, Prologue, pp. 1-4.
[5] Chibnall (1984), p. 170.
[6] Ibid., pp. 172-73.
[7] *HP*, pp. 83-85; *The Letters and Charters of Gilbert Foliot . . .* , ed. A. Morey and C.N.L. Brooke (Cambridge, 1967), pp. 65-66; Chibnall (1984), pp. 172-73; cf. A. Morey and C.N.L. Brooke, *Gilbert Foliot and his Letters* (Cambridge, 1965), pp. 119-20; G. Constable, ed., *The Letters of Peter the Venerable* (2 vols., Cambridge, MA, 1967), ii, pp. 252-56. The exact interpretation of the discussion before Innocent II in 1136 and 1139 has been in some way confused by John – just how, is not entirely clear; but there does seem a clear discrepancy between Ulger's silence in Gilbert Foliot (an eye-witness), and his eloquent rebuttal in John. On Arnulf, see F. Barlow, ed., *The Letters of Arnulf of Lisieux* Camden Third Series, 61, (London, 1939), introduction; cf. i, p. 195, of *Letters of John of Salisbury*, ed. W.J. Millor, H.E. Butler and C.N.L. Brooke (2 vols., i, Nelson's Medieval Texts, 1955 (and corr. reprint, Oxford Medieval Texts, 1986), ii, Oxford Medieval Texts, 1979) – henceforth *Letters*.

part I cannot believe that a man of such sanctity was not guided by the love of God, or that a bishop of such prudence and learning should commit to writing anything whose meaning was not clear to him, however obscure it might seem to others.[8]

In this celebrated passage, which Jane Austen would not have been ashamed to have written, the irony is clear, and gently applied – he is not talking about Arnulf of Lisieux – and brilliantly successful. One is reminded of his letter to Thomas Becket, archdeacon of Canterbury and royal chancellor, when Archbishop Theobald was on his deathbed, in which the subleties and ambiguities of Becket's position are brilliantly revealed – wholly beholden to two patrons, king and archbishop, not at one in their demands on him.[9] But I am also reminded of many passages in his letters where he runs two arguments in harness and is not so successful in keeping them under control, so that his meaning becomes almost as obscure as Bishop Gilbert's and he drives his translator to despair.[10]

The manuscript names no author; but since Giesebrecht first suggested in 1873 that it was written by John, no one seems seriously to have doubted it.[11] My father, the late Professor Z.N. Brooke, used to reckon it sharper in tone, less charitable, than he would have expected of John, and that is a judgement worth recalling. But the issue of authorship has been discussed in meticulous detail by Dr. John McLoughlin, and I do not propose to resume it here.[12] I am entirely convinced that John wrote it; and that – apart from style and attitude – a major ground for this belief remains Giesebrecht's original observation, that 'the only man with the knowledge and experience to have written it was John of Salisbury'.[13]

The author himself describes his theme (or a major theme) as 'pontificalis historia': 'superest ut ad pontificalem redeamus hystoriam' says he after a particularly long digression;[14] and Marjorie Chibnall pointed out long ago the likely identification of the work with 'Libellus I. Sar' de statu curie Romane' of

---

[8]  *HP*, p. 16.

[9]  *Letters*, i, no. 128; cf. Brooke in *The World of JS*, pp. 15-18.

[10]  E.g. *Letters*, i, no. 112 and exposition ibid., pp. xlvii-l; or the confusion of argument and quotation in ibid., no. 124, which is clarified a little in a modern edition by italics; or the eloquent, but sometimes opaque, shifts and turns in ii, nos. 175-76. On the other hand, i, no. 131 – the report of the Anstey case – is a model of clear exposition of other men's arguments in a complex lawsuit.

[11]  W. von Giesebrecht, 'Arnold von Brescia' in *Sitzungsberichte der philosophisch-philologischen und historischen Classe der k.b. Akademie der Wissenschaft zu München* (1873), pp. 122-54, at pp. 125-26; repr. in *Arnold von Brescia* (Munich, 1893), pp. 6-7.

[12]  J. McLoughlin, 'John of Salisbury (*c*. 1120-1180): The Career and Attitudes of a Schoolman in Church Politics', (Unpublished Ph.D. thesis, Trinity College Dublin, 1988), i, pp. 129-47. I am much indebted to Dr. John McLoughlin for the gift of his thesis and permission to cite it.

[13]  Dr. Chibnall in *HP*, p. xix, paraphrasing Giesebrecht (n. 11): 'So schlecht unterrichtet sind wir nicht in der Geschichte jener Zeit, dass wir einen Mann, der seine Lebensumstände so bestimmt darlegt, nicht erkennen sollten. Der Verfasser ist ohne Zweifel kein anderer, als Johann von Salisbury'.

[14]  *HP*, p. 41.

the fourteenth-century Canterbury library catalogue.[15] Like all his works, it is formless, yet it is inspired by a kind of plan which is evident enough: to describe events as they flowed in and out of the papal curia during the years when John had been a frequent visitor there, and so an eye-witness of much that he narrates. He follows a well-worn path in pretending that his book is a continuation of another chronicle: in his case of an obscure continuation of the chronicle of Sigebert of Gembloux.[16] At first sight this appears an unlikely peg to hang his book on; and it seems to have been chosen for no better reason than that the book he continues ended in 1148, very shortly after John had entered the service of Theobald, archbishop of Canterbury, and probably the year in which John himself was first in the papal curia.[17] This underlines his purpose: to describe events as they impinged on the curia, especially on a frequent visitor to the curia.

The path of John's early life has been traversed even more often than he took the path to Rome.[18] Born in Old Sarum, a student in Paris – and perhaps elsewhere in France – from 1135/6 to 1147, clerk to Archbishop Theobald from 1147 to 1161 (when Theobald died), then in the service of Theobald's successor, and John's close friend, Thomas Becket from 1162. From 1163-64 John was in exile, living in Rheims under the protection and enjoying the hospitality of the man who was perhaps his closest friend, Peter of Celle, then abbot of Saint-Rémi. They lived together from 1164 until John returned to Canterbury in 1170 just before Becket's own return and martyrdom. After a period of resident in Exeter and service in the church courts, John was elected bishop of Chartres, on the initiative of King Louis VII – who was himself prompted by his brother-in-law William of the White Hands, archbishop of Sers, in 1176, and died there in 1180, to be succeeded by Abbot Peter.[19] No one doubts that the *HP* was written in exile in Rheims, and that the 'Peter' addressed within it is Peter of Celle.[20] It cannot be earlier than 1164: Marjorie Chibnall has shown reason to suppose it may have been composed as late as 1167, but the date cannot be precisely determined.[21]

[15] *HP*, pp. xlix-l.

[16] Ibid., pp. 2-3, 95. This may have been Peter's suggestion (Chibnall (1984), p. 171).

[17] John entered Theobald's service in 1147 (A. Saltman, *Theobald, archbishop of Canterbury* (London, 1956), pp. 169-73; *Letters*, ii, pp. x, xii).

[18] First by C. Schaarschmidt, *Johannes Saresberiensis* (Leipzig, 1862); recent studies, to 1980, are summarised by David Luscombe in *The World of JS*, pp. 21-37; cf. also his bibliography, ibid., pp. 445-57; O. Weijers, 'The Chronology of John of Salisbury's Studies in France (*Metalogicon*, ii.10)', ibid., pp. 109-16; K.S.B. Keats-Rohan, 'The Chronology of John of Salisbury's Studies in France: A Reading of *Metalogicon* 2.10', *Studi Medievali*, 3rd series, 28 (1987), pp. 193-203.

[19] Brooke in *The World of JS*, p. 1 and n. 2; *Letters*, p. xlvii n. 2.

[20] He is 'dominorum amicorumque karissime' (*HP*, p. 3), 'mi Petre' (p. 4), 'amicorum karissime' (p. 41). No other Peter was so close to John, nor had he any other friends so likely to be addressed as 'dominorum amicorumque karissime'.

[21] Chibnall in *HP*, pp. xxiv-xxx, supplemented by Chibnall (1984), esp. pp. 174-76 and the foreword to the corrected reprint of *HP* of 1986.

John's principal function in Theobald's curia, anyway in his early years there, was as envoy to the papal court. 'Ten times I have crossed the yoke of the Alps' he tells us in a passage written not later than 1159.[22] This gave him a close knowledge of two popes in particular; Eugenius III, the central character of the *HP* as we have it, and Cardinal Nicholas Brakespear, Pope Adrian IV, the one English pope. There are copious indications that he was particularly close to Adrian IV. Late in 1167 he wrote to Walter, cardinal bishop of Albano – who had succeeded Nicholas Brakespear in that office when the latter was elected pope – and cited Pope Adrian as a link between them.

> He planted you as a strong pillar (so it is hoped) of the holy Roman Church; me by a special bond of charity he loved more than any of our fellow countrymen, and reckoned the chances of my fortune as part and parcel of his own. His affection for me was known to us two and a few others; had not the fates stolen him prematurely from our midst – an event which the Christian world now mourns [especially since it was followed by schism] – it would have been known by now to the world too.[23]

It is hard not to interpret this to mean that John was expecting to be made a cardinal when Adrian died. If the *HP* had not been discovered in the nineteenth century – if a work by John on that subject came suddenly to light today – we would open it with every expectation of finding Adrian IV at its centre, and of being treated to an immortal portrait of that obscure but remarkable pope. But in the *HP*, as we now have it, he is never mentioned. True, the book starts in 1148 and hardly gets into the 1150s. But Nicholas Breakspear became a cardinal, in all probability, in 1149;[24] he could easily have entered the narrative we have. One can only presume that his entry was reserved for a later set-piece – perhaps even for his election as pope. It remains a very puzzling omission.

The central character is Eugenius III. But a subordinate figure of great importance in the narrative is John's patron, King Louis VII. John had evidently hoped in early life for patronage from Henry II of England; and had come within measurable distance of it when he acted as royal as well as archiepiscopal envoy in Rome in 1155-56 and negotiated the pope's approval of Henry II's invasion of Ireland.[25] In the event he negotiated too well: the pope apparently gave Ireland to Henry as a papal fief, or anyway a papal gift, whereas Henry regarded it as his of right; and John was in disgrace. From this affair John's image in Henry's eyes never really recovered. Even at the height

[22] *Metalogicon*, iii, prol., ed. J.B. Hall and K.S.B. Keats-Rohan (*CCCM* 98, Turnhout, 1991), p. 101: ed. C.C.J. Webb (Oxford, 1909), p. 117).

[23] *Letters*, ii, no. 235, pp. 432-35. Cf. *Letters*, i, pp. xiv n. 1, 256; Brooke in *The World of JS*, p. 12.

[24] R.L. Poole in *Essays in Medieval History Presented to Thomas Frederick Tout*, ed. A.G. Little and F.M. Powicke (Manchester, 1925), p. 67.

[25] For this and what folows, *Letters*, i, p. 257; cf. J.A. Watt, *The Church and the Two Nations in Medieval Ireland* (Cambridge, 1970), pp. 35-41.

of the Becket crisis John still hoped for reconciliation with Henry; but his immediate fate was more closely linked to Louis. For in Rheims he was remotely under royal protection, and immediately under the protection of King Louis' brother, the powerful, if erratic, Archbishop Henry of France, formerly a Cistercian monk. Though John was much closer to Abbot Peter, it is evident that he was respected by the archbishop, and greatly respected by his brother: the bishopric of Chartres was no mean reward for an Englishman. That apotheosis came only in 1176; but we should expect in all the circumstances of the 1160s to find John exceptionally favourable to King Louis. To my taste the account of Louis and his first queen, Eleanor of Aquitaine – reigning queen of England when John wrote – is one of the most puzzling features of the *HP*.[26]

The *HP* has several long digressions. Early on, in the midst of the council of Rheims of 1148, he takes time off to discuss in detail the theological opinions of Bishop Gilbert of La Porrée, bishop of Poitiers. But the greatest digression of all is the Second Crusade. True, it was a major event in papal history; its launching was one of the central events of Eugenius III's pontificate; and it was right and natural for it to be given some space. But a large proportion of his narrative is taken up with the relations of Louis and his queen; and indeed the bearing of this on the *HP* in its wider purposes become apparent when the couple return to Rome and Eugenius III attempts to reconcile them

> In the year of grace 1149 the most Christian king of the Franks [it seems that John himself was one of those who helped to consecrate this title for Louis] reached Antioch, after the destruction of his armies in the east, and was nobly entertained there by Prince Raymond, brother of the late William, count of Poitiers. He was as it happened the queen's uncle, and owed the king loyalty, affection and respect for many reasons. But whilst they remained there to console, heal and revive the survivors from the wreck of the army, the attentions paid by the prince to the queen, and his constant, indeed almost continuous, conversation with her, aroused the king's suspicions. These were greatly strengthened when the queen wished to remain behind, although the king was preparing to leave, and the prince made every effort to keep her, if the king would give his consent. And when the king made haste to tear her away, she mentioned their kinship, saying it was not lawful for them to remain together as man and wife, since they were related in the fourth and fifth degrees. Even before their departure [on crusade] a rumour to that effect had been heard in France, where the late Bartholomew, bishop of Laon, had calculated the degrees of kinship; but it was not certain whether the reckoning was true or false. At this the king was deeply moved; and although he loved the queen almost beyond reason he consented to divorce her if his counsellors and the French nobility would allow it. There was one knight amongst the king's secretaries, called Terricus Gualerancius, a eunuch whom the queen had always hated and mocked, but who

[26] Some of what follows resumes part of an article on 'The Marriage of Henry II and Eleanor of Aquitaine', *The Historian*, no. 20 (1988), pp. 3-8 (the genealogical table on p. 5 has several printers' errors, corrected in the next number). I am grateful to Mrs. Irene Collins for her approval of my use of this material here.

was faithful and had the king's ear like his father's before him. He boldly persuaded the king not to suffer her to dally longer at Antioch, both because

'guilt under kinship's guise could lie concealed',

and because it would be a lasting shame to the kingdom of the Franks if in addition to all the other disasters it was reported that the king had been deserted by his wife, or robbed of her. So he argued, either because he hated the queen or because he really believed it, moved perchance by widespread rumour. In consequence, she was torn away and forced to leave for Jerusalem with the king; and, their mutual anger growing greater, the wound remained, hide it as best they might.[27]

The denouement is well known. When the couple reached the papal curia at Tuscolo, Eugenius presided over a dramatic reconciliation. The pope

received (Louis) with such tenderness and reverence that one would have said he was welcoming an angel of the Lord rather than a mortal man. He reconciled the king and queen, after hearing severally the accounts each gave of the estrangement begun at Antioch, and forbade any future mention of their consanguinity; confirming their marriage, both orally and in writing, he commanded under pain of anathema that no word should be spoken against it and that it should not be dissolved under any pretext whatever. This ruling plainly delighted the king, for he loved the queen passionately, in an almost childish way. The pope made them sleep in the same bed, which he had had decked with priceless hangings of his own; and daily during their brief visit [apparently only of two days' duration][28] he strove by friendly converse to restore love between them. He heaped gifts upon them; and when the moment for departure came, though he was a stern man, he could not hold back his tears, but sent them on their way blessing them and the kingdom of the Franks, which was higher in his esteem than all the kingdoms of the world.[29]

Eugenius was Italian by birth, but his happiest days, we may suppose, had been spent as a monk at Clairvaux. It is a moving account; and it is followed, not much later, by a similar effort by Pope Eugenius to restore another broken marriage. He listened in court to the arguments of Hugh, count of Molise, for the annulment of his marriage. Although the count's case was well-prepared – he had bribed the curia, according to a characteristic aside of John's – the pope rejected it:

And then, bursting into tears, he hastened down from his seat in the sight of all, great as he was, and prostrated himself before the count so utterly that his mitre, slipping from his head and rolling in the dust, was found after the bishops and

---

[27] *HP*, pp. 52-53. The quotation is from Ovid, *Heroides*, iv, 138.
[28] See Dr. Chibnall's note, p. 61 n. 2.
[29] *HP*, pp. 61-62.

cardinals had raised him under the feet of the dumbfounded count. And he begged and entreated him, as far as a father's affection, an orator's eloquence and the venerable dignity of the Roman pontiff in the church could prevail, to put aside all ill-will and take back his wife affectionately, not merely in enforced obedience to the law, but with all the trust and love of a husband.

And after some more exhortation, the pope took 'a ring from his own finger [and] placed it on the count's, adding, 'Let this ring, a token of faith and contract, be a witness before God between thee and me, that I have given thee a wife in the sight of the church, and thou hast received her into thy protection'.[30]

It is certain in the case of Louis and Eleanor, and probable in the case of Count Hugh, that the pope's intervention had only short-lived consequences, and that within a few years both marriages had been effectively dissolved. Early in 1152, after much hesitation, Louis summoned a council at Beaugency in which four archbishops and numerous bishops examined the case.[31] They paid no attention to Pope Eugenius, though he was still alive; they simply listened to a recital by the king's friends and relations of proof that king and queen were related within the prohibited degrees. They declared the marriage null; and Eleanor – evading two other suitors at least – took flight to her own land, to Poitiers, where she became the wife of the young Henry, duke of Normandy, count of Anjou, soon to be king of England.[32]

It is extremely improbable that there was any intrigue or affair, in the sense John implies, between Eleanor and her uncle. But it is one of those curious cases in which the historian's errors themselves help to confirm the essential truth of the story he relates. Eleanor had a very strange career as wife and mother. To Louis she was married for fifteen years, and had two daughters and no son. When she married Henry she was in her late twenties, perhaps already thirty; and yet she had seven children at least in the next fifteen years – four

[30] Ibid, pp. 81-82; for the identification of Count Hugh, and the denouement, see *HP*, pp. 99-100.

[31] For this and the whole process the most thorough study is still that of E. Vacandard, 'Le divorce de Louis le jeune', *Revue des questions historiques*,n.s. 3 (1890), 408-32. He gives a table showing Eleanor's relation to Louis on p. 417 which, in spite of his doubts, is only incorrect in calling their common ancestor Thibaut – he was William like almost all the dukes of Aquitaine. For a correct table showing her relationship to both her husbands, see W.L. Warren, *Henry II* (London, 1973), p. 43. See also Brooke, *Medieval Idea of Marriage* (Oxford, 1989), pp. 123-24 and nn.

[32] Robert de Torigny, *Chronica*, ed. R. Howlett, in *Chronicles of the Reigns of Stephen* etc., iv (Rolls Series, London, 1889), p. 165, dates the marriage *about* Pentecost, i.e. *c.* 18 May 1152; cf. Warren, *Henry II*, pp. 42-45.

sons and three daughters who grew up;[33] and Louis meanwhile was begetting children by two other wives. Much the most probable explanation of these curious facts is that for most of the time she was married to Louis she refused to sleep with him. John describes Pope Eugenius's insistence that they sleep together in October 1149; and sure enough, we know from other evidence that the second child, the Princess Alice, was conceived soon after their return from the east. So far, John's testimony fits the facts; but what of the curious scene at Antioch?

By 1152 Louis was evidently exasperated by his wife's treatment of him, and in despair of a male heir. But we may accept John's testimony that Louis had been fond of Eleanor and that it was the queen who had earlier wished for an annulment; and we can well imagine the difficulty of her position. To whom was she to turn for help and protection? To whom was she to go if she succeeded in leaving Louis? She had been the daughter and heiress of Duke William of Aquitaine, and she had no close male relatives to protect her; her uncle of Antioch was her nearest relative. An extraordinary chance had brought her to his court; it was a unique opportunity – it would hardly occur again. For whatever reason, her dislike of Louis must have cut deep if she could be queen of France for so many years and refuse him his conjugal dues (as things were then understood). John's explanation of her anxiety to stay in Antioch is absurd; but the story which lay behind it is very likely indeed to be true. Yet it strange that John, a would-be courtier whose affairs were never far removed from the English court, should speak so disrespectfully of the queen of England – and, in particular, throw such grave doubt on the validity of her grounds of annulment. But if his treatment of Eleanor is strange, his account of Louis is stranger still; for although there are many respectful, even affectionate, references to him, the claim that he loved Eleanor 'in an almost childish way' ['fere puerili modo'] is extremely disrespectful.[34]

Equally surprising is his treatment of Louis' brother, the disciple of St. Bernard who had become a monk of Clairvaux, then bishop of Beauvais, and who by the time John wrote was the archbishop of Rheims under whose sceptre John was living. He gives a whole chapter to his election as bishop of Beauvais, but never hints that he had since become archbishop of Rheims. That is odd. Marjorie Chibnall reasonably observes that 'Peter of Celle did not need to be told of the appointment of his own archbishop', but that hardly applies to any

---

[33] For her first marriage and her children by Louis see A. Luchaire, *Louis VI le Gros* (Paris, 1890), no. 589, p. 268; cf. no. 580, p. 264; M. Bouquet *et al.*, eds., *Recueil des historiens des Gaules et de la France*, nouv. édn., ed. L. Delisle (24 vols., Paris, 1869-1904), xii, p. 127 (birth of Alice after their return from the Crusade); cf. pp. 125, 471; G. Duby, *The Knight, the Lady and the Priest* (trans. B. Bray, New York and Harmondsworth, 1983-84), pp. 190-98. For her children by Henry, see C. Brooke, 'Marriage and Society in the Central Middle Ages', in *Marriage and Society*, ed. R.B. Outhwaite (London, 1981), pp. 17-34, at pp. 19-20 and nn.; *Handbook of British Chronology*, 3rd edn., ed. E.B. Fryde, D.E. Greenway, S. Porter and I. Roy (London, 1986), p. 36.
[34] *HP*, p. 61.

wider audience he might have in mind.[35] Odder still is his treatment of him. There is copious evidence – from John's letters as well as from other sources – that Henry was an impulsive and erratic man; at one time he was at logger-heads with the king, at another with the citizens of Rheims.[36]

'On the death of the bishop of Beauvais, a monk of Clairvaux, Henry, succeeded him because he was a brother of the king of the Franks. But within a short time there was such strife between the brothers that the king summoned an army and was hastening to annihilate Beauvais when prudent advisers – Jocelin, bishop of Soissons, and Suger, abbot of Saint-Denis – and Queen Adelaide [Louis' and Henry's mother] most of all, urged the bishop to be less reckless and made peace between the brothers.' The bishop then went to Rome and was 'welcomed as a friend there' – for the pope too had been a monk of Clairvaux. But 'he pleaded to be allowed to give up the burdens of a bishopric, though whether from inconstancy of character, religious zeal, or knowledge of his limitations is uncertain. But his prayer was not heard, either because he was believed to be inspired by the love of God or through fear of scandal' on account of the difficulties which would follow if he returned to Clairvaux. 'On his return to France he forgot what agreement he had reached with the lord pope: and troubled by conscientious scruples wrote again to ask him what ought to be done, and what they had decided. At this the lord pope, in letters written by his own hand so that they should not come to the knowledge of notaries', insisted that he resume his duties as bishop, 'brushing aside his scruples and soothing him with words of consolation'.[37]

St. Bernard and Gilbert de la Porrée were dead ten years or more before John wrote, and what he said could only do justice and, within certain limits, honour to them. But Archbishop Henry and King Louis and Queen Eleanor and her second husband were all alive – and on her marriages depended the fate of the two kingdoms in which John spent all his life (save when travelling to the papal curia). The *HP* would not have been congenial to any of them; and we can imagine the use Bishop Arnulf might have made of it to blacken John's name if it had fallen into his hands – though indeed one must allow he was not the villain John painted him. Yet the puzzle remains: if the book had become public knowledge, it would have given some hostages to fortune. There are never easy answers to the puzzles John set his readers and posterity. The ceaseless discussion of the identity of Cornificius in the *Metalogicon*, or his attitude to tyrannicide – in an age (as he believed) in which tyrants flourished in

[35] Chibnall (1984), p. 176.
[36] *HP*, p. 69; *Letters*, ii, no. 223, pp. 384-87; cf. pp. 384-85 n. 1. On Henry see *Letters*, ii, p. 6 n. 13 and references; Chibnall (1984), pp. 174-77.
[37] *HP*, p. 69-70.

Germany and England – are eloquent witnesses of the fact.[38] But in this case the best key lies in his relation to Peter of Celle.[39]

It seems that Peter had inspired John with the idea of writing history during his enforced sabbatical leave; and in particular expressed an interest in the council of Rheims of 1148 and the theological opinions of Gilbert of La Porrée.[40] Hence the long digression on this theme. As in his celebrated letter 209 to the count of Champagne (in the preparation of which Peter had also played a part), John was given an agenda, a list of questions as it might be, and set to work to answer them.[41] To a modern audience he seems conspicuously successful. But it may well have appeared to him as he proceeded that in trying to entertain his delightful friend and host he had failed to provide himself with any other audience; indeed it may have been worse than that. For he had allowed himself to be carried away in disrespect of Peter's and his own lords and patrons; and if Peter was a notable exponent of *amicitia*, he was also a spiritual director, a man of God. John's book is often frivolous.[42] It may be that the modern reader is more pleased with it than Peter was. For these or for other reasons, John broke it off short, to our eternal loss.

My purpose has not been to answer, but to pose questions; or rather to reflect on a few of the oddities of this delightful work. I have studied the book so long – and others have written so profoundly and so well about it – that it is too late to say much that is new; but we do well to remind ourselves in handling the books which take us close to the intellectual heart of twelfth-century Europe that they are still full of puzzles; and that is why I have taken the *Historia pontificalis* as the theme of a reflective essay in homage to Margaret Gibson.

---

[38] See the most recent discussion by John McLoughlin (n. 12), i, pp. 89-102.

[39] Revealed in numerous letters between them: cf. esp. John's *Letters*, i, nos. 19, 31-35, 111-12, and on no. 112, ibid. pp. xlvii-lii. Peter's letters, and his concept of friendship, are being studied by Julian Haseldine.

[40] *HP*, p. 41.

[41] *Letters*, ii, pp. 318-19.

[42] But Peter himself engaged in light-hearted banter when writing to close friends, and especially to John: this line of argument must not be overworked. An element of frivolity actually strengthens the case that it was primarily for Peter's ear; it is the extent of, and sharp edge to, the caustic comments which raises doubts whether it was all to Peter's taste.

# 15

## Prescription and Reality in the Rubrics of Sarum Rite Service Books

### Richard W. Pfaff

The subject of this essay is the relationship between service books as they have come down to us and as they seem actually to have been used in English medieval parish churches. Its concrete starting point is the information about books which can be assigned to specific parish churches in N.R. Ker's *Medieval Libraries of Great Britain* and its *Supplement*:[1] For the something like 8,000 to 10,000 parishes and chapels probably operating in England by the end of the middle ages, just over one hundred books of a liturgical sort (including a few books of hours and kalendars) have been identified as having belonged to a specific one. As might be expected, missals are far better represented than any other types of books: forty-two have been so identified, all save two apparently of the Sarum Use, the overwhelming majority from the fifteenth century. All other major types of books together number about the same: eleven breviaries, fourteen psalters, four antiphoners, three graduals, eight manuals, four martyrologies (forty-four in all). About two-thirds are of the fifteenth or early sixteenth centuries; twenty-seven are dated fourteenth or fourteenth/fifteenth; a mere two are of the thirteenth century. There seems to be nothing at all earlier than that.

The survival of such books, and therefore their appearance on this list, is of course a purely fortuitous matter; so that if we look for well-known parish churches from which we might most wish to study service books – for example, Tideswell in Derbyshire, St. Mary Redcliffe in Bristol, Howden in the East Riding, St. Peter Mancroft in Norwich, Escomb in County Durham, all of which would fall into expected categories of noble, beautiful, picturesque or at least very ancient – we will be sadly disappointed. In any case, rather than choosing our books by the churches which possessed them, we shall need to consider the evidence from some of these surviving books – none, as it

[1] N.R. Ker. ed., *Medieval Libraries of Great Britain: A List of Surviving Books*, (2nd edn., London, 1964) [hereafter *MLGB*]: Andrew G. Watson, ed., *Supplement to the Second Edition* (London, 1987).

happens, belonging to churches of any particular fame – in the light of certain aspects of their contents. In doing so, we shall have to assume something not absolutely provable, that on the whole these books were not only owned by but also used in the churches to which they belonged and that it should therefore be possible to consider them as evidence for the practice of the liturgy in those places.

Let us look, to begin with, at a breviary used in the fifteenth century at Launton in north Oxfordshire.[2] The book is very large: 415 by 290 mm. are its present dimensions (but it has been cropped somewhat) it weighs about twenty-eight pounds. It was made somewhere in southern England (i.e., province of Canterbury) in the first half of the fifteenth century. By about 1530 it belonged to John Cottisford, then Rector of Lincoln College, Oxford. At some time in the previous hundred years or so it came to the church at Launton, whose feast of dedication was added to the calendar at 3 October to be kept on the first Sunday of that month, and whose *yconimi* are twice noted as being bound to offer twelve pence to the church at Bicester on the feast day of St. Edburga. Though not elaborately illuminated, it is well enough decorated to have found its way into Pächt and Alexander as 'Good borders and initials. Some borders added xv[med]' – most likely when the book went to Launton, which indicates that a degree of special attention was paid to it at that time.[3]

It would seem a suitable vehicle out of which to conduct the divine office there – physically congruous with, for example, the rubric for the ceremony surrounding the reading of the genealogy of Christ from Matthew at matins of Christmas Day (fo. 30): a rubric which specifies that after the final responsory and its versicle the deacon goes with subdeacon, thurifer, candlebearer and crucifer, all solemnly apparelled, to cense the altar and be blessed by the officiant before mounting the pulpit to sing the lesson. This sort of prescription, implying as it does a liturgical force of three sacred ministers and at least three attendants, naturally leads to an impression of considerably elaborated worship; a feeling that the services at Launton must have been splendid.

Some questions begin to arise, however, when we look at the standard modern printed edition of the Sarum breviary, that of Proctor and Wordsworth, which is for the most part a printing of the 'Great' Breviary of 1531, and see there largely the same rubric:[4] but we note that the rubric continues, as it does not in the Launton breviary, by specifying a second censing of the high altar (apparently with the aid of a second thurifer), the other altars not being censed. Are we entitled to infer from this detail that at Launton a second

---

[2]   Oxford, Bodleian Library, MS Laud Misc., 299.

[3]   O. Pächt and J.J.G. Alexander, *Illuminated Manuscripts in the Bodleian Library*, iii: *English etc. School* (Oxford, 1973), no. 827.

[4]   F. Proctor and C. Wordsworth, eds., *Breviarium ad usum insignis ecclesiae Sarum* (3 vols., Cambridge, 1879-86), i, clxxxvi.

thurifer was not used, or that there were no other altars besides the principal one in that church, or both?

Certainly the latter inference looks dubious in the light of a rubric for first vespers of St. Nicholas, which falls within the Octave of St. Andrew. The Launton breviary's rubric spells out that there should be a procession to the altar of St. Nicholas, during which both the altar and the image of that saint are censed (fo. 309 v). But the rubric in the 1531 Great Breviary specifies that this should happen only (and reasonably) 'si habeatur', if there is such an altar; it makes no mention of an image.[5] In this case does logical inference convince us that at Launton there were such an altar and such an image? That is certainly conceivable, though the church was not dedicated to St. Nicholas but to St. Mary (her Assumption), and it probably had only two altars in addition to the principal one.[6]

If one of the altars was dedicated to Nicholas, was the other to Thomas Becket? Another rather elaborate rubric, at the end of second vespers of Holy Innocents, indicates that after the Boy Bishop ceremonies sometimes associated with that day are concluded there is a procession to the altar of St. Thomas the Martyr (whose first vespers it is also). In neither the Launton (fo. 44 v nor the 1531 breviary (i. ccxlv) is the stipulation 'if there is one' added; how likely does this make the existence of such an altar in a small Oxfordshire parish church?

Similar questions are raised when we turn to a slightly earlier book of the same sort, a breviary used at Denchworth in Berkshire.[7] This is another very large codex, 425 by 375 mm. in present outside dimensions, made in the last decade or so of the fourteenth century, and probably given to the parish church in the Berkshire village of Denchworth by a member of the Hyde family: obits of other members of this family dating back to 1135 were apparently entered in this book out of an older one.[8] Indeed, some such history is suggested by the rubric on fo. 262 v, following the entry about the Translation of Thomas Becket (7 July), in which we read that on the next Sunday after the Translation, 'celebratur festum reliquiarum Sarum ecclesie quod nuper celebratum consuevit in octava die nativitatis beate Marie'. As the change of date for the Sarum Feast of Relics was made in 1319, well over a century before this book was written, the long-obsolete information contained in the present rubric is best explained by its having been copied from an earlier one.

This context intensifies the interest with which we may note the extensive rubric on fo. 283 v dealing with the question of when St. Matthias's feast (usually on 24 February) falls in leap years – a quadrennial problem given that

[5] Procter and Wordsworth, iii.25.
[6] Jennifer Sherwood and Nikolaus Pevsner, *Oxfordshire*. The Buildings of England (Harmondsworth, 1973), p. 681.
[7] Oxford, Bodleian Library, MS lat. liturg., b. 14.
[8] Printed by H.B. Hyde in *Notes and Queries*, 7th ser, v (7 Jan. 1888), pp. 2-3.

the Roman dating-system for the later half of a month works towards the beginning of the next month – and also if it should coincide with Ash Wednesday. There is a fairly standard form for such a rubric, one which appears with only a few variations in wording in, for example, the Launton Breviary (fo. 337 v) and a third parish church breviary, that used at Coltishall church in Norfolk.[9] Yet into the Denchworth rubric is tucked the entire entry from the martyrology for 23-25 February. Of all the breviaries consulted for this enquiry, the Coltishall book is the only other one that has any mention of possible complications in the reading of the martyrology, though somewhat shorter than that of the Denchworth book. Is it likelier to be the case that the incumbents of just these two parish churches, one in the Berkshire Downs and one in the Norfolk Broads, had a particular desire to keep their martyrology reading tidy, or that both breviaries have some distant family likeness witnessed to by this peculiar trait?

Next we consider the question of the rubric 'Ubi vero dedicata est ecclesia in honore'. In most of the late Sarum breviaries there is a direction about the observance of first Vespers on a feast day when it is also what we would call the patronal feast. Since the matter of first vespers is one of the trickiest questions in the higher reaches of liturgical minutiae, this would make good sense were it not for the fact that only two or three feasts are so treated, and these are the same feasts in all the breviaries checked for this detail. Every one of nine large manuscript volumes – the Launton, Denchworth and Coltishall breviaries plus service-books used at Arlingham (Gloucs.), Great Bedwyn (Wilts.) and Ranworth (Norfolk),[10] and three which have no identifiable connection with a specific parish,[11] has such a rubric only for two or three feasts: the Decollation of John the Baptist (29 August); Michaelmas (29 September); and sometimes also Anne (26 July). The 1531 Great Breviary has such a rubric at four places, the three just mentioned plus Andrew (for a slightly different case, when it coincides with the First Sunday in Advent, which would trump even the vespers of the patronal feast). It may be objected that such instruction is necessary for the feast of St. Anne, which came to enjoy universal popularity only from the end of the fourteenth century and which follows immediately another important feast, that of James. But there is no major observance before either Michaelmas or the Decollation of John the Baptist (to which we shall return in another context); and it is thus striking that there is no rubric of this kind for David, Gregory, Augustine of Canterbury, Alban, Etheldreda, Nativity of John Baptist, Peter, Paul, James, Laurence, Bartholomew, Denis, Luke, Martin, Nicholas, Thomas the Apostle, or Thomas Becket – that is, for

---

[9] Durham, University Library, MS Cosin V.i.3, fo. 393 v.

[10] Salisbury, Cathedral Library, MSS 152 and 224, and a manuscript at Ranworth parish church (an antiphonal), respectively.

[11] Oxford, Bodleian Library, MSS Bodl. 976, Hatton 63 and Lat. Liturg., f. 29.

those saints to whom, besides Mary, the vast majority of English churches were in fact dedicated.

This example, while it does not cast any particular doubt on the veracity of the books in which it appears, highlights a somewhat misleading aspect of many manuscript service-books: that, while we tend to think of such manuscripts as to a large extent 'purpose-written' books, any given one will in reality contain a large amount of material irrelevant to the church where it came to be used. In this case we are told what to do on patronal feasts only when the church is dedicated to the Beheading of John Baptist, Michael and sometimes Anne.[12] Since none of these is the dedication in any of the instances in which we know the church where one of these books was used, we must suppose that this rubric was simply passed over, year after year, as an irrelevance. Where it comes to make some sense is, of course, in a printed book like the 1531 edition, presumably made to be circulated to churches of many different dedications. This obvious fact does not explain the appearance of the rubric in manuscript books of a hundred years earlier.

When we turn from breviaries to missals, the situation is even more productive of curiosity; for missals are more likely to contain ceremonial directions – fitfully but, with the fully developed Sarum missals, often in considerable detail. When and how these rubrics, here called ceremonial (what to do, as distinct from what to say), came into the Sarum missal is not yet clear. Nor is the situation ever wholly uniform. By the time of several notable missals which can be connected with specific parishes – as with breviaries, mostly not until the later fourteenth century – several such rubrics are often found, though never uniformly. While their appearance or non-appearance is not coherent enough to be said to tell an entire story in itself, the diversity involved is marked enough to further our argument.

The first 'ceremonial' rubric to attract our attention is found in every manuscript Sarum missal examined. It concerns not action inside the Mass but the location of a Mass. The feast of the Decollation of John the Baptist, 29 August, was also the day on which a virgin martyr of great antiquity, Sabina, was commemorated. Sabina's seems in fact to have been the earlier observance, but the secondary feast of the Precursor (which, along with the tertiary one of his Conception, may have been more popular in England than on the Continent) received the greater liturgical attention. Hence the widely-encountered rubric, which generally reads something like this: 'dicitur missa in cap° [capitulo] de Sancta Sabina virgine post primam ante terciam more solito et missa de Sancto Johanne post sextam dicitur'. The meaning of 'in capitulo' is

---

[12] In fact, there appear to have been virtually no churches dedicated to the Beheading. One possible exception is Coln St. Aldwyn's (Gloucs.); another, but highly dubious, is Tadcaster (Yorks): F. Arnold-Forster, *Studies in Church Dedications*, i (London, 1899), p. 61. But it is notoriously difficult to get accurate information about medieval English parish church dedications. Without question many churches were dedicated to Michael, a few to Anne.

not clear; the likeliest explanation, that there was an altar in the chapter house which could be used for subsidiary masses, is only an explanation *faute de mieux*. It has been observed that chapter houses – that the one at Salisbury is the ultimate point of reference for this rubric is made plain by the addition of the words 'sicut mos est in ecclesia Sarum' in, for example, missals from Closworth (Somerset) and Colwich (Staffs.)[13] – are singularly unsuited to altars, and furthermore that there is no evidence that altars were ever placed there.[14] For our purposes this does not matter greatly, for the one clear point is that the rubric makes sense only where there is a chapter house, however it is (or is not) involved. Every one of the missals we are considering has here a direction which, almost by definition, cannot have been followed in the parish churches in which these books were used.

Then there is the question of the persons, places and vesture involved in certain chants. This can be seen clearly in rubrics often found for the Saturday Ember Mass in Advent – itself an unusually elaborate service involving twelve lessons with appropriate responses. After the epistle, the tract (in place of a gradual during the penitential season of Advent) is to be sung in the following way: 'Duo clerici de secunda forma in superpelliciis ad gradum chori dicant [*or* cantent] hunc tractum . . . Chorus idem repetat; clerici versum chori dicant'. Then, towards the end of this very extensive piece of singing, there is a further instruction that: 'Duo clerici de secunda forma in cap(p)is nigris ad gradum chori simul dicant totum et integrum istum tractum'. Remembering again that our concern is not with the elaborateness of this exercise, as it might have been performed in Salisbury cathedral, but with the relation between the written page in a missal and the parish church in which that missal was used, we observe that this rubric presupposes (a) two pairs of singing clerics (for the 'solo' parts): (b) a larger body of clerics out of which both pairs are of the second form or rank – again, a point the meaning of which is itself not entirely clear: (c) a body of singers (*chorus*) to respond: (d) at least one step (*gradus*) into the architectural feature called the choir; and (e) surplices for the first pair of clerics and *cappae nigrae* ('in habitu quotidiano', as some of the missals gloss this) for the second pair. Of these features a typical parish church would probably have had the last two: a step at the entrance into the choir and a couple of surplices, along with perhaps the *cappae nigrae*. The rest of the rubric is likely to have been honoured only in the breach. This is again a widespread rubric, appearing in missals used all over the country, for example,

[13] Oxford, Bodleian Library, MS Don.b.6, fo. 199 and London, B.L., MS Harl., 4919. fo. 274.
[14] F.H. Dickinson, ed., *Missale ad usum . . . Sarum* (Burntisland, 1861-83), p. vii, note n, with respect to Requiem Masses to be celebrated 'in capitulo'.

in Adderbury (Oxfordshire), Gawsworth (Cheshire), St. Margaret Lothbury (London), and probably Maldon (Essex).[15]

The third Mass rubric to consider is, unlike the previous instance, found only in certain manuscript missals. This is a bit of delicate liturgical symbolism for the feast of the Seven Brothers on 9 July. Here the instruction is that at the Alleluia the two verses should be sung 'a duobus pueris in superpelliciis' – sometimes the words 'sicut in ebdomade pasche domini' being added. Missals in which this rubric appears include ones used at St. Botolph's and St. Laurence Jewry (both in London),[16] as well as the St. Margaret Lothbury, Colwich and Maldon books cited above, and several not at present to be ascribed to specific parish churches but almost certainly used in such a context.[17]

This way of marking the 9 July feast is not found in the three earliest known Sarum missals: the Crawford (mid thirteenth century), Arsenal (early fourteenth), and Bologna (only a little later than Arsenal).[18] The Bologna missal, which is thought to have some possible connection with Oxford, may however reflect knowledge of the practice, because after the words 'Laudate pueri' it continues 'require in sabbato'. The Saturday in question must be Easter Saturday, though on that day there is no special rubric at the Alleluia in the Bologna missal. Yet the printed missals all contain a rubric about the Easter Saturday Alleluia which begins, 'Duo pueri in superpelliciis in pulpito dicant'; after these two boys have sung a 'Haec dies' verse two other boys, also in surplices, stand at the entrance to the choir and sing (with obvious appropriateness), 'Laudate pueri'.[19] By this time, as again in the printed missals show, the practice had spread to the feast of the Seven Brothers, for the rubric for that occasion reads, 'Et dicitur cum utroque versu hac die sicut in Sabbato in hebdomade Paschae',[20] Then the same boys pick up again, alternately with the choir, on the verse, 'Sit nomen domini . . .'

Because the Easter Saturday practice is hinted at, though not specified, in the Bologna missal – why else would the words, 'Require in sabbato', have been added at the Alleluia in the Seven Brothers Mass? – but not in the markedly earlier Crawford or slightly earlier Arsenal missals, we may suspect

[15] Respectively, Oxford, Bodleian Library, MSS Don.b.5, fo. 18 v and Barlow 1, fo. 13; Cambridge, University Library, MS Dd.1.15, fo. 17; and London, B.L., MS Harl. 2787, fo. 22. It is noteworthy that in the printed missals mention of the second pair of clerics is omitted (Dickinson edn., col. 38).

[16] Oxford, Christ Church, MS 87, fo. 207 and London, B.L., MS Arundel 109, fo. 187 v, respectively.

[17] Oxford, Bodleian Library, MSS Barlow 5, fo. 202; Rawl. A. 387[A], fo. 119; Rawl. liturg. c.2, fo. 199 v; Oriel College 75, fo. 246 v; and Pembroke College, 1, fo. 198.

[18] As in J.W. Legg, ed. *The Sarum Missal* (Oxford, 1916): Manchester, John Rylands University Library, MS Crawford lat. 24; Bologna, University Library, MS 2,565; Paris, Arsenal, MS 135. The first is mid thirteenth century, the other two early fourteenth.

[19] Dickinson ed., col. 379.

[20] Dickinson ed., col. 807.

that this bit of elaboration was the invention of a cleric (or just possibly a patron) of the early fourteenth century with a taste for elegant touches in the liturgy. We may suspect also that the inclusion of the Seven Brothers rubric in a limited number of manuscript missals is rather a sign of some affinity between them as books (though not one which can be exaggerated into a close family likeness) than an indication of a sub-use within the Use of Sarum. The printed missals (Caxton's of 1487 is the earliest) seem to have been based on an examplar or examplars which contained the rubric; and so what appears to be a standard if trivial part of the late medieval Sarum rite is in fact attested to in only a small minority of manuscript service-books.

Such conclusion as a preliminary enquiry like the present one can have may be stated briefly. It begins with the observation that the mentality we bring to the study of medieval liturgical manuscripts tends to be coloured by the presuppositions of those who worship according to printed liturgical books, especially if such worshippers are of either the Anglican or the Roman tradition – in both of which the use of authority to mandate uniform observance complements the identity-in-multiplicity which the technology of printing makes possible. This mentality is deeply unhelpful when applied to manuscript service books, characterised as they are by a high degree of individuality. Furthermore, the fact that medieval English service-books tend to be classified by Uses, and that only one such Use (that of Sarum) had any very widespread currency, encourages us to think that there is something like a normative Sarum missal or Sarum breviary as prototypical of the *Book of Common Prayer* or the Roman breviary or missal of 1568/70. In very broad outline this may be true, at least negatively: one can say that a book is not Sarum because it lacks such and such features, and to a degree that it is Sarum because it contains this or that. But the variation among those books nominally classed as of the Sarum rite is enormous.

   Discrepancies of the kind here discussed, between rubrical prescription and (putative) practice, underline the necessity of careful study of individual manuscripts as discrete pieces of evidence each possessing intrinsic worth, rather than as generalised precursors or models for the printed books which emerged at the end of the fifteenth century. Though those books, cut off as they are by the changes of the English Reformation, can easily seem normative to the liturgical scholar, they may in important respects be misleading to the historian.

   Margaret Gibson has commented, addressing another problem, that, 'The relation of the written text of a sermon to the mode and language of its actual delivery is not yet [1984] fully understood'.[21] The same thing can be said of the

---

[21] Her n. 43 on p. 92 of R.W. Hunt, *The Schools and the Cloister: The Life and Writings of Alexander Nequam (1157-1217)*, ed. and rev. by Margaret Gibson (Oxford, 1984).

relation between the written text of a manuscript service-book – at least when used in medieval English parish churches – and the performance of that liturgical worship for which it was meant to provide. In both areas there is plenty of work to be done.

# 16

## Expenses of a Mid Thirteenth-Century Paris Scholar: Gerard of Abbeville*

### R.H. and M.A. Rouse

Paris, Bibliothèque Nationale, MS lat. 16366, fo. 3 (fly-leaf) contains a list of sixty-four household items and the prices paid for them, in a hand of the mid thirteenth century.[1] The list was probably written by the mid thirteenth-century Parisian master Gerard of Abbeville.[2] It is a witness to the expenses, recurring and extraordinary, of a Paris schoolman, the material goods that he owned, their relative costs, and the words used to describe them[3].

* We are grateful to François Avril, Louis Bataillon O.P., Françoise Gaspari, Marie-Thérèse Gousset, Marie-Hélène Tesnières, Jean Vezin and Olga Weijers for their considerate help with various aspects of this essay. We thank the Comité Du Cange (Paris) for use of their files and reference collection. We are indebted most of all to Patricia Stirnemann, who has been actively involved with us in this study from its beginning.

[1] The note is edited below, and see also reproduction of the MS, below; there are 66 entries on the list, two of which have been deleted. In considering this list we turned to the well-known vocabularies of the names of things compiled by the twelfth- and thirteenth-century Paris masters John of Garland and Alexander Nequam, which were edited together by Auguste Scheler, *Lexicographie latine du XIIe et du XIIIe siècle* (Leipzig, 1867); the edition includes as well the *De utensilibus* of Adam of Petit-Pont, which was not germane here. Concerning John of Garland, see A.B. Emden, *A Biographical Register of the University of Oxford to AD 1500*, 2 (1958), pp. 743-44; concerning Alexander Nequam, see R.W. Hunt, *The Schools and the Cloister: The Life and Writings of Alexander Nequam, 1157-1217*, ed. and rev. M.T. Gibson. Both John's and Alexander's lists were in the nature of school exercises; while we found them useful, the distance between classroom and daily life was apparent.

[2] Regarding Gerard of Abbeville see Ph. Gand, 'Le quodlibet XIV de Gérard d'Abbeville', *Archives d'histoire doctrinale et littéraire du moyen âge* 31 (1964), pp. 207-69; P. Glorieux, *Répertoire des maîtres en théologie de Paris au XIIIe siècle*, 2 vols., Etudes de philosophie médiévale 17-18 (Paris, 1933-1934) i, pp. 356-60, no. 174; and W.M. Newman, *Le personnel de la Cathédrale d'Amiens 1066-1306* (Paris, 1972), p. 40, no. 92.

[3] There is no modern study of the social and economic history of Paris and its university in the thirteenth century; see, however, L.-J. Bataillon, 'Les conditions de travail des maîtres de l'université de Paris au XIIIe siècle,' *Revue des sciences philosophiques et théologiques*, 67 (1983), pp. 417-33. Concerning trades and commerce in contemporary Paris, see also Gustave Fagniez, *Etudes sur l'industrie et la classe industrielle à Paris au XIIIe et au XIVe siècle*, Bibliothèque de l'Ecole des hautes études: Sciences philologiques et historiques, 33 (Paris, 1877); Bronislaw

207

MS lat. 16366 is a small volume of the late twelfth century containing Hugh of St. Victor, *De sacramentis*, Book I. In the mid thirteenth century it belonged to Gerard of Abbeville, who bequeathed it to the Sorbonne with his library upon his death in 1272.[4]

Gerard of Abbeville, whose benefices included the position of archdeacon at Amiens (by 1260),[5] was a secular master of theology at the university of Paris from 1257 until his death. In 1262 he held as well the post of protector of the university's privileges. Gerard owes his modern reputation to the fame of his opponents. He succeeded William of St. Amour at Paris as the leading secular polemicist against the Mendicant Orders, and against what the seculars saw as the disproportionate role of the Mendicant masters at the university. His public attacks, in a series of quodlibets (1266-67), evoked specific responses in 1268 and 1269 from both Bonaventure and Thomas Aquinas. Even Gerard's legacy of books to the Sorbonne was largely motivated by his wish to provide secular students and masters in theology (whose centre was the Sorbonne) access to a library that would equal those of their Franciscan and Dominican counterparts.[6]

Geremek, *Le salariat dans l'artisanat parisien aux XIIIe-XVe siècles*, trad. A. Posner and C. Klapisch-Zuber, Ecole pratique des hautes études-Sorbonne, VIe section: Sciences économiques et sociales, Industrie et artisanat, 5 (Paris, 1968); D. Frappier-Bigras, 'La famille dans l'artisanat Parisien du XIIIe siècle,' *Le moyen âge*, 95 (1989), pp. 47-74; R.H. and M.A. Rouse, 'The Commercial Production of Manuscript Books in Late Thirteenth- and Early Fourteenth-Century Paris,' in *Medieval Book Production: Assessing the Evidence*, ed. L.L. Brownrigg (Los Altos Hills, CA, 1990), pp. 103-15; and K. Fianu, 'Familles et solidarités dans les métiers du livre Parisiens au XIVe siècle,' *Médiévales*, 19 (1990) pp. 83-90. A vivid picture of life in London and Paris of an earlier generation, based especially on the vocabularies of Alexander Nequam and John of Garland, is given by U.T. Holmes, *Daily Living in the Twelfth Century* (Madison, WI, 1952).

[4] The ex libris (fo. 47 v) reads 'Iste liber est collegii pauperum magistrorum studentium Parisius in theologia/ ex legato magistri Geroudi de Abbatis Villa precio xx sol./ folii 48, quaterni 6'. Concerning Gerard's association with the Sorbonne see P. Glorieux, 'Bibliothèques de maîtres parisiens: Gérard d'Abbeville', *Recherches de théologie ancienne et médiévale*, 36 (1969), pp. 148-83, and R.H. Rouse, 'The Early Library of the Sorbonne,' *Scriptorium*, 21 (1967), pp. 47-51. Gerard's will is edited from Paris, Arsenal, MS 1228 fol. 518 v by Gand 'Le Quodlibet XIV', pp. 214-18, and by P. Glorieux, *Aux origines de la Sorbonne*, 2, *Le cartulaire* (Paris 1965), pp. 354-58, no. 301. To be precise, this is a *vidimus* (by the *officialis* of Cambrai) of a *vidimus* (by the dean and chapter of Cambrai) of Gerard's will.

[5] The exact number and dates of Gerard's benefices are not known. He was probably a canon of Amiens by 1260, at which time he was archdeacon of Ponthieu in the see of Amiens. His connection with Cambrai, where he was also archdeacon, is known principally through his will, which survived through the Cambrai cathedral archives.

[6] His will says explicitly, 'I want the secular masters of theology to have an abundance of *originalia* and *summas*, at least, because the regulars already have enough' ('Volo autem quod de originalibus et de summis fiat copia magistris theologie secularibus dumtaxat, quia religiosi satis habent'); Gand, 'Le Quodlibet XIV,' p. 215, Glorieux *Aux origines*, 2, p. 355. Gerard leaves his books to all secular students of theology at Paris, both within the Sorbonne and without (although the books are to be housed in and governed by the Sorbonne), to make more pointed his exclusion of the Mendicants; Gand, 'Le Quodlibet XIV,' p. 215, Glorieux, *Aux origines*, 2, pp. 354-55.

Gerard may have left MS lat. 16366 to the Sorbonne loose-stitched in a soft vellum wrapper, since the number of its leaves and quires is noted in the ex libris, 'fol. 48 quaterni 6'. Today it is bound in the green vellum binding applied by the college to its manuscripts in the eighteenth century. Clearly the volume contained no more than Book I of *De sacramentis* even in Gerard's day, since the Sorbonne librarian has added a formal note across the bottom of fo. 45, 'Explicit primus liber de sacramentis Hugonis complete (*sic*) a principio usque ad finem, continens partes 12 et capitula 275', and on the blank fo. 47 v (acknowledging the absence of the rest of the work), 'Hugo de sacramentis incompletus'.[7]

The manuscript, which measures 205 x 135 (165 x 100) mm., was written in northern France in a proto-gothic hand of the late twelfth or early thirteenth century. The ruling and script become markedly narrower and smaller by quire as the manuscript progresses, beginning with thirty-one lines to the page and ending with seventy-three lines. The initials (unflourished) and rubrics are written in a red-orange ink.

The volume opens with three fly-leaves formed of two bifolia, fo. 3*bis* (the conjunct of fo. 1) having been excised. These were part of the original manuscript, since both they and the rear fly-leaves (containing the Sorbonne's *ex libris*) are included in the total of forty-eight folios recorded by the librarian.[8]

The columnar list of goods and services and of the sums dispensed for them is written on unruled parchment, in a small script of the mid thirteenth century, down the left-hand side of fo. 3. The following features of the hand may be noted: terminal 's' is always straight; 'a' is always in teardrop form; round and straight 'r' are employed correctly; the straight 'r' occasionally drops below the line; the tail of the 'g' is closed, as is the loop of the reverse 'c' for *con*. Few abbreviations are used, other than the tilde for suspension and contraction. The tironian 7, uncrossed, is used for *et*. As might be expected in an informal account, little effort was made toward evenness of the left margin, or toward evenness of the finishing strokes of 'e's or of horizontal abbreviation strokes. Twice toward the end of the list the writer crossed out entries, presumably mistakes. The leaf also bears numerous illegible notes in hard point.

One cannot be positive that the accounts are those of Gerard of Abbeville, even though he owned the manuscript at a date appropriate to the hand of the list. A large part of Gerard's library had formerly belonged to Richard de Fournival, physician, poet, and chancellor of Amiens from 1241 or earlier until

---

[7]   The manuscript was to have been recorded as no. 2 in section xxxv, *Originalia Hugonis*, of the Sorbonne's 1338 catalogue, according to the pressmark on fo. 47 v of B.N., MS lat. 16366; but the manuscript was unavailable (on loan, misplaced, or the like) when the compiler of the catalogue was at work and the entry was left blank.

[8]   The '6 quaterni', however, are in fact five quires of 8s and two half-quires (front and back) of 4s.

his death in 1260.[9] Because the twelfth-century MS lat. 16366 could have belonged to him, the list also could have been Richard's rather than Gerard's. That is improbable, however, given both the evident date and the contents of the list: on the basis of script it would be difficult to put the list much before 1250, while its contents clearly suggest a scholar at the schools rather than the chancellor of a cathedral.

Another possibility is raised by a mid or late thirteenth-century note on fo. 46, the first rear flyleaf: 'Magister Andreas de Ambianis pro libris [naturalibus (crossed out)] Salomonis [debet (crossed out)] fratris H. debet totum.' The statement was written at one sitting; in other words, the deletions represent the correction of errors, not two successive debts. The implications of the note are unclear. Perhaps Master Andrew owed the owner of B.N. lat. 16366 a sum for the purchase of the Sapiential Books commented on by a Brother H. (probably Hugh of St. Cher's postills),[10] and the owner jotted a reminder here. Perhaps, instead, Master Andrew left B.N. lat. 16366 as a pledge in exchange for the Wisdom Books, the debt being recorded on a flyleaf of the pledge volume itself, a common occurrence. In the latter case, perhaps the transaction transpired after Gerard had left the book to the Sorbonne, and Andrew, as a Sorbonnist, used a Sorbonne book as pledge.[11] Master Andrew of Amiens is unidentified, but he must have been associated with either the Sorbonne or the Cathedral of Amiens,[12] or, like Gerard of Abbeville, with both; and he could conceivably have been responsible for the list, before B.N. lat. 16366 came into Gerard's possession. When we look for the man whose accounts these are, therefore, Gerard of Abbeville is not the only possibility; but he is the most likely, of those whose names are associated with this manuscript, and we assume hereafter that the expenses refer to him.

The list of expenses was written down at one sitting, and the items in it are not dated, but there is some indication of the length of time they cover. In University of Paris records of the mid thirteenth century, a *bursa* is the payment of weekly expenses, with the exception of rent: 'expenses unius

---

[9]   Regarding Richard de Fournival see R.H. Rouse, 'Manuscripts Belonging to Richard de Fournival,' *Revue d'histoire des textes*, 3 (1973), pp. 253-69, and Newman, *Amiens*, p. 37, no. 80.

[10]   We thank Louis J. Bataillon for this suggestion.

[11]   Records – especially unambiguous records – of transactions of this sort are scarce. A roughly similar case, extending over a period of a dozen years in the fifteenth century, was the repeated use of London, B.L., MS Royal 3 D.I as a pledge by a related group of Cambridge scholars; see R.H. Rouse, M.A. Rouse and R.A.B. Mynors, *Registrum Anglie de libris doctorum et auctorum veterum*, Corpus of British Medieval Library Catalogues (London 1991), pp. xliv-xlv and n. 2, citing the Cambridge Grace Books.

[12]   Andrew's name does not appear in the list assembled by Newman, *Amiens*.

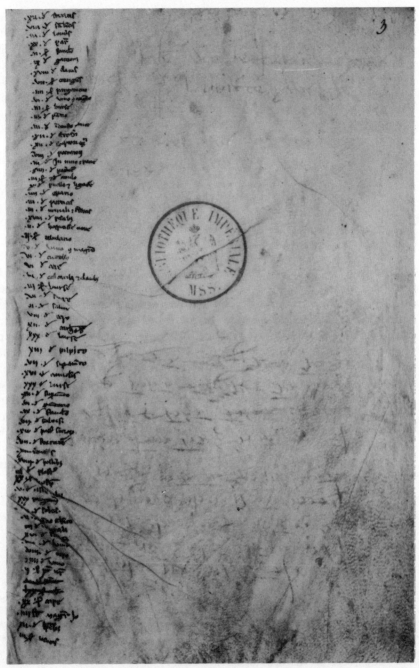

Paris, Bibliothèque Nationale, MS lat. 16366, fo. 3

septimane, quod vulgariter bursa nuncupatur.'[13] *Burse* occur four times in the list (11, 31, 36 and 40), suggesting that the accounts cover a period of four to five weeks. This assumption is supported by the recurrence of other regular expenses: for example, two payments for wine with a master (10 and 27), three other payments for wine (17, 57 and 59), three payments for candles (29, 34, and 58), and perhaps four payments for the removal of waste and garbage (23, 38, 41 and 55). Considering the payments for a cloak (63) and fur lining (46), and the three different purchases of candles,[14] perhaps the list represents expenses in the winter.

In addition to *bursas*, a number of other expenses point to Gerard's life at the schools. Among them are three payments for parchment (4, 9 and 52); a payment for ink and pumice (13); payment to a scribe (15); payment for a lectern or reading desk (37); payment for wooden boards possibly for book binding (51), and skins (48) perhaps for covering the boards; and, as we have noted, two payments for wine with a master.

The mentions of wine with a master, along with the payments of *bursas*, raise the possibility that the list pertains to Gerard's student days before he lived in a house of his own on the Mont Ste-Geneviève.[15] To judge from his expenses, the writer of this list was well-to-do, but that would fit well with Gerard whose family was wealthy.[16] Students in the graduate faculties were mature men and seldom poor.[17] Often theology students had been awarded benefices at the beginning of their graduate careers; and the submission of a *rotula* of names to the pope with a petition for favour later came to be a routine annual exercise of the colleges. A consideration of the list as a whole, however, inclines us instead to think that these accounts refer to Gerard when his student years were past; one master can drink wine with another, and *bursas* were paid by student and master alike. In particular, the purpose for which the list seems to have been written would be more appropriate to a master's state.

We suggest that the list reflects in part the refurbishing of living quarters,

[13] H. Denifle and E. Chatelain, ed., *Chartularium universitatis Parisiensis*, 4 vols. (Paris 1889-1897), i, pp. 258-59, no. 231. For a recent discussion of *bursa* in a university context together with examples of its use, see O. Weijers, *Terminologie des universités au XIIIe siècle*, Lessico intellettuale europeo, 39 (Rome 1987), pp. 93-97.

[14] Concerning the importance of lamps and candles in a scholar's life, see Bataillon, pp. 428-29.

[15] Robert of Sorbon's will mentions 'a certain house situated on the Mont Ste-Geneviève near the house of Master Gerard of Abbeville' ('excepta dumtaxat domo quadam sita in monte Sancte Genovefe prope domum magistri Geroldi de Abbatisvilla'); Glorieux, *Aux origines*, 2, p. 326, no. 279. Gerard at the time of his death owned more than one house in Paris, as the terms of his will reveal: 'Volo quod vendantur domus mee Parisius'; Gand, 'Le Quodlibet XIV,' p. 217, Glorieux, *Aux origines*, 2, p. 357.

[16] We thank Louis J. Bataillon for this suggestion.

[17] For example, a student of canon law in 1290 celebrated the receipt of his licenciate by commissioning for himself a copy of the *Decretum* decorated by the Parisian illuminator Master Honoré; see L. Delisle, 'Notes sur quelques manuscrits de la Bibliothèque de Tours,' *Bibliothèque de l'Ecole de Chartes*, sér. 6, 4 (1868), pp. 596-98.

whether a house or a set of rooms.[18] A number of the purchases, found especially but not exclusively toward the beginning of the list, cannot be considered regular necessities of life, but they could well be extraordinary expenses associated with building: for example, wages (3 *louveris*), nails (7 *clavis*), belts or-straps (8 *corrigiis*), straw (thatching? litter? 14 *stramini*), a workman (21 *operario*), rods (22 *perticis*), a saw (32 *serre*), plaster (49 *plastro*), boards (51 *asseribus*). The removal of waste (38 and 41, *superamento*) may as easily refer to the cost of a builder's clean-up as to the removal of human waste.

Having rebuilt a portion of his house, Gerard would need to acquire additional furnishings. A second group of purchases, toward the middle of the list, are things required on moving in; for example, two chamber pots and cressets (23 *urinali et crassetis* and 55 *urinali*); keys (30 *clavibus*), a chair (35 *cathedre*), a lectern (37 *pulpito*), firedogs or andirons (39 *caniculis*), and even a small statue or figurine (56 *immagine*); and perhaps the various parcels of cloth mentioned (12 and 54 *panno*) were to be used as wall-hangings or drapes, though the sums are relatively small.

While new quarters were being prepared or old ones refurbished, Gerard presumably had to live elsewhere.[19] The list includes two payments to proprietors. That of 2 denarii to the new landlady (25 *hospitissa nova*) was small enough to have been in the nature of a gratuity; but the 80 solidi to the innkeeper or landlord (50 *hospiti*) is the largest amount mentioned on the list. This was probably a payment for lodging, given that a term for rent does not appear elsewhere on the list.[20] This large sum perhaps represents the settlement of Gerard's account at the end of a stay in temporary quarters.

Perhaps Gerard made a separate record of the expenses incurred during a period of four or five weeks while his lodgings underwent repair or remodelling – or perhaps this was a report on such expenses by an agent who handled his expenses and provided him with a written summary periodically, for example, the *famulus* (5) whose pay at 2 solidi is more than double that of the other servants at 9 denarii (6, 43). Either procedure could explain why the list was written at one time. This particular report was written along a blank sheet of parchment, folded once before writing, that later served as a fly-leaf for the *De sacramentis* when Gerard had the manuscript bound. It is worthy of mention, finally, that although the goods and services noted here must surely have been negotiated in the vernacular, they were recorded in Latin.

[18] We thank Patricia Stirnemann for this fruitful suggestion.

[19] The typical Left Bank lodgings of the previous generation, described by Holmes (pp. 74-107, chap. 4, 'Lodgings in the City'), would not have changed much by Gerard's time.

[20] The only other possibility, *bursa*, at Paris in the thirteenth century seems specifically to have meant 'weekly expenses excluding rent', rather than implying both room and board; see Weijers, *Terminologie*, p. 94, citing *Chartularium*, no. 674. See also the passage from the will of Robert de Sorbon in 1270 that explicitly distinguishes 'in bursa et hospicio'; Glorieux, *Aux origines*, 2, p. 326 no. 279, cited by Weijers, p. 95.

Having constructed a case for the master refurbishing his living quarters, we should now acknowledge that identification of a number of items on the list in B.N., MS lat. 16366 is uncertain, and will always remain so. The many growing and laudable dictionaries of medieval Latin are of little help in defining the idiomatic Latin terms particular to a narrowly limited time and place, some of them perhaps slang, in a bald listing without any prose context to give clues to meaning. The interpretations that come to mind if one presupposes the refurbishing of living quarters could have meant something quite other in actuality. The belts or straps (8 *corrigiis*) that might have been related to building may, instead, have been the purchase of decorative belts for personal wear; the fact is, the sum listed seems excessive for either of these contexts. Or perhaps *corrigiis* was a payment for book-binding, for either a very large volume or more probably a multi-volume set; the sum is not unreasonable compared, for example, with the cost of 5 solidi spent to bind the Paris-made Gospel volume of a glossed Bible given to Clairvaux *c.* 1240-50,[21] i.e., at a time and place close to the list of expenses in MS lat. 16366. If 'for binding' is the correct interpretation, then *asseribus* (51) very probably has nothing to do with construction but refers instead to the boards that cover a book; *in asseribus* is the expression most commonly found in contemporary library catalogues to indicate that a book is bound between boards. To continue on this assumption, one would assume that *pellibus* (48) refers to skins for covering the boards. In sum, what one finds in a list such as this depends greatly on what one looks for. When a man's expenses include payments for *strate* and *caniculi* (1 and 39), perhaps he has been travelling, and has paid road tolls and dined out on rabbit – or perhaps he is a stay-at-home who paid for a great deal of bedding and bought andirons for his fire; the terms will bear either interpretation, and it is wise to remind ourselves occasionally how much of historical evidence is choice.

Despite the variables, it is clear that Gerard was an active consumer of goods and services, who purchased a knife (28), a desk (37) and a chair (35), and indulged himself with a ring (19), a fur lining (46) and an inexpensive statue or figurine, probably religious (56). He purchased cloth (12, 54), employed a tailor (42), bought sandals (44, 53) and apparently rode a horse, because he paid for spurs (30); the purchase of straw (14) may be relevant here, as well.[22] Beyond the standard fare entailed in his *bursa*, he paid for fish (24) and perhaps rabbit (39), drank with his teacher or a colleague (10, 27), perhaps ran

---

[21] Recorded in the fly-leaves of Troyes, B.M., MS 157; the accounts for the Gospels include 100 sol. for parchment, 30 sol. for the scribe, 5 sol. to rent an exemplar, and 5 sol. for binding.

[22] When he made his will in 1271, Gerard of Abbeville owned several horses: the testament directs his executors to sell 'my horses' (*equi mei*) to pay his obligations, and leaves 'one of the best of my nags' (*unum de melioribus ronsinis meis*) to his cook; Gand, 'Le Quodlibet XIV,' p. 217, Glorieux, *Aux origines*, 2, pp. 356-57. Probably this was not unusual, among churchmen of his rank.

an account (26), and dined with friends (45). He employed servants (5-6, 43) and a workman (21), and paid interest on his debt (66).

Manufactured goods, almost always paid for in solidi – such as the cloak for 20 solidi (63), the belts-straps-binding for 7 solidi (8), 3 solidi for a ring (19), 2 solidi for a rosary (60) – are more expensive than food or services, ordinarily stated in denarii.[23] Weekly board varied between 30 and 36 denarii (i.e., 3 solidi; 11, 31, 36 and 40), perhaps dependent upon whether he dined five, or six, days at the house in the week. It would be interesting to know the purpose for the large sum of 4 pounds paid to Master John (64), perhaps the payment of a debt, the purchase of some books – or something completely unsuspected. It might be even more interesting to know about the girl and the binding (20).

For the 64 items on the list (excluding the two that have been excised), the median expenditure was only 10 denarii.[24] But the range was wide, with the largest expenses (4 pounds, the equivalent of 960 denarii) exceeding in multiples of several hundreds the outlay of 2 denarii for the smallest purchases, to the extent that, in contrast to the median, the average purchase was 4 solidi 1½ denarii. In the period of four or five weeks covered by these accounts, Gerard spent more than 247 solidi – the equivalent of 12 pounds 7 solidi 7 denarii. Of this, his four *burse* together cost him only 11 solidi, a little over 4 per cent of his total outlay. The bulk of his spending went for living quarters, material goods, services and entertainment.[25] The expense list is a useful reminder of the dependence of pre-industrial society on human labour to haul and serve, and conversely of the number of people who earned their living by this means, whether delivering messages, carrying heavy goods, or removing human waste.

Two thirteenth-century records of trades and professions in Paris, Etienne de Boileau's mid century *Livre des mestiers* and the Paris *taille* books of 1292-1313,[26] give a picture of lay urban commerce. Largely absent from these documents is the university, the students and masters, who were seldom taxable (and thus seldom mentioned) because of their clerical status. A list such as that in B.N., MS lat. 16366 attests that these two worlds actually inhabited the same space, with people crossing over from one world to the

---

[23] He also bought a cheaper one for 14 denarii (no. 18).

[24] See the appendix below, with the list rearranged according to the amounts, from smallest to largest.

[25] Still useful in this regard is G. d'Avenel, *Histoire économique de la propriété, des salaires, des denrées, et de tous les prix en général depuis l'an 1200 jusqu'en l'an 1800*, 6 vols. (Paris, 1894-1912).

[26] R. de Lespinasse and F. Bonnardot, eds., *Le livre des métiers d'Etienne Boileau* (Paris, 1879); H. Géraud, ed., *Paris sous Philippe-le-Bel . . . Le rôle de la taille . . . 1292* (Paris 1837); Karl Michaëlsson, *Le livre de la taille de Paris . . . 1296*, Göteborgs Universitets Arsskrift, 64, no. 4 (Göteborg, 1958); idem, *Le livre de la taille de Paris . . . 1297*, ibid., 67, no. 3 (Göteborg 1962); and idem, *Le livre de la taille de Paris . . . 1313*, ibid., 57, no. 3 (Göteborg, 1951); the unedited taille books for 1298-1300 are preserved in the Archives Nationales in Paris, numbered KK. 283. Géraud's alphabetical list of *métiers* (pp. 483-549) is especially helpful, although his explanations and etymologies are not reliable.

other many times a day. Among the tradesmen and craftsmen referred to in the Old French of the *taille* rolls, therefore, are a number whose counterparts appear in the Latin of the list: for example, *parcheminiers* or parchmenters (4, 9, 52), *ecrivains* or scribes (15) and *encriers* or ink-makers (13); *paternostriers* or makers of rosaries (18 and 60), *ciriers*, sellers of wax and makers of candles (29, 34 and 58), *serruriers* or *claceliers*, locksmiths (30), *taverniers* or *osteliers*, landlords (25, 50), *aneliers* or makers of rings (19), *bufetiers* or wine merchants (10, 17, 27, 57, 59), *couteliers* or makers of knives (28), *peletiers* or dealers in skins and furs (46), *porteurs* or porters (16), *segiers* or chair makers (35), *tailleeurs* or tailors (42), *telemeliers* or bakers (17), *chaumeeurs* or sellers of straw (14), *esperonniers* or spur-makers (30).

The items enumerated in the list reflect a complex urban society composed of labour, craft, proprietary and clerical groups, actively serving each other, forming a consuming society accustomed to buying and selling the desired goods and services with hard coin.

Paris, B.N., MS lat. 16366, fo. 3

1.]   xii d.              stratis

Perhaps 'for bedding', in the sense of mattress stuffing (from *stratus*; cf. Du Cange = Charles Dufresne, seigneur du Cange, *Glossarium mediae et infimae latinitatis* [Paris 1840-1850 etc.] s.v.); the sum is excessive, unless several mattresses are being filled. Other contemporary meanings include 'road tolls'; see A. Blaise, *Dictionnaire latin-français des auteurs du moyen-âge* = Corpus christianorum continuatio mediaevalis, *Lexicon latinitatis medii aevi* (Turnhout, 1975), p. 869.

2.]   viii d.            sa ... lentis (?)

One possible reading is 'scintilentis,' perhaps in the sense of tallow candles; one would have expected 'scintilentibus.' The price agrees well with other purchases of candles, however (see 34, 58 and cf. 29).

3.]   iii d.             louveris(?)

This may read *louveris*, from *loyerum* (cf. Du Cange, 'praemium, merces, Gall. *loyer*') akin to the Old French *louier*, 'for hire' or 'for wages', given that it approximates the sum listed below paid to a workman (21); or possibly it reads *lomentis*, 'for soap'.

4.]   xx d.             par[gameno]

'for parchment' (see 9, 52).

5.]   ii s.            famulo

'to the servant' (see 6, 43).

6.]   ix d.            garcioni

'to the serving boy' (see 5, 43); cf. Du Cange, and Blaise 412. Nequam uses the term to refer to the stable-boy (p. 90).

7.]   xviii d.         clavis

'for nails,' perhaps, although the sum recorded should have bought a very large store of nails; perhaps instead 'a key', one of the rare nouns in the nominative case (cf. 18, 60), although again the sum is large compared to another payment for keys (see 30). Nequam (p. 102) lists things necessary for building a house, a list beginning 'Clavis, asseribus . . . .'

8.]   vii s.           corrigiis

'for belts' or straps, or possibly 'for bookbinding' (cf. 51); see W. Wattenbach, *Das Schriftwesen im Mittelalter*, 3rd ed. (Leipzig, 1896; repr. Graz, 1958), p. 331. The large sum involved would suggest the first, lavishly adorned; for *corrigia* as belts or girdles or money-belts see *Dictionary of Medieval Latin from British Sources*, fasc. 2, p. 501. The word is defined by John of Garland as belts only (p. 23, para. 10).

9.]   iiii s.          pargameno

'for parchment' (see 4, 52).

10.]   vi d.           vino cum magistro

'for wine with a master' (see 27, and cf. 17, 57, 59).

11.]   iii s.          burse

'for weekly board' (see 31, 36, 40); the payment varied between 30 denarii and 36 (= three solidi), perhaps dependent upon whether he dined five, or six, days at the house. John of Garland (p. 24, para. 18, n. 7) mentions this as a literal, physical purse ('vendunt . . . bursas de corio cervino, ovino, bovino et porcino'); but it is unlikely that Gerard would have bought four purses, consecutively, all at about the same price.

12.]   iii d.          panno

'for cloth' (see 54, 61).

13.]   iii d.          incausto, punice

'for ink, pumice'; see O. Weijers, ed., *Vocabulaire du livre et de l'écriture au moyen-âge* (Turnhout 1989) pp. 31, 32, and Wattenbach pp. 175, 193-203; for *punex* as a variant of *pumex* see R.E. Latham, *Revised Medieval Latin Word-List* (London 1965), p. 383. They are included by Nequam among the necessities for writing (pp. 112-13), and for John of Garland see the note to 35, below.

14.]   xii d.         stramini

'for straw', a large sum.

15.]   xii d.         scriptori ex$^{ri(?)}$

'to an external scribe', i.e., someone not of the household? The extension of the abbreviation is not certain.

16.]   viii d.        portatori

'to a porter or messenger'.

17.]   iii d.          in vino et pane

'on wine and bread' (see 57, 59, and cf. 10, 27).

18.]   xiiii d.        pater noster

'a rosary'; another rosary cost nearly twice this sum (see 60).

19.]   iii s. et(?) d. anulo

'for a ring,' probably not of gold for this amount. There seems to be no number of pence stated in the price column. Possibly the symbol before *d.* was intended as an arabic 7; but none of the other amounts on the list are written in arabic figures, and the symbol is identical in appearance with the writer's tironian *et*. No other sum on the list is expressed in both solidi and denarii, odd amounts in other cases being translated into pence (cf. 4, 7, etc.).

20.]  x d.  puelle et ligature

'to a servant girl, and for binding'; perhaps *puelle* is a slip for *pelle*, skin to be used for a book binding.

21.]  iiii d.  operario

'to a workman' (cf. 3); see *Novum glossarium mediae latinitatis* s.v.

22.]  iii d.  perticis

'for rods' or poles; cf. Latham, p. 346, and Blaise, p. 680. John of Garland treats a *pertica* solely as a horizontal rod from which things hang – he mentions (p. 23, para. 9) a man coming to sell shoes which are hanging on a rod, 'tulit in pertica una ad vendendum sotulares ad laqueos', and he names (p. 32, para. 59) the clothing that hangs 'super pertica magistri Johannis'. Nequam also (pp. 88, 91) thinks of a *pertica* particularly in terms of a rod from which to hang things, but he mentions the word as well as a perch for one's falcons (p. 91).

23.]  iii d.  urinali et crassetis

'for a chamber pot and lamps or torches' (see 55). For *urinale* see Blaise, p. 940. *Crassetus* or *crassetum* appears in numerous dictionaries of medieval Latin with the meaning 'small grease lamp' or 'torch' (cf. the English 'cresset'); see *Dictionary of Medieval Latin from British Sources*, fasc. 2, p. 511; J.F. Niermeyer, *Mediae latinitatis lexicon minus* (Leiden 1976), p. 283; Blaise, p. 263. The combination would have been a peculiar one for which to make a single payment. Among the 'green glass products' made by English medieval glassmakers one finds both urinals – *vases de nuit*, not simply the physician's vial – and glass hanging lamps; see R.J. Charleston, 'Vessel Glass,' in *English Medieval Industries: Craftsmen, Techniques, Products*, ed. J. Blair and N. Ramsay (London 1991), chap. 10, esp. pp.258-260 and figs. 114, 117-118, 124. However, not only is this example exclusively English, but, more to the point, a wall lamp made of glass is a considerable remove from the standard meaning of 'cresset' or *crassetus*. Unlikely, then, but not impossible. Perhaps, instead, the particular meaning in thirteenth-century Paris of the word used here was related to another facet of the modern French *crasse*, which has a range of meanings similar to the English 'filth', so that the phrase would simply say 'for emptying the chamber pot.' We can offer no corroboration for such an interpretation.

24.]  xviii d.  piscibus

'for fish', a large sum for food (cf. 39). However, this was an especially important part of the diet of a community of clerics. John of Garland (p. 31

para. 72) lists varieties of edible fish sold in contemporary Paris; Nequam mentions 'little fish cooking in a sauce' ('pisciculi coquendi sunt in salsamento,' p. 87), for which he gives a recipe (p. 93).

25]   ii d.          hospitisse nove

'to the new landlady' or housekeeper; see the *Dictionary of Medieval Latin from British Sources*, fasc. 4, p. 1178 for thirteenth-century examples.

26.]   ii s.          tabulario

'for the account'; alternatively, a *tabularium* can be a market stall or shop, and the *tabularius* the vendor there – neither of which meanings is far afield from 'the account' or 'tab'. A *tabularius* can also be a scribe, a notary (cf. *tabellio*), or a tax collector, and a *tabularium* a notary's office; see the range of possible thirteenth-century meanings in Du Cange s.v., in Blaise, p. 902, and in Niermeyer, p. 1011.

27.]   v d.          vino cum magistro

'for wine with a master' (see 10, and cf. 17, 57, 59).

28.]   vi d.          cutello

'for a knife'; for thirteenth-century examples see *Dictionary of Medieval Latin from British Sources*, fasc. 2, pp. 529-30.

29.]   vi d.          cere

'for candles' (see 34, 58); for thirteenth-century examples see *Dictionary of Medieval Latin from British Sources*, fasc. 2, p. 316.

30.   vi d.          calcaribus et clavibus

'for spurs and keys'; the sum is small for careful iron work, but the price is similar to that for the saw (see 32, and cf. also 7). Gerard's were obviously not the fancy 'calcaria argentata et aurata' mentioned by Garland (p. 23 para. 15).

31.]   iii s.          burse

'for weekly board' (see the note at 11 above, and see 36, 40).

32.]   vi d.          serre

'for a saw'.

33.]   ii d.            saline(?)

'for salt'; the reading is uncertain.

34.]   viii d.          cepo

'for tallow' to be used for candles (see 29, 58); see Latham s.v. *sebum*.

35.]   xii d.           cathedre

'for a chair.' John of Garland (p. 31 para. 55) includes *cathedra* in the list of objects one should find in the lodgings of a 'probus homo'; he distinguishes it from *ferculum*, folding chair. He includes *cathedra* as well (p. 31, para. 56) in the list of implements needful for *clerici*, along with *pulpita* (see 37), *cepum* in the sense of 'candle' (see 34, 58), *incaustum* and *pumex* (spelled 'pinex'; see 13), and *asser* (see 51). Nequam also includes *cathedra* among the equipment needful for writing (p. 112).

36.]   xxx d.           burse

'for weekly board' (see the note at 11 above, and see 31, 36).

37.]   xiii d.          pulpito

'for a lectern' or reading desk.

38.]   vii d.           superamento

'for [removal of] waste', by extension from *supero* and *superat* (see 41).

39.]   xvi d.           caniculis

'for andirons ['firedogs']', as seen in the inventory of the estate of Gerard of Montaigu, canon of Notre Dame, in 1339 (Paris, Archives Nationales, S 6458, no. 8); another contemporary meaning would be 'for rabbit', since this spelling is a common enough variant for *cuniculis*; see for example *Dictionary of Medieval Latin from British Sources*, fasc. 2, p. 534 and Latham, both s.v. *cuniculus*, and Blaise, p. 270 s.v. *cunicula*. The cost is within the range of expenses on this list both for food (see 24) and for ironmongery (see 30). Without knowledge of the context in which this word was written down, it is hard to say which is the more likely.

40.]   xxx d.           burse

'for weekly board' (see the note at 11 above, and see 31 and 36).

41.]   xii d.          superamento

'for [removal of] waste' (see the note at 38).

42.]   vi d.          permentario

'to the tailor'; see Du Cange s.v. *permentarius*.

43.]   ix d.          famulo

'to the servant' (see 5, 6).

44.]   vii d.          soleis.

'for sandals' (see 53); see P. Contamine, *La vie quotidienne pendant la Guerre de Cent Ans: France et Angleterre (XIVe siècle)* (Paris 1976), p. 202. Curiously, neither Garland nor Nequam use *soleis* for footwear, although they mention a number of other sorts (cf. Garland p. 23 para. 9, Nequam 89).

45.]   xii d.          pastu sociorum

'for a dinner with friends', probably just the writer's share of the cost.

46.]   vii d.          forrature

'for fur trimming', perhaps a cloak-lining; see *Dictionary of Medieval Latin from British Sources*, fasc. 4, p. 970 and Blaise, p. 391, both s.v. *foderatura*.

47.]   xii s.          [illeg.]

48.]   xviii d.          pellibus

'for skins,' possibly for book-binding (see also 51); for *pellis* as parchment see Latham, p. 338 and Weijers, pp. 29, 66, 95. The core meanings of 'pellis' changed little from classical Latin, '[animal] hide', 'leather', and 'parchment'; see, e.g., *Oxford Latin Dictionary*, s.v.

49.]   x d.          plastro

'for plaster'.

50.]   $\overset{\text{iiii}}{\text{xx}}$ s.          hospiti

'to the innkeeper';' see *Dictionary of Medieval Latin from British Sources*, fasc. 4, p. 1176 for thirteenth-century examples; 80 solidi (here and 64) is the largest sum in the account.

51.]    v d.            asseribus

'for wooden boards' probably for book-binding; see Wattenbach, pp. 246, 328, 331-332, 346, and Weijers, pp. 58, 64; in a different context it could also refer to lumber, specifically rafters, to be used in construction (see *Dictionary of Medieval Latin from British Sources*, fasc. 1, p. 140, or Blaise, p. 75), but the price is very modest for such an interpretation. John of Garland (p. 31, para. 56), among the names of things needed for reading and writing (books, lectern, lamp, ink, pumice, scraper, chalk, quill, lead, ruler, chair, etc.) includes *asser*, in the singular; his meaning is not clear, but Alexander Nequam makes it plain that in the context this means a lapboard: 'in cathedra sedeat, ansis utrimque elevatis . . . asserem sustinentibus' (p. 112). However, Nequam also uses *asseres* in the context of building a structure (p. 102), and of constructing a wagon or coach (*currus*, p. 101).

52.]    xxx [d.]        pargameno

'for parchment' (see 4, 9).

53.]    viii d.          soleis.

'for sandals' (see 44).

54.]    ii d.            panno . . . h . . . ico(?)

'for cloth'; the indecipherable word probably refers to type or colour (see 12, 61).

55.]    viii d.          urinali

'for a chamber pot', or for emptying the chamber pot (23).

56.]    xvi d.          immagine

'for a statue', though probably small and of wood considering the relatively small cost; see Victor Gay, *Glossaire archéologique du moyen âge et de la renaissance*, ed. H. Stein and M. Aubert, 2 vols. (Paris 1887-1928) ii, pp. 45-46.

57.]    iiii d.          vino

'for wine' (see 17, 59).

58.]    viii d.          cepo

'for tallow' to be used for candles (see 29, 34, and cf. 2).

59.]   et(?) vii d.   vino

'for wine' (see 17, 57, and cf. 10, 27).

60.]   ii s.        pater noster

'a rosary'; the cost is almost twice that of the other rosary on the list (see 18), probably reflecting a difference in material or in workmanship.

61.   iii s.        panno [the whole crossed out]

'for cloth' (see 12, 54).

62.]   lxx s.       [illeg., the whole crossed out]

63.]   xx s.        cape

'for a cloak'.

64.]   iiii lb.      magistro Johanni

'to Master John'; the large size suggests repayment of a debt, or payment for a purchase.

65.]   xii d.       speciebus

'for spices' or medicines; see Du Cange, s.v. *species* no. 6, and also Blaise, p. 857, Latham, s.v., Niermeyer, p. 983. John of Garland (p. 28 paras. 43-44) names a variety of spices and herbs sold by apothecaries ('gallice dicuntur *epiciers*' as an early gloss adds: H. Géraud, *Paris sous Philippe-le-Bel* . . . [1837], repr. with intro. by C. Bourlet and L. Fossier [Tübingen, 1991], p. 596, paras. 42-43), and Nequam mentions 'species aromaticae' in the kitchen (p. 87).

66.]   iii s.        usuris

'for interest'; this is a serious sum, although a relative figure meaningful in a modern context would be hard to name.

# *Appendix*

Following are the expenditures on fo. 3 of Paris B.N., MS lat. 16366 rearranged in twenty-three categories according to amount (excluding the excised entries 61 and 62). The median expenditure was 10 d. (in category 9), the average 4 sol. 1½ d. (in category 19).

(1)
ii d.   hospitisse nove
ii d.   saline
ii d.   panno . . . h . . . ico

(2)
iii d.   lomentis
iii d.   panno
iii d.   incausto, pumice
iii d.   in vino et pane
iii d.   perticis
iii d.   urinali et crassecis
iii d.   vino

(3)
iiii d.   operario

(4)
v d.   vino cum magistro
v d.   asseribus

(5)
vi d.   vino cum magistro
vi d.   cutello
vi d.   cere
vi d.   calcaribus et clavibus
vi d.   serre
vi d.   permentario

(6)
vii d.   superamento
vii d.   soleis.
vii d.   forrature
vii d.   vino

(7)
viii d.   sa-lentis(?)
viii d.   portatori
viii d.   cepo
viii d.   soleis.
viii d.   urinali
viii d.   cepo

(8)
ix d.   garcioni
ix d.   famulo

(9)
x d.   puelle et ligature
x d.   plastro

(10)
xii d. (i s.)   stratis
xii d.   stramini
xii d.   scriptori ex*ri*
xii d.   cathedre
xii d.   superamento
xii d.   pastu sociorum
xii d.   speciebus

(11)
xiii d.   pulpito

(12)
xiiii d.   pater noster

(13)
xvi d.   caniculis
svi d.   immagine

(14)
xviii d.   clavis
xviii d.   piscibus
xviii d.   pellibus

(15)
xx d.   par[gameno]

(16)
ii s.(xxiv d.)   famulo
ii s.   tabulario
ii s.   pater noster

(17)
xxx d.   burse
xxx d.   burse
xxx [d.]   pargameno

(18)
iii s.(xxxvi d.)   burse
iii s.   burse
iii s.   usuris
iii s. &?   anulo
(19)
iiii s.   pargameno
(20)
vii s.   corrigiis

(21)
xii s.   [illeg.]
(22)
xx s.   cape
(23)
$\overset{\text{iiii}}{\text{xx}}$ s.   hospiti
iiii lib.   magistro Johanni

# 17

## Reflections on the Role of the Medieval Universities in Contemporary Society

### Alan B. Cobban

The medieval university was rooted in utilitarian soil. Europe's earliest universities were born of the need to harness the intellectual advances of the eleventh and twelfth centuries to the professional requirements of an increasingly urbanised society. Their precursors, the cathedral and other types of urban schools, were far more attuned to the demands of the secular world than had been the long-established monastic schools. While these urban schools had attempted educational programmes which transcended practical community wants, their basic *raison d'être* had been to service the practical imperatives of professional life.[1] As such, the cathedral and municipal schools contributed to the transformation of a monastically dominated education into one in which the immediate professional concerns of society became central to the educational system. The weakness of the cathedral schools lay in their ephemeral character and the random nature of their instructional diet. Their reputation was too closely geared to the movements of individual masters. The sudden departure of an eminent teaching master could result in the lapse of a specialism which had been maintained with distinction for a number of years. The fast-expanding demand for advanced education in the twelfth century could not be met satisfactorily by the cathedral and municipal schools which, at best, attained heights of quixotic brilliance but whose overall performance was limited and patchy.[2] A more permanent institutional form was required in order to enshrine the intellectual advance of the twelfth century, to channel student talent more effectively through structured courses of study leading to a specific degree, and to deploy teaching masters and resources on a more

---

[1] For the cathedral schools see G. Paré, A. Brunet and P. Tremblay, *La renaissance du xiie siècle: les écoles et l'enseignement* (Paris and Ottawa, 1933); E. Lesne, 'Les écoles de la fin du viiie siècle à la fin du xiie' in *Histoire de la propriété ecclésiastique en France*, v (Lille, 1940); S. d'Irsay, *Histoire des universités françaises et étrangères des origines à nos jours*, i (Paris 1933).

[2] See e.g. L. Boehm, 'Libertas scholastica und negotium scholare: Entstehung und Sozialprestige des akademischen Standes im Mittelalter' in *Universität und Gelehrtenstand, 1400-1800* (Limburg an der Lahn, 1970), pp. 24-25.

rational and disciplined basis. The institutional response came in the shape of the earliest universities which, as Europe's first collectivised educational venture, were cast in the role of supports for the professional, ecclesiastical and governmental needs of society.

The medieval universities were largely vocational schools.[3] They were expected to give value for money by responding and adapting to community demands. The concept of study for its own sake was confined to a minority of scholars who could be described as the opinion-makers of society. These included the legal theorists, theologians, philosophers, logicians and natural scientists who made such a profound contribution to the rich complexities of medieval thought. One may here highlight the efforts which theologians and philosophers made to reconcile the polarised elements of Christian learning and Aristotelian philosophy; or one may emphasise the glittering achievements of the galaxy of Roman and canon lawyers who made such an inestimable addition to European political and legal theory; or one may stress the fundamental work done within the field of the natural sciences and the evolution of what was essentially the modern method of scientific inquiry. Enduring accomplishments of this kind do not negate the premise that the medieval universities were wedded primarily to the canon of utility. Opportunities always existed for scholars of outstanding abilities to pursue non-utilitarian lines of investigation which, in the short term, seemed to have little relevance for transient community need. The colonies of Franciscans and Dominicans domiciled within medieval universities afford a powerful example of scholars who, with the security and resources of their orders behind them, could apply themselves to areas of scholarship irrespective of contemporary educational values.

For the majority of students, however, education was a severely practical matter. The medieval universities trained students in the mastery of areas of knowledge and techniques which could be applied in the secular professions such as law, or teaching, or medicine, or in governmental and ecclesiastical employment. This utilitarian emphasis was reinforced by the general level of underfunding of university education in the medieval period. After receiving core provision from the relevant authority, whether a monarchy, a principality, a commune, a municipality, or senior ecclesiastics or members of the nobility, most universities had to struggle along on the basis of fee income and private donations and endowments. The uncertain nature of university finances would be exacerbated if it were deemed that the university was not giving value for money and support was temporarily withdrawn. The highly utilitarian and changeable attitude of the Florentine Signoria towards the

---

[3] Discussion of this theme is provided by A.B. Cobban, *The Medieval Universities: Their Development and Organization* (London, 1975), esp. pp. 218-34. See also F.M. Powicke, *Ways of Medieval Life and Thought* (London, 1949), pp. 198-212 and G. Leff, *Paris and Oxford Universities in the Thirteenth and Fourteenth Centuries* (New York, 1968), esp. pp. 1-11, 116-18.

medieval university of Florence is a case in point.[4] The fact that there was little surplus wealth available for non-vocational courses of study had a profound effect upon the student mentality. The average student was dependent on a parent, guardian or patron for his finances and felt himself to be fortunate if he managed to win through to a first degree.[5] The constant insecurity with which many students had to grapple must have conditioned his social and political outlook. It is true that as part of his university training the medieval student would debate the central theological and political issues of his age;[6] he would doubtless scrutinise contemporary structures; and he would be a ready critic of established norms. But while at university the average student would have little incentive to change the world in which he lived. The business of survival was altogether too hard to permit of the intellectual indulgence generated by a state-aided system of education. Most students seem to have gone to university to qualify for lucrative employment within the safety of the established order, whether in the church or in an area of government service or in one of the organised professions. In his later career, the graduate's skills might be utilised, for example, in the shaping of propagandist material on behalf of papal, imperial or royal ideologies.[7] To this extent, the university student might ultimately be bound up in movements which led to adjustments within the social order. At the university stage, however, the world of the average student was attuned to conservative modes of thought.

It is sometimes argued that there were students who did not fit the establishment mould and who led an itinerant life of anarchical protest. Much attention has been lavished upon the alleged 'Order of the Wandering Scholars', upon the 'Goliards', the followers of Golias, the symbol of vice, ribaldry, lawlessness and anti-authoritarianism.[8] That wandering loose-living clerks were perennial features of medieval society cannot be contested: the ecclesiastical authorities made frequent legislative attempts to curb their activities.[9] It is true that these *clerici vagantes* may have included students in their company. From the early thirteenth century, however, such itinerant students would not have been recognised as *bona fide* members of their universities and would not

---

[4] G.A. Brucker, 'Florence and the University, 1318-1434' in *Action and Conviction in Early Modern Europe*, ed. T.K. Rabb and J.E. Seigel, (Princeton, 1969), pp. 220ff.

[5] On the conditions and aspects of life of medieval students see C.H. Haskins, *Studies in Medieval Culture* (New York, 1929; repr. 1958), chaps. 1-3. For English student life see A.B. Cobban, *The Medieval English Universities: Oxford and Cambridge to c. 1500* (Berkeley, CA, and Aldershot, 1988), ch. 9.

[6] See e.g. the list of late thirteenth-century *quaestiones* in A.G. Little and F. Pelster, *Oxford Theology and Theologians, c. A.D. 1282-1302* (Oxf. Hist. Soc., xcvi, 1934), pp. 104ff.

[7] On the close relations between the Italian law schools and secular and papal government see W. Ullmann, *Principles of Government and Politics in the Middle Ages* (London, 1961), p. 290.

[8] H. Waddell, *Wandering Scholars* (London, 1954), *passim*; J.H. Hanford, 'The Progenitors of Golias', *Speculum*, 1 (1926), pp. 38ff.

[9] F.J.E. Raby, *A History of Secular Latin Poetry in the Middle Ages*, ii (Oxford, 1934), p. 339.

have met the criteria for matriculation.[10] A few restless spirits of this genre may have lived a shadowy existence on the periphery of the academic community but their attitudes can hardly be taken as representative of the student population. Moreover, the widespread phenomenon of student power among the universities of Italy, provincial France and the Iberian Peninsula was directed towards specific ends such as a greater degree of protection for members of student guilds or the winning of university autonomy from external ecclesiastical dominion.[11] Nowhere is there any indication that direct student action within the medieval universities was channelled towards the reformation of the wider community. It would be anachronistic to imagine that medieval students regarded the university as a microcosm of society in the sense that radical restructuring within the academic community would be a prelude to a similar reshaping of society at large. Medieval student power did not embrace this degree of political and social sophistication.

Just as student power movements were not directed towards revolutionary change in the community, so too they were not much concerned with the selection of the elements of the curriculum.[12] There was an agreed core of authorised texts in the medieval universities which were hallowed by time and supplemented by the glossatorial and disruptational literature. The mastery of a challenging discipline, the sharpening of the critical faculties, the ability to expound logically, the careful digestion of approved knowledge – these were the hallmarks of the average university education. Teaching and learning were conservative experiences and, at the ordinary student level, questioning was encouraged both as a form of training and as a means of elucidation within a largely *a priori* intellectual system.[13] Only in the most advanced university circles could expression be given to ideas of the universality of learning upon which medieval education was theoretically based. For the average student the universities mounted a study regime designed to perpetuate received doctrine rather than to stimulate independent inquiry. Before the advent of printing memory work and rote learning loomed large in the absorption of the basic material. It is true that in selected faculties in at least eleven universities the *exemplar-pecia* system, a cheap utilitarian method of manuscript production which enabled multiple copies to be made of texts, commentaries, lectures and disputations, must have alleviated the student's claustrophobic dependence on

---

[10] Most of the early universities enacted legislation to exclude from their communities students who were unattached to a definite master and who did not follow an approved course of study. See e.g. the problems faced by the schools of Erfurt in trying to distinguish between genuine and false scholars: G.C. Boyce, 'Erfurt Schools and Scholars in the Thirteenth Century', *Speculum*, 24 (1949), esp. pp. 11-12.

[11] See A. B. Cobban, 'Medieval Student Power', *Past and Present*, 53 (1971), pp. 28ff.; idem, 'Episcopal Control in the Medieval Universities of Northern Europe', *Studies in Church History*, 5 (Leiden, 1969), pp. 1ff.; idem, *The Medieval Universities*, chaps. 3,7.

[12] Cobban, 'Medieval Student Power', p. 31.

[13] Ibid., pp. 31-32.

the lecturer's every word and permitted a degree of private study in a more relaxed environment.[14] But only a small proportion of Europe's student population would have enjoyed the benefits of such a system. The extent to which medieval students were accorded a passive role in the educational process helped to make them broadly acquiescent in contemporary assumptions about their education', and none of their rebellions had, as an objective, a radical transformation of the curriculum. It was not until the growing appeal of humanist learning became irresistible in the late medieval period that pressures for this kind of reform materialised.[15]

The medieval universities, then, were perceived as primarily vocational institutions which provided intellectual fare and disciplined training considered to be germane to the life of the community. They were essentially teaching academies. They could not be described in any strict sense as centres of research. Although significant contributions to learning were made by scholars within the universities, this was largely done on an individual basis. the universities, as corporate bodies, offered neither research degrees nor research appointments in any way comparable to those in modern universities. The generality of university benefactors expected returns for their investments in utilitarian coin. They did not give of their wealth to subsidise ivory towers or the more esoteric branches of learning. It needs to be stressed, however, that medieval notions of educational utility were of a more expansive nature than those which depress the modern university. Here one must not fall into the propagandist trap set by some of the humanist scholars of the fifteenth and sixteenth centuries who argued that most of the education of the preceding university age had been socially irrelevant.[16] Doubtless there is a grain of truth in the humanist criticism that an immoderate adherence to Aristotle and his Jewish and Arabic commentators could lead to logical excesses and stifling pedantry. But to dismiss medieval university education, on the basis of a number of inbred defects, as wanting in community value, would be misleading to the point of caricature. A rigorous training in logical analysis, which underlay all university disciplines, allied to the adversarial techniques of the disputation, were deemed to comprise a valuable groundwork for the oral and written requirements of a wide range of occupations within the medieval

[14] For the *exemplar-pecia* system see J. Destrez, *La pecia dans les manuscrits universitaires du xiiie et du xive siècle* (Paris, 1935) and G. Pollard, 'The *Pecia* System in the Medieval Universities', *Medieval Scribes, Manuscripts and Libraries: Essays Presented to N.R. Ker*, ed. M.B. Parkes and A.G. Watson, (London, 1978), pp. 145ff.

[15] See e.g. Cobban, *The Medieval English Universities*, pp. 243-56; J.M. Fletcher, 'Change and Resistance to Change: A Consideration of the Development of English and German Universities during the Sixteenth Century', *History of Universities*, 1 (1981), pp. 1ff.; J.K. McConica, 'Humanism and Aristotle in Tudor Oxford', *E.H.R.*, 94 (1979, pp. 291ff.

[16] See e.g. H. Rashdall, *The Universities of Europe in the Middle Ages* 3 vols., 2nd ed., ed. F.M. Powicke and A.B. Emden (Oxford, 1936), iii, pp. 453-54; M.H. Curtis, *Oxford and Cambridge in Transition 1558-1642* (Oxford, 1959), pp. 21-22, 65ff.

society. In a legally-orientated society of competing rights and privileges conferred by a hierarchy of authorities, there was unlimited scope for the application of that exactitude of mind which was shaped and refined by logical training.

As vocational academies, the medieval universities appear to have succeeded fairly well in supplying the trained personnel for the manifold needs of secular and ecclesiastical government. University graduates are found at all levels within the hierarchies of state and church.[17] They held the principal offices of government, and served as royal councillors and king's clerks, and they were prominent among Europe's bishops, deans of cathedrals and head of religious houses. They also found careers as diplomats, as judges in both secular and ecclesiastical courts, as members of parliamentary institutions, as senior officials, canons and prebendaries of cathedrals, as the officials of bishops and archdeacons, and as the holders of offices within aristocratic households. On a lesser plane, university graduates became schoolmasters, notaries public, parish clergy, chantry priests and domestic chaplains. It is clear that in the later medieval period the universities were performing an indispensable role in buttressing Europe's political, administrative, legal and ecclesiastical structures. It is further apparent that the majority of Europe's graduates could be described as technicians who oiled the wheels of the established order and who seldom offered revolutionary challenge.

While this utilitarian emphasis was less than ideal in terms of a broadly based education, students had the satisfaction of pursuing what were generally reckoned to be socially relevant courses. Moreover, they were not constrained by the curious modern notion of a cultural breach between the sciences and the arts. The polarisation between classical and Christian learning was indeed an ever-present source of cultural contrast which the medieval student could not evade. But at least he was not conscious of an intellectual chasm dividing the study of mathematical and scientific data and the contents of the arts curriculum. Such a separatist view of the seamless web of scholarship would have made little sense in medieval universities considering, for example, that the course leading to the M.A. degree was an integrated mixture of arts, mathematical and scientific subjects which had to be studied in easy association. The lack of false dichotomy between the arts and sciences ensured that medieval

[17] For an analysis of career patterns in medieval Oxford and Cambridge see Cobban, *The Medieval English Universities*, pp. 393-99; T.H. Aston, 'Oxford's Medieval Alumni', *Past and Present*, 74 (1977), pp. 3ff.; T.H. Aston, G.D. Duncan and T.A.R. Evans, 'The Medieval Alumni of the University of Cambridge', *Past and Present*, 86 (1980), pp. 9ff.; J. Dunbabin, 'Careers and Vocations', *The History of the University of Oxford*, i, *The Early Schools*, ed. J.I. Catto (Oxford, 1984), pp. 565ff.; G.F. Lytle, 'The Careers of Oxford Students in the Later Middle Ages', *Rebirth, Reform and Resilience: Universities in Transition 1300-1700*, ed. J.M. Kittelson and P.J. Transue, (Columbus, OH, 1984), pp. 213ff. See also A.B. Cobban, *Universities in the Middle Ages* (Liverpool Historical Essays, Liverpool, 1990), p. 30.

students were not subjected to the narrowing compartmentalism which is experienced by many of their modern counterparts.

Although the medieval universities functioned, for the most part, as service agencies for community life, they nevertheless harboured deep-seated aspirations to win and retain a large degree of autonomy. The essence of the university was the academic guild designed for the defence of its members and for the organisation of the teaching regime. As legal corporations with elected officers and statutes, the guild of masters, or of students, or of masters and students combined, made perennial claims to autonomous status. The reality, however, was often very different. The emergence and early development of the medieval universities was a phase which was frequently punctuated by conflict arising from struggles with external ecclesiastical or secular authorities. The need on the part of the academic guilds to combat external encroachments helped to formulate more sharply ideas of corporate university autonomy. these notions were fundamental to the image of the university as a separate estate within the medieval community and ranking alongside the principal forces by which Christian society was directed: the spiritual (*sacerdotium*) and the temporal (*imperium*).[18] The early period of university history was characterised, especially in northern Europe, by the attempted stifling of university autonomy by bishops within whose dioceses the universities lay.[19] All too often episcopal power was channelled in a direction which was antithetical to the growth of the corporate independence of the universities. This was so because many of the bishops in the thirteenth and fourteenth centuries had tended to classify the north European universities as virtual ecclesiastical 'colonies', almost as the physical possessions of the local bishops and their representatives. That is to say, the universities were not regarded as evolutionary organisms but as ecclesiastical appendages, as the most advanced educational form yet to emerge under the umbrella of the church. As such, they were to be integrated into the ecclesiastical structure and kept in a more of less permanent tutelage.

This static and dependent role mapped out for the universities was one wholly incompatible with the objectives of the academic guilds. In order to obtain an acceptable degree of autonomy several of Europe's early universities such as Paris, Montpellier, Angers, Orleans, Oxford and Cambridge had to mount protracted struggles to win their emancipation from episcopal and archiepiscopal jurisdiction.[20] In the later middle ages, however, Europe's episcopate had come to a general acceptance of the principle that a university was an autonomous entity standing outside the ecclesiastical hierarchy.

[18] Cobban, *The Medieval Universities*, p. 22; also H. Grundmann, 'Sacerdotium, Regnum, Studium', *Archiv für Kulturgeschichte*, 34 (1952), pp. 5ff.

[19] On this see Cobban, 'Episcopal Control in the Medieval Universities of Northern Europe', pp. 1ff, and *The Medieval Universities*, pp. 75-76.

[20] Cobban, 'Episcopal Control', pp. 1ff, and 'Medieval Student Power', pp. 49-55.

Indeed, episcopal aid made a signal contribution to new university foundations in the fifteenth century. For example, the Scottish universities of St. Andrews, Glasgow and Aberdeen could scarcely have survived without the enlightened treatment which they received at the hands of their episcopal sponsors. The Scottish episcopal founders gave their wealth in the realisation that adequate endowments and organisational maturity would inevitably bring independent status for their creations.[21] Moreover, episcopal dominion was not much of an issue in most of the universities founded in the late fourteenth or fifteenth centuries in provincial France, Germany, the Low Countries and Scandinavia.

The winning of university freedom from ecclesiastical domination was to prove to be something of a false dawn. In the case of the old-established universities of northern Europe varying degrees of state control were eventually substituted for episcopal power, and in those of southern Europe university autonomy was generally surrendered to the communes or other municipalities in return for the endowment of salaried lectureships and protective supervision.[22] Many of the universities which were founded in the later medieval period were subject to secular authority from their inception. Universities such as Prague (1347-48), Vienna (1365), Heidelberg (1385) and Leipzig (1409) owed their origins and sustained support to the initiative of kings and local rulers. Others such as Cologne (1388) and Rostock (1419) were the outcome of municipal enterprise.[23]

Whereas several of the early universities, including Bologna, Paris, Montpellier and Salamanca, had been cosmopolitan centres of learning which transcended national boundaries and local allegiances, universities of the later medieval period were founded by kings, princes and city authorities as symbols of national, provincial or civic prestige. Stripped of their supranational character, universities were viewed increasingly as integral parts of political territorial units, designed to serve the requirements of national institutions and to be of benefit to the local community. In this way Europe's universities came to be trapped within the orbit of secular controls. The concept of university autonomy had proved to be something of a chimera. The poverty of imaginative response which was often displayed towards the intellectual challenge of the medieval universities, from both ecclesiastical and state authorities, is but an early foretaste of the unending struggle of the universities to carve out for themselves a truly independent enclave within society. The universities were to discover that the winning of a measure of academic freedom could turn out

[21] Cobban, *The Medieval Universities*, p. 76.
[22] Cobban, 'Medieval Student Power', pp. 47, 48.
[23] Cobban, *The Medieval Universities*, p. 119.

to be no more than an ephemeral gain.[24] Nevertheless, the concept of academic freedom which was formulated in the initial phase of university history has been the touchstone of university aspirations from the middle ages to the twentieth century. It is the idealised model of the medieval university as an autonomous intellectual association which has been such an inspirational point of reference for universities over the centuries, and especially for those which have been the victims of state repression.

The decline in the autonomous position of the late medieval universities was accompanied by an ever-increasing involvement by members of the academic staff in political, business and ecclesiastical affairs. This was very marked between the fourteenth and sixteenth centuries. These combined developments seriously undermined the idea of a cohesive professional scholarity, at least *de facto* if not *de iure*. The closer entanglement of university teachers in community activities was expressed symbolically by the attempt to rank the academic order on a par with that of knighthood. From the fourteenth century this equivalence was manifested, for example, with reference to the legal profession. As a recognition of the value which society placed upon lawyers, both academic lawyers and those engaged in the administration of the law, titles such as *seigneur ès lois, chevalier ès lois* and *chevalier en lois* were conferred upon prominent academic lawyers and practising jurists alike.[25] In 1420 Alfonso V of Aragon granted all the privileges of knights to all the doctors and licentiates of civil law at the university of Valencia;[26] in the sixteenth century the doctoral college of Bologna was given the right to confer the status of knighthood upon teaching doctors, a privilege conceded by the Emperor Charles V;[27] and in the later medieval period the Salamancan doctors of law acquired some of the financial and ceremonial privileges of the nobility.[28] What was here projected was the idea of an aristocracy of merit, an intellectual nobility which deserved to enjoy the privileges appropriate to its contribution to society. This academic nobility did not usually acquire the

[24] This is well illustrated by the history of the university of Paris. The winning of university independence from the local ecclesiastical authorities in the early thirteenth century was followed by a protracted and bitter dispute with the mendicants at Paris which led to papal intervention and the curtailment of the powers of the university guild. Although the guild of masters had recovered many of its privileges by the early fourteenth century, it was increasingly subjected to the control of the French monarchy. In the fifteenth century Paris University had lost much of its cosmopolitan character and was now firmly cast in the role of a national institution which was devoid of significant levels of autonomy.

[25] R. Cazelles, *La société politique et la crise de la royauté sous Philippe de Valois* (Paris, 1958), pp. 292-93; J. Goff, *Les intellectuels au moyen âge* (Paris, 1957), p. 145; J. Verger, *Les universités au moyen âge* (Paris, 1973), pp. 185-86.

[26] V. de La Fuente, *Historia de las universidades, colegios y demás establecimientos de enseñanza en España* (4 vols., Madrid, 1884-89), i, pp. 234-35, 328-29; G. Ajo y Sáinz de Zúñiga, *Historia des las universidades hispánicas* 8 vols., (Madrid, 1957-72), i, pp. 546-47.

[27] Rashdall, *Universities of Europe*, i, pp. 228-29, n. 2.

[28] R.C. Kagan, 'Universities in Castile, 1500-1700', *Past and Present*, 49 (1970), p. 58.

privileges pertaining to an aristocracy of birth: the equivalence was not commonly with a blood aristocracy but with the military order in society.[29] There are, however, notable exceptions. In 1319 Henry II of Castile and Léon conceded to every master who had taught for forty years all the privileges enjoyed by dukes, marquises and counts, including the right to bear arms in public and private and the right to keep four laymen or slaves armed with swords.[30] In this instance, the academics were evidently to enjoy the privileges of an aristocracy of birth.

The idea that advanced education ennobles, that an intellectual elite formed a species of nobility in society, found an interesting embodiment in an educational treatise, written by an anonymous mature German student at Paris University and dated *c.* 1347-65.[31] In this work, the author argues that in a fully-fledged university the teaching masters are dubbed knights and are crowned lords of science, and that they are rightly revered by the lay and ecclesiastical authorities from whom they received well-merited rewards. The author then draws a distinction between the masters in authentic universities, who are true knights, and those who are employed in schools which do not have full university status and who have not yet acquired the dignity of a knight. In the statutes of Vienna University of the late fourteenth century a ceremonial bath is prescribed for a candidate on the eve of his taking a bachelor's or master's degree.[32] This makes an arresting parallel with the ritual of knighthood. In several of the Spanish universities newly created doctors were invested with a sword and other military insignia in clear imitation of knightly ceremonial.[33]

As teaching masters became heavily enmeshed in community affairs outside the university a price had to be paid; generally speaking, Europe's students judged that price to be unacceptably high. Absenteeism among lecturers who were engaged in extra-university business reached significant proportions in the later medieval period.[34] Normally an absentee lecturer was required to arrange for a substitute lecturer to discharge his office. the substitute system was organised on an extensive basis in the universities of southern Europe and

---

[29] See e.g. the opinion of Petrus Rebuffus, *Privilegia universitatum collegiorum, bibliopolarum, et omnium qui studiosis adiumento sunt* (Frankfurt, 1585), pp. 158-59.

[30] La Fuente, *Historia de las universidades*, i, pp. 314-15; Ajo y Sáinz de Zúñiga, i, p. 291, n. 500. See also A.B. Cobban, 'Elective Salaried Lectureships in the Universities of Southern Europe in the Pre-Reformation Era', *Bulletin of John Rylands University Library of Manchester*, 67 (1985), p. 681.

[31] The text and translation are supplied by L. Thorndike, *University Records and Life in the Middle Ages*, Records of Civilisation, xxxviii (New York, 1944: repr. Octagon Books, New York, 1971), pp. 409ff. (text), 201ff. (translation).

[32] R. Kink, *Geschichte der kaiserlichen Universität zu Wien*, 2 vols., (Vienna, 1854), ii, p. 55.

[33] Rashdall, *Universities of Europe*, i, pp. 228-29, n. 2; Verger, *Les universités au moyen âge*, p. 180.

[34] On absenteeism among academic staff in medieval universities see Cobban, 'Elective Salaried Lectureships', pp. 670-75.

the scale of this problem has been little appreciated. This matter of substitutes was among the most common of the criticisms voiced by students in the medieval universities. The undesirability of substitutes had been anticipated in the *Siete Partidas*, the legislative code of Alfonso X of Castile, which was compiled between 1256 and 1263 and which incorporated one of the earliest attempts to legislate on the nature of a university. It is here enacted that substitutes are to be tolerated only in the case of the illness of lecturers. They were to be paid by the lecturers themselves or, in the event of death, by their heirs.[35] It is clear, however, that Alfonso's legislation failed to stem the tide of substitutes employed in the universities. Students frequently complained that the excessive use of substitutes could lead to discontinuity in the course and the alienation of the student audience. Students were prone to believe that they were being fobbed off with second best and cast aspersions upon the professional competence of the substitutes, many of whom were young and inexperienced.[36] Indeed it sometimes happened that lecturers absented themselves without providing substitutes of any kind.[37] Given the abuses to which the substitutes system was liable, some universities attempted to limit by statute the conditions under which substitutes might be engaged.[38] Substitute lecturers were employed according to need, the duration of service ranging from brief spells over a session to longer periods of one or more years. For example, in 1314 James II of Aragon hired a law lecturer from Lérida University for diplomatic business and arranged for a substitute to perform his duties for at least fifteen days;[39] and at the Portuguese university of Lisbon and Coimbra in the late fifteenth century law lecturers were permitted to employ substitutes for lectures for the space of two months each year to given them time to prepare their repetitions or review exercises.[40]

Despite the multifarious criticisms of the substitute system it had the advantage that it could provide a pathway to the rank of tenured lecturer for at least some of those graduates who aspired to an academic career. In general, however, the extent of the substitute system is a pointer to the harm which can

[35] *Las Siete Partidas del rey don Alfonso el Sabio*, 3 vols., ed. for the Royal Academy of History (Madrid, 1807), ii, title xxxi (pp. 339-46), law 4.

[36] In 1457 the Venetian Senate (Padua University was then subject to Venice) alleged that declining student numbers at Padua were caused mainly by the neglect of the teaching doctors and that the quality of the substitute lecturers did not meet with student approbation: P. Kibre, *Scholarly Privileges in the Middle Ages* (Medieval Academy of America, London, 1961), pp. 76-77.

[37] For example, in 1486 the parlement at Toulouse deprived two law lecturers because they had not lectured for two or three years and had not provided substitutes: J. Puget, 'L'université de Toulouse au xive et au xve siècles', *Annales du Midi*, 42 (1930), p. 375.

[38] See the detailed discussion of the statutes of Valladolid University regarding substitutes by Cobban, 'Elective Salaried Lectureships'. pp. 671-72.

[39] Ajo y Sáinz de Zúñiga, *Historia de las universidades hispánicas*, i, pp. 473-74.

[40] Ibid., i, pp. 590-1; T. Braga, *Historia da Universidade de Coimbra*, 4 vols. (Lisbon, 1892-1902), i, pp. 166-67.

be caused to the workings of universities when large numbers of teaching staff
are deflected from their primary purpose by being excessively involved in
community affairs. Certainly universities have an obligation to respond to such
needs. But when that response is disproportionate and causes disruption to the
teaching regime and a diminution in the quality of instruction it is hard to avoid
the conclusion that teaching staff, in those circumstances, have prostituted
themselves for lucrative reward and career advancement. The driving force of
educational utility led to this situation in the later medieval period: universities
and governments towards the close of the twentieth century would do well to
heed this lesson from the past.

Another expression of the symbiotic relationship which existed between the
medieval universities and their surrounding communities was the fact that,
even before the impact of movements such as humanism, the universities were
prepared to make curricular adaptations to meet fresh challenges thrown up by
society. This point may be illustrated with reference to the Italian universities
and the university of Oxford. The connecting link here is the science of written
rhetoric.

In the thirteenth-century Italy the classical art of rhetoric had re-emerged as
an important attribute of civic, papal and imperial affairs. There was a demand
for spoken rhetoric in the world of the Italian communes with their aggressive
republicanism and entanglements in papal and imperial politics. Specially
designed handbooks, containing model speeches for the benefit of officials of
the communes and for university lecturers, bear witness to the rhetorical
revival which engulfed Italian life in the early phase of university development.
The Italian universities may well have made teaching provision for training in
oratory, but it was in the field of written rhetoric or *dictamen* that the
universities evinced particular interest.

*Dictamen* (*ars dictaminis*, *ars dictandi*), the science of letter-writing and of
other types of literary composition, dates as an art from at least the treatises of
Alberic of Monte Cassino in the second half of the eleventh century.[41] It was
not, however, until *dictamen* became a indispensable prerequisite for clerks in
papal, imperial, royal and episcopal service that it was elevated to a position of
primacy in the arts faculties of the Italian universities.[42] Despite the promotion of the craft of *dictamen* by *dictatores* of the calibre of Buoncompagno and
Guido Faba, the *ars dictandi* was never entirely separated from the arts
courses. But the specialised offshoot of *dictamen*, the *ars notaria* (*ars notarie*),
which concerned the professional work of the notary, seems to have attained
what was tantamount to separate faculty status, first at Bologna by 1250 and at

---

[41] Haskins, *Studies in Medieval Culture*, pp. 171-73.
[42] For the teaching of the *ars dictandi* and the *ars notaria* in Italy and France see L.J. Paetow,
*The Arts Course at Medieval Universities* Illinois University Studies, iii, no. 7 (Urbana-Cham-
paign, 1910), pp. 67ff.

other Italian universities later in the thirteenth century.[43] This development is an eloquent instance of curricular adaptation in order to accommodate a popular professional demand. Notarial courses in the Italian universities were a combination of both theoretical and practical elements and many of the teachers of the *ars notaria* were notaries in the town and members of the notarial guild.[44] The end-product of these notarial courses was not a degree but a licence to practice as a notary. Hybrid courses of this character were clearly designed to cement the university-community nexus and to project the Italian universities as vocationally relevant institutions.

The *ars notaria* was not taught in England in any official sense and neither the *ars dictandi* not the *ars notaria* developed separate faculty status at Oxford or Cambridge. But subjects which were akin to these disciplines were taught at Oxford, albeit in an adulterated and semi-official form.[45] Since English society was largely geared to the common law, there were far fewer outlets for notaries than on the Continent. Nevertheless, from an early date, Oxford University made instruction available in elements of *dictamen* and the *ars notaria*. Such business courses were tailored to students who did not intend to follow an official degree course but who attended university to undertake a practical training aimed at specific lines of employment. In modern parlance, it could be said that students of this kind were engaged in courses which came under the umbrella of 'university extension'. From the beginning of the reign of Henry III until the mid fifteenth century there was present at Oxford a colony of teachers who specialised in the 'useful subjects': those which had a direct application to diverse areas of business administration. The teachers of these courses were not necessarily university graduates but they set up their schools in the town of Oxford and they were subject to the jurisdiction of the university. The courses which were taught covered such matters as the drafting of charters, wills and letters, conveyancing, the keeping of accounts, court procedure and heraldry.[46] The aim of this type of study at Oxford was not to produce a student who was fully qualified for a practical area of employment. Rather it was to provide a solid foundation for the many facets of a business or administrative career. This training might take no more than six months, although it was of an intensive nature.

It is evident, then, that for about two hundred and fifty years Oxford

[43] Ibid.
[44] I. Hajnal, *L'enseignement de l'écriture aux universités médiévales*, end ed., L. Mezey, (Budapest, 1959), p. 155.
[45] For a detailed discussion of this theme see Cobban, *The Medieval English Universities*, pp. 334-48.
[46] See H.G. Richardson, 'Business Training in Medieval Oxford'. *A.H.R.*, 46 (1940-41), pp. 259ff.; 'An Oxford Teacher of the Fifteenth Century', *Bulletin of the John Rylands University Library of Manchester*, 23 (1939), pp. 436ff. On similarities between Italian notarial manuals and the subject matter taught at Oxford see J.J. Murphy, 'Rhetoric in Fourteenth-Century Oxford', *Medium Aevum*, 34 (1965), pp. 15-17.

University offered what were in effect university extension courses. These formed a bridge between the official academic curriculum and the business affairs of the wider world. There is here a pale and unsystematic reflection of the more organised and sophisticated teaching of business studies in the Italian universities. It is unlikely that Oxford stood alone among the universities of northern Europe with regard to activities of this kind. Much, however, remains to be discovered about this elusive area of medieval university life.

Mention has been made of the status of knighthood given to members of university staffs in recognition of their community value. In addition, many common privileges were accorded to the academic population as an indicator of the contribution which universities could make to the public good. In general, these privileges were formulated by legal commentators in France and Italy. They were based upon texts in Roman and canon law and on Frederick I's Authentic *Habita* of 1158 which, at the hands of juristic interpretation, came to acquire an ecumenical significance as the origin and fount of academic freedoms in the middle ages.[47] A number of privileges related to the accommodation of scholars. For example, the French civilian, Guilielmus de Cuneo, argued that scholars ought to be compulsorily billeted on townspeople if there were a shortage of lodgings. The justification here was that greater public utility resided in the profession of scholar than in the private need of a landlord.[48] It was further asserted by the commentator Petrus Rebuffus that landlords might not seize a scholar's books in place of rent because of the high utilitarian worth of books: indeed he reached the conclusion that all writers of books were, *ipso facto*, automatically rendered privileged persons in society.[49] Moreover, the jurists held the opinion that study ought to be conducted in a suitable environment and that nuisances such as noise or bad odours ought to be absent from the university schools and from the vicinity of student's lodgings. At least some jurists argued that scholars even had the right to expel an offending artisan from their immediate environment on the grounds that the public good of scholarship would thereby be advanced.[50] Following a provision in the Authentic *Habita*, it was also judged to be in the public interest that a scholar be specially protected when journeying to and from his university.[51] Broad privileges of this nature were of a theoretical character and their practical application in the medieval universities varied according to particular circumstances. Collectively, however, they furnish an insight into the public perception of the utilitarian value of the universities as

[47] See W. Ullmann, 'The Medieval Interpretation of Frederick I's Authentic "Habita"', in *L'Europa e il diritto romano: studi in memoria di Paolo Koschaker* (Milan, 1954), pp. 101ff.; Cobban, *The Medieval Universities*, pp. 51-54.

[48] Ullman, 'The Medieval Interpretation', p. 117; Kibre, *Scholarly Privileges in the Middle Ages*, p. 13.

[49] Ibid., pp. 14-15.

[50] Ibid., pp. 15-16.

[51] Cobban, *The Medieval Universities*, pp. 52f.

expressed through juristic sources. The generality of legal opinion reckoned that scholars formed an aristocracy of labour in society, whose scholarship and wider activities merited privileged protection because they made such a notable contribution to the common good.

As against the idea of the medieval universities as service agencies catering for diverse community needs, there were, as in every age, a number of scholars who sought to endow education with a higher purpose and who strove to provide a broader alternative to the concept of educational utility.[52] By their treatises they endeavoured to publicise the notion of education as a life-long process and as a means of developing the full potential of the individual. Writers such as John of Salisbury, Hugh of St. Victor, Vincent of Beauvais, and many of the later humanist scholars, adopted the common stance of rejecting much of the materialism in which the universities were so clearly implicated. It is evident that their educational programmes went far beyond what could be achieved by any but the most exceptional of disciples. The scale of such schemes often demanded a universality of knowledge and powers of comprehension which transcended the realistic objectives of any educational system. But the perpetuation of educational notions which ran counter to the idea of education as a marketable product and feeder of immediate community wants at least helped to keep the debate about education alive on however limited a plane. It was important to voice, and to go on voicing, the question as to whether or not a university can successfully or even meaningfully function on a purely technical or professional diet. There is little doubt that in the later middle ages the principle of educational utility predominated and the universities were viewed as essentially service agencies. It is refreshing, however, to discover that the role generally ascribed to the medieval universities was not everywhere accepted. It was periodically subjected to searching intellectual challenge by some of the ablest scholars in medieval society.

[52] E.g., ibid., pp. 225-29.

# 18

# 'God is no Respecter of Persons': Sacred Texts and Social Realities

## John Van Engen

In January 1147 Bernard of Clairvaux charged the clergy at Cologne with leading a 'disordered' (*informem*) life – a charge he had raised at Paris eight years earlier in a sermon *Ad clericos de conversione*. While he never issued in written form what he argued in person at Cologne, Geoffrey of Auxerre, monk at Clairvaux (1140-53) and secretary to Bernard, subsequently composed a 'Dialogue between Peter and Jesus' (*Colloquium Symonis et Jesu*) said to be based upon *reportatio* of this exchange.[1] The aim of the original confrontation, and of the written treatise, was to persuade 'disordered' secular clerics to join the 'ordered' life of a Cistercian cloister; the argument hinged entirely upon an interpretation of Matthew 19:27-29. There the apostle Peter had asked Jesus a question of direct concern to medieval religious: 'Behold, we have forsaken all and followed; what shall we have therefore?' Jesus promised that when he came into his kingdom the apostles would 'sit upon twelve thrones, judging the twelve tribes of Israel', further that those who truly forsook all for his name's sake would 'receive a hundredfold and inherit everlasting life'.

Invoking this text, Bernard appealed to his hearers and Geoffrey to his readers with an argument of relative advantage, highlighting the promise of greater rewards still to come, including the power to judge. 'What secular honour can be conceived that would not seem vile by comparison? They are to preside with Christ as judges, not over one city or people or even over one region, but over everything. Those who disdain for a time the mere mist of

---

[1] See Jean Leclercq, 'Saint Bernard et ses secrétaires', *Revue Bénédictine*, 61 (1951. pp. 221-24; and Henri Rochais, ed. *Geoffroy d'Auxerre, Entretien de Simon-Pierre avec Jésus* (Sources chrétiennes, 364, Paris 1990), pp. 9-18, who lists 86 manuscripts.

present glory will [eventually] judge people and even angels'.[2] The apostles
and all those who live an apostolic life of renunciation may expect judicial
power in the end. Negligent human beings, pitiable creatures, are slumbering
through such a promise,[3] ignoring him who offers a greater and more certain
reward (*certior copiosiorque remuneratio est*). But the 'human conscience'
counters that the waiting is too long. To abandon one's earthly lot without as
yet obtaining any celestial reward is to incur torment beyond what can be
sustained, a sorrow beyond consoling.[4] Thus the argument proceeded, back
and forth, advancing towards a final appeal to the reward of eternal life. Both
monks assumed throughout its central premise: in return for present renuncia-
tions not only a 'hundred-fold reward' but also a future power to sit alongside
Christ as judge. Hearers were warned therefore not to 'preside' in earthly
power but 'to sit down with Christ'.[5]

Bernard and Geoffrey assumed the central point because they had read it,
and in the very books that informed them of Christian tradition. Any culture
that has at its centre an authoritative written text – a divine word, a legal norm,
a political constitution – will acquire a body of interpretation built up around
that text. In the course of the eleventh and twelfth centuries, a set of
'standardised interpretive notes' (the Ordinary Gloss) became attached to the
text of Holy Scripture. That gloss rested upon much older tradition, and down
to the end of the middle ages all clergymen took that interpretive construct for
granted in their reading of the Bible.

All three verses in Matthew were central for the understanding of religious
life during the middle ages, but one phrase will occupy this essay: 'Sedebitis et
vos super duodecim sedes, iudicantes duodecim tribus Israel' (v 28). The Gloss
explained that the twelve seats in this case referred to all who would judge, the
twelve tribes to all who would be judged. More concretely, it explained,
drawing upon surrounding verses, those who leave everything and follow the
Lord will be the judges, those who make legitimate use of this world's goods

[2] 'Quis vero saecularis honor excogitari potest, qui non prorsus in tantae sublimitatis comparatione vilescat? Non unius siquidem civitatis aut populi regionis unius sed universitatis iudices
habent praesidere cum Christo. Non solum homines sed et ipsos angelos iudicabunt [see I Cor. 6:3,
which also played a role in developing this teaching], qui parentem ad modicum vaporem
praesentis gloriae dedignantes et exsufflantes, improperium Christi universis praeferunt titulis
dignitatum.' *Entretien*, 41 (n.1 above) p. 224.
[3] 'Haec enim est perfectorum gloria singularis, inter ipsos etiam eminere fideles et ceteris
quoque salvandis praeeminere auctoritate iudiciariae potestatis. . . . Quid istud miseriae est, quod
ad verbum tantae promissionis negligentia humana dormitat!' *Entretien*, 42 (n. 1 above), p. 230.
[4] 'Magna quidem divina promissio, sed longa nimis dilatio et molesta exspectatio est. Terre-
nam deserere sortem et necdum obtinere caelestem, afflictio est intolerabilis et inconsolabilis
dolor.' *Entretien*, 44 (n. 1 above), p. 234.
[5] A typical 'Bernardian' play on words: 'Insipiens tu qui praesidere eligis quam consedere,
quaerens in itinere diverticula'. *Entretien*, 31 (n. 1 above), p. 188.

the judged, thus two 'orders' among the good.[6] The origin of the Gloss in this exact form has yet to be determined, though its crucial distinction comes closest to the wording in Bede's commentary.[7] The essential idea went back at least to Augustine,[8] and then to Gregory, who further developed distinctions between the judges and the judged by way of Matt. 19:28 and 25:34-36.[9] The wording that most nearly anticipated that found in the Gloss appeared first, notably, in a sermon by Bede celebrating Benedict Biscop, the founder of his monastery; here too an exposition of the religious life and its rewards turned entirely upon an interpretation of Matt. 19:27-29.[10] This was the passage Hrabanus Maurus took over for his commentary,[11] which may have been the more immediate source for the Gloss.

There was, however, an alternative tradition of interpretation, one closer to

[6] '*Super sedes*: Per duodecim sedes universitas iudicantium, per duodecim tribus universitas iudicandorum intelligitur. Qui reliquerunt omnia secuti sunt Dominum, hi iudices erunt; qui licita habentes recte usi sunt, iudicabuntur, quibus dicitur: *Venite benedicite patris mei, Esurivi enim et dedisti mihi manducare* [Matt. 25:34, 35]. Duo enim sunt ordines bonorum.' All quotations [hereafter simply *Gloss*] are taken from the 'Rusch Bible' printed at Strassburg before 1480: *Biblia latina cum glossa ordinaria* (Strassburg: Adolph Rusch for Anton Koberger) = Goff B-607. Compare *PL* 113:149.

[7] 'Quia enim duodenario saepe numero solet universitas designari, per XII sedes apostolorum iudicantium omnium numerositas et per XII tribus Israel universitas eorum qui iudicandi sunt ostenditur.' Bede *In Matheum*: *PL* 92:87. Compare n. 10 below for a fuller version found in a homily.

[8] 'Qui ergo iudicabunt cum Christo, principles ecclesiae sunt, perfecti sunt. Talibus dixit: *Si uis esse perfectus, uade, uende omnia tua, et da pauperibus*. Quid est, *Vis esse perfectus?* Vis mecum iudicare et non iudicari. Ille contristatus abscessit; sed multi hoc fecerunt, et multi hoc faciunt; ergo isti cum illo iudicabunt. Sed multi promittunt sibi quia iudicabunt cum Christo quia dimittunt omnia sua et sequuntur Christum. Sed habent praesumptionem de se. . . .' *Enarrationes in Ps.*, 90:9 *CCSL* 39. p. 1262 (commenting upon Ps. 90:7).

[9] 'Ex electorum uero parte alii iudicantur et regnant, qui uitae maculas lactimis tergunt, qui mala praecedentia factis sequentibus redimentes, quicquid illicitum aliquando fecerunt ab oculis iusicis eleemosynarum superductione cooperiunt. Quibus iudex ueniens in dexteram consistentibus dicit: *Esuriui.* . . . Alii autem non iudicantur et regnant qui etiam praecepta legis perfectionis uirtute transcendunt, quia nequaquam hoc solum quod cunctis diuina lex praecipit implere contenti sunt, sed praestantiori desiderio plus exhibere appetunt quam praeceptis generalibus audire potuerunt. Quibus dominica uoce dicitur: *Vos qui reliquisitis . . .* [Matt. 19:28]. His itaque in extremo iudicio iudicantur et regnant, quia cum auctore suo etiam iudices ueniunt.' *Moralia* 26.27.51, *CCSL* 143B, pp. 1305-06. This passage was taken over by Taius, *Sententiae*, 2.21, *PL* 80:806-08.

[10] 'Sciendum namque est omnes qui ad exemplum apostolorum sua reliquerunt omnia et secuti sunt Christum iudices cum eo uenturos, sicut etiam omne mortalium genus esse iudicandum. Quia enim duodenario saepe numero solet in scripturis uniuersitas designari, per duodecim sedes apostolorum omnium numerositas iudicantium et per duodecim tribus Israhel universitas eorum qui iudicandi sunt ostenditur. Unde notandum quod duo sunt ordines electorum in iudicio futuri, unus iudicantium cum Domino (de quibus hoc loco commemorat) qui reliquerunt omnia et secuti sunt illum, alius iudicatorum a Domino qui non quidem omnia sua pariter reliquerunt sed de his tamen quae habebant cotidianas dare elemosinas pauperibus Christi curabant. Unde audituri sunt iudicio: *Venite.* . . .' Bede, *Homelia*, 1.13, *CCSL* 122, pp. 89-90.

[11] *PL* 107: 1023-24.

several patristic authors and preserved by Jerome. It construed the difference
between the judges and the judged more broadly as that between believers and
unbelievers (especially Jews), and it emphasised as the main mark of disciple-
ship the imitation of Christ rather than renunciation of goods.[12] Those
Carolingian authors who attempted original interpretations of Matthew
tended to follow this line. Paschasius Radbertus summarised a host of earlier
interpreters (visible in the new edition),[13] and Christian of Stavelot elaborated upon Jerome. But Christian's comments presupposed the other tradition
of teaching – judges as those elevated by keeping precepts of a higher order –
and he directly opposed it, though he was himself a monk.[14] His enthroned
judges represented all the elect, as in Jerome they were all the believers
(*credentes*).[15] But this more learned tradition, more *recherché*, if you like, dug
out of late antique works by Carolingian intellectuals, was not to prevail. It was
the tradition which highlighted the extraordinary acts and rewards of monks,
the tradition of Augustine, Gregory, Bede and Hrabanus, that became the
standard reading of this text.

Early twelfth-century authors, all of them likewise monks, simply assumed
it, in part no doubt because they read it in the margins of their Bibles.
Honorius, in a work which became widely read in Latin and then in various
vernacular translations, reduced it to a neat formula: apostles and martyrs [in
earlier days], monks and virgins [now] will do the judging, while those who are
properly married and carry out works of mercy and redeem their sins with alms
will be among those (favourably) judged.[16] Rupert of Deutz, around the year
1115-16, explained that those committed to the active life (that is, the married
and propertied) incur sins, redeem them with alms, and stand in the end
among the judged, while those who give up worldly things for the contempla-

[12] Jerome, *In Matheum*, 3, *CCSL* 77, pp. 172-73.

[13] Paschasius Radbertus, *In Matheum*, *CCCM* 56B, pp. 967-72.

[14] 'Nam et monachi, quamvis aliquid plus videantur facere quam in evangelio scriptum est,
tamen eamdem normam et ipsi tenere debent. Et si aliquid eis plus praeceptum est, ad nihil aliud
praeceptum est nisi ut Domini regula possit custodiri. . . . Non enim beatus Benedictus alterius
imitator fuit, nec plusquam Dominus facere voluit, quia sufficit discipulo ut sit sicut magister euis,
et erit tunc perfectus. . . . Omnes tamen habent Christum in exemplum et apostolos eius quos
imitari debent. Laici autem habent Nicodemum, Gamaliel, Joseph; et si potentiores sunt, possunt
in scripturis divinis invenire quem imitentur et in potentia seculari et in mansuetudine et humilitate
Christi.' Christian, *Expositio in Matheum* 43, *PL* 106:1419-20.

[15] '*Iudicantes duodecim tribus Israel*: Sicut per duodecim apostolos omnis electorum numerus
exprimitur, ita per duodecim tribus omnes gentes et Iudaei intelliguntur propter duodenarium
numerum, qui perfectus et apud paganon et consecratus in divinis scripturis invenitur.' *PL*
106:1421.

[16] 'Qui sunt qui iudicant? Apostoli, martyres, monachi, uirgines. . . . Qui sunt qui iudicantur:
Qui opera misericordiae in legitimo coniugio exercuerunt uel qui peccata sua poenitentia et
eleemosynis redimerunt.' Yves Lefèvres, *L'Elucidarium et les elucidaires* (Paris, 1954), p. 459.

tive life take no part in the active life and sit at the end as judges.[17] It was tradition inscribed in commentaries and glossed Bibles, central to the monks' understanding of their place in the divine plan, that Bernard invoked in his polemical appeal.

Once inscribed, the teaching could never be ignored or gone entirely around – one of the points of this essay. But what seemed so clear to these monks met with renewed questioning from schoolmen, most of whom belonged to the circles of those secular clergy Bernard was attempting to convert. An early scholastic commentary on Matthew, once attributed to Anselm of Laon, cited the basic phrases from the Gloss but focused its attention on other matters.[18] Cardinal Robert Pullen's entire discussion of the judgement was little other than an attempt to make sense of the Gloss, quoted and paraphrased throughout (not manifest in the Migne edition). The real point, he suggested, was *knowledge* of salvation, virtually certain for those who had given up everything, still in doubt for those who used the things of this world – and judgement here referred to this knowledge of their final destiny.[19] Even as schoolmen eased away from the monks' blunt equation of renunciation in this life and judgeship in the hereafter, Peter Lombard, compiling his *Four Books of Sentences* in large part from the Ordinary Gloss on the Bible (as the new edition makes clear), included one element of the idea drawn from Matt. 19:28, thereby assuring that all theologians to the end of the middle ages would perforce be confronted with it. Peter asked whether in the Judgement 'saints' would judge with Christ and how that could happen. Predictably he cited Matt. 19:28, explicated not by the standard gloss, however, but by another text

---

[17] ' . . . aciuae uitae inseruiunt et peccata quidem contraxerunt, sed eadem elemosynis redimere studuerunt. Nam qui contemplatiuae uitae dediti sunt, eorum non est iudicari sed iudicare. Immo sicut eorum non est quidquam in hoc saeculo possidere sed omnia pro Christo reliquisse, sic eorum non est esurientem pascere, sitienti potum dare, hospitem colligere, nudum operire, infirmum et in carcere positum uisitare. . . . Notandum igitur ubi dicitur, *Venite benedicti Patris mei, possidete regnum*, non huiusmodi rationem subiungi, propter me enim omnia reliquistis et me secuti estis, sed nec istas – non enim occidistis, non meochati estis, non furtum aut rapinam fecistis, siue non concupistis – sed *esuriui enim et dedistis mihi manducare* etc., ut intelligamus illos esse iudicandos et in maximo timore futuros qui peccauerunt negotiis saecularibus implicati, sed peccata sua, ut iam dictum est, elemosynis redimerunt, et in iudicio esse saluandos; illos autem, quia omnia reliquerent et Dominum secuti sunt, iudicaturos.' Rupert, *De sancta Trinitate*, 42.14, *CCCM* 24.2115-16.

[18] *Enarrationes in Matheum*, *PL* 162:1416.

[19] 'In sanctis quoque quorundam iam salus scitur, quorundam autem usque ad finem nescitur. Fidei enim christianae professores, illorum salutem iam novimus qui omnia pro Christo reliquerunt, unde Dominus illis qui eum secuti omnia reliquerunt ait [Matt. 19:28] . . . qui omnia relinquit suo modo iam iudicatus est, uidelicet ad salutem; quia sua reservat, nondum iudicatus est; quoniam quod de illo, ut in hac uita potest propter eminentem uitam cognoscitur, hoc de altero propter saeculi multiplicationes ignoratur. Atque ideo dicitur quod qui relinquunt omnia et sequuntur Dominum, ii cum Domino iudices erunt, qui uero licita habentes recte utuntur iudicabuntur.' Robert Pullen, *Sententiae* 8.30, *PL* 186:1005, 1006.

attributed (misleadingly) to Augustine – perhaps the Gloss as he knew it.[20] He affirmed further that the saints 'would judge with power and authority', though (again that distancing) he considered the mode and reality of this beyond knowing until actually seen.[21]

It would lead far afield to follow this notion through all the subsequent commentaries of the schoolmen, who generally proved more circumspect, often attempting to recover the broader tradition that went back to Jerome and sometimes – John Duns Scotus, for instance – ignoring the passage altogether. But they were bound to the idea, both by the Gloss in their Bibles and the *distinctio* in Lombard's *Sentences*. Thomas Aquinas provides an outstanding example. He took up the question whether 'other men will judge with Christ.' His discussion first proposed numerous objections to such a notion, countered by a bare citation of Matt. 19:28, and concluded with a cursory determination of 'it seems so.'[22] Next he raised strong objections – like those of Jerome and Christian – to the direct link between voluntary poverty and the power to judge, countered by two texts, above all Matt. 19:28 and its gloss (cited specifically), and then determined with an 'as above' (*et sic idem quod prius*). In short, Thomas felt bound to the idea, chiefly by way of the Gloss on Matt. 19:28, though he plainly had no taste for it and poured all his energies into articulating objections – including one which speculated that any presumed co-power to judge would befit masters better than monks.[23] His *summa* breaks off just at the point where this issue would have arisen, but it seems clear that he had already ascribed all power to judge to Christ himself, leaving no room for co-judges.[24]

In the early Franciscan tradition, and in much of the school tradition, this matter received fuller theological treatment; and while presuming the Gloss it also articulated further the implicit social or legal metaphor. Thus Alexander of Hales pointed out, as nearly all later schoolmen would, that the power of

[20] 'Per duodecim igitur sedes perfectio tribunalis, idest universitas iudicantium intelligitur, scilicet omnes perfecti qui relictis omnibus secuti sunt Christum; per duodecim tribus, universitas iudicandorum.' Peter Lombard, *Sententiae* 4.47.2, 3rd ed. Spicilegium Bonaventurianum (Grotta-ferrata, 1971) pp. 537-38. This text is not from Augustine in this form. He treated the verse from Matthew on several occasions: his sermon on Psalm 90 (n. 8 above); a concluding chapter in his *De civitate Dei* 20.5, *CCSL* 48, pp. 704-5, taken over in Julian of Toledo's *Prognosticon* 3.13, *CCSL* 115, p. 90; and his sermon on Psalm 49, *CCSL* 38, pp. 582, 584.

[21] 'Iudicabunt uero sancti non modo comparatione sed etiam auctoritate et potestate. . . . Si uero quaeritur quae erit eorum potestas uel auctoritas in iudicando, puto non ante posse sciri quam uideatur, nisi divina reuelatione quis didicerit.' *Sententiae* 4.47.2, p. 538. This phraseology suggests that he might have been working at this issue through commentaries on I Cor. 6:3 (see his own in *PL* 191:1576.

[22] 'Ergo uidetur quod etiam alii iudicabunt cum Christo.' *In Sent.* 4.47.2, (Parma, 1859), 7, p. 1154.

[23] 'Ergo ex hoc quod aliquis proponit legem uel uerbum exhortationis ad instructionem morum, habet quod iudicet contemnentes. Sed hoc est doctorum. Ergo doctoribus magis competit quam pauperibus'. Ibid.

[24] See *Summa theologiae*, iii, q. 59.

judging resided in the Triune God alone and was conferred by extension upon the humanity of Christ. This theological point he elucidated in terms of a legal metaphor drawn from canon law: the Trinity possessed supreme 'authority', Christ the 'power of execution'.[25] As for the notion of 'co-judges', he described the apostles as judges mainly by association, 'companions' in power who had imitated Christ and were to act as 'witnesses' and 'assessors'.[26] The theological distinctions, bound by the text and its gloss, were rendered more precise in part by refining the legal metaphor, which presupposed a full knowledge of how courts, whether ecclesiastical or civil, worked in their day. So Bonaventure cited the Gloss on Matt. 19:28 as his authority, and then explained that the 'apostolic men' will be judges in the sense of those who 'assist and advise' the judge actually pronouncing the sentence, themselves bearing by association the name and dignity of a judge, an honour they acquired by keeping the supererogatory counsels of perfection.[27] What began as the exposition of a biblical image (*super sedes*) addressed to the apostles was perpetuated and elucidated by an image of contemporary courts (*honorabilem consessionem*) applied to apostolic men.

This was not peculiar to Franciscan authors. Indeed other Dominicans were less reluctant than Thomas to take up this notion. A good example, which may be stand for many others, if offered by Peter of Tarantaise (d. 1276 as Innocent V). He skillfully accounted for all the theological possibilities implicit in the text and its gloss by invoking the accepted modes of legal teaching and practice: the 'ordinary power' to judge of Christ as God; the 'delegated power' of Christ as man; the 'accessory dignity' of those 'assisting' the judge (a pithy summary of Bonaventure); an 'approving' judgement by all the elect (the older patristic position); and the 'comparative' judgement of the less bad over the worse (another position found in schoolmen and related to interpretations of Luke 11). The 'perfect' will sit with the judge as those who have a better grasp

---

[25] ' . . . Trinitas iudicat auctoritate, Christus homo iudicat exterius potestate sua exequendo.' Alexander of Hales, *Summa theologica* 3.8.2, (Quaracchi, 1948), 4, p. 309. For this distinction in canon law, which derives from Rufinus, see Robert L. Benson, *The Bishop-Elect* (Princeton, 1968).

[26] 'Ipsi apostoli iudicabunt per associationem, quia scilicet socii sunt Christi in hoc quod ipsum imitati sunt, ut sicut associati erant Christo in imitatione passionis et tribulatione, ita erunt associati in potestate. . . . ' 'Item, ipsi dicuntur iudices quia testes vel assessores, quia per imitationem Christi testificabuntur ipsum iudicem,' Ibid.

[27] ' . . . assistit ferenti [sententiam], secundum quod aliqui iudices assistunt et quodam modo consulunt iudici principali. . . . Qui autem assistunt iudicanti etiam nomen et dignitatem iudicantis sortiuntur; et tales sunt viri perfecti qui ultra opera necessitatis praeceptorum supererogaverunt perfectionem consiliorum; tales autem sunt apostoli principaliter tanquam capita et eorum perfecti imitatores. Assistentia autem illa non erit ad consulendum, quia Dominus consilio non indiget; sed erit tanquam ad quendam honorem et appropinquationem ad iudicem, quam possumus appellare iuxta verbum Domini honorabilem consessionem.' Bonaventure, *In Sent.* 4.47.2, (Quarrachi, 1889) 4, p. 971.

of the law and customs of the kingdom of God.[28] Much the same explanation
may be found in the slightly later Franciscan theologian, Richard of Middleton.[29] These theologians attempted to render the idea they inherited in the
text and its gloss more intelligible by transposing the image of the Judgement
into that of a sophisticated legal arrangement (known especially from canon
law): ordinary judicial power (God); delegated judicial power (Christ the
man); assessors and witnesses (the perfect); approbation (all the elect); juries
of good men.

To make this brief story complete: What the masters worked out in their
*summae* and *questiones* by way of dealing with this text and its gloss, Nicholas
of Lyra, in his *Postils* completed by 1333, entered summarily into his glossed
Bible, a standard resource in the later middle ages and beyond:

> Advertendum quod iudicare accipitur tripliciter. Uno modo principaliter sicut iudex
> qui prefert sententiam, et hoc modo solus Christus iudicabit; alio modo pro sedere in
> loco eminenti iuxta iudicem sicut assessores iudicis, et hoc modo apostoli et alii
> perfecti cum Christo iudicabunt; tertio modo large accipitur, scilicet per sententiam
> iudicis approbatur, et hoc modo omnes iudicabunt quia sententiam iudicis approba-
> bunt. Considerandum etiam quod licet iudiciaria potestas que competit alicui per
> modum assessoris conueniat apostolis et perfectis ratione sue perfectionis supra
> alios eminentis, tamen magis attribuitur uoluntarie paupertati quam aliis uirtutibus,
> et hoc per quandam correspondentiam, sicut supra dictum est, quia sicut exaltatio
> correspondet humilitati, sic iudiciaria potestas paupertati, quia pauperes in hoc
> mundo conculcantur et peruerse iudicantur, quia etiam eorum bona in malum
> interpretantur, ideo e contrario eminentia sedis iudiciarie competet eis in
> regeneratione.[30]

Nicholas managed to include every element: the theological refinements about
Christ alone as judge; the contemporary legal image to make the text intelligible; the linkage to voluntary poverty (reaffirmed here as a Franciscan); and
the original notion of a spiritual-social inversion, humble renunciation in this
life in return for the power to judge in the next. The last phrase – about the
poor being trampled and misunderstood in this life – remains somewhat
ambiguous, referring probably to the recent woes of the Franciscans, but
possibly meant to include the involuntary poor.

The medieval clergymen who treated Scripture expected its texts both to

[28] 'Sicut iudici attribuitur [actus iudicandi] Christo; et hoc dupliciter, quia iudicabit iurisdictione
ordinaria, ut Deus cum tota Trinitate, et iurisdictione delegata, ut homo. Sicut assessori: sic
attribuitur viris perfectis qui cum iudice eminentius residebunt, tanquam melius scientes leges et
consuetudines regni Dei, quibus totaliter implendis sciendis operam dederunt. Imperatiue dupliciter, uel iudici consentiendo et approbando: Sic iudicabunt omnes sancti, et etiam angeli; uel
iudicandorum culpam manifestando: Sic iudicabunt minus mali.' Innocent V, *In Sent.* 4.47.2
(Toulouse, 1651). 4, p. 451.

[29] Richard of Middleton, *In Sent.* 4.47.2, (Brixen, 1599), 4, p. 628.

[30] *Biblia latina cum glossa ordinaria . . . et cum postillis et moralitatibus Nicholai de Lyra* (Basel,
1498: Johann Froben et Johann Petri = Goff, B-609), hereafter: Nicholas, *Postils*.

shape and to explain the reality within which they lived. Required to render intelligible the drama of divine judgement, they drew upon images which made sense to themselves and their hearers. They had first to make the images of Jewish apocalypticism – twelve followers of the Christ seated as judges over the twelve tribes of Israel – pertinent to a body of believers that embraced the whole of the Roman Empire. The fathers of the church, echoed by the Carolingians and some later authors, exploited number symbolism to have the twelve include the whole of the elect. But some focussed upon the apostles' promised position as judges and the injunction to pursue the life of perfection, a linkage rendered explicit by Augustine, who had himself in the last stage of his conversion set out in pursuit of the perfect life and then as bishop imposed that life upon his fellow clerics in Hippo. From the early sixth to the later twelfth century both the spiritual and the social lines hardened: divine judgement loomed ever larger; the identification of the apostolic life with forms of monasticism grew ever firmer (despite resistance from people like Christian of Stavelot); and the equation between giving up power in this life and acting as judges in the next became ever more explicit. Two biblical images merged, that of the twelve judges on the Last Day and of the twenty-four elders gathered around the throne of Christ singing praise: the social referant for both was the monk in choir. Here, beginning with Gregory, there was a kind of inversion of the social order, earthly judgement (the heart of social power both at the royal and the local level) exchanged for divine judgement. The unnuanced way in which Rupert, Bernard, and many others took over Augustine's phrase about 'judging rather than being judged' may simply reflect the language of the biblical text and its gloss; but it may have been animated, made intelligible in the hearer's mind, by the plentitude of judges with relatively 'royal' powers at every social level in the early middle ages, something Bernard and Rupert both knew and even participated in as abbots. The schoolmen, bound to the Gloss, introduced the image of a contemporary court to nuance the idea theologically, distinguishing various powers to judge according to various contemporary legal distinctions. Their image was that of a court, whether ecclesiastical or royal; the 'perfect men' acted now as 'counsellors' and 'assessors', not as judges in their own right. It was this image that Nicholas of Lyra subsequently took over as 'standard' in his later form of the Gloss.

A crucial notion about the privileges of the 'perfect', anchored in a biblical text and its gloss, underwent refinement therefore not only through increased theological reflection but also through a shift in the interpretive social (legal) image. But the Bible and its interpretive apparatus was equally expected to exert pressure on social reality. To suggest, it must be conceded, that the teachings of a biblical text and gloss, however irremovable and unavoidable, necessarily worked their way into the social realities of medieval Europe is to claim more than most medieval historians would risk these days. There was, rather, a constant tension between sacred texts and social realities, which may be illustrated, in a kind of counterpoint to the previous example, with still another text and its glosses.

In Deuteronomy 16:18-19 God ordered that judges be established at the gates to every town and that they not 'respect' persons or gifts ('nec accipies personam, nec munera'). In this they were to reflect God himself described in an earlier text (Deut. 10:17) as 'respecting' no person and taking no bribes ('Deus magnus et potens et terribilis. qui personam non accipit. nec munera'). New Testament writers took over this theme of 'divine impartiality'.[31] Peter learned in a vision that God was not a 'respecter of persons' (Acts 10:34, 'comperi quia non est personarum acceptor Deus') and that he was to visit the gentile Cornelius. Peter's Letter describes God as judging everyone, without respect of persons, according to their deeds (I Peter 1:17, 'qui sine acceptione personarum iudicat secundum uniuscuiusque opus'). Paul likewise argued that God brings tribulation upon those that do evil and glory upon those that do good, whether they be Jew or Greek, for there is no respect of persons with God (Rom. 2:11, 'non enim est acceptio personarum apud Deum'). In the moral injunctions that typically concluded Paul's letters, he twice urged this ideal upon believers in imitation of God, reminding masters to treat their servant well (Eph. 6:9, 'scientes quia et illorum et vester Dominus est in caelis, et personarum acceptio non est apud eum'), and servants that they will be rewarded according to their deeds (Col. 3:25, 'Qui enim iniuriam facit, recipiet id quod inique gessit, et non est personarum acceptio apud Deum'). But the most powerful invocation of this idea comes in James 2:1-9, where believers were enjoined not to make distinctions between the rich and the poor in their assemblies (i.e. churches) lest their new faith in Christ show respect of persons (Hebr. 2:1, 'Fratres mei, nolite in personarum acceptione habere fidem Domini nostri Iesu Christi gloriae') – thus bringing to bear upon the early Christian community the ideal first imposed upon the ancient Hebrews.

Any axiom repeated so often in the Bible was sure to work its way into the teachings of medieval Christians. Commentary on the Pauline texts mostly emphasised the theological notion that God offered his salvation impartially to Jew and Gentile alike, according to their deeds.[32] The moral injunction, the notion of impartiality as a divine attribute to be worked out in human society, operated as a maxim among medieval Christian writers. In an influential passage Gregory the Great characterised *acceptio personarum* as making judgements on the basis of circumstantial matters (such as wealth or clothing)

---

[31] See Jouette Bassler, *Divine Impartiality: Paul and a Theological Maxim*. (Chico, CA, 1981).

[32] One representative example, the Gloss on Rom. 2:11: 'Coaequo iudaeum et gentilem in pena et gloria, quia Deus iudicat non secundum personas sed secundum merita, quia utrosque secundum modum peccati damnat.'

rather than on the merits of the person.[33] Louis the Pious ruled about 817 that bishops should be elected 'without respect of persons or gifts' – a royal capitulary Gratian (and many other canonists) judged worth of the church's law on elections.[34] The Council of Tribur in 895 ruled that any complaints made by laity against priests or priests against laity should be handled under the auspices of the bishop without respect of persons ('episcopo precipiente sine personarum acceptione finiatur') – a canon also taken over by Gratian; and therefore familiar to subsequent lawyers.[35] Bernard of Clairvaux, warning Eugene III against becoming entangled in the evil ways of the papal curia, noted that 'respect of persons' tripped up many judges; the pope should not count it a mere venial sin to judge cases according to personalities rather than their merits.[36]

What could be stated so axiomatically required nuance when it was put into social practice. Thus, of the canon in the Council of Tribur, Rufinus, writing about 1160, noted that there was indeed no respect of person with regard to the sentence imposed; but since the complaints of priests were to be received on their word alone, those of lay people only under oath, there was an acceptable inequality in the actual form of the proceedings.[37] Peter the Chanter, commenting a generation later on II Samuel 18:12 ('Even if a thousand shekels were weighed out into my hands, I would not lift my hand against the king's son'), observed that 'honour and reverence' were owed to the sons of noblemen, and this represented no respect of persons;[38] just as it was not to bury a king's daughter (II Kings 9:34), for honour was due to her (Rom. 13:7)[39] – one axiom here cited over against another. Thomas Aquinas insisted in several different places, including three quodlibetal questions, that one must take care

---

[33] 'Ipsa humanae conditionis qualitas indicat quam longe rebus ceteris praestat. . . . Et tamen . . . plerumque hominem non ex eo quod ipse sit, sed ex his quae circa ipsum sunt ueneramur. Cumque non intuemur quid ipse sit sed quid possit, in acceptione personarum, non ex personis sed ex rebus adiacentibus, ducimur. . . . Sed omnipotens Deus uitam hominum ex sola qualitate interrogat meritorum, et saepe inde plus punit. . . . ' Gregory, *Moralia* 15.1.1, *CCSL* 143B, p. 1230.

[34] *MGH Leges* 1.206 = *Decretum*, D. 63 c. 34.

[35] *Decretum*, C. 2 q. 5 c. 4 = c. 21 in the Council of Tribur.

[36] 'Sed est quod non minus saepe, ne noxie minus, insidiari iudicantibus solet, de quo maxime, quid in tua lateat conscientia, latere te nolim. Quid illud sit quaeris? Acceptio personarum. Non parvi te reum peccati existimes, si facies peccatorum sumis et non potius causas iudicas meritorum,' Bernard, *De consideratione* 2.14.23: *Opera sancti Bernardi*, 3, p. 430.

[37] ' . . . *sine personarum acceptione*: quoad articulum sententie, non quantum ad formam cause; nam quantum ad formam cause ad imparia presbiter et laicus iudicantur, cum illi solummodo verbo, isti non nisi iuremento credatur.' Heinrich Singer, ed., *Rufinus von Bologna, Summa Decretorum* (Paderborn, 1902; reprinted 1963) p. 250.

[38] '*Balteum*, utpote primo percutienti in filium. Ergo honor et reverentia debetur filiis nobilium, nec est aceptio persone.' Oxford, Bodleian, MS Bodl. 371, fo. 27ra. For this reference and that in n. 39, I am deeply indebted to Dr. Phillipe Buc of Stanford University.

[39] '*Sepelite eam quia filiam regis Syrie est*: Non fuit acceptio persone; cui honorem honorem.' Paris, Arsenal, MS 44, fo. 405b.

to distinguish the object of the respect: it is wrong to favour someone in a dispute just because he is more literate, but appropriate when it comes to promoting him as a master – and so also with matters concerning wealth.[40]

Respect of persons was, in sum, a known vice; making distinctions by social class and political office a no less compelling reality; the latter necessarily nuanced the reading of biblical texts on this axiom. But the Gloss, too, influenced the way intellectuals confronted and interpreted texts about respect of persons. The question is whether such social pressures became evident in the Gloss itself. The moral injunction was unmistakable, and about its first declaration in Deut. 10:17 the gloss added between the lines asserted: 'quem debetis imitari'. The interlinear gloss on Col. 3:25 observed that 'no one would be excepted for his greater status' ('nulli parcetur pro maioritate sua'), and that on Eph. 6:9 established God himself as the measuring rod: 'Deus enim iustus iudex causas discernit, non personas'. Nicholas's *Postil* on this same text asserted that lords and servants would be punished alike, with lords held to a higher accountability: 'Ita enim puniet dominum sicut servum, et etiam gravius, ceteris paribus, quia quanto status altior, tanto casus gravior, propter quod dicitur Sap. 6, potentes potenter tormenta patientur'. In interpreting I Peter 1:17 both Hugh of St. Cher and Nicholas of Lyra invoked the notion of equity in justice.[41]

This axiom presupposed a principle, that all human beings enjoyed a common status under an impartial God. The most dramatic statements of it with regard to respect of persons come in the text that followed Col. 3:25, ('Domini, quod iustum est et aequum, servis praestate; scientes quod et vos Dominum habetis in caelo' Col. 4:1). The Gloss (and later Peter Lombard) noted of *aequum* simply that it was 'by nature, so you [lords] regard them [subjects] as human beings' ('per naturam, ut scilicet homines reputetis').[42] The commentary ascribed to Bruno the Carthusian noted likewise that lords were to acknowledge servants as 'human beings like you' ('ut pensetis eos aeque homines esse sicut vos').[43] In the early thirteenth century Hugh of St.

---

[40] 'Accipere enim causam est iudicium formare ex aliquo quod facit ad causam, quod laudabile est; accipere uero personam est formare iudicium ex aliqua conditione personae quae non facit ad causam, quod uitium est [a more sophisticated statement of Gregory's point in n. 33 above]. Unde contingit quod ex eadem conditione personae considerata quandoque fit iudicium iustum, quandoque est acceptio personarum. Sicut si in aliqua controversia detur sententia pro aliquo quia est litteratior, erit acceptio personarum. Si autem ex hac consideratione in licentiando ad magisterium aliis praeferatur, non erit acceptio personarum. Si ergo aliquis honor diuiti exhibeatur propter causas ad quas diuitiae aliquid faciunt, non erit acceptio personarum.' Thomas, *Quodlibeta*, 10 q.6 a. 12, (Parma, 1859), 9, p. 608.

[41] Hugh of St. Cher, *Biblia cum postillis Hugonis de sancto Caro* (Basel, 1598-1602, Johann Amerbach for Anton Koberger -Goff, B-610): 'Et tangitur ibi quinta ratio [for doing good], scilicet discretio et equitas iudicii ubi unusquisque recipiet secundum opus suum.' Nicholas, *Postil*: 'in aequitate iustitiae'.

[42] *PL* 192: 286.

[43] *PL* 153:395.

Cher's *Postil* elaborated upon the same essential idea, stressing the notion of 'equal by nature'.[44]

Commentators tended to associate particular texts with fuller discussions, a device for memory and for systematics: for respect of persons that text was James 2. The interlinear Gloss summarised the main point of the passage: whoever selected a wealthy person for his wealth alone and repudiated a poor person sinned against both.[45] Material for the marginal glosses derived mostly from early Christian writers, but the so-called Catholic Epistles, including James, had received little in the way of continuous commentary. Bede was among the first: his interpretation of James 2 supplied much – in some places all – of the marginal Gloss. Its opening statement, frequently cited in later literature, he drew from a letter of Augustine.[46] Bede (and Augustine) clearly condemned the promotion of the wealthy for their wealth alone. Yet a close comparison of the Gloss (in its 1480 printed edition) with Bede's commentary reveals a noteworthy sharpening of tone. The Gloss begins with a passage not found in Bede, contrasting Christ's way with those of the world, the one caring for the poor and the other for the rich.[47] Both commentary and Gloss warned lest those who are wealthier in this world be regarded as better in the divine judgement,[48] but the Gloss went on to draw concrete inference – 'et ideo non sunt preferendi, nam Deus non diuites sed pauperes eligit' – before going on to paraphrase the end of Bede's passage. Similarly in paraphrasing and abbreviating the biblical sentence that begins with *Nonne*, where Bede offered a definition of the poor ('Pauperes uocat humiles et qui pro contemptu rerum uisibilium . . . '), the Gloss had the point stand on its own ('Nonne pauperes eligit Deus'). The Gloss likewise quoted the sharp language of vv. 6 and 7 about the wealthy using their power to oppress and to judge (something also done by Bede, but as part of a larger explanation), and then drew another concrete inference not found in Bede: 'Et est alia causa quare non sunt eligendi. quia mala inferunt fidelibus'. Finally, for the sentence beginning

---

[44] '*Et equum*: idest quandam equalitatem propter naturam, et non uiles eos habeatis, sed equales per naturam uobis reputetis, maxime si boni sunt.' Hugh, *Biblia cum postillis*.

[45] *Gloss*: 'Quicumque divitem propter divitias elegit et propter paupertatem obiicit utrobique peccat.'

[46] *Gloss*: '*Tu sede*: Si hanc distantiam sedendi et standi ad honores ecclesiasticos referamus, non est putandum leue esse peccatum in personarum acceptione habere fidem domini nostre Iesu Christi gloriae. Quis enim ferat eligi diuitem ad sedem honoris ecclesiae, contempto paupere instructiore atque sanctiore? Si autem de cotidianis consessibus loquitur, quis non hic peccat, si tamen peccat, nisi cum apud semet ipsum intus ita iudicat, ut ei tanto melior quanto ditior uideatur?' See Augustine, *Epistola* 167: *CSEL* 44, pp. 605-06; and compare Bede, *In epistolas septem catholicas*: *CCSL* 121, pp. 191-92.

[47] 'quasi Dominus diuites inuitaret ad fidem et pauperes despiceret. Non ita est, quia dominus pauperes elegit in hoc mundo et eos fide donauit. Mundus pauperem abiicit, diuitem colit; fides Christi econtra docet, quia *omnis gloria* diuitum *tanquam flos faeni* [1 Peter 1:24], misericordia in pauperes floret in aeternum.'

[48] *Gloss*: '*Audite*: Diligentius attendite, quia non qui ditiores in seculo [Bede: ad saeculum], hi meliores in diuino examine. . . . ' Bede, *CCSL* 121, p. 194.

*Si tamen* (v. 8) Bede offered no commentary, but the Gloss observed that even if the wealthy are not to be elected for their wealth's sake, they are not less deserving of love for God's sake.[49] For the Gloss, unlike Bede, the point of this passage about not showing ecclesiastical preference to the wealthy had come down to the question of their election to office – which, for the remainder of the middle ages, the glossed Bible forbad. In the early twelfth century, when the Gloss assumed its final shape, that in Bede which most needed sharpening was precisely these strictures against favouritism in clerical elections.

So much for the biblical injunction and the glosses that reinforced it; but what of the social dilemmas inherent in its implementation? In contrast to the earlier biblical passage treating the apostles' position in the divine judgement, this passage about impartiality in human judgements never made it into Peter Lombard's *Sentences*, possibly because he concentrated upon theological rather than ethical topics. No pattern of commentary and exposition arose therefore in the context of Sentence commentaries. But the matter was far too prominent in Scripture and too important in social practice not to receive continued attention. Reflections went on in two places: in subsequent scriptural commentaries (where James was treated), and in systematic works with an ethical component.

Hugh of St. Cher, assembling biblical material for his Dominican brothers in Paris in the 1220s, prefaced his treatment of James 2 with a lengthy systematic analysis of *acceptio personarum*:

Accipitur autem persona quandoque in malo, quandoque in bono [edition: malo]. [1] In malo accipere personam est statum malum uel conditionem pro humano fauore uel amore acceptare uel potius commendare. Item, preferre minus dignum magis digno propter favorem persone uel statum uel conditionem uel circumstantiam que est in ipso inquantum in ipso. Unde Gregorius: *Accipere personam est hominem non quia homo sed propter aliquid quod circum ipsum est honorare* [apparently an axiomatic version of Gregory's teaching in n. 33]. [2] Item, in bono acceptio persone est honoris debita exhibitio seruato gradu dignitatis et officii. Dicitur autem hic persona substantia rationalis indiuidua suis proprietatibus substantialibus a ceteris segregata, inter quas tamen exigitur aliqua proprietas preeminentior ceteris, ratione cuius si debeatur honor qui ex diuitiis solis contrahi non potest nec debet sed ex potentia collata ad officium aliquod in ecclesia uel in secularibus secundum instituta ecclesie et mores patrie. Et propter hoc dixit Dominus quibusdam Lucas 20, *reddite ergo que sunt Cesaris Cesari, et que sunt Dei Deo*; Eph. 6, *Serui, obedite dominis carnalibus cum timore et tremore* etc. [3] Sed nonne omnis potestas a Deo est? Ita contra Rom. 13, *omnis anima potestatibus sublimioribus subjecta; non enim est potestas nisi a Deo*. Ergo obediendum est potestati et honoranda est potestas, et sic persona eius accipienda. Solutio: Verum est quod propter officium uel dignitatem honoranda est persona et non propter

[49] *Gloss*: '*Si tamen*: . . . etsi diuites propter diuitias non sunt eligendi, non tamen propter Deum minus sunt diligendi.'

*God is no Respecter of Persons*

diuitias aut ornatus uel huiusmodi, quia non sunt data homini ut presunt propter illa sed ex illis usum et necessitatem impleat. [4] Item, obicitur: Preferre personam persone in iudicio est accipere personam, et hoc est peccatum; ergo a simili preferre personam persone in collatione ecclesie uel in datione elemosyne est accipere personam et peccatum. Quid est quod dicit Eccles. 12. . . . Solutio: Non est simile quia iudicium respicit merita causarum, opus uero misericordie conditiones perso-narum. [5] Item, quare magis excluditur hoc uitium a Deo quam alia, Sap. vi . . . Act. x, Rom.ii, et in multis locis scripture. Solutio: quia acceptio personarum declinat in partem; Deus autem universalis est et redemptor et creator. [6] Item, dictum est quod homo propter officium uel dignitatem honorandus est. Quid est ergo quod dicit Gregorius quod *accipere personam* in malo *est hominem non quia homo sed aliquid quod circa ipsum est honorare*? Nonne enim officium uel dignitas circa hominem est? Solutio: non est officium uel dignitas circa hominem sed supra. Ostendit autem que sunt illa propter que non est accipienda uel honoranda persona, scilicet ornatus uestium, abundantia diuitiarum, dicens. . . . [the Ordinary Gloss begins][50]

For everyone who used Hugh's glossed Bible, meaning most Dominican preachers and confessors at the very least, the passage from James could no longer be read without calling to mind a systematic analysis of the nature of this vice. Hugh's fundamental distinction between the person and that which was circumstantial to the person rested upon his understanding of Gregory – and provided the material for Thomas's formulation. He regarded the vice of *acceptio personarum* as singled out in Scripture by its frequent mention because it tended to 'party interests' and violated the universal character of God's creation and redemption [5]. But to accommodate an acceptable 'respect of persons' – and thereby to account for social reality – he approved honour and respect paid an office, whether ecclesiastical or secular [2], never to be confused with the trappings of the person or the office [3]. Indeed, a false respect of persons would begin with honouring mere trappings such as clothing and wealth [6]. Admonitions against showing respect of person applied in the first instance to rendering judgements, not the showing of mercy [5]. Hugh only noted in passing [4] the classic instance, favouritism in promotion to church office, which he doubtless took for granted as repudiated in the Ordinary Gloss. Following this lengthy preface, he added relatively little to the Gloss itself, focusing mainly upon the key point of the biblical passage, preference shown the wealthy. This, he observed, was forbidden on two grounds: because it rested ultimately on human rather than divine judgement ('tale iudicium non est a Deo sed ab homine'), thus violating the universality of God and the common created nature of humans, and because it contradicted the 'example of Christ', who preferred the poor, choosing even to be born of poor people.

At virtually the same time that Hugh prepared his *Postils*, William of Auxerre composed a *summa* of theology (subsequently called the *Summa*

---

[50] Hugh, *Biblia cum postillis*.

*aurea*). The penultimate to his fifteen 'tractates' on sin took up *acceptio personarum*, considered a species of 'evil judgement' (*de pravis iudiciis*) and treated just before the 'sin against the Holy Spirit'.[51] His treatment, divided into four questions, used James 2:1-4 as its point of departure. He knew other standard scriptural references to respect of persons (Deut. 10:17; Acts 10:34; Rom. 9:13), and proceeded through them somewhat haphazardly at the end of his discussion, arguing simply that people should not be preferred for money or any other unworthy cause. But the focal point of his consideration was social practice. He began with respect of persons shown the wealthy. 'We must honour the wealthy more than the poor', he states as a self-evident truth, 'only to avoid scandal.'[52] To honour them for their wealth is to have that pre-empt the image of God, possessed as well by the poor ('preponunt ymagini Dei que est in paupere'), for – here he challenged the text from Rom. 13: 'cui honorem, honorem' – people are to be honored only for their image and likeness to God ('tantum propter ymaginem vel similitudinem Dei sit honorandus'). The rich have no greater measure of that; they are as a point in a line; and to honour them for their wealth is to dishonour the image of God.[53]

William's second situation was presented as a case: Of two persons equally deserving of a prebend, the bishop chose his kin, making him apparently guilty of respect of persons. But William argued to the contrary, citing Paul's injunction that we do good to all, 'especially those in the household' (omitting 'of faith', Gal. 6:10). So long as the two were equally deserving, thus guaranteeing that carnal considerations were not preferred to spiritual, the bishop simply followed 'ordered charity' in selecting a kinsman.[54]

Then William set a harder case and had social reality triumph even more dramatically over scriptural principle. The choice again concerned preference to a church post, the one person common but well-lettered, the other noble but illiterate ('ignobilis bene litteratus, alter nobilis illiteratus'). Rejecting what he too regarded as the obvious first choice, William settled for the nobleman as better able to keep peace in the church and thus to resist attacking wolves.[55] He was quick to qualify. If the post entailed cure of souls, and the man was truly illiterate, he would not stand for it. These options were in fact false and extreme (*excedentia et excessa*). On occasion the commoner could be preferred if the church had enough powerful people to defend the church ('quando

[51] *Magistri Guillelmi Altissiodorensis Summa Aurea* Liber II, Tractatus XXIII, ed. Jean Ribaillier, Spicilegium Bonaventurianum 17, (Grottaferrata, 1982), 2, pp. 686-90.
[52] 'Divites etiam magis debemus honorare quam pauperes propter scandalum vitandum tantum.' Ibid., p. 688.
[53] 'Divitie enim non se habent in aliqua proportione ad ymaginem et similitudinem Dei, sicut punctus ad lineam. Unde propter eas [divitias] non est aliquis magis honorandus; et ideo cum aliquis propter eas tantum aliquem honorat plus alio, derogat ymagini Dei.' Ibid., p. 688.
[54] 'Preterea ordinata caritas est quod magis diligamus domesticos quam extraneos; ergo iste non peccat preponendo consanguineum suum illi, cum in aliis sint pares.' Ibid., p. 689.
[55] 'Talis nobilis melius pacem ecclesie conservat et melius resistit lupo venienti; ergo est preferendus.' Ibid., p. 690.

ecclesia habet sufficienter alias personas defendere potentes ecclesiam'); the nobleman, moreover, was not preferred for his nobility but for what followed from it, power to keep peace in the church ('propter consequens, scilicet propter pacem ecclesie').

The fourth case concerned two people judged acceptable for a post, though one clearly better (*duo boni, sed alter melior*): is it respect of persons to promote the other? William reluctantly conceded that it was, though he made an exception again for keeping peace in the church. Then he concluded by asking why this vice was reproached so vigorously in humans, and God made so excellent for not showing respect of persons. The answer, he says, is that it would constitute a sin against God's largesse (*contra largitatem*), made manifest in his being a God of the gentiles as well as the Jews. A powerful social value in aristocratic society had come to shape the understanding and defence of this scriptural principle.

The cases William posed became part of a standard repertory; indeed he may have inherited them. What marked his own discussion was a certain plainness, even bluntness, in confronting text and society. He insisted upon the principle, grounding it in people's image-likeness to God, yet at every point he found good reasons to defend the social realities of kinship and power, especially on grounds of maintaining peace in the church.

A decade after Hugh and William, about 1235-45, the *Summa fratris Alexandri*, commonly ascribed to Alexander of Hales, likewise devoted an entire section to 'respect of persons' as a species of sin, particularly of evil judgement. He too introduced the section by citing James 2 and the Augustinian passage in the Gloss (without identifying it as from the Gloss: everyone would have known that). He distinguished three forums for respect of persons: promotion to office; making judgements; and showing honour. With respect to kinship and promotion, he noted that kin could of course receive temporal benefices; that is, Alexander raised no objections to an hereditary earthly order. But in conferring spiritual benefices a distinction was to be made: kinship of fleshly consideration could be only secondary (*secondaria*) in awarding a spiritual benefice with temporalities attached, and could not be considered at all in awarding a purely spiritual benefice, though it could still be conferred on kin if that generated no scandal.[56] With regard to the preference of a nobleman to a lettered man, Alexander came to the same conclusion: that on some occasions the socially more powerful man is necessary for the peace of the church.[57] With respect to making judgements, Alexander determined quite simply that there must always be equity. As for the matter of showing

---

[56] Alexander, *Summa theologica* (Quaracchi, 1930), 3, p. 379.

[57] 'Ad quod dicendum quod, licet litteratura siue scientia sit praeferenda simpliciter nobilitati, eo quod ipsa necessaria est in regimine ecclesiae, nihilominus tamen in casu praeferri potest ipsa nobilitas personae, ad hoc ut arceantur lupi, qui non tantum pacem temporalem, immo etiam spiritualem ecclesiae pacem impediunt . . . ' Ibid., p. 380.

honour, it was owed to prelates by reason of their receiving power from God (*ratione qua a Deo acceperunt potestatem*), and to evil prelates by reason of their office. As for showing honour to wealthy people, the heart of the biblical passage, he cited the standard materials and arguments, then qualified the moral strictures by conceding that it might be done to avoid scandal, so long as the poor were not thereby held in contempt or the wealthy fostered in their sin.[58] Lastly, he asked, as William did, why this vice received special attention in Scripture; and his answer was essentially the same, though his word for the divine virtue it revealed was 'liberality'.

Alexander's notion of the balance between biblical axiom and social reality fit perfectly with William's. But Alexander deepened his analysis by raising the hard question implicit in some of the argumentation already deployed. If ordained power comes from God and the power conferred by God is that being honoured in a powerful man, could not the same argument be made for a wealthy man? Is there then any real case of respect for persons? Alexander and his contemporaries plainly found such an argument, reinforced by a social order which they both took for granted and regarded as God-given, very compelling. But Alexander insisted upon a distinction between power, conferred by God and essential to the rule of all things, and wealth, which, he said, arose from usurpation. Even in power, in so far as it involved rule over people and human vanity, there could also be respect of persons.[59] His was hardly a vigorous indictment of the ruling social order, yet he makes a distinction between 'ordained' power and 'usurped' wealth which befits a Franciscan.

By the mid thirteenth century the discussion concerning respect of persons, whether biblical or systematic, was largely structured. Though considerable nuance could be added by exploring more commentaries and treatises, this essay will end by noting two works, a *summa* and a gloss or postil, significant for their later influence. In his *Summa theologiae* Thomas Aquinas treated *acceptio personarum* (II, ii, qu. 63) as the first and major vice set in opposition to the cardinal virtue of justice. Thomas understood it as a matter of distributive justice that people be awarded honours or offices according to properties

[58] 'Si tamen hoc fiat pro uitatione scandali, ita tamen quod pauper non contemnatur, uel diues in peccato suo non foueatur, licitum est.' Ibid., p. 383.

[59] 'Et sicut potestas datur a Domino, ita et diuitiae dantur a Domino et alia bona quae dicuntur fortunae. Et sicut honorari potest Dominus in bono potentiae dato, ita in bono diuitiarum et sic in aliis bonis. Cum ergo non dicatur acceptio personae si honoretur Deus potens in homine potente, sic non dicatur acceptio personae si honoretur Deus dives in homine divite, et Deus nobilis in homine nobili. [Sed] . . . aliter dicendum est de potestate et diuitiis et huiusmodi bonis fortunae. Per potestatem enim gerit homo uicem Dei sine potestate ordinata non regitur universitas, et ideo ei per se debetur reuerentia. Diuitiae autem quasi ex quadam usurpatione prouenerunt. . . . Est tamen considerare potestatem dupliciter: uel in quantum ordinata sit sub Deo uel in quantum est super homines. Si ultimo modo, uantis est in potestate sicut in diuitiis, et illo modo posset esse acceptio personae.' Ibid., p. 383.

in the person, thus, to use the first example that came to his mind, that someone be made a master for his learning, not because he is a certain person; respect is paid to the grounds, not to the person as such ('hic attenditur causa debita, non persona'), for which he cited as his authority the gloss on Eph. 6:9 (quoted above). Thomas then dealt briefly and pithily (a. 2) with the exemplary social cases reviewed by William and Alexander; as his *'sed contra'* he cited the text from James 2 and an Augustinian sentence from the Gloss. Thomas conceded that it was customary in the church to promote kin ('cum hoc ex consuetudine praelati faciunt'), but condemned it as an end in itself. He silently avoided the noble/literate choice, and his firmly declared the promotion of the less worthy 'respect of persons', while acknowledging that choices were necessary at times to avoid scandal. He also opted for the election of the 'better' and not merely the 'good enough'. Thomas raised one concrete case not encountered previously: The rich and powerful receive dispensations from marriages contracted within the forbidden degrees far more easily than do others. The point of such dispensations, he argued, was to preserve the bonds of peace, which in the case of exalted persons had greater bearing upon the common good.[60] With regard to showing honour, Thomas argued more clearly than ever that honour pertained to the virtue inherent in a person, not the person as such, or to that in another person they represented: thus to princes and prelates as bearing the *persona* of God and placed over the community; to parents and lords as participating in the lordship of God; to the aged for the virtue inherent in their age; and to the wealthy for the greater place they held in their communities.[61] At all points Thomas upheld the biblical injunction, especially against favouritism for the wealthy, but he also made allowance for the necessary compromises with social reality, particularly for the bearers of power.

Already Alexander, raising questions about ordered power, seemed to limit impartiality to the sphere of ecclesiastical relations. This was increasingly true for other schoolmen as well. Respect of persons seemed too much the way their social world worked to imagine any massive extension of the principle outside the church – certainly not into the arrangements of hereditary power where kinship was, in Thomas's reading of Romans 2, a legitimate

---

[60] '. . . principaliter fieri consueuit propter foedus pacis firmandum, quod quidem magis est necessarium communi utilitate circa personas excellentes. Ideo cum eis facilius dispensatur absque peccato acceptionis personarum.' *Summa* II, ii, q. 63 a, 2. (Rome, 1897), 9, p. 64.

[61] 'Sciendum tamen quod aliquis potest honorari non solum propter virtutem propriam, sed etiam propter virtutem alterius. Sicut principes et praelati honorantur etiam si sint mali, inquantum gerunt personam Dei et communitatis cui praeficiuntur. . . . Et eadem ratione parentes et domini sunt honorandi, propter participationem divinae dignitatis, qui est omnium Pater et Dominus. . . . Divites autem honorandi sunt propter hoc quod maiorem locum in communitatibus obtinent. Si autem solum intuitu divitiarum honorentur, erit peccatum acceptionis personarum.' Ibid., a. 3, 9, p. 65.

consideration.[62] Responding to the prescriptions of James 2 and its gloss in the midst of one quodlibet, Thomas noted that *acceptio personarum*, preferring the rich to the poor, had no place in the administration of the sacraments; but where the support of the world was required, it was necessary to carry on in the world's customary ways.[63] Balancing sacred mandates and social realities called for compromise: for all his moral clarity and his firm juxtaposition of this vice with the virtue of justice, Thomas and other schoolmen edged towards reducing 'respect of persons' to a relatively lesser charge, the prejudicial treatment of a single individual, without challenging in any way the built-in respect of persons which was the social reality within which they lived.

Finally, and even more briefly, the case of Nicholas of Lyra, whose *Postils* shaped biblical scholarship into the early modern period. Here the dialectic between biblical and systematic thinking came full circle. Thomas had consistently cited the relevant scriptural text and its gloss as a key element in his argument, frequently as his '*sed contra*' or as the main element in his '*determinatio*'. Now Nicholas quoted and summarised Thomas for his postil on James 2 (without acknowledging his source) – right down to Thomas's first example ('si cancellarius Parisiensis promoueat aliquem . . .'). He began with a summary of the *determinatio* Thomas offered in his article 1, then went on to the discussion of honour in article 4 (n. 61 above). He concluded his opening treatment of James 2 with a remarkable paragraph, his own or drawn from yet another source. Here he addressed forthrightly the seeming casuistry which had the rich and powerful still receiving honour without facing any charge of respect or persons. Where this served the ends of divine honour, the good of the church and the devotion of the faithful, Nicholas argued, it did not constitute respect of persons. He cited the case of Constantine: by his example many came to the church, helping it spread throughout the world. To work for the conversion and fostering in faith of the rich and powerful more than of the poor was not to commit the sin of respect of persons but to look to the good which can arise more from them than from the poor.[64]

---

[62] ' . . . puta, si aliquis det alicui propter consanguinitatem plus de bonis patrimonialibus, non est acceptio personarum, quia consanguinitas est conueniens causa propter quam de talibus bonis debeat habere. Si autem propter consanguinitatem aliquis praelatus det alicui plus de bonis ecclesiasticis, potest hoc ad acceptionem personarum pertinere, si alia idoneitas non concurrat; non enim consanguinitas est ratio conueniens distributionis bonorum spiritualium.' *Expositio in Rom.*, 2.2, (Parma, 1862), 13, p. 27.

[63] 'Ad primum [a citation of James 2 and its Gloss] ergo dicendum, quod in his quae ad fidem Christi pertinent, peccatum est diuites pauperibus praeferre, sicut sunt ministrationes sacramentorum, et alia huius modi; sed in his quae mundi conuictus requirit, oportet mundo gerere morem.' *Quodlibeta* 10 q. 6 a. 1 (12): ed. (Parma, 1859) 9, p. 608.

[64] ' . . . si autem attendatur ad honorem diuinum et ecclesie bonum et deuotionem recipientis fidem uel exhortationem, non est acceptio personarum in talibus, si predicta magis exhibeantur aliquibus quam aliis secundum maioritatem deuotionis eorum uel honoris diuinc et ecclesie. Sicut conuersio Constantini ad fidem, ex cuius exemplo ualde multi uenerunt ad fidem et ex eius facto

The intellectuals who reflected on *acceptio personarum* were constrained by two realities, both of them in some sense divine. The biblical texts and their glosses, written down under the aegis of God's Spirit and therefore authoritative, demanded that they set as their ideal the model of divine impartiality. And they took it seriously: the moral injunctions in their glosses were forceful, and known to every learned reader of the Scriptures; they were cited or paraphrased matter of factly in the course of the masters' theological expositions. Even though this biblical axiom was left out of Lombard's textbook, masters found innumerable ways, in scripture commentaries, in extended prefaces to postils, in sermons, and in *summae* to take up the ethical issues.

Yet they were no less constrained by a social order which they accepted as in large measure ordained by God, dividing people into the ordained and the laity, lords and subjects, those who command and judge, those who obey and are judged. To recognize these distinctions was not to violate respect of persons; it was to respect or honour the arrangement of power and authority established by God. The social practices these intellectuals chose to explore and in large measure to justify, together with Thomas's overt remarks (n. 63 above), suggest that they held out little hope of implementing a 'divine impartiality' in the world at large. They could and did address its manifestations in ecclesiastical society, but often simply to account for present practice, kin chosen over the lettered to keep peace in bishoprics and exercise inherited powers, the wealthy and powerful shown honour for the sake of expansion in the church and stability in the commonwealth. Perhaps intellectuals have always, to a larger degree than they admit, worked not only to hold out alternative ideals but also to render intelligible present realities. Yet no one can reckon how much the steady pressure of this ethical teaching, and its concomitant sense of a basic human quality before God, restrained the worst excesses of raw power and human favouritism; how often it made possible, particularly inside the church, judgements or advancements based on merit rather than kinship or wealth.

Both sets of texts and glosses treated in this essay reinforce the basic, but crucial, point that scholars must take seriously the influence of the Gloss in determining the topics upon which medieval intellectuals were forced to reflect. In both cases a spiritual ideal encapsulated in the Gloss helped to leaven a relatively closed social order. The Gloss on the text from Matthew encouraged people to give up their wealth, their families, their self-will and their bodies, all the elements of social power in this life, in return for the opportunity to reign as judges alongside Christ in the next. The texts on

est ecclesia promota et honorata quasi per totem orbem, sic etiam laborare ad conuersionem et nutritionem in fide diuitum et potentum magis quam pauperum non est personarum acceptio, attendendo ad bona que ex eis prouenire possunt magis quam ex pauperibus.' Nicholas, *Postil* on James 2.

*acceptio personarum* encouraged people to think in terms of common humanity under a universal God and to judge in terms of merit in a society where the distribution of social power according to kinship and wealth was widely taken as given, even God-given. Both upheld notions of merit, of the human will striving to follow a divine plan that transcended the social order. Yet social realities, legal notions of judgement and the customary practice of social relations powerfully blunted the force of these teachings and nuanced the way intellectuals explained them. All the same, without these biblical texts and the particular interpretive thrusts given them by the Gloss there might have been no creative friction, no forced reflection at all.

# 19

# Lending Books: The Growth of a Medieval Question from Langton to Bonaventure

## Lesley Smith

'Not to lend your books is homicide'. An uncompromising statement by Stephen Langton, Paris theologian and later archbishop of Canterbury, is the rather blunt starting point of this little investigation. So arresting was the image (and apparently so out of context) that I was impelled to search out the background of Langton's unexpected contention, and of the attitude to books and the lending of them of some of the scholars of the late twelfth and thirteenth centuries.

Langton's opinion occurs in a biblical commentary, and the Bible itself, although it has little to say on lending, displays a remarkably consistent line (remarkable because the Bible can be made to support opposite arguments on almost any chosen subject) summarised in Luke 6:35: 'lend, hoping for nothing thereby.' Questions of lending which raise any controversy are those involving lending money and charging for it. Key texts such as Lev. 25:36 and Deut. 23:20, which forbid lending at interest to your 'brother' (interpreted as fellow-Christians) were used to justify the prohibition of Christian money-lending and were part of the circumstances which forced the Jews to their characteristic profession in the middle ages. The *Glossa ordinaria* makes little of these passages beyond the obvious, and initial checks through various scholastic commentators suggested that they followed suit. Of course, they do discuss usury, often at length, but when no money is involved, interest plummets.[1]

Theological commentary on lending seemed to be yielding few results. What, then, of the other angle – the history of books and libraries? As might be imagined, there is a long history of reluctance to lend books. Everyone knows that books were objects of high value, acquired with glee, and so dear as themselves to be used as securities in loans. The difficulty and expense of making parchment is drilled into us, and the laments of generations of poor

---

[1] For an intensive discussion of usury in the Schools see J.T. Noonan, *The Scholastic Analysis of Usury* (Cambridge, MA, 1957).

scribes ring familiar in our ears: they complain about the cold, stiff fingers, aching backs, bad light, long hours, and boring text:

> Here ends the second part of the title work of Br. Thomas Aquinas of the Dominican Order, very long, very verbose, and very tedious: thank God, thank God, and again, thank God.[2]

Parchment may be durable in everyday use, but it can be burnt, torn or cut, and is susceptible to vermin and mould. However, people are undoubtedly more of a danger than mere age or natural damage. Richard of Bury (writing in 1345) warns his readers not to lend books to students in the winter: their noses are bound to run and drip all over the pages. Again, 'the cleanliness of decent hands would be great benefit to books as well as to scholars, if it were not that the itch and pimples are characteristic of the clergy'.[3] It is an ecumenical problem: writing in 1190 Rabbi Judah ben Samuel Sir Leon Chassid forbids anyone to do his accounts on the pages of a book.[4] Moreover, medieval books were subject to vicissitudes that ours are not. Peter the Venerable writes to the abbot of the Grande Chartreuse asking to borrow his copy of Augustine's correspondence with Jerome: the Cluny copy had been eaten by a bear.[5]

If he were making a copy, the borrower might well be expected to make an extra one to give back with the original in payment. Making unauthorised copies was frowned upon, as we know from the famous story from the life of St. Columba. Without permission, Columba made a copy of a psalter borrowed from his teacher Finian. Finian demanded the return not merely of the psalter but of the copy too: the copy must go with the book, 'as the calf must go with the cow'.[6] Columba's refusal on principle forced war and exile.

In those religious communities where reading books was part of the Rule, special care was taken. Benedict's Rule assumes the existence of a library and book lending to monks.[7] Monastic customaries specified the duties of the

---

[2]   M.B. Parkes, *English Cursive Book Hands 1250-1500* (Oxford, 1969), p. xiii. The quotation is from Oxford, New College, MS 121, fo. 376v.

[3]   *Philobiblon: Richard de Bury*, Text and translation by E.C. Thomas, edited M. MacLagan (Oxford, 1960), c. xvii, pp. 157, 161. The chapter contains some wonderful complaints against medieval readers.

[4]   From the *Sefer Chasidon* (Regensburg, 1190), quoted in M. Drogin *Anathema!* (Totowa, NJ, 1983), p. 25.

[5]   *The Letters of Peter the Venerable* ed. Giles Constable (Cambridge, MA, 1967) i, letter 24, p. 47.

[6]   Adamnan's *Life of Saint Columba* ed. W. Reeves (Edinburgh, 1874), p. xlii,

[7]   *Benedicti Regula* ed. R. Hanslik *CSEL* 75, c. 48, pp. 114-19.

librarian, where and how the books were to be kept, and how and when they were to be lent out.[8] Books were borrowed for set periods – in some houses from Lent to Lent, more frequently in others. On the day appointed for their general return we know that some communities laid a carpet on the stone floor: the monk or nun knelt on the bare floor but the books were returned to the carpet.[9] Benedictines at Monte Cassino, who were not normally allowed handkerchiefs, could use them to cover their hands when reading books, and some customaries had monks turn down their sleeves so that hand and book might not meet.[10]

Attitudes to lending outside the community obviously varied over time, but religious houses, where there was most likely to be some kind of library, were generally wary of books being borrowed by non-members. The Rule of a community of French third order Franciscans reads: 'No outsider, whether monk or secular priest can take a book outside of this monastery, in case the book is destroyed'. Or, from the college of Bernardines in Paris: 'No one, irrespective of rank, may take a book outside of this library, whether for himself or for someone else, inside the college or out, without the highest penalty'.[11] Where books could be borrowed from the library of a religious house a pledge – not just a token but something of value – had to be left in exchange. Indeed, although the thirteenth-century statutes of the Franciscan province of Aquitaine forbade demanding pledges from fellow friars, evidence suggests that the rule was ignored.[12]

The most famous medieval library was that of the college of the Sorbonne, which in 1290 listed 1,017 volumes in its catalogue.[13] The library was in two parts: the *grande* library, where the more-used books were chained and rarely lent out; and the *petite* library, which housed duplicated and little-used

[8] J.W. Clarke, *The Care of Books* (Cambridge, 1902; repr. London, 1975), esp. chap. 2, pp. 51-94. Other general information can be mined from K. Christ, *The Handbook of Medieval Library History*, rev. by A. Kern, transl. & ed. by T.M. Otto (Metuchen, NJ and London, 1984) and E.A. Savage, *Old English Libraries* (1911; repr. NY, 1970).

[9] Clarke, *Care of Books*, pp. 57-58, quotes the decrees given to English Benedictines in 1070 by Archbishop Lanfranc.

[10] Ibid., p. 66.

[11] K.W. Humphreys, *The Book Provision of the Medieval Friars (1215-1400)* (Amsterdam, 1964): 'The Library Regulations of the Dominicans', pp. 18-45; 'The Library Regulation of the Franciscans', pp. 46-66. See also, especially for non-mendicant regulations, Clark, *Care of Books*, esp. chap. 2.

[12] Humphreys, *Book Provisions*, pp. 64-65.

[13] L. Delisle, *Le Cabinet des manuscrits* (Paris, 1874), 2, p. 180, n. 3, and p. 182 for the 1338 catalogue. Christ, *Handbook*, p. 241. for the Sorbonne in general, Delisle, *Cabinet*, 2, pp. 42-204; 3, (Paris, 1881), pp. 8-114.

volumes which, under certain conditions, could be borrowed. Some of the books acquired as gifts were only available for use by members of certain nations, or even of a particular person.[14]

Commonly, books from religious institutions had marks *Ex libris*, and by the fourteenth century the Sorbonne at least charged fines – borrowers had to make this pledge:

Hunc librum accomodavi a collegio Sorbone Parisius, et promisi reddere sibi, vel duo scuta Francie cum dimidio pro ipso.[15]

With all this in mind, Stephen Langton's statement is the more remarkable. In his commentary on Deuteronomy, in the section on the Ten Commandments, writing on 'You shall not kill', he says: 'not to lend books is a type of homicide', and actually it is the only type of homicide he mentions.[16] Following the advice never to apologise or explain, Langton promptly changes the subject. About twenty-five years later, in one of his acts as archbishop of Canterbury, we catch him putting money behind his bookish views by giving over the revenues of Lower Halstow church for the repair and correction of books.[17]

About the same date as Stephen Langton's grant, Robert Courson, of the university of Paris, in the statutes of the synod of Paris of 1212, writes:

Besides this we prohibit any cleric or ecclesiastical person from making an oath that he will not lend books to those in need, since lending is outstanding amongst the works of mercy . . . If anyone ignores this prohibition he will be suspended from his benefice, if he has one, or else be excommunicated.[18]

In fact, Robert repeats the injunction about lending books to the needy, stating it once in those provisions addressed to clerics and again (as above) in those addressed to religious.[19] Furthermore, he declares that books cannot be

[14] Delisle, *Cabinet*, 2, pp. 185-86.
[15] Ibid., 2, p. 186, quoted from Paris, B.N., MS lat. 15946.
[16] Commentary on Deut. 5:17 in Oxford, Trinity College, MS 65, fo. 258 rb: 'Interlinearis: "Re vel voluntate vel subtrahendo alii quod potes prestare". Ergo genere homicidii est quaternos non accommodare.' [A later hand has written *nota* in the margin at this point.]
[17] *Acta Stephani Langton: Cant. Archiep. A.D. 1207-1228*. ed. Kathleen Major. (Canterbury and York Society, vol. 50; Oxford, 1950), no. 10 (13 November 1214).
[18] J.D. Mansi, *Sacrorum conciliorum nova et amplissima collectio* (Venice, 1778), 22: Concilium Parisiense A.D. 1212, part 2, c. 23, col. 832.
[19] Ibid., 22; Concilium Parisiense A.D. 1212, part 1, c. vii, col. 821.

put under anathema and all current anathemas are declared invalid.[20] Robert goes on to order that religious houses should provide a sort of free library of some of their books, as the abbot made available ('secundum providentiam abbatis'[21]). Incidentally, although Humphreys doubts that this provision was much – if ever – used, these were the first libraries open to poor scholars.[22] Somewhat later in the century, Delisle has recorded gifts of books to the library of the abbey of Saint-Victor, expressly for the use of poor scholars:

> Gervase Anglicus: 'Hos omnes libros dedit ad usum claustralium et pauperum scolarium'.
> John of Abbeville gives books worth seventy Parisian pounds 'ad usum fratrum et pauperum scolarium'.[23]

So we have practical examples of books being lent out and the examples of the sort of regulation this called forth; but following Langton, where were other examples of the theological issue of lending books to be found in scholastic interpretation? Other commentaries on the Decalogue yielded nothing similar. Eventually, something came to light amongst questions *On scandal*. To scandalise someone in this moral theological sense is to do something which incites him to sin, or provides an occasions for him to sin (especially mortal sin) – and thus to be damned.[24] The scandaliser is himself also damned. Thomas Chobham, in his *Summa confessorum* (written around 1220), says:

---

[20] Anathemas, the wonderful curses against thieves that people have been writing in books since the year dot, shed an interesting sidelight on borrowers' morals:

> For him that steals or borrows and does not return this book from its owner, let it change into a serpent in his hand and rend him. Let him be struck with palsy and all his members blasted. Let him languish in pain, crying aloud for mercy, and let there be no cease to this agony till he sing in dissolution. Let bookworms gnaw at his entrails in token of the worm that never dies. And when at last he goes to his final punishment, let the flames of hell consume him forever.
> (From the monastery of San Pedro in Barcelona.)

Hear, too, the rather plaintive:

> Take me, open me, read me, do not harm me, close me, and *put me back* ['Tolle, aperi, recita, ne laedas, claude, repone.']
> (Part of a colophon commonly used by Reginbert, abbot of Reichenau.)

Both in Drogin, *Anathema*, p. 22.
[21] 'Sed adhibita consideratione diligenti, alii in domo ad opus fratrum retineantur, alii secundum providentiam abbatis, cum indemnitate domus, indigentibus commodentur,' Mansi, *Conciliorum*, as n. 18.
[22] Humphreys, *Book Provisions*, p. 16.
[23] Delisle, *Cabinet*, 2, p. 212, 215.
[24] For a summary of the issues surrounding scandal see, for example, Thomas Aquinas, *Summa theologica*, II, ii, q. 43, (Rome, 1895), 8, pp. 322-30.

For Augustine says that whenever we can do so without sin we should avoid scandal, because we ought to love the soul of our neighbour infinitely more than temporal things. Therefore, if anyone is scandalised because I claim back what I am owed, or because I do not give him my book . . . which he asked for, then since I could do this without sin I scandalise my neighbour and sin mortally.[25]

Later he adds some further rules making the lender's position somewhat easier, but as far as books go he is fairly clear. Listen, however, to William of Auxerre, writing at much the same time:

Am I held to give my book to another if I see that he will be scandalised unless I do? It seems so, as I am held to give my bodily life for another's soul. Again, if I see my neighbour dying, I am held to give whatever I can to stop him. But spiritual death is infinitely worse than corporal death. Therefore, I must give my book if I see he will spiritually die without it – and to be 'scandalised' is to die spiritually.[26]

*Solutio*: If the man asks to borrow your book with no good reason then there are two grounds for refusing: 'to reprimand the temerity of his asking' and for the public good, for it is to the public good that dominion over things is not transferred without good reason. If a man asks reasonably, you must consider your relative positions. If you both have an equally good claim then you, as owner, may refuse, 'to reprimand the temerity of his asking' and 'on account of the order of charity' (*propter ordinem caritatis*) since you ought to love yourself before you love your neighbour. If both you and he have good reason for wanting the book, but yours, as owner, is better, then you should refuse: 'to reprimand his temerity in asking' and 'for the public good', since everything should be used to its best advantage. If the claimant has better reasons, but you as owner propose to give the book to a third party in even greater need, then you should refuse, 'to reprimand his temerity . . . etc.' If the claimant has better reasons but the owner believes that a third party with greater need will soon appear then he should refuse, 'to reprimand . . . .' Finally, if the claimant has the better case and there is no one either now or in the future who seems to have a better claim, then the claimant should be given the book. A far cry from Langton's blanket prescription.

Alexander of Hales has no question on lending books but he does ask whether in time of famine a theologian-preacher should immediately sell his many books on theology to feed the hungry. It seems so – *sed contra*: corporal almsgiving is good, but spiritual almsgiving is better. At this point I was – and I trust my readers are also – all cynicism; but we do Alexander a disservice. You don't need books to preach, he says, and if *you* do, you should seriously ask

[25] *Summa confessorum* ed. F. Broomfield (Analecta Mediaevalia Namurcensia, 25; Louvain/Paris, 1968), art. 7, d. 13, q. iiia, pp. 568-69.
[26] *Summa aurea* ed. J. Ribaillier (Spicilegium Bonaventurianum XVIIIB; Grottaferrata (Rome)/C.N.R.S. (Paris), 1986, bk. iii, t. ii, tr. lii, c. v, pp. 1028ff, Cf. On giving alms bk. 3, t. 7 (clxiii) and on selling knowledge bk. 3, 6. 21 (ccxxixv).

yourself if your people will suffer very much if you cease to preach for a while until you can afford new ones. However, if you really think the laity will be damned without your sermons, you can keep your texts, but on account of zeal for their souls, not cupidity of books.[27]

Sadly, Alexander is an oasis in the desert. The Dominican Roland of Cremona, who, like Alexander, was his Order's first Paris master, presents a different picture. He devotes an entire question in his *summa* to whether or not you must lend your Bible (he is specific) lest the petitioner be scandalised.[28]

At first it seems so, since you must love your neighbour – and, in particular, his soul – more than your own body. But if we follow this reasoning, says Roland, anyone can ask anything of me, even my life and, if he will be scandalised if I do not do it, then I am enjoined to give it. 'Who will be saved', he asks, 'if this is so?' And what of the masters who ask about the fellow who requests, reasonably enough, to borrow my book, but is *not* scandalised if I refuse? Does he not have a claim? Other masters say that, if his request is *un*reasonable then I do not have to lend the book: 'to reprimand his temerity in asking' and 'for the public good'. Readers will remember where we heard that line of argument before.

It seems to Roland that if anyone is scandalised because I do not give him my Bible, it is not *I* who have scandalised him but *his* malice, already in him, coming out because I did not give him the book. The consequences would be infinitely worse if I were obliged to give to whoever asked me.

The question proceeds following William of Auxerre's reasoning, but Roland takes it several steps further. If my Bible is necessary to me but more necessary to a petitioner, I do not have to lend it, since the order of charity (so-called) says that I should love myself more than I love him. It seems to me, he says, that I am not obliged to give my Bible to him at all simply on account of his being scandalised. 'Nor can I think of any case in which I am obliged to give, except by reason of its superfluity to me and because I believe that I will not, in the present or the future, be able to give it to someone who will use it for the honour of God and the profit of the church.' But the situation is not all bleak: 'And, apart from these conditions, since God orders it, I am obliged to give my Bible.' One wonders what conditions could possibly be left.

As far as scandal is concerned, if we do not intend to scandalise anyone, then we do not – it is up to them if they take offence. After this, Roland, no doubt for the sake of comprehensiveness, says that if we see someone spiritually dying and do not give all that we have to save him then we kill him, although not, of course, because he is scandalised – this is his own fault.

Of the opinions we have examined so far, three seem to stand out in their

---

[27] *Summa theologiae* (Quaracchi, 1930), 3, *De avaricia* inq. iii, tr. iv, S. ii, Quaest. i, Tit. v, c.x.iv (no. 584), p. 572.

[28] *Summae magistri Rolandi Cremonensis, O.P.*, ed. A. Cortesi (Bergamo, 1962), cap. cdxl, pp. 1301-4.

generosity: Thomas Chobham, Robert de Courson and Stephen Langton. Aside from their association with the university of Paris, the obvious thing that they have in common is the man we think was their teacher – Peter the Chanter. From the work by John Baldwin on the Chanter and his circle at Paris,[29] we know that Peter and his pupils were particularly interested in how the interpretation of the Bible affected the more everyday questions of medieval life. Grabmann called them the 'biblical moral school'. Few subjects could be more everyday than lending books; after all, we have amongst books of sample letters for students forms for writing to someone who has borrowed your book and not returned it.[30]

So it was disappointing to find no explicit trace of lending books discussed in the Chanter's own *Summa*. But I did find something else. In a section on doing justice to your neighbour, Peter raises a series of questions on 'How many ways we leave our neighbour wretched'.[31] The first way is by neglecting to carry out the works of corporal mercy – feeding the hungry, clothing the naked, visiting the sick and so forth. The second way is by leaving our neighbour in spiritual misery:

> For if I do not restore him to eating the bread of the word of God, as I am able, but abandon him to wretchedness, I know that I am not immune from sin. For every single one of us who is able to ought to give: to the ignorant and less knowledgeable the word of doctrine and learning; to the slack of word of revivification and excitement; to those who do good the word of exhortation if they need it; and to those who wander from the path the word of correction and refutation.[32]

Surely this eloquent exhortation would encompass lending one's book. In support, here is the Chanter's exposition of a slightly different topic, from further on in the *Summa*:

> Similarly, in the case where your brother is in need and seeks a loan from you, but you do not wish to give it to him although you are able to give him a loan from your money; but instead you hang on and he is compelled, out of necessity, to sell his inheritance to you. Should you not, if he is subsequently forced to break up his inheritance into pieces and sell it to you or others, be obliged to restore to him what he has lost because you would not show him the kindness you should have?[33]

The answer is yes; and the opinion is important to Peter. Shortly after he asks the question again: 'We repeat it', he says, 'so that we can add something'. What he adds is an even stronger statement on restitution than the first: you

---

[29] J. Baldwin, *Masters, Princes, and Merchants: The Social Views of Peter the Chanter and his Circle* (Princeton, 1970), 2 vols.

[30] See, e.g., C.H. Haskins, *Studies in Mediaeval Culture* (Oxford, 1929), p. 31.

[31] *Summa de sacramentis et animae consiliis*, ed. J.-A. Dugauquier (Analecta Mediaevalia Namurcensia, 7; Louvain/Lille, 1957), sections 127-28, pp. 258-68.

[32] *Summa*, s. 127, p. 259.

[33] Ibid., s. 128, p. 262.

are bound to make reparation even to a third party who has been harmed by your initial refusal to grant the loan.

Couple these unequivocal opinions on lending with the earlier reference to spiritual sustenance and I believe we can be confident of what Peter the Chanter's position on lending books would be, and of what his pupils might have learned from him. Certainly they clarify Robert de Courson's statement in the decrees of the synod of Paris. Robert, rather oddly, refers to loans as one of the chief works of mercy. In the light of the passage from his master, this tradition is somewhat clearer.

Here then is a line of discussion from Peter the Chanter and some of his pupils. Ought there not to be another, more obvious, line of interest very much on the lenient side of lending and opposed to owning? When the two great mendicant orders set themselves up in the theology faculty at the university of Paris (which they both did soon after their inceptions), they came in for a great deal of criticism from both inside and outside their Orders over their use and apparent ownership of possessions, which of course both – and the Franciscans especially – had vowed not to have. Amongst the most noted of these possessions were books. Richard de Bury again tells us he made sure that he kept on the right side of mendicants, so that he would have an entrée into their libraries:

> But whenever it happened that we turned aside to the cities and places where the mendicants we have mentioned had their convents, we did not disdain to visit their libraries and any other repositories of books; nay there we found heaped up amid the utmost poverty the utmost riches of wisdom . . . . And to pay due regard to truth . . . although they lately at the eleventh hour have entered the lord's vineyard . . . they have added more in this brief hour to the stock of sacred books than all the other vine dressers . . . . [34]

Moreover, Richard de Bury was especially full of praise for Dominicans as lenders:

> yet we must laud the Preachers with special praise, in that we have found them above all the religious most freely communicative of their stores without jealousy, and proved them to be imbued with an almost divine liberality, not greedy but fitting possessors of luminous wisdom. [35]

Things may have changed by the mid fourteenth century, or perhaps one side is buttering up the other here – whether Richard or the Dominicans is hard to say. Yet the friars were very cautious indeed in their own provisions for books brought into convents and provinces by novices or through gift, for the lending of books between houses and for books willed away at a friar's death. The rules are detailed, covering such cases as what happens to the books of a friar from

---

[34] *Philobiblon*, c. 8, p. 91-93.
[35] Ibid., c. 8, p. 93.

one province who died whilst in another. The rights of his home province are guarded jealously.[36]

Give these beginnings, we might have expected to find some juicy references to owning and lending books among mendicant theologians. Although various regulation and provincial statutes treat of books with some concern, there are fewer references to lending as such, as a theological question, in academic treatises (although in some cases they would have been written by the same people). We have seen Roland of Cremona's solution, hedged around with all manner of qualifications. Alexander of Hales' was a view much closer to the ideal of apostolic poverty, but Alexander became a Franciscan only late in life and he may not himself have written the opinion on selling books we have read.[37] I cannot claim to have made an exhaustive search, since the availability of material varies, but so far I have found no other mention of books until we reach Bonaventure.

Bonaventure became minister-general of the Franciscans just at the time when the debate over apostolic poverty had reached its height. In the Narbonne constitutions, which were formulated for the Franciscans in 1260, Bonaventure writes under the heading, 'The Observation of Poverty':

> Again, no deposit [gift] shall be retained in the brothers' house in gold or silver, gems, *or any other precious thing*, with the sole exception of books . . . . [38]

And further on:

> We firmly prohibit taking out a loan or debt for the construction, moving, or expansion of buildings, *or even* for writing or emending books.[39]

That this is expressly forbidden is particularly suggestive: the brothers seen to be taking the pursuit of knowledge rather too seriously. Friars rarely copied books for themselves, generally buying them or being given them as gifts, *ad usum* of course; and, as we have noted, each province guarded its own collection with care. In a question whose authorship is uncertain – although it has been attributed to Bonaventure or a close companion – comes the answer to why friars are so slow to lend out their books: one really cannot be blamed for being unwilling to lend books, the writer says, since:

> he who is quickest to ask is slowest to return; and having been asked repeatedly gives

---

[36] See Humphreys, n. 5 above.

[37] Alexander worked on the *Summa* with a team of Franciscan theologians. He died in 1245 when it was incomplete. It was finished by William of Meliton and others. Although Alexander may not himself have written the question on selling one's books, we can say that it came from the circle of Franciscan scholars under his direction and tutelage.

[38] *Constitutiones Narbonenses*, rubr. 3 'De observantia paupertatis' in *Opera omnia* (Quaracchi, 1898), 8, p. 452, my italics.

[39] Ibid.

it back with much murmuring and ingratitude in return for kindness shown. Often the book has been written in or torn; or it will be lent to someone else without your permission, who lends it again, and this fourth person does not know who you are or how to return it to you. Or this person may move too far away to return it. It cannot be entrusted to a messenger or he fears it will be destroyed on the journey. Or else the person who is supposed to return it wants to read it himself or lends it to another, and *he* ends up by denying he ever had it. Sometimes the book is bound in a volume with other works and the thing is pulled apart to get at the section the borrower wants. Or if you agree to lend the the book to one person, others will be angry that you did not lent it to them too, so you are compelled to wait a long time until they all see it; or finally, having passed through many hands, it comes back dirty or destroyed altogether.[40]

We must admit that this is a familiar and convincing summary of reasons not to lend books, but it certainly contrasts with Francis himself who, so the story goes, one day found a Gospel and distributed the pages among his brothers so they might all enjoy it at once. It is interesting, too, that this opinion comes in a Determined Question, giving a magisterial view of a topical problem. Appearing to answer a keenly contested debate, the author specifies that these reasons for refusing to lend books are *irreprehensibiles*, and friars who do not lend in such circumstances cannot be judged to lack charity to their neighbour. And with this we return to scandal. For by scandalizing our neighbour we cause him spiritual degradation, and if charity obliges us to assist our neighbour temporally our obligations to his spiritual well-being are much more strong. By not lending books, we sin against charity to our neighbour, and are brought back to Stephen's Langton's placement of book lending amongst the Ten Commandments, whose precepts deal with love for God and for neighbour.

Yet, though we appear to have come full circle, we are surely distant from Langton's blanket pronouncement, which laid down no such conditions on charity. What, apart from the scarcity of human generosity, might this little issue of book lending tell us?

The evidence falls into two phases, before and after the entry of the mendicants into teaching positions in the university of Paris. The lack of secular discussions after this event may well be more a question of availability of material than a real distinction – the mendicant take-over of theology being swift and comprehensive. I must admit that questions on book-lending have been hard to find, and editions of mendicant authors are more available than those of seculars. That said, however, among the mendicants lending books seems to be more an issue for Franciscans than for Dominicans and this clearly must be because 'The question of ownership of books played an important part

---

[40] *Determinationes Quaestionum*, pt. 2, qu. 21 in *Opera omnia* (Quaracchi, 1898), 8, p. 372.

in disputes over the vow of property'.[41] Although both orders of friars were vowed to poverty, for the Dominicans this was secondary to their commitment to preaching the Gospel. They could argue that possession and use of books was a necessary part of their vocation; but the Franciscans made their first vow to poverty – Francis' withdrawal from the world embraced Lady Poverty as an end in herself. Their enemies deplored this Franciscan position as an affectation, an attempt to inhabit the holier-than-thou high ground. They seized on the Franciscans' buildings and goods – and the transformation of the Order and its splitting into two parts, conventual and spiritual Franciscans, occurred very soon after Francis' death, as the band of brothers minor became a major international organisation – as a weak point in their castle of moral superiority. The Franciscans felt the issue keenly, for the question provoked an internal struggle as well as an external fight. Christ notes that 'The order's leadership sought to disarm charges from the spiritualist faction that the cloisters owned too many books . . . .'[42] Even so, the question was not so straightforward, and the Franciscan positions we have looked at here were for internal consumption and argument, rather than necessarily being directed at the outside world. The roots of bibliophilia grow deep and strong. Even Peter Olivi, embroiled in the *usus pauper* controversy of the 1280s, speaks of goods with a special spiritual usefulness, which might lie outside the normal prohibitions: 'In a moment of self-disclosure Olivi notes that books are of spiritual benefit and are needed in quantity if we are to investigate the many things to be known. Thus excess is harder to judge in this area than in others unless it is a question of multiple copies or ornamentation serving vanity rather then spiritual advancement'[43]. That the issue continues to puzzle interpreters is clear from a comment made by Burr in discussing the Determined Question on the need for large buildings in order to protect goods for Franciscan use: 'These are, of course, rationalizations, but the total argument is quite consistent'. How, then, to distinguish between 'rationalization' and 'truth'? When we read in the Franciscan *Speculum disciplinae ad novitios* (possibly by Bonaventure, possibly by his secretary Bernard of Besse) a chapter on the cleanliness and circumspection needed for the care of goods 'chiefly books', for 'Indignus est libro, qui negligit custodire',[44] are we able to judge rationalisation from good sense and sensible housekeeping? And yet the avidity of Franciscans for books was such that, by the 1280s men making their wills to dispose of their property before entering

---

[41] K. Christ, *Handbook*, p. 257. The question of the possession and use of goods by the friars minor was settled at least temporarily by the bull *Quo elongati*, published by Gregory IX in 1230 (and rescripted 1245, 1279, 1288). It is suggestive that we have discussion of book lending up to around that time, and then a lull until the *usus pauper* debates.

[42] Christ, *Handbook*, p. 257.

[43] D. Burr, *Olivi and Franciscan Poverty: The Origins of the Usus Pauper Controversy* (Philadelphia, 1989), p. 69. Burr is summarising question 9 of Olivi's treatise on *Usus pauper*.

[44] *Speculum disciplinae ad novitios* in Bonaventure's *Opera omnia* (Quaracchi, 1898), 8, part 2, c. 4, p. 619: *De rerum custodia*.

the Order willed themselves money in order to buy books – and the sums were substantial.[45]

For Franciscans, then, there are clear reasons for their interest in the question of book acquisition and lending. For Dominicans, this side of life was rather easier. Although the issue is important enough to be mentioned in various statutes and regulations, there is not the same urgency of tone.[46] Their right to use books in pursuit of their primary aim, preaching, was much clearer to them. Never were they faced with persecution over poverty in the same way; so for the Preachers the anxiety was internal: keeping books in their appointed place and in good order; acquiring more books at least cost in time and effort (Dominicans were less likely to copy books themselves than Franciscans); and not losing valuable tools to other provinces. It is indicative that, as far as I can tell, Thomas Aquinas has no discussions of book lending and acquisition, in contrast to his contemporary, Bonaventure.

With the secular authors before the mendicant admission to university chairs, however, the issue is different. Those scholars whose opinions I have been able to determine seem to be associated with Peter the Chanter. The question of ownership and possession is not central to them. Rather, the problem must be part of the possibility of selling knowledge – of turning the gifts of God into commodities in the market place – that were important to Peter and his circle. If it was illicit for usurers to charge for money-lending because they were receiving payment solely for *time*, which belongs only to God, could it be allowed to teachers to ask a fee for sharing their understanding of the created world? Was it not also one of God's gifts to be shared freely with any who asked? The commandment to love one's neighbour and to prevent him from suffering spiritual harm seems to order gratuitous instruction, but how then could unbeneficed teachers live? John Baldwin retails the arguments of four of the theologians who discussed lending: Peter the Chanter, Thomas Chobham, Robert Courson, and Stephen Langton.[47] In all cases there were two pertinent questions: Did the teachers have another source of income, such as a benefice, and what subject did they teach? It was agreed that theology teachers were in a more sensitive position than teachers of mechanical skills and arts. (We should note that, of our examples, the only writer who specifies what kind of books are under discussion is Roland of Cremona, who speaks of lending one's *biblia*. For the others we must imagine that books useful for spiritual instruction and preaching are intended; and indeed to a Paris theologian of the day, a glossed Bible would be as close to authoritative as the simple text.) Among the Chanter's circle it was assumed that a teacher of theology would be beneficed. But what of those who were not so lucky?

---

[45] Burr, *Olivi*, pp. 11-12. Burr quotes figures which are ten or more times that needed to live meagrely for a year.

[46] See n. 11.

[47] J. Baldwin, *Masters*, 1, pp. 124-28.

> If a master of arts could collect fees, asked Stephen Langton, why not also the doctor
> of theology? . . . he concluded that a theologian should not because of the dignity of
> his subject (*propter privilegium operis*), but if he was without prebend he might
> accept contributions from his students provided that he made no contract for the
> amount. Robert of Courson concurred with his countryman . . . although a
> theologian could not contractually sell the science of God, he was permitted to
> accept sufficient temporal sustenance to carry on his spiritual activities . . . . [48]

Baldwin characterises Robert Courson as most comprehensive and Langton as
attacking the question 'on a theoretical level',[49] remarks certainly reminiscent
of their attitude towards lending books: Courson's careful statutes and Langton's sweeping and unsupported general statement.

As we have seen, the questions on lending books tend to appear in wider
discussions on treatment of one's neighbour and on scandal, how one's own
behaviour might affect the immortal soul of another person. In the extreme
case, Langton even used the forum of the Decalogue precepts about one's
neighbour as a place for the question. The relationship between scandal and
charity to one's neighbour makes it clear why Langton, not usually an
innovator, should put this opinion in his Decalogue commentary. What is
interesting here is that lending books is dealt with as an issue of behaviour, of
outward action, rather than of virtue and vice – inward acts of avarice or
generosity, greed or magnanimity. Only rarely, such as in Peter the Chanter's
note in the *Verbum abbreviatum* that the brother who wishes to become
librarian should not be allowed the job, since it will only bring out his miserly
qualities,[50] or Humbert of Romans' statement that it is reprehensible to have
too much affection for books, because you will not want to lend them out,[51] do
we hear the inner voice speak. We should remember that this more niggardly
attitude to book lending comes about during the time when books were in
greater supply. The universities – and particularly the Dominicans working in
them – had brought about streamlined book production, faster handwriting,
abbreviations, university booksellers, more accessible libraries, and so on.
Combined, this meant that books were much more readily available to scholars
and teachers. Our sources intimate a corresponding decrease in generosity: the
more they had, the more protective of it they became.

This little question brings us very close to the medieval mind. There are
times when medieval society may as well have been peopled with creatures
from outer space: the daily circumstances of medieval life are so far away from
ours, the theological questions too obscure for us to understand their moment,
the outlook too strangely credulous for us to imagine possible. But this
question of lending books leads us straight into minds that function just like

---

[48] Ibid., i, p. 127.

[49] Ibid., i, p. 124.

[50] *Verbum abbreviatum*, c. 153: *De proprietate monachorum*, PL 205: 368.

[51] *Expositio in regulae B. Augustini*, c. 4, in *Opera de vita Regulari*, ed. J. Berthier (Rome,
1888), 1, pp. 449-50.

our own. We cannot say there was a single medieval attitude towards lending books. Even when they are posing the question in the same words, for the seculars around Peter the Chanter and for the mendicant friars the intent and meaning of the question is different. And although we may have gained a little more insight into why Langton gives his blanket order where and when he does, his opinion still stands out in its liberality. Rather, as scholars are able to have greater numbers of personal books for private use, their zeal for possession increases. The involved explanation of why out Franciscan *would* lend his book if he could is exactly the way we explain *away* our own reluctance to lend to others. It is illuminating that the commentators choose to deal with the question under the headings of scandal and poverty – outward behaviour – rather than avarice or largesse. Reflecting on inward disposition brings the issue far too close to home. Few of us remember the order of charity in the face of a borrowed – and unreturned – favourite.

# 20

# The Diffusion of the Doctrinale of Thomas Netter in the Fifteenth and Sixteenth Centuries

## Margaret Harvey

The *Doctrinale* of Thomas Netter of Walden, prior provincial of the English Carmelites, one of the most successful polemics against Wycliffite ideas in the fifteenth century, continued to be reproduced in the sixteenth because its historical approach and its arsenal of authorities came to be seen also as an answer to Protestantism.[1] The present essay is an interim report on many years of cogitation about the process by which the work was spread.[2]

Netter's vast enterprise was in three parts: Volume 1, Books I to IV, which dealt with God, the church and authority, was begun at the suggestion of Henry V, probably when Netter returned from a diplomatic mission to Poland, thus about 1421.[3] A copy of this was presented by John Kenynghale, O. Carm., to Pope Martin V, just as the pope was preparing to send Cardinal Giordano Orsini to Germany, as legate for a crusade against the Hussites, thus probably early in 1426, so that the legate took a copy with him.[4] A copy also went at the same time to Archbishop Chichele of Canterbury.[5] The second

---

[1] Margaret Gibson made much of the research for this essay possible by frequently lending me her flat. Dr. Kathleen Scott supplied some of the information on manuscripts and Dr. Ian Doyle lent me his notes on the English ones. I give fairly cursory notes here because Dr. Scott and I intend to collaborate on a more detailed study soon. Dr. David Bagchi drew my attention to John Eck and supplied most of the information on him.

[2] I have used the photo-reprint of the Venice edition of 1757, ed. B. Blanciotti, produced by Gregg in 1967. The citations are from its volume numbers, with column references.

[3] For dates of the different books and suggestions for the order of writing them: A. Hudson *The Premature Reformation: Wycliffite Texts and Lollard History* (Oxford, 1988), pp. 50-52.

[4] The pope's letter of acknowledgment to Netter was dated 1 April, 1426, printed Blanciotti, i, xviii: see M. Aston, 'William White's Lollard Followers,' in *Lollards and Reformers: Images and Literacy in Late Medieval Religion* (London, 1984), p. 76, n. 22. Orsini's appointment had already been decided by 16 January, 1426: E. König, *Kardinal Giordano Orsini* (Freiburg im Br., 1906), p. 48. He set off on 21 March, p. 49. At the same time Netter also wrote to the cardinal protector of his Order and to Father Bernard Vaqueri, proctor of the Order: B. Zimmerman, *Monumenta Historica Carmelitana* (Lerins, 1905), i, p. 445.

[5] Zimmerman, *Monumenta*, ibid., p. 445.

volume, *De sacramentis* (Book V), was still being finished then and a copy
went to the pope the following year, perhaps again delivered by Kenynghale.
The pope acknowledged it on 8 August 1427, saying that he had had it
examined and approved by Juan Cervantes, cardinal priest of St. Peter and
Bernard la Roche Fontenille, OFM., M. Th., bishop of Cavaillon, between 17
June and 23 July.[6] The first volume *De sacramentalibus* (Book VI), was sent
before Netter died in 1430.[7] These early copies are not known to exist now,
though there is no evidence to prevent one guessing that some of the existing
copies may be these. Those presented to Chichele may be the copies of
Volumes I-V which were in All Souls College in his lifetime.[8] The whole
work, now in three volumes in the Vatican Library, cannot be that sent by
Netter, since its Volume II (Book V) is dated 1431.[9]

The work was first and foremost spread in England in the fifteenth century
by the Carmelite Order. Manuscript nos. 1, 2, 3, 8, 10, 13 and probably 12 in
my Appendix are English and Carmelite. Several of the volumes of *De
sacramentis*, even to the inexpert eye, seems to have been uniformly produced,
including the frequent practice of putting a scribe's name at the end of *De
eucharistia* and illuminating the beginning of each sacrament, though, as will
be seen, in some copies the illuminations were pictures of the sacraments being
conferred, whereas in others they are floral designs. Most of the remaining
copies are expensive parchment volumes. In the one case (nos. 4 and 5), where
we know how much the books cost we can see that the outlay was considerable,
but presumably there was a market, and not just within the Order itself. No. 13
suggests that the Carmelite provincial was responsible for some of the diffusion. No. 24b, the reduction by Walter Hunt of the book to conventional
scholastic *questiones*, even suggests that, as was certainly the case in Europe in
the sixteenth century, Netter was already being used as a scholastic text book
in the midcentury.[10] This may explain why John Whethamstede, abbot of St.
Alban's, gave nos. 4 and 5 to Gloucester College, the major Benedictine house
of study in Oxford and perhaps why no. 6 seems to have a connection with
Wymondham, a daughter house of St. Alban's. In mid fifteenth century
Oxford Thomas Gascoigne certainly knew the *Doctrinale* (he left notes in

[6] The letter acknowledging it is dated 8 August, 1427, Blanciotti, i, pp. vxiii-xix; Aston, p. 76, n. 22. The pope explained that he entrusted the examination to the two named prelates, for whom see C. Eubel, *Hierarchia catholica medii aevi* (Münster, 1913), i, pp. 45, 179. For Bernard see also H. Müller, *Die Franzosen, Frankreich und das Basler Konzil*, 2 vols. (Paderborn, 1990), i, p. 435.

[7] *BRUO*, ii, pp. 1343-44.

[8] N.R. Ker, *Records of All Souls College Library, 1437-1600* (Oxford, 1971), p. 6, nos. 69 and 70.

[9] Appendix, no. 15.

[10] On Hunt, M. Harvey, 'Harley Manuscript 3049 and Two *Questiones* of Walter Hunt, O.Carm.', *Transactions of the Architectural and Archaeological Society of Durham and Northumberland*, new series, 6 (1982), pp. 45-47. In n. 29 the whereabouts of the second volume, no. 5 in the appendix below, is wrongly given.

no. 1) and was also aware of a certain amount about Netter's life.[11] In England the book continued to be valued as a weapon against heresy at the end of the century, as Bishop Russell's paraphrase shows, (no. 24a) and the early reformers knew and used it, as witness Cranmer's ownership and use of nos. 6 and 7.

In the early sixteenth century, when Leland examined libraries, the Oxford and London Carmelites both had Netter, Oxford in two volumes and London *in tribus maximis voluminibus*.[12] St. Paul's, London also contained it.[13] Whether any of these are among those now extant it is impossible to know. Dr. Ker found evidence among pastedowns of at least two Netters from the fifteenth century.[14]

On the continent the work must have become known both because Netter sent it to the pope and because it was used at the council of Basel. The Cracow volumes, (nos. 20 and 21), completed in Basel in 1434, are only one testimony to its diffusion. We know that through these particular volumes Wyclif's ideas, as well as Netter's, became known in Poland.[15] At the council Cardinal Cesarini had a copy which he lent to Procop, one of the leading Hussites, who in turn lent it to Peter Payne, the ex-Oxford scholar turned Hussite.[16] *Doctrinale* was therefore used by Rockycana, another Hussite, in various replies,[17] and by John de Ragusio, against Rockycana on communion under both kinds, and in his *De ecclesia*.[18] Henry Kaltenstein, on the side of orthodoxy, quoted Netter frequently in the same debates when discussing preaching.[19]

The publicity from Basel and the knowledge of the work sent to the pope is sufficient to explain why Cardinal Piero Donato had a copy in his library,

[11] Oxford, Lincoln College, MS Lat. 117, pp. 23, 24, 161, 168; MS Lat. 118, p. 372, including something on his life. Notes in Gascoigne's hand in Lincoln, MS Lat. 106 (no. 1 in appendix) fos. 307, 307 v, 315, with his characteristic *Jesus Maria*, and fo. 359 v some notes on Netter's life.

[12] J. Leland, *De rebus Britannicis collectanea*, ed. T. Hearne, 6 vols. (Oxford, 1715), iv, pp. 53, 59. K.W. Humphreys, *Corpus of British Medieval Libraries: The Friar's Libraries* (London, 1990), pp. 182, no. 32, 192, no. 13.

[13] Leland, *Collectanea*, iv, p. 48.

[14] N.R. Ker, *Fragments of Medieval Manuscripts used as Pastedowns in Oxford Bindings, c. 1515-1620* Oxford Bibliographical Society Publications, new series, 5 (Oxford, 1954), nos. 605 and 1591.

[15] See notes at appendix nos. 20 and 21 for diffusion.

[16] E.F. Jacob, 'The Bohemians at the Council of Basel', *Prague Essays*, ed. R.W. Seton-Watson (Oxford, 1949), pp. 81-123, esp. p. 92; *Monumenta conciliorum seculi decimi quinti, concilium Basiliense scriptorum* i (Vienna, 1858), p. 307.

[17] *Monumenta conciliorum*, i, pp. 327, 344. See also W. Krämer, *Konsens und Rezeption: Verfassungsprinzipien der Kirche im Basler Konziliarismus*, Beiträge zur Geschichte der Philosophie und Theologie des Mittelalters, new series 19 (Münster, 1980), p. 121.

[18] On both kinds *Monumenta conciliorum*, i, pp. 327, 344; *De ecclesia*: *Magistri Johannis Stojkovic de Ragusio O.P. Tractatus de ecclesia*, ed. F. Šanjek, A. Krchňák, M. Biškup, Croatia Christiana, Fontes, i (Zagreb, 1983), pp. 298, 310.

[19] See for instance Vatican Library, MS Vat. lat. 5609, fo. 132 r-v, 153 v. The MS was made at Basel in 1434, and belonged to cardinal Juan de Torquemada, see fos. 213 v, 182 v.

according to the inventory made between 1439 and 1445,[20] as did Cardinal Domenico Capranica, who died in 1458, according to the 1468 inventory of his books.[21] So the work was known in Italy very early.

This may explain why there was a manuscript copy of the whole *Doctrinale*, in three volumes, in the Carmelite convent of St. Paul in Ferrara. These, together with the Vatican volumes (nos. 14, 15, and 16), were used by Blanciotti for his edition of 1759, which is the best to date.[22] The volumes were in the Ferrara convent already in 1561, when the Carmelite general, Antonio Ricci, wanted them searched for there during the council of Trent, for use against Protestant arguments; the work may have been in the library since the fifteenth century.[23] The Ferrara library was famous, built up by G.M. Varrati, a notable anti-Protestant, who died in 1563, but begun by Battista Panetti, who died in 1497.[24] The Netter volumes are not known to exist now.

The work of Netter was also known very early in the Netherlands, as can be seen from the favourable remarks quoted in the chronicle of Gilles de Roye, O.Cist. written at Dunes in Flanders from 1459. He was a former professor of theology in the college de St. Bernard in Paris and had been abbot of Royaumont in 1453. The chronicle mentions a Dominican, Nicholas Jaquier, who used *Doctrinale* in his writing against the use of the chalice for the laity and said that to purchase Netter's work one should sell precious vessels. No library should be without it.[25] This sort of opinion probably explains the existence of nos. 17, 18, 19 and 23.

*Doctrinale* therefore was known in the early Reformation period, in England and elsewhere, as a useful weapon against heretics. No. 5, given to Merton by a conservative in 1558 and no. 23, given to Trinity Hall in 1551 by Robert Hare who was prominently a recusant, are witness to this trend. As will

---

[20] P. Sambin, 'La Biblioteca di Pietro Donato (1380-1447)', *Bolletino del Museo Civico di Padova*, 48 (1959), pp. 53-98, esp. pp. 72, 87 n. 120.

[21] A.V. Antonovics, 'The Library of Cardinal Domenico Capranica', *Cultural Aspects of the Italian Renaissance: Essays in Honour of Paul Oskar Kristeller*, ed. C.H. Clough (Manchester, 1976), pp. 141-59, esp. p. 142 and n. 41, where the author cannot identify Thomas (Naldi) the Carmelite who presented a work to Martin V, here vol. 68.

[22] *Doctrinale*, i, p. x. For the volume *Tesori delle biblioteche d'Italia: Emilia e Romagna*, ed. D. Fava (Milan, 1932), p. 46; F.A. Zaccaria, *Iter litterarum per Italiam* (Venice, 1762), Part i, chap. 10, p. 160: *Thomae Waldensis Carmelitae Doctrina fidei seu ecclesiae contra Wiclephistas et Hussitas. Tomis tribus, f. comprehensa.* I thank Professor A.C. de la Mare for this reference.

[23] H. Jedin, *Geschichte des Konzils von Trient*, 4 vols. (Freiburg, 1949-75), iv, p. 313. Blanciotti, i, p. xi, says that an inscription in the volumes said that they were for the use of a learned Carmelite who died in 1466.

[24] A. Bargellesi-Severi, 'Due Carmelitani a Ferrara nel Rinascimento', *Carmelus*, 8 (Rome, 1961), pp. 63-131, esp. p. 103.

[25] *Chroniques relatives à l'histoire de la Belgique sous la domination des ducs de Bourgogne*, ed. K. de Lettenhove, 3 vols. (Brussels, 1870), i, pp. 209-10, with notes on the author, pp. vi-vii. For Jaquier see T. Kaeppeli, *Scriptores ordinis praedicatorum medii aevi*, 3 vols. (Rome, 1970, 1975, 1980), iii, pp. 172-75. He wrote a Dialogue on Communion in 1466 (p. 175). He was an inquisitor in France and Flanders and died in Ghent in 1472.

be seen below, the most probable reason for its popularity was its historical method, which was a useful counter-measure to that of the early reformers who constantly tried, as Wyclif had done, to show that doctrines and practices of the current church had no foundation in early history. Netter had collected a formidable weight of authorities to disprove this. The perceived usefulness of Netter's approach easily explains the earliest printed editions, which were produced in Paris by Josse Badius, with prefaces which give their genesis.

The first printed by Badius was Book V, *De sacramentis*, published in Paris on 13 October, 1521, dedicated to Sigismund Gonzaga, cardinal protector of the Carmelites, by Louis de Lira, prior of the Paris Carmel. The dedication states that faced with the threat of heresy Lira and Father John Hotte, O.Carm, a professor of theology, searched their library and found two Netter manuscripts, *De sacramentis* and *De sacramentalibus*, and decided to publish *De Sacramentis* first.[26] Almost certainly therefore they were using no. 18. The second volume, *De sacramentalibus*, doubtless based on no. 19, appeared in 1523, with a dedicatory epistle from John Roch *Carmeli Meldunen' Prior*, that is prior of the Carmel at Melun, (not Meaux, though that is what the Latin suggests), to Stephen Poncher, archbishop of Sens, dated Melun, 25 December, 1523.[27] It had an *imprimatur* from the Sorbonne, dated 13 December, and a title specifically aiming it against the Lutherans. It was printed by Badius, for Francois Regnault, a bookseller with English connections, who paid for it.[28] Finally Badius published books I-IV, with a letter of dedication to Pope Clement VII, dated 5 September 1532, explaining that the general of the Carmelites, Nicholas Audet, when in Paris the year before, had told him that the Carmelites house in Ghent had a copy of the first part of Netter's work, and had arranged to have the manuscript sent to Paris, with permission of the prior of Ghent, Baldwin Brocard. Badius himself was a native of Ghent. It is possible, therefore that the manuscript was no. 23, although I cannot prove it.

The background to the printing is thus clear. The Carmelite house in Paris was also the general house of study in the Order.[29] Under Louis de Lira from

---

[26] P. Renouard, *Bibliographie des impressions et des oeuvres de Josse Badius Ascensius*, 3 vols. (Paris, 1908), iii, pp. 387-88; Extant copies listed idem, *Inventaire chronologique des éditions Parisiennes du XVIe siècle*, iii, *1521-30* (Paris, 1985), no 187; Idem, *Imprimeurs et libraries Parisiens du XVIe siècle*, II, nos. 491, 526, 696. For Hotte: L van Wijmen, 'Carmelite Licenciates at the University of Paris (1373-1788)', *Carmelus*, 19 (1972), pp. 134-75, esp. p. 146. He graduated in Paris in 1520.

[27] Renouard, *Badius*, iii, p. 388; list of copies: *Inventaire*, no. 558. For Roch: van Wijem, 'Carmelite Licenciates', p. 146. He graduated in 1522.

[28] Renouard, *Badius*, iii, pp. 389-90. There should have been an *imprimatur* for the first volume: F.M. Higman, *Censorship and the Sorbonne: A Bibliographical Study of Books in French Censured by the Faculty of Theology of Paris, 1520-1551*, Travaux d'Humanisme et Renaissance, 222 (Geneva, 1979), p. 23.

[29] L. Van Wijmen, *La congrégation d'Albi, 1499-1602*, Textus et Studia Historica Carmelitana, 11 (Rome, 1971), pp. 37-39.

Hainault it was reformed and, not without considerable friction, joined the strict Congregation of Albi in 1519.[30] The publication of work against heretics was seen by these early reformers as part of their task of improving the level of the church. Hotte and Roch both joined the Albi Congregation and Roch became prior of Melun which had been a very early addition to it.[31] Poncher, formerly bishop of Paris, had much to do with attempts to reform religious houses and combat heresy.[32] Nicholas Audet, who helped Badius with the last volume, was the main reformer of the French Carmelites as a whole and favoured the Congregation of Albi. He was in Paris for their chapter in early 1531.[33]

The effect can be instantly observed. When Jean Clichetove, who knew the Carmelites well and sympathised with the reforming branch, published his *Anti-Lutherus* in Paris in 1524,[34] he pointed out that in the newly published *De sacramentalibus* Walden defended rites and ceremonies, and advised the reader to go and look at it.[35] In *Propugnaculum* (Paris, same publisher, 1526), he again referred to *De sacramentalibus* and to *De sacramentis*.[36]

The *Doctrinale* thus entered the mainstream of anti-Protestant polemic from this printing. John Bale used this edition,[37] and so did John Eck, the foremost Catholic disputant of the early Reformation.[38] In the introduction to the *Enchiridion* (Landshut, 1525) Eck listed Netter as the only non-contemporary work he had used; many implicit references, giving Netter's authorities, occur throughout the work.[39] In his 1526 work on the Sacrifice of the Mass he

[30] Ibid., pp. 45-47.

[31] Ibid., pp. 30-31 for Melun, not Meaux as in Renouard; pp. 81 n. 73, 88 n. 93 for Hotte and Roche. J.G. Farge, *Biographical Register of Paris Doctors of Theology, 1500-1536*, Subsidia Medievalia (Toronto, 1980), pp. 394-95.

[32] A. Renaudet, *Pré-réforme et humanisme à Paris pendant les premières guerres d'Italie (1494-1517)* (Paris, 1953), index under Poncher.

[33] Van Wijmen, *La Congrégation*, pp. 109, 110; A. Stäring, *Der Karmelitangeneral Nikolaus Audet und die Katholische Reform des XVI Jahrhunderts*, Textus und Studia Historica Carmelitana, 3 (Rome, 1959), p. 112.

[34] For the edition, Renouard, *Inventaire*, iii, no. 635 and idem, *Bibliographie des éditions de Simon de Colines, 1520-46* (Paris, 1894), p. 62.

[35] *Anti-Lutherus* (Simon de Colines, Paris, 1524), fos. 3, 53 v.

[36] *Propugnaculum* (Simon de Colines, Paris, 1526), fos. 13.5, 15.5, 70.11. For Clichetove, J.-P. Massaut, *Critique et tradition à la veille de la Réform en France*, Collection de Pétrarque à Déscartes, 31 (Paris, 1974), p. 87, n. 19; idem, *Josse Clichetove, l'humanisme et la réforme du clergé*, 2 vols, Bibliothèque de la Faculté de Philosophie et Lettres de l'Université de Liège, 183 (Paris, 1968), i, pp. 385-94. For the edition Renouard, *Inventaire*, iii, no. 959; *Bibliographie de Colines*, p. 80.

[37] A. Hudson, 'John Purvey: A Reconsideration of the Evidence', *Lollards and their Books* (London, 1985), pp. 85-110, esp. p. 96, n. 51.

[38] David Bagchi supplied much information on Eck.

[39] *Johannes Ecks Enchiridion locorum communium adversus Lutherum et alios hostes ecclesiae (1525-43)*, Corpus Catholicorum, 34, ed. P. Fraenkel (Münster in Westfalen, 1979), pp. 1, 378, cited by name, and see also pp. 440-51, for borrowings.

acknowledged his use of Netter's collection of authorities.[40] In the *Confutatio confessionis Augustanae* (1530), the official Catholic reply to the Augsburg Confession, Netter's authorities were used on confession, on the worship of Saints, on communion under both kinds and on marriage of priests.[41]

This early use ensured that at the council of Trent Netter was recognised as a Catholic authority. Antonio Ricci, the Carmelite general, quoted him verbatim in 1547,[42] but so did the Jesuits Salmeron and Jay,[43] and in 1551 he was quoted on communion under both kinds.[44] A Spanish bishop also referred to him on the ceremonies of the Mass.[45]

This doubtless explains why a new printing was undertaken. In 1556 in Salamanca Johannes Maria de Terra Nova and Jacobus Archarius printed *De sacramentalibus*, dedicating it to the rector of the university.[46] They explained that they had just set up a press to accompany their existing bookshop. In 1557 they published *De sacramentis*, similarly dedicated. De Terra Nova was a Florentine, agent in Spain for the enormous Florentine/Lyons book firm of the Giunti.[47] This particular edition seems essentially a reproduction of the Paris edition, with the Sorbonne *imprimatur*, the letter to Poncher and Louis de Lira's letter in their appropriate volumes.[48] Probably as a result copies of Netter are to be found in many Carmelite convents in later sixteenth-century Spain.[49]

The final sixteenth-century edition was produced in Venice in 1571. It was a reprint of all three volumes of the Paris edition, but with an added apparatus of references. The major part of the work seems to have been done by the Carmelite Nicholas Aurificio of Sienna, with help for the second volume by the

---

[40] E. Iserloh, *Johannes Eck (1486-1543): Scholastiker, Humanist, Kontroverstheologe*, Katholisches Leben und Kirchenreform, 41 (Münster in Westfalen, 1981), p. 56.

[41] *Die Confutatio der confessio Augustana vom 3 August 1530*, ed. H. Immenkötter, Corpus Catholicorum, 33 (Münster in Westfalen, 1979), pp. 71, 124, 133, 135, 144, 148-49, 151, 155, with other reminiscences. See also P.O. Kristeller, *Iter Italicum*, 3 vols. (London, 1963, continuing), ii, p. 338 for reference to a commentary on Netter in Vatican MS Lat. 6216. I have not yet seen this MS.

[42] *Concilium Tridentinum: diariorum, actorum, epistolarum, tractatuum nova collectio*, ed. Görres-Gesellschaft (Freiburg, 1901 seq), vi/2, pp. 370-71, 472, 473.

[43] Ibid., vi/3, pp. 159, 527.

[44] Ibid., vii, pp. 173, 175.

[45] Ibid., p. 419.

[46] I have used the volumes in the British Library: BM 3678 f 8 where vol. i is the Badius edition of 1532. I have also looked at the Durham volumes.

[47] P. Bolugas, *El libro Español* (Barcelona, 1962), p. 157; W. Pettas, *The Giunti of Florence* (San Fransciso, 1980), pp. 109, 111.

[48] The letter of Louis de Lira is printed in vol. ii and that of Roch in vol. iii.

[49] J. Smet, 'Carmelite Libraries of Spain and Portugal at the End of the Sixteenth Century', *Carmelus*, 19 (1972), pp. 251-301, esp. p. 261, Coimbra; p. 264, Moura; p. 270, Lisbon; p. 293, Seville; p. 299, Utera.

prior of the Venice Carmelite convent.[50] A life of Netter was included. The moving spirit seems to have been Giovanni Battista de Rossi (Rubeo), the general from 1564-78, with the printers.[51] Rossi was a staunch supporter of Audet at Trent. He commended the work to Pius V and to his fellow Carmelites.[52] The printers were Vincentio Valgrisi and his son-in-law Giordano Ziletti, both flourishing Venetian printers, who, however, were somewhat suspect for their relations with foreigners and heretics and may have been glad to print someone so orthodox as Netter.[53]

From then onwards Netter became an established 'authority,' so much so that Thomas Stapleton quoted him abundantly and he figures in Bellarmine's *De controversiis*.[54] In 1575 the *Doctrinale* was included in the curriculum of Carmelite students and William Allen thought that all young seminary priests intending to go from Douai to England ought to read him.[55] I wonder how many did?

## Appendix of Manuscripts

This is not intended to be a complete description of each manuscript, especially where a reliable catalogue entry exists. It is intended to give, if possible, place and date of production, name of scribe, and something about the history of the volume.

---

[50] I have used Cambridge University library E$^x$ 9 15(c). The details come from vol. i, fo. 2 r-v, Rossi's letter to Pius V and fo. 3 r-v his letter to the Carmelites, with the preface in vol. ii from Aurificío to Rossi. The life of Netter is i, fo. 4 r-v.

[51] For Rossi see *Lexikon für Theologie und Kirche*, 9, (Freiburg, 1964), col. 81, article by A. Stäring, under Rubeo.

[52] Fos. 2 r-v, 3 r-v.

[53] P.F. Grendler, *The Roman Inquisition and the Venetian Press, 1540-1605* (Princeton, NJ, 1977), pp. 166, 189-90.

[54] For Stapleton and Netter: H. Schützeichel, *Wesen und Gegenstand der kirchlichen Lehrautorität nach Thomas Stapleton: Ein Beitrag zur Geschichte der Kontroversetheologie im 16 Jahrhundert*, Triere Theologische Studien, 20 (Trier, 1966), pp. 24, 32, 66, 177, 241, 311, 341. For Bellarmine, R. Bellarmine, *De controversiis* (Paris, 1613), i, cols. 502, 599; ii, cols. 2, 238, 314, 321, 741, 834.

[55] *The First and Second Diaries of the English College, Douay*, ed. T.F. Knox (London, 1878), p. xliii, from a letter of Allen in 1578 or 1580: 'Thomas Waldensis, who has most learnedly refuted all the tenets of modern heretics in their parent Wickliff'. For the continental Carmelites: K.S. Smith, 'The Ecclesiology of Controversy: Scripture, Tradition and Church in the Theology of Thomas Netter of Walden, 1372-1430' (unpublished Ph.D. thesis, Cornell, 1983), p. 174; G. Wessels, *Acta capitulorum generalium ordinis fratrum b.v. Mariae de Monte Carmelo*, i, (Rome, 1912), p. 506. See also MS Vat lat. 1165, fo. 103, mentioned by G. di S. Teresa, *Archivum bibliographicum Carmelitanarum*, 4 (1959), p. 217, no. 97, a late sixteenth-century epigram on Netter. Also MS Vat lat. 3919, fo. 293, mentioned as an authority against Luther: *Archivum* as above, 6 (1961), p. 196, no. 141. And see also note 41 above.

1.   Oxford, Lincoln College, MS Lat. 106: Book V, *De sacramentis*.

Presented to the college by the founder Richard Fleming, who died 1431.[56]
Made by Carmelite: fo. 206 v (the end of *De eucharistia*) has *Westakyr
Carmelitus*, as the signature of the scribe, who must be Reginald Westakyr,
whom Dr. Doyle finds in Paris, B.N., MS lat. 2473. A very sumptuous copy,
with an illumination for the beginning of each sacrament, showing the sacrament being administered. Royal arms over the first initial, It was used by
Thomas Gascoigne (see fos. 307, 359 v, 307 v). Parchment.

2.   Oxford, Merton College, MS 319: Book V, *De sacramentis*.

Another fine copy, with a very similar layout. Signed in several places by John
Holt, Carmelite. At the end of *De eucharistia* (a favourite place in these
copies): 'Dextram scribentis benedicat lingua legentis. Scriptus per manum
fratris Johannis Holt, carmelite.' He signs again at the end, fo. 323 v and he has
signed corrections. The book was in Merton in 1507.[57] According to Drs.
Doyle and Scott this scribe wrote part of Trinity College, Cambridge, MS
O.9.33, signing fos. 64 and 101, with other scribes, one a Carmelite (John Eye,
Aylesford in 1451).

3.   Oxford, Magdalen College, MS 157: Book V, *De sacramentis*.

Another fine copy, now mutilated, probably by water but carefully repaired.
Begins: *Epist. ad Victorianum* (II, x, col. 29), and ends *prius committente
potestas* (col. 907, on penance). A Carmelite production. At the end of *De
eucharistia* (fo. 179 v): 'Dextram scribentis benedicat lingua legentis. Amen
dicat omnis homo. Ffreton.' Ffreton is in red, the rest black. See no. 16 below.
Each sacrament begins with a floral design. Parchment.

4.   British Library, MS Royal 8 G. X: Books I and II.

5.   Oxford, Worcester College, MS 233: Books III and IV with other
contents.

Nos. 4 and 5 were given to the monks of Gloucester College by John
Whethamstede, in his first period as abbot from 1420 to 1440, at a cost of £6 13s

[56] *BRUO*, ii, p. 698.
[57] F. M. Powicke, *The Medieval Books of Merton College* (Oxford, 1931), p. 225, no. 1140. the
pages are largely unnumbered. Holt has signed a correction at the end of chapter 12. The other
information on him comes from Drs. Scott and Doyle.

4d.[58] No. 4 has a note of the gift fo. 1 v and fo. 2 has Whethamstede's arms. It belonged to Lord Lumley.[59] No. 5 is still in the original binding, with clasps. It came after the dissolution to Robert Serles, formerly of Merton College, an opponent of Cranmer, who presented it to Merton in 1558.[60] In 1938 Merton returned it to Worcester College. Both parchment. Dr. Kathleen Scott tells me that the hand is the same in MS Royal 8 G. X fos. 21-203 and in Oxford, New College, MS 49, fos. 14-40 v, 57v-159.[61]

6.   Oxford, Bodleian Library, MS Bodley 261: Book V, *De sacramentis*.

Incomplete, ending 'sequitur aliqualiter pro omnibus' (ii, col. 915). SC 2436 dates this end quarter of the fifteenth century; probably meaning 'second.' Belonged to Cranmer, like no. 7 below and after him to Lord Lumley as nos. 4 and 7. Presented to Bodley by Lumley in 1600 with no. 7.[62] At fo. 10, just under the gathering number is a tiny note saying *Wymondham*, probably repeated fo. 156, but now cut off. Wymondham was a St Alban's cell, which became an independent monastery. Parchment.

7.   Oxford, Bodleian Library, MS Bodley 262: Book VI, *De sacramentalibus*.

SC 2437 dates this second quarter of the fifteenth century. Incomplete, ending fo. 263 v 'Esto ergo eciam bellando pacificus' (iii, col. 1006). Fo. 264 has extracts from ii, cols 36, 37. Fo, 265, from *De sacramentis*, ii, cols. 60-64. The volume has notes by Cranmer. Dr. Scott does not consider the hands of nos. 6 and 7 the same. Parchment.

8.   Oxford, Magdalen College, MS 153: Books I-IV.

A fine volume, with illuminated capitals, produced by the Carmelites. fo. 319 v has: 'scriptus per manum fratris Ricardi Wetyng eiusdem ordinis professi,'

---

[58] For Whethamstede see M. Harvey, 'John Whethamstede, the Pope and the General Council', *The Church in Pre-Reformation Society: Essays in Honour of F.R.H. du Boulay*, ed. C.M. Barron and C. Harper-Bill (Exeter, 1985), pp. 108-122. A.G. Watson, *Catalogue of Dated and Datable Manuscripts 435-1600 in Oxford Libraries*, 2 vols. (Oxford, 1984), p. 148, no. 881. The scribe of fos. 14-40 v and 57 v-150 also wrote New College, Oxford, MS 49. Initials here and in MS Bodleian Auct. F. inf. I. 1 are in the same hand. For the cost: *Annales monasterii S. Albani a J. Amundesham*, 2 vols. ed. H.T. Riley, Rolls Series 28 (London, 1871), ii, p. 269.
[59] *The Library of John Lord Lumley: The Catalogue of 1609*, ed. S. Jayne and F.R. Johnson (London, 1956), p. 116.
[60] Powicke, *Medieval Books*, no. 1201 and p. 231. For Serles: A.B. Emden, *Biographical Register of the University of Oxford, 1501-1540* (Oxford, 1974), pp. 510-11. He gave evidence against Cranmer in 1555.
[61] According to a typed note in the volume. See N.R. Ker, *Medieval Manuscripts in British Libraries*, 3 vols. (Oxford, 1969-83), iii, pp. 732-33.
[62] As note 59 above.

after the name of the author. Given to the college in 1614 by Bartholomew Jessop but formerly belonged to Bishop Alnwick of Norwich (1426-36) and Lincoln (1436-49).[63] Parchment.

9. Cambridge, University Library, MS Dd.8.16: Books I-IV.

A Carmelite production; see no. 10. This and no. 10, both parchment, were given by Mathew Parker in 1574. Dr. Doyle thinks the hand is different from no. 10.

10. Cambridge, University Library, MS Dd.8.17: Book V, *De sacramentis*.

A Carmelite production, signed at fo. 186 (the end of *De eucharistia*: 'Scriptum totum istud volumen per manum fratris Thome Rychard ordinis Marie genetricis Dei Monte Carmeli et complevit anno domini m°cccc°xxx primo. Virgo ferens natum tu Thome tolle reatum.' He repeats this at the end of confirmation fo. 220 v. and signs again at fo. 315 v, the end.[64] The illuminations for the beginning of each sacrament are not depictions of the administration, but naturalistic designs.

11. British Library, MS Sloane 168: Book V, *De Sacramentis* and other contents, originally not part of this volume.

The Netter is fos. 135-354, incomplete, ending with the words 'substanciarum materialium,' mid-chapter lxxiii (ii, col. 446). Fo. 354 v is blank. The rest of the MS with different numbers of lines per page, is medical treatises: Galianus di S. Sophia, *Simplicia pulcherrima*, fos. 1-116 v, and Petrus de Abano, *De venenis*. fos. 117-134 v.[65] The Netter is a careful production, with carefully drawn initials, in red and brown. Paper.

12. Cambridge, Corpus Christi College, MS 90: Books I-IV.

Incomplete, ending Book IV, chapter xlii, *oportet clericos specialiter*. In production very like no. 3, and therefore probably Carmelite. There is a *nota bene* in the margin at fo. 209, at Book II, chapter 72, next to a mention of Carmelites. Parchment.

---

[63] J.R. Bloxham, *A Register of the Presidents, Fellows, Demies . . . of Magdalen College, Oxford* (Oxford, 1853), i, p. 20; and information from Dr. Doyle.
[64] P.R. Robinson, *Catalogue of Dated and Datable Manuscripts c. 737-1600 in Cambridge Libraries*, (Bury St. Edmunds, 1988), addenda, p. 112, no. A 1.
[65] L. Thorndike, P. Kibre, *A Catalogue of Incipits of Medieval Scientific Writings in Latin*, Medieval Academy of America, Publication 29 (rev. ed. London, 1963), cols. 10 and 1357.

13.   Paris, Bibliothèque Nationale, MS latin 3378: Book V, *De sacramentis*.

A Carmelite production, probably English, with picture illuminations for the beginning of each sacrament. At the end of *De eucharistia*, fo. 204 v: 'Parce domine Johanni Erlham clerico provincialis scriptori.' who may have been the rubricator. fo. 358 has: 'parce domine parce fratri Roberto Freton Carmelite scriptori,' who I take to be the scriptor of no. 3 above. Parchment. From the Paris Carmel, see fo. 1: 'ad usum pp. Carmelitarum 1551', no. 9 in their 1672 catalogue.[66]

14.   Vatican Library, MS Vat. lat. 904: Books I-IV.

Signed at every gathering of eight by the scribe John Novel, O.Carm. Some illuminations, eg. fos. 247, 254. Lacks several folios.

15.   Vatican Library, MS Vat. lat. 905: Book V, *De sacramentis*.

Signed by John Novel, and dated fo. 305: 'scriptus per manum fratris Johannis Novel ordinis genetricis dei de Monte Carmel anno domini m°cccc°xxxi°. Illumination for the beginning of each sacrament.

16.   Vatican Library, MS Vat. lat. 906: Book VI, *De sacramentalibus*.

Without signatures, but so like nos. 14 and 15 as to leave no doubt that they are by the same scribe. Illumination fo. 17. Fos 2 and 7 missing.
In view of their date this set cannot be those sent by Netter to the pope. They were among the manuscripts used for the printed edition of 1759.[67] They may be English. All are parchment.

17.   Paris, Bibliothèque Nationale, MS lat. 3377: Books I-IV.

End of the fifteenth century. According to an inscription on fo. 321 written by Wolfardus Petri: 'Fardus Wol verte, sic scribam noscis aperte, ordine pari tripe vult cognominari.' The volume has not been completely finished; notes to the rubricator still exist, not completely carried out, fos. 1-8, 248.[68] Paper.

---

[66] *Bibliothèque Nationale: catalogue générale des manuscrits latins*, 5 (Paris, 1966), pp. 316-17.
[67] *Doctrinale*, p.x. G. di S. Teresa, *Archivum bibliographicum carmelitanum*, 2 (1957), pp. 249-51, nos. 27, 28, adds nothing to the Vatican catalogue.
[68] C. Samaran and R. Marichal, *Catalogue des mss en écriture latine, portant des indications de date, du lieu ou de copiste* (Paris, 1962), ii, *Bibliothèque Nationale: fonds latin*, p. 533; B.N., *Catalogue générale*, pp. 315-16.

18.   Paris, Bibliothèque Nationale, MS lat. 3379: Book V, *De sacramentis*.

A copy of no. 137?, made *c*. 1456, same hand as no. 19 below, also from the Paris Carmel.[69] Parchment.

19.   Paris, Bibliothèque Nationale, MS lat. 3380: Book VI *De sacramentalibus*.

According to fo. 206: 'Finitum et completum per manus Oliverii Deryani, nati diocesis Trecorensis (Treguier), anno domini millesimo quadringentesimo quinquagesimo sexto, die antepenultima Augusti.' From the Paris Carmel as nos. 13, and 18.[70] Parchment.

20.   Cracow, Biblioteka Jagiellonska, MS 1760: Books I-IV and other contents.

The scriptor was Michael Koyer, who signed his name fo. 172 v. At fo. 216: the explicit is 1434 'in concilio Basiliensi.' The rest of the contents are part of the discussion with the Bohemians at the council.

21.   Cracow, Bibliotheka Jagiellonska, MS 1759: Books V and VI.

At fo. 215: 'Michael Koyer scriptor huius libri. orate pro eo Michael Koyer.' The Deputy Director of the Library very kindly informed me that though MS 1759 has no marks of ownership, MS 1760 has in several places the name of Nicolaus Kozlowski, (fos. 340 v, 342 v, 349 v, 350). He was one of the foremost Polish theologians of his day and certainly brought home works of Netter from Basel, which he gave to the library of the Faculty of Arts in 1439.[71]

22.   Munich, CLM., MS 6501: Books I-IV.

Late fifteenth or early sixteenth century, in several hands. From Freising cathedral library. No marks of ownership nor of scribe.[72] Paper.

23.   Cambridge, Trinity Hall, MS 3: Books I-IV.

A Carmelite production from the Ghent Carmel, written in 1500, according to an inscription on the final folio: 'Finit feliciter prima paras reverendi magistri

[69] *Catalogue générale*, p. 317.
[70] Samaran et Marichal, ii, p. 171 and plate cxviii; B.N. *Catalogue générale*, pp. 317-18.
[71] For Kozlowski: C. Morawski, *Histoire de l'université de Cracowie*, 3 vols. (Paris/Cracow, 1900-1905), i, pp. 92, 295-97, 306; M. Schlauch, 'A Polish Vernacular Eulogy of Wycliff', *Journal of Ecclesiastical History*, 8 (1957), pp. 53-73, esp. p. 68; *Codex diplomaticus universitatis studii generalis Cracoviensis* (Cracow, 1870), i, pp. 139, 160, 190-94; ii, no. 157, pp. 110-12.
[72] Dr. Sigrid Krämer kindly examined this for me.

Thome Walden in doctrinale tocius ecclesie catholice contra blasphemias Wiclef per me fratrem Livinum de Preestere alias Presbiteri ordinis gloriose dei genetricis Marie de Monte Carmeli pro fratribus eiusdem ordinis conventus Gandensis conventum prefatum priorante venerabille patre Petro de Brune Anno domini mccccc xvjᵃ die septembris. Orate fideliter pro scriptore.' According to an inscription in the front of the manuscript it was given to the college in 1551 by Robert Hare, a benefactor who may have been a recusant.[73] The volume has been carefully used by someone who tried to verify Netter's references. e.g. at fo. 62 v, (ii, c, xii) where there is reference: 'Augustinus . . . prima parte sermonum, sermone xxix,' the margin has: 'decima parte tractatu.'

Apart from these manuscripts there are some containing parts.

24a.   Oxford, University College, MS 156: Paraphrase from Book VI, *De sacramentalibus*.

The compilation is explained by a note at fo. 1, where John Russell, bishop of Lincoln, explains that in 1491, worn out by all the heretics in Oxford, he compiled this at Woburn, to aid those attacking heresy.
It is a paraphrase of parts of Book VI: on non-written traditions, prayer to saints, prayer in common, chant, canonical hours, vigils, the sacramentals of the mass, baptism, order and penance.[74]

24b.     British Library, MS Harley 3049.

Fos. 237 v-240 are two *questiones*, on predestination and on the role of Peter, which are rearrangements of sections from Netter's first volume. They appear to be from ordinary lectures in the schools, and are the work of Walter Hunt, O.Carm., who was teaching in Oxford *c*. 1450. The manuscript was given to the library of Durham cathedral in 1458, by the prior, William Ebchester, who had been warden of Durham College, Oxford.[75]

---

[73] M.R. James, *A Descriptive Catalogue of the Manuscripts in the Library of Trinity Hall*, (Cambridge, 1907), pp. 5-6; Robinson, *Dated and Datable Manuscripts*, no. 392, p. 106 and plate 348.

[74] Watson, *Dated and Datable Manuscripts*, p. 147, no. 877.

[75] See n. 10 above.

# 21

## Christopher Columbus and the Friars

### Valerie I. J. Flint

Christopher Columbus's affection for the friars is well known. The Franciscan friars of the convent of La Rabida, on the Rio Tinto not far from Seville, solaced the great admiral and cared for his little son Diego at the very outset of the admiral's adventures.[1] The head of the Franciscan sub-province of Seville, Antonio de Marchena, advised the original (and successful) approach to the duke of Medina Sidonia for support for the westward voyage to the Indies. The intercession of Fray Juan Perez, prior of La Rabida, may have been crucial in persuading Isabella of Aragon to encourage Columbus, and thus pivotal to the enterprise as a whole.[2] The bond of sympathy between Columbus and the orders of friars remained strong throughout the admiral's life and continued, notably through the sympathetic work of the Dominican historian Bartolomé de las Casas, well after his death. Both morally and materially, then, the friars were essential to Columbus's great voyages of discovery. They are essential too to our own understanding of these voyages.

Given these clear and close associations and this moral and material support, Columbus might reasonably have been expected to have drawn upon the intellectual life of the friars, and especially upon that in their writings which bore upon his own treasured project. The contribution of the Dominican and Franciscan friars to the intellectual vigour and creativity of the later middle ages was, after all, outstanding in quantity even if it varied in excellence, and the Franciscans had, in addition, been in the forefront of the overland missions to, and exploration of, Columbus's 'Indies'. Little detailed attention has so far been paid, however, to the question of how many of the written materials produced by the friars were actually read by the admiral; this despite the facts that these materials were often relevant both to his journeys and to his

---

[1] The outlines of the 1485 visit of Columbus and Diego to La Rabida can be reconstructed from Garcia Fernandez's account of the admiral's important 1491 visit: *trans*. S.E. Morison, *Journals and Other Documents on the Life and Voyages of Christopher Columbus* (New York, 1963), p. 18.

[2] For bibliography upon, and references to, the important interventions of these two Franciscans see P.E. Taviani, *Christopher Columbus: The Grand Design* (London 1985), pp. 439-40; translated from the Italian *Cristoforo Colombo: la Genesi della Grande Scoperta* (Novara, 1974).

ambitions as a Christian trader and coloniser, and that many of them circulated widely in the later fifteenth century.[3]

We might attribute this lack of attention in one part to our poor knowledge of the extent of Columbus's library, and to the dearth of good and available editions and modern translations of the books he knew. The tremendous endeavours of the quatercentenary celebrations produced only five books of which we can be certain, through the presence in them of his annotations, the admiral himself possessed and read.[4] There is the compendium known as *Imago mundi*, put together between c. 1410 and 1414 by Cardinal Pierre d'Ailly (1340-1420)[5], the *Historia rerum ubique gestarum* of Aeneas Silvius Piccolomini (Pope Pius II, pope 1458-64), a copy of Pliny's *Natural History* in an Italian translation by Cristoforo Landino published in Venice in 1489, and another of Plutarch's *Lives*, this time translated into Castilian by Alfonso Palencia and printed at Seville in 1491.[6] Columbus had also a printed edition (Antwerp 1485/86) of the Latin rendering of the *Travels* of Marco Polo, translated by Fra Pippino of Bologna (perhaps between the years 1302-14) as the *De consuetudinibus et conditionibus orientalium regionum*.[7] We may be reasonably certain, in addition, that Columbus had (and enjoyed) a copy of Seneca's *Tragedies*[8], and that he read (and probably also enjoyed) the *Book of Sir John Mandeville*.[9] The list as we have it is of the first interest, and the annotations are doubly so. They show that the admiral was an eager and

[3] Attention has been paid, certainly, to the general influence the friars exercised upon the admiral, and to the relevance of Franciscan apocalypticism to his projects. See J.L. Phelan, *The Millennian Kingdom of the Franciscans in the New World* (Berkeley and Los Angeles, 1970), P.M. Watts, 'Prophecy and Discovery: On the Spiritual Origins of Christopher Columbus's "Enterprise of the Indies"', *American Historical Review*, 90 (1-2) (1985), pp. 73-102, and, especially, A. Milhou, *Colon y su mentalidad mesianica en el ambiente Franciscana Español* (Valladolid, 1983).

[4] The annotations are printed, together with those portions of the original works to which they refer, in C. de Lollis, *Scritti di Cristoforo Colombo: raccolta di documenti e studi pubblicati dalla r. commissione columbiana*, I, ii (Rome, 1894).

[5] A facsimile of this incunabulum has been published; *Imago Mundi by Petrus de Aiaco with Annotations by Christopher Columbus* (Massachusetts Historical Society, Boston 1927). The latin texts of d'Ailly's *Imago mundi*, *epilogus mappae mundi*, and *Compendia cosmographiae Ptolomaei* have been edited and published, complete with Columbus's annotations and a translation of the whole into French, by E. Buron, *Ymago mundi de Pierre d'Ailly* (Paris, 1930).

[6] No modern edition of these last three items as yet exists.

[7] We have a modern translation of this into Italian, together with Columbus's Latin *postille*; L. Giovannini, *Il Milione con le postille di Cristofero Colombo* (Rome, 1985). This is an odd, and unsatisfying, combination. Columbus read Marco Polo in a Latin abridgement, not, as Dr. Watts suggests ('Prophecy . . . ', p. 75), in an Italian one.

[8] S. de la Rosa y Lopez, *Libros y autographos de D. Cristobal Colon* in *Discurso leidos ante la Real Academia Sevillana de Buenas Letras*, i (Seville, 1891), p. 21.

[9] Andreas Bernaldez, for instance, was sure that Columbus had read the notorious work, and the admiral's son, Ferdinand, certainly knew it, and implied that his famous father did. Trans., C. Jane, *Select Documents Illustrating the Four Voyages of Columbus*, i (London, 1930), pp. 130-31. Trans. B. Keen, *The Life of the Admiral Christopher Columbus by his son Ferdinand* (London, 1960), pp. 42-44.

attentive reader, that he profited from the newly discovered art of printing, and that he turned to a variety of manuscripts and printed sources for help both before and during his voyages. But the list is also a short one and, apart from the effort at translation by Friar Pippino, there is little in it on the surface to direct us especially towards the friars. The redoubtable Friar Odoric of Pordenone both travelled to the east and returned a full report on his journey; yet the only certainty we have at present that Columbus knew of this report rests on the latter's reading of Mandeville, who incorporated much of Odoric.[10] Columbus did know several passages from the *Opus maius* of Roger Bacon. One of them stands behind a part of the famous letter he wrote to his sovereigns after the third voyage.[11] But all of Columbus's knowledge of Bacon to which we can at present point could have been gleaned from Pierre d'Ailly.[12] This is a very disappointing total.

A small portion of the blame for this gap in our knowledge must be laid upon the interests of the admiral's biographers, and upon the predispositions of some of the editors of his works. The portrait Morison so consistently painted, for instance, though in many ways admirable, is limited and, to some, discouraging. Morison's rehabilitated Columbus emerges as a seaman and practical navigator of genius, and an entrepreneur, if not of genius, at least of enthusiasm and persistence; but he is a man with little mental time left over for anything but mystical fancies, fancies held in place by an unreflective and ill-informed conservatism.[13] Jane is, on this level, even more dismissive[14] He specifically associates the 'strain of mysticism' he finds in Columbus, further-

---

[10] C. Deluz, *Le livre de Jehan de Mandeville, une 'géographie' au XIVe siècle* (Louvain-la-Neuve, 1988), pp. 51-52 suggests that Odoric was a more important source for Mandeville than was Marco Polo.

[11] The passage concerned may be conveniently read in translation in J. Cohen, *The Four Voyages of Christopher Columbus* (Harmondsworth, 1969), pp. 223-24, or with Spanish text and translation together in C. Jane, *Select Documents Illustrating the Four Voyages of Columbus*, ii (London, 1933), pp. 40-43. In it Columbus expresses strong Baconian views upon the proportion of water to land upon the surface of the earth.

[12] Buron scrupulously identifies the relationship between the views Columbus expressed in his letter to his sovereigns and their ultimate sources. E. Buron, *Ymago*, i, pp. 212-13.

[13] Morison explains, for instance, both Columbus's mistaken reading from the Pole Star and his famous claim to have discovered the Terrestrial Paradise (both on the third voyage) in this way: '[He] did not draw the proper conclusion from his own observations. It was another instance of the curious dualism in his nature; a scientific capacity to observe, fighting against a scholastic habit of mind which squeezed all observed phenomena into pre-conceived ideas.' S.E. Morison, 'Columbus and Polaris', *American Neptune*, 1 (1941). p. 133. Morison opposes Columbus's paradisaical conceits' to the latter's expertise in 'practical navigation'; ibid., *Admiral of the Ocean Sea*, ii (Boston, 1942), p. 558.

[14] 'His imagination was at once vivid and untutored. He had in a marked degree the poetic temperament . . . But while he was thus imaginative, Columbus was also a man of no more than imperfect education; whatever practical or theoretical knowledge he had gained, he had not acquired the power, and he had perhaps no great desire to possess the power, of cold and systematic reasoning,'; C. Jane, *Select Documents Illustrating the Four Voyages of Columbus*, i (London, 1930), pp. cvii-cviii.

more, with the admiral's attachment to the Franciscan Order.[15] Casts of mind
of this type rarely attract the attention of intellectual historians. Nor do the
attitudes and writings of the religious orders who appear to sustain them.
Lastly, Columbus has been seen, and often quite rightly, as in essence a symbol
of transition; as a bridge, this is, between the old world and the new. Bridges
are all very fine in their way but, once in place, they rarely claim the direct
concern of the persons or places they unite. Columbus's intellectual interests,
spanning those of Renaissance scholars and medievalists, of Romance linguists
and of Latinists, of historians of America and historians of Christian Europe,
have not yet engaged any of them fully. This in part explains the lamentable
lack of modern editions and translations both of the texts he did read and of
those he may have done.

Yet arresting clues exist and have existed for some time. Over sixty years ago
Buron printed, translated and traced the source of Columbus's annotations to
d'Ailly's *Imago mundi*, annotations which showed that Columbus had access,
independently this time of d'Ailly, to the written works of at least two other
especially famous Franciscans: Nicholas of Lyra (1270-1349) and Francis of
Meyronnes (1295-1325).[16] Columbus's interest in Francis may lie in that
reverence for the Virgin so manifest in the naming of so many of the admiral's
discoveries; perhaps Francis had helped to inspire the reverence.[17] Nicholas
was an even more popular commentator upon the Bible. His *Postillae perpe-
tuae sive brevia commentaria in universa biblica* was the first such commentary
to be printed.[18] Nicholas's works were widely accessible in late medieval
Spain,[19] and Columbus makes reference to him more than once.[20] The
writings of each of the two may very well throw much needed further light
upon the admiral's character and interests. Then again, over one hundred
years ago now, S. Rosa y Lopez found, among the books offered to him as
belonging to Columbus, a *Filosofia natural* (*sic*) of Albertus Magnus, printed
in a Latin edition at Venice in 1496; and a *Summula confessionis* of 'San

[15] ' . . . there was in him a profound strain of mysticism . . . But it is not therefore to be
concluded that Columbus was converted into a mystic by the misfortune which he suffered; on the
contrary it would seem that he was mystical by nature. That he was so is suggested by his marked
attachment to the Franciscan Order,'; ibid., p. liii.

[16] Annotation to c. 8; Buron, *Ymago*, i, pp. 206-15. Meyronnes was a distinguished theologian
and Mariologist.

[17] According to Las Casas, Columbus referred to Francis of Meyronnes in his journal of his
third voyage too; Morison, *Journals*, p. 279.

[18] It was printed at Rome in 1471-72.

[19] See K. Reinhardt, 'Das Werk des Nicholas von Lyra im mitterlalterlichen Spanien', *Traditio*,
43 (1987), pp. 321-58, especially 325-41. Columbus is not numbered, however, among the many
figures this author singles out as readers of Nicholas's work. Again Columbus has failed to catch
the attention of medieval intellectual historians.

[20] In his note to c. 24 of the *Imago Mundi*, too, for instance, Buron, *Ymago*, i, pp. 306-7. Phelan
draws attention to the references reported in the *Raccolta*; *The Millenial*, p. 132, n. 31.

Antonio de Florencia', printed in the same city, again in Latin, in 1476.[21] The
first was the *Philosophia naturalis* (usually known as the *Philosophia pauperum*) of the Dominican friar Albertus Magnus (d. 1280), printed by Geor-
gius Arrivabenus at Venice in 1496; a compendium of five books of Albertus
upon the constitution of the world and the soul – subjects very dear to the heart
of the admiral.[22] 'San Antonio de Florencia' was the Dominican friar Antoninus Florentius (1389-1459), founder of the convent of San Marco in Florence,
and archbishop of the same city. The *Summa confessionis* was his *Confessionale*, first printed in Venice in 1474 by Johannes de Colonia and Johannes
Manthen and, because of its enormous popularity, reprinted in 1476.[23] The
evidence that Columbus read the writings of Nicholas of Lyra and Francis of
Meyronnes is better, of course, than that which connects him with these last
works; but cumulatively it is all interesting. It is time, especially for intellectual
historians and historians of medieval texts, to attempt a little bridge-repair.

This essay seeks to bring one small plank (and perhaps the odd nail) to this
repair; and it launches an appeal for many more. It is now possible, I think, to
argue that Columbus read at first hand, and quoted to his sovereigns, the
writing of at least one more Franciscan friar. Support for this proposition
comes primarily from the happy conjunction of two widely separated pieces of
evidence. It comes on the one hand from a source long known but little
explored and, on the other, from a source discovered only very recently. As a
result of this conjunction of old and new material, it may be possible to test
these propositions about Columbus's 'strain of mysticism' and its supposed
relationship with his reading from the friars – even to make a few tentative
different suggestions. Such suggestions will also, I hope, show how very much
more there is still to know about him.

The friar in question is Friar John of Marignolli; the writing is his *Chronicle*.
John, of the aristocratic Florentine house of Marignolli, was a Franciscan friar
at Santa Croce in Florence. In 1338 he was sent as papal legate to the court of
the Great Khan, and he remained in the east until 1353. On his return,
dissatisfied, it seems, with his appointment to the see of Bisignano in Calabria,
he joined the service of the Emperor Charles IV; this in 1355. He died in 1358/
59.[24] John wrote his *Chronicle* whilst he was in the emperor's service and so

[21] Rosa y Lopez, *Libros y autographos*, pp. 20-21.
[22] The five books of Albertus from which the compendium was made are the *Physica*, *De
elementis*, *De coelo et mundo*, *Meteora*, *De anima*.
[23] On the popularity of the *Confessionale* see the *Catalogue of Books Printed in the Fifteenth
Century now in the British Museum*, iv (London, 1916), pp. 226-27. There are over 102 incunable
editions of it, often in pocket-book form and largely, it seems, designed for the lay market.
[24] The essential facts about John's career may be found in L. Oliger, 'De anno ultimo vitae Fr.
Iohannis de Marignollis Missionarii inter Tartaros atque Episcopi Bisinianensis', *Antonianum*, 18
(1943), pp. 29-34.

within the last three or four years of his life.[25] It was written to please his
patron and was devoted primarily therefore to the history of Bohemia,
especially to the demonstration of Bohemia's proud place among the history of
nations. To this end John chose the well-tried pattern of the Christian world
chronicle; a history, that is, which begins with the first chapters of the Book of
Genesis and discusses, before the individual nation with which it is concerned,
the vicissitudes of the race of Adam, from whose stock all Christian kingdoms
spring. The choice of this pattern gave John, as a missionary friar, great scope
for further comment: the nature of this comment endowed the *Chronicle* with
a special interest for Columbus, for in these early chapters John tells at first
hand of his experiences in the east.

The opportunity is readily provided by the story in Genesis 2:8 of the
planting by God of 'a garden in Eden, in the east', and the placing there of
Adam. 'Plantaverat autem deus paradisum voluptatis a principio, id est in
parte orientali', says John, 'qui locus dicitur Eden ultra Indiam.'[26] The last two
words are, of course, an addition to the biblical text, and they preface an
account of his own adventures in these very parts. He tells with great
excitement of his mission to the court of the Great Khan, of Cambaluc, the
Khan's capital, and of the great cities and riches of the Khan's empire as a
whole. He dilates upon the friendliness of the Khan towards the Christian
religion. He recounts the journey he himself made through the Khan's
province of Mangi in Cathay, to the pepper forests of India and the Christian-
ised lands of St. Thomas the Apostle. John claims to have visited the realms of
the Queen of 'Saba' (often identified with the biblical country of Sheba, *Saba*
in the Vulgate), and to have crossed from them to 'Seyllanum', perhaps
Ceylon, and to this island's great mountain, a mountain which, says John,
stands opposite the Terrestrial Paradise. John of Marignolli's account of this
part of his travels, of the mountain, and of the lands to be found on the edges of
the Terrestrial Paradise, must be quoted at some length, for they are of central
importance to my attempt to demonstrate that Columbus did indeed have a
use for John's *Chronicle*:

> perrexi ad famosissimam reginam Saba . . . deinde perreximus per mare ad Seylla-
> num, montem gloriosum ex opposito paradisi, et de Seyllano usque ad paradisum, ut
> dicunt incole ex tradicione patrum, sunt miliaria ytalica quadraginta, ita quod, ut
> dicitur, auditur sonitus aquarum fontis cadencium de paradiso.

In a passage of the first interest, John describes this Paradise, the sound of
whose great fountain could so clearly be heard in 'Seyllanum':

> Est autem paradisus locus in terra circumvallatus mari oceano in parte orientali ultra
> Indiam Columbinam, contra montem Seyllanum, locus altissimus super omnem

---

[25] The *Chronicle* is edited by J. Emler, *Kronika Marignolova, Fontes Rerum Bohemicarum*, iii
(Prague, 1878), pp. 492-604.
[26] Ibid., p. 494.

terram, attingens, ut probat Johannes Scotus, globum lunarem, ab omni altercatio-
nem remotus, locus omni suavitate ac claritate amenus. In cuius medio oritur fons
. . . Fons autem ille derivatur de monte et cadit in lacum . . . et intrat sub alia aqua
spissa et post egreditur ex alia parte et dividitur in quatuor flumina, que transeunt
per Seyllanum, et hec nomina eorum; Gyon, qui circuit terram Ethiopie . . . Phison,
qui circuit omnem terram Evilach Indiam et descendere dicitur per Cathay, et ibi
mutato nomine dicitur Caramora, id est nigra aqua, quia ibi nascitur bedellium et
lapis onichus, et puto quod sit maior fluvius de mundo aque dulcis . . . Tercius
fluvius vocatur Tygris . . . Ultimo pervenimus ad quartum fluvium, nomine
Eufrates.[27]

A little further on in the narrative John comes back to the great mountain near
to Paradise:

In isto eciam altissimo monte est cacumen supereminens, quod raro videri potest
propter nebulam . . . Dicunt incole . . . quod illuc nunquam ascendit diluvium.[28]

The area round about Paradise is incredibly rich and fertile, helped by the
rivers which carry fruits and aloes and jewels and precious stones from
Paradise itself:

In eodem monte versus paradisum est fons maximus, bene decem miliarium
ytalicorum, aquis optimis, perspicuis, quem dicunt derivari de fonte paradisi et ibi
erumpere, quod probant, quia aliquando erumpunt de fundo quedam folia ignota et
in magna copia et lignum aloes et lapides preciosi sicut carbunculus et saphirus et
poma quedam ad sanitatem.[29]

John's initial description of Paradise leads him, by an evident logic, to discuss
the creation and fate of Adam and Eve, their lives and their sorrows. His
account of these events is especially well-spiced with Genesis legends of the
utmost interest, legends which would reward a deal of further investigation.[30]
We must here confine ourselves for the moment, however, to that in his
*Chronicle* which bears specifically upon the east. Filled as it is with information
about the Khan's friendliness to Christians he much wanted to hear, and with
information about the Indies and their riches he so much wanted his patron to
believe (I have quoted only a little of this), this part of the *Chronicle* was
certainly of an order greatly to Columbus's taste. In all of these features John's

[27] Ibid., p. 497.
[28] Ibid., p. 500.
[29] Ibid., pp. 500-1.
[30] Adam, John tells us, after his Fall, was promptly taken by the arm by an angel and deposited
upon the mountain in Ceylon where John himself had been – on the edge, that is, of Paradise. As
he fell from grace Adam left an enormous footprint upon the rock, 'et usque hodie perseverat'.
Eve was deposited upon a mountain nearby. A great statue of Adam survives on the mountain, as
does his house, made of great marble slabs like a sepulchre, ibid., pp. 499-500.

reports are similar to the reports of Friar Odoric. With the help of the newly discovered source, it is now possible at least to propose that Columbus consulted Marignolli's *Chronicle* directly.

This second source is the *Libro copiador de Cristobal Colon*. The *Libro copiador* is a sixteenth-century copy-book of letters by Columbus himself; a copy-book which may draw directly upon the admiral's own archives. It is probably Italian in origin, and was found in a private collection from the island of Majorca. It has nine letters in all; five *cartas-relaciones*, or narrative letters about the voyages to the 'Indies', all previously unknown; two short personal letters from Columbus to his sovereigns, also unknown until now; and additional texts of two further *cartas-relaciones*, one of the third voyage and one of the fourth. Each of these last narrative letters is, by contrast with the others, well known, but in forms which vary in certain particulars from those given by the *Libro copiador*.[31]

We shall be concerned here with Columbus's famous letter to his sovereigns about the third voyage, (May 1498-October 1500), the voyage from which he returned in chains, of which he reported that he had skirted the Terrestrial Paradise. This letter, readers may recall, compares previous reports of the area around the Terrestrial Paradise with the area (Trinidad, the coast of Venezuela and the mouths of the Orinoco river), Columbus and his crews had actually explored. The relevant passage in the *Libro copiador* version of this letter reads as follows (I italicise the variant sentences as de Armas does):

San Isidro y Beda y Damasceno y Estrabon y el maestro de la Ystoria Escolastica y San Ambrosio y Escoto y todos los sacros teologos todos conciertan quel Parayso terrenal es en fin de oriente, *el qual oriente llaman el fin de la tierra; yendo al oriente, en una montana altissima que sale fuera deste ayre torbolento, adonde no llegaron las aquas del dilubio; que alli estan Elias y Enoque, y de alli sale una fuente y cae aque en el mar, y alli haze un gran lago del qual proceden los quatro rrios sobredichos; que bien questo lago sea en oriente y las fuentes destos rrios sean divisas en este mundo, por ende que proceden y vienen alli deste lago por catar antes debajo de tierra, y espiran alli donde se been estas sus fuentes; la qual aqua que sale del Paraiso terrenal para este lago, trahe un tronido y rroqir mui grande, de manera que la gente que naze en aquella son sordos.*[32]

A second variant passage in the same letter tells of the special attention Columbus paid to the rushes and depth of sweet water off the coasts of that

[31] The whole has been discussed, and the texts reprinted, by A. Rumeu de Armas, *Libro copiador de Cristobal Colon: Correspondencia inedita con los reyes catolicos sobre los viajes a America* (Madrid, 1989), but the editor has paid little attention to the question of the possible sources of Columbus's accounts. I am deeply indebted to Professor John Elliott, both for drawing my attention to this collection in the first place and for lending me his personal copy.

[32] Rumeu de Armas, *Libro*, i, p. 360. For the well-known version of this part of the letter, see Jane, *Select*, ii, p. 2-47 (on pp. 36-37). Jane identifies the sources given in the above section, although John Scotus Eriugena is not the same as Duns Scotus, as Jane suggests. The attribution to Strabo should, of course, be to Anselm of Laon.

land he increasingly supposed to be the island of the Terrestrial Paradise. He
measured the depth of this water with his plumb-line, taking enormous care:

> Y si alli del Parayso no sale, paresce aun muy maior maravilla, porque no creo que
> sepan en el mundo de rio tan grande y tan fondo, *al qual no pude llegar; en alqunos*
> *lugares es en el pie largo con ochenta brazas de cordel e colgado del doze libras de*
> *plomo.*[33]

Some of the material in this letter about the Terrestrial Paradise is certainly
drawn from d'Ailly's *Imago mundi*, and some from *The Book of Sir John
Mandeville* – further proof, if any were needed, of Columbus's reliance upon
this latter work. The idea that Paradise is raised above the general level of the
lands of earth, so high indeed that the waters of the Flood were unable to cover
it is, for instance, to be found in the *Imago mundi*, c. lv. So are many of the
authorities Columbus cites here, as is also the notion that the great crashing
and roaring of the rivers of Paradise, as they pour through and out of the great
lake which at first contains them, deafens all the surrounding inhabitants.[34]
Mandeville reinforces these propositions in c. xxxiii of his *Book*[35], and lays
especial emphasis upon the impossibility of humans ever reaching these great
rivers.[36] Mandeville also speaks, in this same chapter, of the plunging of the
rivers of Paradise underground when they have poured from the lake, as does
the first of the variant passages I have quoted from the *Libro copiador*. The
relevant portion from Mandeville has, in Letts's translation, considerable
charm:

> In the midst of Paradise is a well out of which there come four floods, that run
> through divers lands. These floods sink down into the earth within Paradise and run
> so under the earth many a mile, and afterwards come they up again out of the earth
> in far countries . . . And ye shall understand that no man living may go to Paradise
> . . . Many great lords have assayed divers times to pass by those rivers of Paradise,
> but they might not speed of their journey; for some of them died for weariness of
> rowing and over travailing, some waxed blind and some deaf for the noise of the
> waters, and some were drowned by the violence of the waves of the waters . . .[37]

So far d'Ailly and the *Book of Sir John Mandeville*, books we know Columbus
read, may reasonably be believed to have been his sources here, even though,
as we have seen, John of Marignolli draws in places close to them both. There
are three small sections of the letter, however, one which is in both versions

---

[33] Ibid., pp. 360-61.
[34] Buron, *Ymago*, pp. 458-60. Columbus annotates these passages. Ultimately the idea that
such rivers induce deafness goes back to a passage in Pliny's *Natural History*, vi, c. 35, in which this
capacity is attributed to the cataract of the Nile.
[35] It may be, indeed, that d'Ailly himself drew on Mandeville for this section of his *Imago mundi*
– further evidence that Mandeville's *Book* was taken seriously by geographers.
[36] M. Letts, *Mandeville's Travels: Texts and Translations* (London, 1953), pp. 214-17.
[37] Ibid.

and two which occur only in the passages I have quoted from the *Libro copiador*, which I have been unable to trace back, either to these two sources or to any other of Columbus's known readings. All of them are to be found in the *Chronicle* of John of Marignolli: the mention of 'Escoto' (John Scotus Eriugena); the emphasis upon the quite extraordinary depth and sweetness of the river of Paradise Columbus thought he had discovered (of the waters at the mouth of the Orinoco, that is); and the mention of 'Elias y Enoque'.

Marignolli alone among the possible authors I have examined cites John Scotus Eriugena as a source; indeed, John Scotus is the only source John does cite for his description of the land around Paradise. Marignolli, too, lays an especial stress upon the River 'Phison', or Ganges, and its rush of sweet waters, 'maior fluvius de mundo aque dulcis'. This emphasis was sustained also, it seems, in Columbus's journal of his third voyage.[38] Most interesting of all, however, is Columbus's reference, in the variant passage in the *Libro copiador*, to 'Elias y Enoque'. 'Elias', the prophet Elijah whom God raised up in a fiery chariot (II Kings 2:11-12) and 'Enoque', Enoch, who 'walked with God' and whom God took to himself Genesis 5:24), were well-known figures of biblical legend.[39] Both had left the world of men and must await the end of the world in some especial place. One sentence in the Vulgate version of Ecclesiasticus 44:16 allowed the identification of this place; it stated that Enoch 'translatus est in paradisum'. This could not be the Paradise promised by Christ at the end of the world, however, for Enoch had not died as men die. It must therefore be the Terrestrial Paradise. The city of Enoch is found at the gates of the Terrestrial Paradise on medieval *mappae mundi*,[40] and Elias, or 'Eli', and Enoch are sometimes identified with the two witnesses who, in the Apocalypse 11:3-12, await the coming of Antichrist.[41]

Columbus could, of course, have come across their names with ease and often; but they are to be found in singularly appropriate places in the *Chronicle* of John of Marignolli – places which associate them very clearly with the Terrestrial Paradise and Columbus's 'Indies'. John speaks of both, together with their vigil near Paradise, when he tells of the line of Seth and, interestingly, says how near is the life of present-day Brahmins ('religiosi de Seyllano') to the religious practices of that line.[42] Then again, near the end of his *Chronicle*, John returns to his visit to 'Saba' and speaks of yet another high mountain there. On this mountain reside Eli and Enoch:

---

[38] Morison, *Journals*, p. 275.

[39] And to monastic biblical legend especially it seems. See M. Esposito, 'An Apocryphal "Book of Enoch and Elias" as a Possible Source of the *Navigato Sancti Brendani*', *Celtica*, 5 (1960), pp. 192-206.

[40] It is found on the famous Hereford Map, for instance.

[41] This identification is a very early one; cf. G. Orlandi, *Navigatio Sancti Brendani*, i (Milan 1968), p. 122.

[42] Ed. Emler, *Kronika*, pp. 504-5.

Helias, tamen, ut dicunt, ibi mansit voluntate dei absconsus . . . et ipse raptus est in celum curru et equis igneis, expectans cum Enoch prelium Antichristi . . . [43]

The extra references could well have been taken, therefore, directly from John Marignolli, from passages in the *Chronicle* which closely shadow Columbus's particular concerns. This evidence may not be alone conclusive; one extra small, but crucial, piece I think makes it so. After the second mention of Eli and Enoch, John goes on. He had badly wanted, he tells us, to climb up the mountain where the two waited so patiently for Antichrist. He had drunk, indeed, at the spring at its foot where Elijah himself also drank, and the inhabitants of 'Saba' had told him that sometimes Elijah appeared. But he could not climb the mountain. His drink had been poisoned by thieves trying to seize his possessions, and he lay there gravely ill. He was eventually cured with the help of the queen of Saba's doctor (seemingly a woman); but he languished for eleven months. The opportunity was lost.[44] In his abstract of Columbus's journal of the third voyage (the only form in which this journal has reached us), Bartolomé de Las Casas tells of the perilous departure of Columbus and his little fleet from the gulf of Paria and the coast of Venezuela; from the area, that is, Columbus was to describe to his sovereigns as the area of the Terrestrial Paradise. Las Casas purports to paraphrase the admiral's own words. Here is what he says (I have placed the crucial passage in italics):

> When the wind fell, they feared lest the fresh water or the salt cast them on the rocks by their currents, and there they would have no hope. It pleased the goodness of God that from that very danger sprang safety and liberation, for the same fresh water, overcoming the salt, swept the vessels out, without a scratch; and thus they were saved; for when God wishes that one or many should live, *water becomes their medicine instead of their poison.*[45]

It seems at the least, then, highly probable that Columbus had direct access to the *Chronicle* of Friar John of Marignolli. Well and good. We may extend the admiral's reading list by one more book, and explain his interest in it by the encouraging information about the east this book contained. We may note, in addition, that this book was by a Franciscan friar; and with this we might, with all satisfaction (and perhaps some wisdom) stop. Yet there could be a little

---

[43] Ibid., p. 583.

[44] 'Helias tamen, ut dicunt, ibi mansit voluntate dei absconsus usque ad tempora illa. Dicunt eciam illi de Saba, quod ibi nunc eciam aliquando apparet, et est ibi fons, unde dicunt eum bibisse in pede montis, et ego bibi de fonte illo, non tamen potui ascendere montem illum beatum, gravatus infirmitate propter fortissimum, quod biberam in Colombo michi propinatum ab hiis, qui volebant rapere, que habebam, quamvis proicerem frustratim spolia, carnes omnium intestinorum cum infinito sanguine et passus fuerim tercie speciei incurabilem dissenteriam mensibus quasi undecim, de qua forte nullus dicitur alius evasisse. Deus tamen misertus est mei, ut referrem, que videram, et auxilio cuiusdam medice illius regine evasi, que cum sucis herbarum tantum et abstinencia me curavit,' ibid., p. 583.

[45] Trans. Morison, *Journals*, p. 277.

more of interest than this alone. Columbus's use of John Marignolli offers us, on the very lowest assessment, the opportunity to think again about the ideas Columbus gained from, and the uses to which he put, his reading of books by the friars.

There has been one very spirited recent attempt to rescue the admiral's mental world from the limbo in which Jane and Morison left it. In an article briefly mentioned at the beginning of this essay[46], Pauline Moffat Watts set herself to enquire far more deeply into the religious dimensions of Columbus's thought and planning. As a result of a thorough and skilful investigation, Dr. Watts came to the conclusion that:

> Columbus's apocalyptic vision of the world and of the special role that he was destined to play in the unfolding of events that would presage the end of time was a major stimulus for his voyages.[47]

According to this view, Columbus's intellectual formation led him to direct his energies towards preparing for an imminent, and divinely predestined, end of the world. The Apocalypse (or Book of Revelation), aided by associated prophecies, preoccupied him above all other books, including all other books of the Bible, and effectively filled his mental vision:

> In his mind . . . the New World was identified with the end of the world – the first heaven and earth passed away, there was no more sea – and the journey of the *viator*, which had begun in the deserts of the Old Testament prophets was surely almost over.[48]

That mystical side of Columbus's personality which Morison tried so hard to keep in the background emerges here with such force as to carry all before it. It has gained in dignity in the process, it is true. It has taken to itself all of the writings Columbus possessed, including those previously thought at least quasi-scientific, like the *Historia* of Pius II or the *Imago mundi* of Pierre d'Ailly. It is a very well-informed species of mysticism indeed, far removed from that of which Morison and Jane spoke. But it is still mysticism; and it is now all-pervading. Navigational expertise, intellectual and practical curiosity and apocalyptic fervour become one, all subsumed beneath this newly eluci-dated, well-read and all-powerful religious dimension to Columbus's persona-

---

[46] Above, n. 3.

[47] Watts, 'Prophecy', p. 74. 'Guided more often than not by prophecies regarding the appear-ance of an emperor-messiah, the conversion of all the peoples of the world to Christianity, the final recovery of the Holy Land from the infidel, and the advent of the Antichrist, Columbus and his contemporaries sought to discover and play out their historical roles in a cosmic drama they perceived as inexorably unfolding from the moment that Adam and Eve had been expelled from the Garden of Eden.' Ibid., p. 79.

[48] Ibid., p. 102.

lity. And in the forefront of the formation of this religious dimension, we are led to infer, were the millenarian writings of the friars. On this reckoning, the main influence of the friars upon Columbus lay in their intellectual reinforcement of this all-absorbing apocalypticism.

Well, perhaps. Certainly it is a beautifully developed argument; but we might straightaway notice two things about it, both of which are a little unsettling. Firstly, the pendulum has swung backwards a very long way indeed. Other-worldliness is now absolute, and is to be seen as the single most powerful directive force of all of the admiral's enterprises; this, moreover, from their very beginning. Secondly, and more importantly within the context of this essay and its plea for more work upon the friars, this is not the message of the *Chronicle* of John of Marignolli.

John's *Chronicle* is very firmly written in and for *this* world. From the very first words where, in a preface resplendent with a range of impressive authorities from Cicero to the *Song of Songs*, John stresses the responsibilities of prudent rulership ('Tunc enim rempublicam constat esse felicem, quando rectores ipsius prudentes esse constituit vel vacare prudencie') to the very end, where he dilates upon the glorious gifts showered upon the cathedral in Prague by Duke Wratislaus of Bohemia ('coronam auream in ea suspendit pondere marcarum XII, argenti vero octoginta, es et ferrum sine numero optulit, pavimentum politis lapidibus exornavit et Romana ecclesia privilegiis communivit'),[49] John's interest is in the development and government of societies here and now, and in the very present rewards good government might offer. He has remarkably little to say about the end of the world or the preparations necessary to it and, beyond the mentions of Eli and Enoch noticed above, when he does refer to the Apocalypse he does so primarily to derive biblical support for the temporal authority and material status of the Christian priesthood.[50]

John's main biblical preoccupation in his *Chronicle* is in fact not with the Apocalypse but with the Book of Genesis. All of the precious information he offers about his experience in the east, and about his legation there, is offered within the context of this single Book of the Bible, with its story of the early sins and (importantly) the later semi-recovery of the stock of Adam and Eve. John's *Chronicle* bears upon the life of Man *in* creation, and, above all, upon the possible improvement of his state in the created world throughout history – not upon the world's imminent demise. In passages which clearly demonstrate his indebtedness to John Scotus Eriugena, John moves from the creation of the angels to the creation of Adam, then launches himself into his first description of his travels to the east just as we prepare to hear about Adam's fall. But we in fact hear little about the Fall, still less about the Judgement. We hear far more

---

[49] Ed. Emler, *Kronica*, pp. 492 and 604.

[50] ' . . . spirituale sacredotium a Christo sumpsit exordium, sicut scribit Johannes in principio Apocalypsis: Fecit eis regnum et sacerdotes . . . '; ibid. p. 577. The reference is to Apocalypse 1:6.

about the land in which the miscreants Adam and Eve eventually found themselves. And that land was and is a *pleasant* land; one of extraordinary riches. The area leading to, and all around, Eden is clearly very desirable indeed by John's account, and the inhabitants both friendly and magnificently hospitable. He seems especially delighted by the likely cash-value of the entertainment he and his company received there, and of the status and physical situation in these lands of the Friars Minor.[51] When John speaks of the east, in short, he speaks of it within the context of a line of Adam redeemable in worldly terms well before the redemption proper in the Second Coming. When he describes the region round about the Terrestrial Paradise, he is far more inclined to tell of the glories of this world than of those of the next. Man might enjoy the gold and jewels of the rivers of Paradise and gather fruits similar to those of the trees of Paradise *now* fruits some of them with healing qualities close to the miraculous.[52] Set about as they are among such descriptions, the effects of the Fall and the threat of the Judgement seem more than mitigated by the uses Adam made and Man might still make of God's good gifts; especially of those gifts God gave to the eastern parts of his creation from the beginning of time.

We can to some extent explain John's emphasis upon the Book of Genesis, and the views he expresses in his *Chronicle*, in terms of his own personality and hopes. John was himself by no means an unworldly man, unappreciative of the finer things of life. He loved bells and banners, well-furnished churches and houses, good living and good entertainment; and he was not averse to trade.[53] He was in addition writing a history, not a plan for the future, and a history for a powerful and worldly patron. Such patrons do not always wish to hear about the Apocalypse and the Day of Judgement. John of Marignolli seems to have written from the heart, but also as befitted an experienced missionary friar. He was aware both of his need of the help of powerful rulers and of the part of the prospect of God's material rewards might play in the encouragement of this help. We have a great deal still to learn about the attitude of medieval friars towards the Book of Genesis and its use in the reinforcement of these particular aims. But in none of these predilections was John necessarily

---

[51] The Great Khan assigned them a princely residence and two noble attendants, says John, 'qui nobis omnibus necessitatibus habundantissime ministrabant in cibis et potibus et usque ad papirum pro laternis, deputatis servitoribus et ministris de curia et sic per annos quasi quatuor servierunt infinitis semper honoribus, vestibus preciosis pro nobis et familiis extollendo. Et si bene omnia computarem ultra valorem expendit quatuor milium marcarum pro nobis . . . habent enim fratres minores in Ca[m]balec ecclesiam cathedralem inmediate iuxta pallacium et solempnem archiepiscopatum et alias ecclesias plures in civitate et campanas et omnes vivunt de mensa imperatoris honorifice valde.' Ibid. p. 496.

[52] Ibid., pp. 497-98, 501-2.

[53] He delighted in Zayton, for instance, 'portus maris mirabilis, civitas nobis incredibilis, ubi fratres minores habent tres ecclesias pulcherrimas, optimas et ditissimas, balneum fundatum, omnium mercatorum depositorium. Habent eciam campanas optimas et pulcherrimas, quarum duas ego feci fiere cum magna solempnitate,' ibid., p. 500.

untypical[54]; and perhaps especially not among the friars of La Rabida, men such as Fray Juan Perez of Fray Antonio de Marchena, the friars Columbus knew. Columbus may, indeed, have turned to John of Marignolli after the tragedies of the third voyage precisely because of John's well-known skill with his royal patron. The audience for whom John of Marignolli wrote had much in common with that to whom Columbus directed his own letter.

The *Chronicle* of John of Marignolli warns us against the idea that Franciscan teaching was inevitably millenarian, and it persuades us, at the very least, to look to the character of their writings on the Book of Genesis as well. The possibility that Columbus read John's *Chronicle* and used it in a crucial letter to his sovereigns may encourage us, too, to look again at the influence of the friars in general, both upon the great admiral's reading and upon his reporting to his patrons. We should, in the first place, enquire more carefully into the contents, and the messages, of those other Franciscan works we know Columbus actually read. In the second place, we should allow ourselves at least to doubt whether it was to the millenarian element in Franciscan spirituality that Columbus was primarily, or even often, attracted.

The similarities between the intellectual life and aims of Columbus and the intellectual life and aims of the Franciscan friars may lie, in fact, rather in the flexibility of each than in the single-mindedness of either. The mark of the friars may best be found in the range and popularity of the reading upon which Columbus drew, and the many different ways in which he employed it. Both Columbus and the friars were, above all, disposed to confront novel and fluctuating circumstances and peoples. Both needed a varied stock of information; varied enough to meet the changing demands which would be made on it. Both could draw upon this stock as and when it suited them, and due perhaps most importantly of all, as and when it suited their supporters and protectors. Columbus could certainly find a place for apocalyptic teaching and for a 'strain of mysticism', as, manifestly, could the Franciscan friars. The materials lay there ready in his books, and in abundance. When his plans seemed to fail, when support for his ventures dwindled almost to nothing, then it may well have seemed worth thundering at his sovereigns with the thunders of the Day of Judgement and the prospect of a New Heaven and a New Earth, and putting together a convincing *Book of Prophecies*. But, like the friars, he could also have need of far more immediate and this-worldly sources of inspiration, and more enticing works: works like the *Travels* of Marco Polo, with their promise of instant material gain; or the *Chronicle* of John of Marignolli. And as John called on Cicero, moreover, Columbus too could draw upon non-Christian

[54] See, for example, Milhou, *Colon*, especially pp. 118-25.

writings to achieve his ends.[55] One of the items on the admiral's known reading-list, for instance, is a copy of Plutarch's *Lives*: and his annotations suggest that Columbus took its messages, on occasions, very seriously. There is nothing millenarian about the *Lives*; indeed, there may be grounds for suggesting that they bore chiefly upon Columbus's colonial ambitions and plans for governorship, and that that is why he read them.

Columbus, in short, suited many of his ideas to his ends. He acquired and employed his mental freight as befitted a sailor and trader. He selected it for the returns it might bring and made use of it as the prospects offered or the circumstances of the voyage required. He trimmed his intellectual sails so as to catch and use the winds which prevailed among his crew, or among others who might help him. Columbus's mental equipment, like that of the missionary friars, was varied because it had, like theirs, so many and such varied *immediate* tasks to perform in time. Intellectual choices and behaviour of this kind present the very best of challenges to the historian of ideas.

---

[55] Many of the names John cites in his preface – Aristotle, Virgil and Augustine, for instance – are, incidentally, names of which Columbus was also fond. We may have here a parade of common stock comforting to the potential audience.

# Index of Manuscripts

# Index of Persons

Abbo of Fleury 99
Abelard, Peter 134, 186
Adalard, count of Tours, lay-abbot of
  St. Martin 3-5
Adalbert, abbot of Hornbach 22
Adam of Petit-Pont 207 n.1
Adamnan 266 n.6
Adelaide, wife of Louis VI, king of France
  194
Adelaide, wife of Roger I, king of Sicily
  122
Adrian IV, pope 189
Agapetus II, pope 35 n.10, 52
Agobard of Lyons 26, 31 n.36
Ailly, Pierre d', cardinal 296, 297, 298,
  303, 306
Aimeric, chancellor 84-5
Airaud of Portes, archbishop of Lyons 86,
  90
Alberic of Monte Cassino 238
Albertus Magnus 298-9
Alcuin 48, 50 n.71a, 62; *and see*
  Pseudo-Alcuin
Alexander II, pope 71, 160
Alexander III, pope 182
Alexander of Hales 248-9, 259-60, 261-2,
  270-1, 274
Alfonso V, king of Aragon 235
Alfonso X, king of Castile 237
Alger of Lüttich 168 n.42
Allen, William 288
Alnick, William, bishop of Norwich,
  Lincoln 291
Ambrose, St. 31, 44, 90, 127, 131, 132,
  163, 302; *and see* Pseudo-Ambrose
Ambrosiaster *see* Pseudo-Ambrose
Anacletus II, anti-pope 92
Andrew of Amiens 210
Angelomus of Luxeuil 28

Anselm, St., archbishop of Canterbury 34,
  92-3
Anselm of Laon 179, 247, 302 n.32
Anselm of Lucca 167 n.36
Antelm, St., bishop of Bellay 88 n.22
Antoninus Florentius, archbishop of
  Florence 299
Aquinas, Thomas 208, 248, 249, 253-4,
  257, 260-2, 263, 266, 269 n.20, 277
Archarius, Jacobus, printer 287
Aristippus, *see* Henry
Aristotle 134, 228, 231, 310 n.55
Arnold of Villanova 145-6, 150, 152, 154-6
Arnulf, bishop of Lisieux 186, 187, 194
Arnulph, emperor 49 n.71
Aschettin, chancellor 120
Atto, layman 4 n.19
Audet, Nicholas, Carmelite general 285,
  286, 288
Audoen, bishop of Evreux 167 n.37
Augustine, St., archbishop of Canterbury
  200-1
Augustine, St., bishop of Hippo 8, 9-10,
  14, 20, 24, 36, 37, 38, 40-1, 42-3, 44, 45,
  46-7, 51, 55, 56 n.94, 57, 58, 59, 68-9, 73
  n.11, 79-80, 90, 126-7, 130-1, 132, 133,
  135, 137, 162, 168, 245-6, 247-8, 251,
  255, 259, 261, 266, 270, 294, 310
Aulus Gellius 31
Aurificio, Nicholas, O.Carm. 287-8

Bacon, Roger 147 n.8, 153-4, 156, 297
Badius, Josse, printer 285-6, 287 n.46
Bale, John 286
Barthélemy, canon of Grenoble 90 n.35
Bartholomew, bishop of Laon 190
Bartholomew, notary 4 n.21
Bartholomé de las Casas, O.P. 295, 305

315

# List of Subscribers

Prof. Christopher Allmand
Lewis Ayres
Dr. John and Dr. Caroline
 Barron
Prof. Robert Bartlett
Neil Beckett
Dr. Jonathan and Dr.
 Maureen Boulton
Dr. Leonard E Boyle
Martin Brett
Prof. Christopher and Dr.
 Rosalind Brooke
Prof. C. Brooks
James Campbell
Dr. J. I. Catto
Dr. E. G. Clark
Dr. C. H. and Dr. M. A.
 Clough
Alan Cobban
Giles Constable
H. E. J. Cowdrey
Anne Crew
Dr. J. C. Crick
J. E. Cross
Dr. Richard Cross
Dr. D. L. d'Avray
Elizabeth Danbury
Dr. P. J. Davey
Prof. J. K. Davies
Dr. R. P. Davis
Christopher de Hamel
Prof. A. C. de la Mare
Prof. Ruth M. Dean
Prof. Jeffrey Denton
A. I. Doyle
Dr. Jean Dunbabin
D. H. Farmer
Dr. B. E. Ferme
Prof. E. C. Fernie
Mirella Ferrari
R.A. Fletcher
Valerie I. J. Flint
Dr. Sarah R. I. Foot

R. M. Franklin
Karin Fredborg
Prof. Karlfried Froehlich
Dr. David Ganz
Prof. Peter Ganz
George Garnett
Anne-Marie Genevois
Dr. V. A. Gillespie
Dr. Diana Greenway
Dr. Susan Hall
Prof. Alan Harding
Barbara Harvey
Margaret Harvey
T.A. Heslop
Dr. J. R. L. Highfield
Prof. Ivan Hlaváček
Prof. C. Holdsworth
Prof. Anne Hudson
Dr. Tony Hunt
Colette Jeudy
Martin Kauffmann
John Kentleton
Joan M. Kenworthy
Steven B. Killion
Dr. Sigrid Krämer
Dr. E.S. Leedham-Green
Andrew Lewis
Prof. and Mrs Karl Leyser
Dr. E. A. Livingstone
F. Donald Logan
Prof. Derek W. Lomax
Dr. G. A. Loud
Ann L. Mackenzie
Prof. R. A. Markus
Prof. Janet M. Martin
Prof. Ann Matter
Prof. D. J. A. Matthew
Henry Mayr-Harting
Rosamond McKitterick
Christa Mee
Rev. John Mullett
Dr. M. E. Mullett
Alexander Murray

Janet L. Nelson
Oliver Nicholson
Prof. Thomas F. X. Noble
Prof. Marina Passalacqua
Prof. Richard Pfaff
Mark Philpott
A. J. Piper
R. Vander Plaetse
Prof. Julian G. Plante
Helen Powell
Dr. Jean F. Preston
Dr. Peter Raedts
Nigel and Marian Ramsay
Marjorie Reeves
Caroline Reynolds Pestieau
Richard and Mary Rouse
Prof. J. E. Sayers
Prof. P. G. Schmidt
Dr. Richard Sharpe
Prof. Michael A. Signer
Dr. Julia M. H. Smith
Dr. Lesley Smith
Sir Richard Southern
E.A. Southworth
Dr. Pat. Starkey
Prof. T. S. Stevens
Dr. William P. Stoneman
Dr. John Taylor
Dr. Alan Thacker
Dr. R. M. Thomson
Dr. John van Engen
Dr. K. M. Waller
Dom Henry Wansbrough
Sister Benedicta Ward
Prof. Andrew Watson
Dr. Teresa Webber
Prof. S. Weinfurter
Drs. M. and M. Whitby
Dr. Roger H. White
Charles Williams
Abby Wolfson
Dr. Roger Wright
Prof. H. Zimmermann

## DATE DUE

| APR 21 95 | | | |
|---|---|---|---|
| | | | |
| | | | |
| | | | |
| | | | |
| | | | |
| | | | |
| | | | |
| | | | |
| | | | |
| | | | |
| | | | |
| | | | |
| | | | |
| | | | |
| | | | |
| | | | |

HIGHSMITH 45-220